Line in the Sand

AMERICA IN THE WORLD

SVEN BECKERT AND JEREMI SURI, *Series Editors*

Martin Klimke, *The Other Alliance: Student Protest in West Germany and the United States in the Global Sixties*

Andrew Zimmerman, *Alabama in Africa: Booker T. Washington, the German Empire, and the Globalization of the New South*

Ian Tyrell, *Reforming the World: The Creation of America's Moral Empire*

Rachel St. John, *Line in the Sand: A History of the Western U.S.–Mexico Border*

David Ekbladh, *The Great American Mission: Modernization and the Construction of an American World Order*

Thomas Borstelmann, *The 1970s: A New Global History from Civil Rights to Economic Inequality*

Donna R. Gabaccia, *Foreign Relations: American Immigration in Global Perspective*

Line in the Sand

A HISTORY OF THE WESTERN
U.S.–MEXICO BORDER

Rachel St. John

PRINCETON UNIVERSITY PRESS

PRINCETON AND OXFORD

Published by Princeton University Press, 41 William Street, Princeton, New Jersey 08540
In the United Kingdom: Princeton University Press, 6 Oxford Street,
Woodstock, Oxfordshire OX20 1TW
press.princeton.edu

Third printing, and first paperback printing, 2013
Paperback ISBN 978-0-691-15613-2

The Library of Congress has cataloged the cloth edition of this book as follows

St. John, Rachel C., 1976–
Line in the sand : a history of the Western U.S.-Mexico border / Rachel C. St. John.
p. cm. — (America in the world)
Includes bibliographical references and index.
ISBN 978-0-691-14154-1 (hardcover : acid-free paper) 1. Mexican-American
Border Region—History. 2. United States—Boundaries—Mexico.
3. Mexico—Boundaries—United States. 4. United States—Relations—
Mexico. 5. Mexico—Relations—United States. I. Title.
F786.S767 2011
972'.1—dc22   2010054533

British Library Cataloging-in-Publication Data is available

This book has been composed in Sabon

3   5   7   9   10   8   6   4

CONTENTS

ACKNOWLEDGMENTS

I COULD NOT HAVE WRITTEN THIS BOOK without the support and encouragement of many people and institutions. Although I can never thank them enough, I am going to attempt to express some small measure of my appreciation and gratitude here.

A number of institutions provided generous financial support to fund the research and writing of this book. This project would not have been possible without the support of the Stanford History Department, the School of Humanities and Science, the Research Institute of Comparative Studies in Race and Ethnicity, and the Mellon Sawyer Seminar on Settlement, Racial Formation, and Partial Sovereignty in North America, South Africa, and Israel/Palestine at Stanford University; the John Randolph Haynes and Dora Haynes Foundation, the W. M. Keck Foundation, and the Andrew W. Mellon Foundation through The Huntington Library in San Marino, California; and the Harvard History Department, the Charles Warren Center for Studies in American History, and the David Rockefeller Center for Latin American Studies at Harvard University.

The history that unfolds in the following pages emerged from books, photographs, manuscript collections, and microfilm reels in archives and libraries throughout the United States and Mexico. I am indebted to the knowledgeable and patient historians, archivists, and librarians who gave me access to and guided me through these sources, including: William O. Hendricks and Jill Thrasher at the Sherman Library in Corona del Mar, California; David Piñera Ramírez, Edna Aidé Grijalva Larrañaga, María de Jesús Ruiz, and Héctor Mejorado de la Torre at the Instituto de Investigaciones Históricas at the Universidad Autonóma de Baja California in Tijuana; Jesús Zamora Aguirre, Alicia Barrios Valencia, and the rest of the staff at the Archivo General del Estado de Sonora in Hermosillo; Teresa Leal and Axel Holm at the Pimería Alta Historical Society in Nogales, Arizona; Robert Ritchie, Peter Blodgett, Daniel Lewis, Bill Frank, and everyone in Reader Services at The Huntington Library in San Marino, California; and the archivists, librarians, and staff of the Arizona Historical Society, Tucson; the University of Arizona, Special Collections Library; the San Diego History Center, the Mandeville Special Collections Library at the University of California, San Diego; the Library of Congress; the National Archives in Washington, DC, and College Park, Maryland; the Stanford University Library; and the Harvard University Libraries.

I was ably assisted in this research by a number of excellent research assistants. Benjamín Alonso Rascón and Jonathan Larrañaga Morales provided invaluable help in the archives in Mexico City, Hermosillo, and Tijuana. At Harvard, Diana Kimball, Paul Katz, Elizabeth Cabrera, Jeremy Zallen, and Jason Robison tracked down books and documents and generally made my life much easier.

At Princeton University Press, Clara Platter, Sarah Wolf, Leslie Grundfest, Dawn Hall, Sven Beckert, and Jeremi Suri have been a pleasure to work with. I am also indebted to Ezra Zeitler for producing the beautiful maps in this book.

Parts of this manuscript have been published in different form in two volumes published by Duke University Press—"Divided Ranges: Trans-Border Ranches and the Creation of National Space along the Western Mexican-U.S. Border," in *Bridging National Borders in North America*, edited by Benjamin Johnson and Andrew Graybill (Durham, NC: Duke University Press, 2010) and "Selling the Border: Trading Land, Attracting Tourists, and Marketing American Consumption on the Baja California Border, 1900–1930," in *Land of Necessity: Consumer Culture in the U.S.-Mexico Borderlands*, edited by Alexis McCrossen (Durham, NC: Duke University Press, 2009). They appear here with the permission of Duke University Press. I am also grateful to the editors of those collections, Benjamin Johnson, Andrew Graybill, and Alexis McCrossen, and all of the authors included in the volumes for their comments on earlier versions of my work.

Many other people generously offered suggestions and support. My professors and mentors at Stanford University—Richard White, Albert Camarillo, Richard Roberts, Jack Rakove, George Fredrickson, John Wirth, David Kennedy, and Gordon Chang—provided guidance and encouragement and taught me how to be a historian. I am particularly indebted to Richard White who, in addition to being a model historian, is an exceptionally committed, generous, and patient mentor. He has supported me and this work in innumerable ways, contributing his insights in ways that are impossible to footnote and helping me to face down all of my academic El Guapos.

Many people read parts of the manuscript, discussed this project with me, and improved it through their comments and suggestions. I am grateful to Stephen Aron, Shana Bernstein, Matthew Booker, Mike Bottoms, John Bowes, John Broich, Vincent Brown, Flannery Burke, Peter Cahn, Ryan Carey, Alicia Chavez Greany, Connie Chiang, Kareem Crayton, Cynthia Culver Prescott, Lawrence Culver, Grace Delgado, William Deverell, Colleen Dunleavy, Sterling Evans, Alison Frank, Andrea Geiger, Andrew Graybill, Amy Greenberg, Camille Guerin-Gonzalez, William O. Hendricks, David Holland, James Honey, Elizabeth Jameson, Benjamin Johnson, S. Deborah Kang, Dorothy Pierson Kerig, Amalia Kessler, Matthew Klingle, Shelley Lee, Patricia Nelson Limerick, Malinda Maynor

Lowery, Peter Mancall, Alexis McCrossen, Kathryn Morse, Andrew Needham, Mae Ngai, Stephen Pitti, Jenny Price, Arthur Ralston, Emma Rothschild, Martha Sandweiss, Virginia Scharff, Lise Sedrez, Jennifer Seltz, Ajantha Subramanian, Jeremi Suri, Joseph Taylor, III, Cecilia Tsu, Conevery Bolton Valencius, Tamara Venit Shelton, Lissa Wadewitz, David Weber, Barbara Welke, Michael Witgen, Jack Womack, and many other people at conferences, workshops, and seminars where I have presented parts of my work. I am particularly indebted to Sven Beckert, Geraldo Cadava, Jared Farmer, Karl Jacoby, Walter Johnson, Maria Montoya, and Samuel Truett, each of whom read the entire manuscript. Samuel Truett's enthusiasm and knowledge about borderlands history have been both inspiring and especially helpful.

At Harvard University I have been fortunate to have an impressive group of brilliant, engaging, and generous historians as colleagues who have supported this work and my professional development in countless ways and made me thankful that I had the good luck to land at Harvard. They include David Armitage, Sven Beckert, Ann Blair, Vincent Brown, Joyce Chaplin, John Coatsworth, Lizabeth Cohen, Nancy Cott, Caroline Elkins, Alison Frank, Andrew Gordon, Evelyn Brooks Higginbotham, Maya Jasanoff, Andrew Jewett, Walter Johnson, James Kloppenberg, Jill Lepore, Mary Lewis, Malinda Maynor Lowery, Erez Manela, Lisa Mc-Girr, Ian Miller, Susan O'Donovan, Emma Rothschild, Daniel Smail, Laurel Thatcher Ulrich, and Jack Womack. Andrew Gordon, Lizabeth Cohen, and James Kloppenberg have not only gracefully handled the challenging job of chairing the History Department but have also gone out of their way to support me and my work. Janet Hatch and the rest of the History Department staff have consistently gone beyond the call of duty to improve the quality of my work and life. With Vincent Brown, Alison Frank, Malinda Maynor Lowery, and Ajantha Subramanian, I have shared both written work and the ups and downs of academia and life.

All of my students at Harvard University, but particularly those in my North American Borderlands History seminars and freshman seminars on the history of the U.S.-Mexico border, have also contributed immensely to this project and my thinking about the border and its history. I thank them for their hard work, engagement, and enthusiasm. I would especially like to acknowledge Winsie Carroll, Andrea Flores, Sarah Honig, Paul Katz, Diana Kimball, Tony Meyer, Julia Renaud, Gabe Scheffler, Kirby Tyrrell, April Wang, Benjamin Weintraub, and Netasha Williams who gave up some of their free time to read parts of my manuscript and gave me very helpful comments.

Finally, I am indebted to friends and family for providing support, lodging, and intellectual, emotional, and nutritional sustenance over the years during which I researched and wrote this book. Ella Booker, Clara Booker, Matthew Booker, Aranzazu Lascurain, Vicki Sandin, Gordon Chang, Chloe Chang, Maya Chang, Charlene Aguilar, Luis Fraga, and Tomás Aguilar Fraga were my surrogate family at Stanford while I was beginning this project. As I completed it in Cambridge, Zareen Brown, Anisa Brown, Vincent Brown, and Ajantha Subramanian welcomed me into their family and provided more meals than I can count. Karen and Oscar Malik gave me a home in Tucson. Mike Malik and Cindy and Paul McCreery have done the same many times in Southern California. And, through all my moves, Jennifer Seltz, Cindy McCreery, Martha Alvers Rodriquez, and Kareem Crayton shared this journey, providing encouragement, helping me overcome obstacles, and celebrating my successes.

I am truly blessed with a family that has provided unfailing support and unconditional love (leavened with mockery) not only for the duration of this project but also for my entire life. Academia is a profession that seems strange to many of us who choose it, let alone to those who do not. Despite the unfamiliarity of my career path, my entire extended family has consistently celebrated my career choice and achievements. I am particularly indebted to my parents, John and Jane St. John, and my grandparents, Harold and Jerry Gegenheimer and John and Barbara St. John, who through their own histories and constant encouragement made it possible for me to go into academia and supported me emotionally and materially along the way. My mom and dad have been there for me through every stage of this project, listening to innumerable stories about the border, encouraging me in my research and writing, and, perhaps most importantly, patiently refraining from asking when I would be done. My sisters, Laura and Liz St. John, have kept me grounded, accompanied me on diversionary excursions to the mountains, beach, and lake, and even on occasion done some research and cite checking for me. My brother, Jeff St. John, has been one of my greatest supporters, as well as a tireless editor. I am fortunate to have such a skilled writer and generous and compassionate person as a brother.

To all of you who have supported me and this book, once again, thank you.

Line in the Sand

Introduction

THE LAND BORDER BETWEEN THE UNITED STATES AND MEXICO is hard to miss these days. It rises out of the Pacific Ocean in the form of metal pilings that cast a shadow across a beach where families gather and Border Patrol jeeps leave tracks in the sand. It then cuts east across coastal bluffs until a dense tangle of traffic erupts around it at the San Ysidro port of entry. There, helicopters circle overhead and street vendors wind their way through the long lines of cars that wait to pass through an array of electronic scanners and vehicle barriers and to be inspected by a host of customs and immigration officials. This scene is repeated again at towns along the length of the boundary line—at Otay Mesa, Tecate, Calexico, Nogales, and other ports of entry where border crossers and buildings crowd the line. But for most of its length the border stands lonely of human activity, save for the barriers erected to prevent crossings—a patchwork of steel mesh, picket fencing, vehicle barriers, and barbed wire that rise above the desert floor marking the boundary line's course from the Pacific Ocean to the Rio Grande.[1]

Although some stretches of the border are still marked by no more than a five-strand barbed-wire fence that can easily be cut or climbed over, it is the image of an imposing physical barrier that comes to mind when most people think of the U.S.-Mexico border today. Walls and fences have become both physical realities and metaphors for the stark divide between the United States and Mexico and the attempts to control undocumented immigration and illegal drug trafficking that many people associate with the border.

But the border has a history. In the nineteenth century there were no border fences. The U.S. government did not prevent Mexican immigrants from crossing the border or even record their entries. In 1900 the U.S. and Mexican officials who patrolled the streets of border towns were occupied with collecting customs duties, not chasing drug runners or migrants. In 1870 there were few border towns west of El Paso and Apaches challenged the United States and Mexico for control of the sparsely settled borderlands. Just a few decades before that, this border did not exist at all.

This book is a history of how and why the border changed. Focusing on the western border between the United States and Mexico from its creation in 1848 through the early years of the Great Depression, it traces the transformation of the once-unmarked boundary line into a space of gates, fences, and patrols that allowed the easy passage of some people, animals, and goods, while restricting the movement of others. It tells the story of how the border shifted from a line on a map to a clearly marked and policed boundary where state agents attempted to regulate who and what entered the nation.

The history of the border began in the early nineteenth century with a collective act of imagination. Long before the border existed as a physical or legal reality it began to take form in the minds of Mexicans and Americans who looked to maps of North America to think about what their republics were and what they might someday become. Their competing territorial visions brought the United States and Mexico to war in 1846. Less than two years later, the border emerged from the crucible of that war. With U.S. soldiers occupying the Mexican capital, a group of Mexican and American diplomats redrew the map of North America. In the east, they chose a well-known geographic feature, the Rio Grande, settling a decade-old debate about Texas's southern border and dividing the communities that had long lived along the river. In the west, they did something different; they drew a line across a map and conjured up an entirely new space where there had not been one before.

The western border stands out as being entirely a creation of the U.S. and Mexican nation-states. Unlike the eastern half of the border, which followed the course of the Rio Grande, the desert border running from west of El Paso to the Pacific Ocean did not correspond to any previously existing geographic feature. In 1848 U.S. and Mexican officials determined its location by simply drawing straight lines between a few geographically important points on a map—El Paso, the Gila River, the junction of the Colorado and Gila rivers, and San Diego Bay. The one part of this boundary line that corresponded to a natural geographic feature, the Gila River, was made obsolete by the renegotiation of the border in the Gadsden Treaty of 1853. From that point on, with the exception of a small stretch of the boundary line that runs along the Colorado River, the western border was made up of a series of imaginary lines.

The delimitation of the western half of the boundary line created an entirely new space in the west. The Rio Grande had drawn people to its banks for trade, travel, and settlement long before it became part of an international border, but on the site of the western border there had simply been no *there* there before the Treaty of Guadalupe Hidalgo. In the years following the boundary line's creation, government agents would mark the desert border with monuments, cleared strips, and, eventually, fences to make it a more visible and controllable dividing line.[2] Although the treaty negotiators had known very little about the lands they divided with this line, with a stroke of the pen they began to transform them into sites of national significance and contested power.

This did not happen easily or all at once. The western boundary line runs through a region of mountains and deserts where water is often scarce and travel can be treacherous. From the Rio Grande it cuts west through a landscape of high-desert grasslands, rugged mountains, and seasonal river valleys. Not far from the point where it begins its diagonal trajectory toward the Colorado River, the border enters the Sonoran Desert, an arid expanse where temperatures can rise and fall by more than fifty degrees in a single day. The Colorado River provides one last respite before the boundary line continues across the desert and through the craggy mountains of the Peninsular Range to the Pacific Ocean.[3]

This is a demanding environment in which unprepared hikers and immigrants still lose their lives today. It was similarly perilous for the U.S. and Mexican officials who were first sent to survey the boundary line in the 1850s. Accustomed to the more well-watered and densely settled landscapes of the eastern United States and central Mexico, few of these men imagined that this unfamiliar territory in which they sweated, toiled, and repeatedly lost their way would ever attract a substantial population or require much government oversight. To the contrary, wrote one of the members of the Joint United States and Mexican Boundary Commission, "much of this country, that by those residing at a distance is imagined to be a perfect paradise, is a sterile waste, utterly worthless for any purpose than to constitute a barrier or natural line of demarcation between two neighboring nations."[4]

But history would prove them wrong. Rather than repelling people, the boundary line would draw people to it. Over the next eighty years the western border would experience dramatic changes and take on new meanings as a result of historical developments in the region, the continent, and the world. Shaped by the forces of capitalism and the expansion of state power, the "sterile waste" would become at different times a marker of military sovereignty, a site of transborder trade, a home to binational communities, a customs and immigration checkpoint, a divide between political and legal regimes, and even, at times, a battlefield. What began as a line on a map became a space of evolving and multiple meanings and forms.

The transformation of the border began with the work of the boundary commission but quickly drew an array of state agents and private actors to the boundary line. Even as the boundary surveys went forward, U.S. and Mexican soldiers battled to establish military sovereignty over the line. To do so they had to defeat both Apache Indians who exercised military dominion over the border region and American and European filibusters who imagined that they could build empires of their own in the borderlands. It was only with their defeat that the western boundary line became a clear marker of military authority.

This conquest of the borderlands made it possible for transnational capitalists to transform the region. As ranchers, miners, investors, laborers, and railroad builders arrived in the borderlands in the late nineteenth century, they incorporated the border into a landscape of property, trade, and towns. In this new capitalist context, the boundary line took on significance as a divide between legal regimes and a customs and immigration checkpoint. The U.S. and Mexican nation-states dispatched officers to enforce national customs and immigration laws, and smugglers, immigrants, and businessmen began to develop both legal and extralegal ways to get around them. Yet at the same time that government agents began to carve out a space of state surveillance on the boundary line, growing numbers of local people also claimed the line through the construction of ranches, railroads, businesses, and homes. By the early twentieth century, a number of new border towns had emerged as busy sites of commerce, community, and government oversight.

While social and commercial exchanges would continue to define the border, by the second decade of the twentieth century, the nation-states' presence on the boundary line expanded dramatically and the border became increasingly significant as a divide between Mexicans and Americans. The change began with the first battles of the Mexican Revolution in 1910. Over the next ten years the Mexican Revolution and World War I ruptured transborder ties and temporarily turned border towns into battlefields. These conflicts, along with the decline in U.S.-Mexican relations and the concerns about national security that they created, also had more long-term effects on the border. During the war years, both nation-states initiated heightened crossing restrictions, dispatched soldiers to patrol the line, and built fences between border towns. While the war's end saw many of the restrictions lapse and most of the soldiers sent home, the fences continued to define the border and divide transborder communities. By the 1930s these fences, along with the other parts of the border control apparatus, had become firmly entrenched on the boundary line where government officials put them to use in the service of new state priorities, including the regulation of American morality and the restriction of Mexican immigration. The legacy of this early version of the modern border control apparatus and the United States' imperfect attempts to use it to control Mexican immigration and smuggling are still evident on the border today.

However, while both the U.S. and Mexican governments gradually expanded their presence and power on the border over the course of its history, this is not a history of how either nation-state managed to close the once-open border, but rather of how the border evolved, often into forms and meanings that neither nation-state could predict or fully control. The boundary line began as a means for the United States and Mexico to claim territory they had yet to conquer. When both nation-states went to war with the region's Native inhabitants, it became significant as a jurisdictional boundary that determined where each military had the right and responsibility to operate. With the growth of trade and settlement the border emerged as a divide between property regimes and a customs barrier. It was only at the beginning of the twentieth century that the boundary line began to become the obstacle to immigration and the stark divide between the United States and Mexico that most people in the twenty-first century imagine it to be. The history of the western U.S.-Mexico border shows that while nation-states have always desired boundaries, the significance and shape of those borders have changed over time.

While much of this narrative highlights the dramatic transformations of the border between its creation and the emergence of the modern border control apparatus in the 1920s and 1930s, there are also continuous themes that run through it. History is always a balance between change and continuity, and the history of the border is no exception. Questions about the control of space, the negotiation of state sovereignty, and the significance of national identities have been entangled with the boundary line since its creation and continue to define the border today. Focusing on these themes not only helps us to understand the U.S.-Mexico border but also to gain broader insight into how nation-states and borders function.

Rather than a clear line that defined the limits of national territory and state power, the border was a space where categories blurred and power was compromised. These themes resonate with other histories of North American borderlands that are replete with "middle grounds," "fugitive landscapes," and "peoples in between."[5] This book builds on the work of a generation of borderlands historians who have explored histories of conquest and cultural interaction in the contact zones at the edges of empires and surrounding international boundaries. Blending Spanish colonial borderlands history with the analytical approaches of Native American, Chicano/a, and western history, recent borderlands histories have drawn attention to broad processes of conquest, colonization, and cultural interaction and exchange and have become models for transnational history.[6] However, as borderlands historians have emphasized historical processes that transcend national boundaries and have expanded their focus to include zones of interaction outside of the U.S. Southwest and Mexican north, they have often treated the border itself as an irrelevant or incidental part of the borderlands.[7] By contrast, I emphasize the centrality of the boundary line in the processes of market expansion, con-

quest, state building, and identity formation with which many borderlands historians are concerned.[8]

Although located at the periphery of the nation, this border, like
boundaries all over the world, was central to state projects of territorial
sovereignty, economic development, and the construction of the boundaries of the body politic.[9] In the years following the creation of the
boundary line in 1848, the U.S. and Mexican nation-states expanded
dramatically, extending their reach to the outer limits of their territory
and into new regulatory arenas. As they grew, they set increasingly ambitious and wide-ranging objectives for the border and simultaneously improved their ability to achieve these goals. While in the 1850s it had been
all either nation could do just to survey the boundary line and build
monuments to mark its course, by the early twentieth century both nation-states had large numbers of agents and physical structures on the
line that allowed them to collect tariffs, inspect prospective immigrants,
arrest smugglers, and perform other duties that brought the boundary
line into closer conformity with state goals.

The boundary the nation-states created was conditional. Depending
on government policies, it denied access to some people, goods, and animals while easing the entry of others. Neither government set out to close
the border, but rather to improve its ability to manipulate spatial controls to reflect state priorities. In pursuit of the perfection of this system,
both nation-states adopted a range of spatial controls in the form of both
physical parts of the built environment, such as boundary markers,
cleared strips, customs houses, and fences, and government regulations,
including immigration restrictions, customs regulations, and international law, which channeled and limited transborder movement.

As a result, throughout its history the changes in the border's meaning
and the nation-states' power were reflected in the transformation of the
border's physical form. Boundary surveys imprinted the imaginary line of
the Treaty of Guadalupe Hidalgo on maps and marked it with boundary
monuments on the ground. When capitalists invested in land, mines, and
railroads in the borderlands they transformed rangelands into ranches
and contributed to the emergence of border towns. Customs and immigration officers established ports of entry for the compliant, but also patrolled the line in search of smugglers and illegal immigrants. During the
Mexican Revolution and World War I, U.S. and Mexican troops took up
arms along the border, turned border towns into battlefields, and threatened to shoot anyone who dared cross the line outside of official channels. When soldiers proved inadequate to regulate all transborder movement, government officials began building fences. By the 1920s and
1930s, the laws that regulated transborder movement were bolstered by
an array of physical structures and government agents that did not com-

pletely close off the border, but did make it possible for the nation-states to use it for new agendas, including morality regulation and immigration restrictions. This landscape of fences and patrols, although it would shift and evolve over the next eighty years, is still with us in the twenty-first century.

State power, however, was never absolute. Although the nation-states became stronger and more entrenched on the border over time, they never achieved complete authority over it. What emerged on the border was a form of negotiated sovereignty in which both nation-states modified their plans in response to practical difficulties, transnational forces, local communities, and the actions of their counterparts across the line. The binational context of the border meant that it was impossible for either nation-state to exercise unilateral authority over it. Despite the legacy of the United States' conquest of northern Mexico and an imbalance of national power that consistently favored the United States, U.S. and Mexican officials repeatedly discovered that they needed to adopt binational strategies to achieve their goals of state control on the boundary line. At times the two nation-states worked together, cooperating to mark the border, suppress transborder raids, and facilitate the flow of trade and investment. At others they only grudgingly accepted that there were limits to their ability to control events across the line (limits that were greater for Mexico than the wealthier and more powerful United States) and adjusted their policies accordingly. In either case, whether in a spirit of binational cooperation or feeling backed into a corner, the United States and Mexico established state power in dialogue.

Some of these conversations took place among diplomats in Washington, DC, and Mexico City, but they more often took the form of informal arrangements crafted by local consuls, military commanders, and customs officials on the border. A critical part of the development of state power was the ability of nation-states to operate on a variety of scales—making wide-reaching policy on a national level, but utilizing the discretion of individual agents to give nuance to those policies on the local level.[10] While in the early years of the border, the discrepancy between how diplomats viewed the border and the reality on the ground reflected a weakness of state power, by the twentieth century the ability of local officials to loosely interpret laws and make exemptions had become a strength. The divergences between how goals were articulated in Mexico City and Washington, DC, and how they were carried out on the border did not always represent fissures in state power, but rather the ability of local officials to prioritize different aspects of enforcement and maintain sovereignty without constantly resorting to force.

This was particularly important in light of the many local challenges to state power that developed as U.S. and Mexican aspirations of border control ran up against the reality of Native peoples' dominance, transnational capitalism, and binational border communities. If the form and relative success of government strategies revealed state priorities and binational compromises, it was the ability of individuals and corporations to negotiate them that reflected the larger landscape of power that existed on the border. As they moved, invested, smuggled, shopped, and socialized across the boundary line, border people created alternative spatial orders and binational communities that challenged national definitions of space and identity. For years, Apaches successfully manipulated the border to evade the U.S. and Mexican militaries. Complaining that customs duties added an undue burden to transborder trade, smugglers created an underground economy that allowed them to profit by evading state regulations. In response to a Mexican law that restricted the land ownership of noncitizens, American capitalists crafted Mexican corporate identities that allowed them to own land on the Mexican side of the boundary line. On the border, people lived within the confines of state-imposed and nationally significant parameters, yet they produced spaces and identities that reflected national and binational agendas of their own.

The negotiation of state power left a lasting mark on the border, shaping the interactions and identities of the people who moved along and across it. On the boundary line, national identity was not just an abstract concept but a critical component of everyday life. Throughout the border's history national membership determined where a person could own property, if he could cross the border, who he could turn to for protection or representation, and, at times, even if he might live or die. The relevance of national identity changed dramatically over time in response to state policy. For instance, while in 1900 Mexican nationals could cross the border with ease, by the 1930s U.S. immigration officials were stopping Mexican laborers at the boundary line and subjecting them to physical inspections and literacy tests or simply denying them entry outright. The significance of American identity was similarly changeable. American mining engineers welcomed with open arms by Mexican officials at the turn of the century faced a surge of anti-American sentiment that threatened their lives by the time of the Mexican Revolution. Nationality was not just important for Mexicans and Americans. Native people who had long identified themselves on the basis of their ties to places and kinship groups struggled to assert their rights in a new national context in which citizenship was an important source of power and privilege. Immigrants from around the world arrived on the border where state officials and local people categorized them on the basis of their national origins. In the face of these state restrictions, people not only confronted the privileges and limitations of their nationality but also learned to game the system. Some of those, like some Native Americans and Chinese, and later Mexican, immigrants who lacked the ability to officially navigate this landscape of power and privilege became skillful fence hoppers, developing intricate smuggling operations and fluid binational identities that evaded national definitions of space. Nationality did not always determine if someone could cross the border but almost always influenced how they did so.[11]

The history of the border brings together the stories of hundreds of crossings with the forces that constrained them. Apaches or immigrants, capital or cattle, alcohol or bullets, every person or thing that crossed the boundary line bore witness to its changing meaning and its incomplete but increasing power. Tracing the way the border changed from the time the first people stepped foot across it to the early 1930s when drug smugglers and Mexican deportees made their way past fences and patrolmen, *Line in the Sand* reveals the hidden history of the boundary line and the many other meanings and shapes it had before it became the border that we know today.

In recounting this history I move across space and time. The book begins with the creation of the boundary line in the mid-nineteenth century and continues to the early 1930s, by which time the outlines of the modern border, with its emphasis on restricting the entry of Mexican immigrants and illegal drugs into the United States, were apparent. By focusing on this period, I contribute to a growing body of scholarship spanning the divide between histories of the Spanish colonial borderlands and the social science and humanities literature on the late twentieth-century U.S.-Mexico border.[12] *Line in the Sand* demonstrates not only that the border lay at the center of a borderlands region in which private individuals and government agents continued to contest the limits of state authority and national identity long after the establishment of fixed national boundaries, but also argues that the border itself is a critical site for understanding the evolution of government priorities and the negotiation of state power in Mexico and the United States more broadly.

The geographic focus of the narrative also shifts subtly over the course of the book. While this is a history of the entire western U.S.-Mexico boundary line stretching from west of the Rio Grande to the Pacific Ocean, different parts of the border rise to the foreground at different points in time in order to highlight central themes and developments. In pursuit of an understanding of how Native people used the boundary line to evade military defeat, we will follow Chiricahua Apaches as they moved between reservations in Arizona Territory and the Mexican Sierra Madre. The construction of railroads will take the story first to Nogales on the Arizona-Sonora border in the 1880s and then a few decades later to the California–Baja California boundary line. While Nogales and the nearby Arizona-Sonora border towns of Naco, Douglas, and Agua Prieta are the best places to look for evidence of how ranching and mining transformed the border, Tijuana achieves prominence with the rise of border vice. This narrative geography reflects both the diversity of experience along the boundary line and how the border changed over time.

The book is organized both chronologically and thematically. Focusing on the delimitation and demarcation of the boundary line, chapter one details the diplomacy and warfare that led to the determination of the location of the boundary line and the trying process through which the Joint United States and Mexican Boundary Commission attempted to survey and mark the boundary on the ground. The story then shifts to the United States' and Mexico's efforts to back up their territorial claims by asserting military authority over the boundary line. Focusing on the violent histories of Mexico's defenses against filibustering and both nation-states' wars against Native peoples, chapter two explores both the alternate versions of spatial organization and power that persisted and evolved in the borderlands and how the nation-states managed to suppress them in the first four decades of the border's existence.

With the establishment of military sovereignty in the 1880s, the border entered a new phase of capitalist transformation. Chapter three describes how ranchers, miners, investors, laborers, railroad executives, and innumerable economic actors integrated the border into an emerging transnational economy and began to create binational communities on the boundary line. Looking at the economic and social spaces produced in the late nineteenth and early twentieth centuries, this chapter explores how the border became the centerpiece of a landscape of binational interaction and exchange. In chapter four I delve into the government efforts to regulate, tax, and restrict transborder movement and enforce jurisdictional boundaries within this context of social and economic integration. Concentrating on early customs, immigration, and law enforcement, this chapter shows how state agents adapted their agendas to local conditions and embraced binational cooperation.

Beginning with the eruption of the Mexican Revolution in 1910, the negotiations and compromises that had allowed the transborder economy and binational communities to flourish became increasingly untenable. Chapter five turns to the decade of war that included both the Mexican Revolution and the United States' participation in the First World War, describing how war transformed the border from a site of interaction and cooperation to one of conflict and division—a transformation that was reflected spatially in transborder battles and the erection of border fences. This burgeoning border control apparatus took on new meaning in the 1920s as the United States and Mexico adopted contrasting approaches to the regulation of public morality. Chapter six describes how U.S. prohibitions prompted the growth of border vice districts and alcohol and drug smuggling along the boundary line and explores the conflict that arose on both sides of the border over how the nation-states could or should use border controls to stymie these developments. Chapter seven connects the history of the boundary line to the contemporary focus on controlling immigration. Building up to the Great Depression and the mass deportations of people of Mexican and Chinese descent from the United States and Mexico, respectively, this chapter traces the emergence of an immigration-control apparatus on the boundary line and how political and economic conditions influenced how and against whom the nation-states used it. As U.S. immigration laws increasingly defined Mexicans as outsiders who could not freely cross the boundary line, the divisive power of the border became more apparent. This sense of division between the United States and Mexico and the United States' ongoing attempts to assert its authority over when and how Mexican immigrants cross the border, which reached one peak in the deportations of the Great Depression, continue to define the border today.

This is the story of how two nation-states, their citizens, and a host of historical forces transformed an undistinguished strip of land into a site of capitalist production and a meaningful marker of state power and national identities. It traces the borderlands' metamorphosis as the U.S. and Mexican governments restricted Native people to reservations and new arrivals moved into the region and asserted their own claims to the boundary line. It reveals how dramatically the U.S. and Mexican states changed over the course of the nineteenth and early twentieth centuries, growing from adolescent republics with tenuous control of their territory to sophisticated bureaucracies that regulated, if imperfectly, the movement of people, animals, commodities, and capital across their shared border. This is the history of how a line in the sand became a conditional barrier between two nations and their people.

Chapter One

A NEW MAP FOR NORTH AMERICA

Defining the Border

On paper one easily draws a line with a ruler and
pencil; but on land it is not the same.[1]
—*José Salazar Ylarregui, Mexican surveyor, Joint
United States and Mexican Boundary Commission*

ON SEPTEMBER 6, 1851, the four highest-ranking members of the Joint
United States and Mexican Boundary Commission met on a high desert
plain about sixty miles southeast of Tucson. Their respective governments had sent them to survey and mark the new boundary line between
the two republics. U.S. boundary commissioner John Russell Bartlett had
only arrived on the border earlier that year. The others, Mexican boundary commissioner Pedro García Conde, Mexican surveyor José Salazar
Ylarregui, and U.S. surveyor Andrew B. Gray, had been at this work for
over two years, during which they completed an arduous survey of the
California–Baja California boundary. Their difficulties, however, were
only beginning.

Salazar Ylarregui started the meeting by announcing that he had completed the demarcation of the first part of the Chihuahua–New Mexico
boundary line. Then Gray made a disheartening declaration—he dis-
agreed with García Conde and Bartlett's location of the initial point at El
Paso del Norte and thus the entire trajectory of the line Salazar Ylarregui
had just surveyed. The initial point on the Rio Grande, Gray argued,
should have been farther south and west. Salazar Ylarregui, he concluded, had drawn the line too far north.

García Conde, with the support of the other members of the commission, informed Gray that his protests were too late and moved ahead
with the commission's other business.[2] The larger issue, however, would
not go away so easily. Gray's continued objections would later lead to
his dismissal from the commission. By then, however, Gray's complaints
and U.S. sectional politics had led southern politicians to denounce
Bartlett for agreeing to the initial point. They refused to ratify the boundary line, hoping to secure more territory and, more importantly, a southern transcontinental railroad route. In 1853 their efforts would culmi-

nate in the negotiation of the Gadsden Treaty and the redrawing of the boundary line.

Of course, the boundary commissioners, preoccupied with the tasks at hand, could not foresee this outcome on that late summer day in 1851. Beyond their responsibilities for making astronomical measurements, building boundary monuments, and gathering information about the surrounding territory, they also had to keep the joint commission of more than one hundred men alive in an unfamiliar, desert landscape populated by Native people who did not recognize their right to be there. Survival was foremost on the commissioners' minds as they left the site of their meeting. While the surveyors proceeded to the Gila River to begin surveying, García Conde and Bartlett set out to secure supplies in the northern Sonora village of Santa Cruz. The commissioners anticipated a short trip but soon lost their way. With only enough food for a few days, they resorted to hunting and scavenging in the orchards of the ominously abandoned settlements through which they passed. Struggling to cut through the Santa Rita Mountains south of Tucson, they wandered well out of their way. Rain soaked them in camp and made it difficult to cross the swollen streams and muddy plains. The commissioners also traveled in fear of Apaches. While they did not meet any Indians face-to-face on this leg of their journey, the sight of a group of riders in the distance sent a soldier in Bartlett's party scurrying into a ravine to hide. By the time they arrived in Santa Cruz, the commissioners had endured more than two weeks of hard travel.[3]

Their experiences took a toll on the commission. Shortly after arriving in Santa Cruz, a number of its members, including both commissioners, became sick. Bartlett spent the next two months recovering in Sonora before continuing by sea to rejoin the commission in San Diego. García Conde was not so fortunate. After a brief recovery he fell ill again and died in December in Arizpe, the same Sonoran town where he had been born.[4]

These travails marked the beginning of what would prove to be the nadir of the decade-long process of drawing the boundary line between the United States and Mexico. Between 1851 and 1853, García Conde's death, the commission's troubles in the field, and political challenges to the boundary line in the United States left the survey in shambles. The men who had set out for the border as confident representatives of sovereignty found themselves fending off political assaults, fearing Indian raids, and struggling to simply stay alive. Rather than establishing the border, they seemed to be searching for it.[5]

From its very beginnings the border eluded state control. Long before smugglers challenged the border's authority, the land and Native people who lived on it resisted the United States' and Mexico's attempts to force them to conform to their sovereignty. From the diplomatic chambers where disagreements over territorial limits devolved into war, to the deserts where men struggled to mark the boundary line, the creation of the border was not easy. The process of delimiting, or drawing, the boundary line on paper, simple as it may seem, was the culmination of decades of conflict and diplomatic negotiation. The territorial limits that the U.S. and Mexican peace commissioners wrote into the Treaty of Guadalupe Hidalgo at the conclusion of the Mexican-American War were laden with national significance, symbolizing a great national triumph for the United States and an even greater loss for Mexico. Having fought for so long to establish the position of the boundary line, Mexican and U.S. officials assumed that its demarcation, or marking on the earth, would be a mere formality. However, as Salazar Ylarregui had emphasized when he made the distinction between drawing the line on paper and marking it on the ground, what on paper appeared to be a fairly simple task could be a dangerous and disorienting ordeal in the field. The difficulties faced by the boundary commission not only impeded the commissioners' work, but also fundamentally challenged the national sovereignty under which they operated. The discrepancy between the ability of the nation-states to delimit the boundary line in the treaty and to demarcate it on the ground marked the beginning of a long history in which the border would repeatedly reveal the divide between the states' aspirations and their actual power.

In delimiting the border, U.S. and Mexican officials imagined that they could easily separate sovereign space. Along with defining national membership, the ability to establish the territorial boundaries of the nation and state sovereignty was considered a fundamental function of the nation-state. In Washington, DC, and Mexico City, politicians controlled this process, but on the ground it rested in the hands of men like Bartlett and García Conde, whose struggles suggested that neither nation-state actually controlled the territory that they claimed.

"On paper one easily draws a line": Imagining the Border

The creation of the boundary line did not begin with the arrival of the boundary commission in the field. The line first began to form in the minds of politicians and pundits over the nearly three decades between Mexican independence in 1821 and the ratification of the Treaty of Guadalupe Hidalgo in 1848. Throughout this period, Mexico struggled to maintain the extensive territorial boundaries that it had inherited from New Spain in the face of growing pressure not only from the United States but also from a number of aggressive European empires, making it impossible to predict where the border would lie and even which nation-states or empires it would divide.

In order to understand how the border came to be where it is today, we first have to understand the context of territorial competition from which it emerged. Territorial competition defined North America in the early nineteenth century. At the beginning of the century, the continent was still very much up for grabs. In the south, the decline of the Spanish Empire created an opening for a revolutionary challenge that began with the Grito de Dolores in 1810 and concluded with Mexican independence in 1821. As the Mexican Republic took form it asserted claim to territory reaching from the Yucatán to a line drawn from the Gulf of Mexico through the Great Plains and the Rocky Mountains to the Pacific Ocean along which the United States and Spain had divided North America in the Adams-Onís Treaty of 1819. In the northeast, the young United States did not have much of a head start on Mexico, having gained its independence only a few decades before. Yet despite its youth, the United States was proving to be a dynamic nation, acquiring Louisiana from the French in 1803, fighting the British to a stalemate in the War of 1812, conquering Native peoples, and more than doubling its size in its first fifty years. In the west, however, with a patchwork of imperial and national claims and on-the-ground evidence of Native sovereignty, the future of the continent remained uncertain.[6]

By the 1830s, people in both the United States and Mexico had come to believe that controlling this territory was critical to each of their nation's destinies. Spanish settlers and missionaries had made limited inroads into Mexico's far north, but the potential for the development of agriculture, ranching, trapping, mining, and trade along the Pacific Coast and in the North American interior was widely acknowledged. In the wake of Mexican independence, the old Spanish settlements in New Mexico had become the linchpin in a trading network extending from central Mexico into the Great Plains and to the western edge of the United States. At the same time, American and British ships expanded their operations in the Pacific, tapping into California's resources and spreading news of the fertile land and deepwater ports to be found there. Finally, although no one could have known that gold would soon be discovered at Sutter's Mill in California, Mexico's northern borderlands were known to have mineral deposits. All of these advantages made northern Mexico attractive to any number of powers, including not just Mexico and the United States, but Great Britain, Russia, and expansive Native polities as well.[7]

For Mexico this land was more than strategically and economically valuable, it was part of the national homeland. With independence Mexico had claimed dominion over Spain's vast territorial claims in

North America. Under the Constitution of 1824, Mexico incorporated the northern half of this territory as the states of Chihuahua, Sonora y Sinaloa, and Coahuila y Tejas, and the territories of New Mexico, Alta California, and Baja California. Although distant and disconnected from the national centers of population and political power, Mexicans saw these states and territories as integral parts of the nation.

Mexico's land was both its greatest strength and its greatest weakness. Exercising control over the far-flung reaches of the nation was an administrative nightmare. Thousands of miles of deserts and mountain ranges separated Mexico City from the sparsely settled and weakly defended northern territories. Communication and transportation were slow and insecure. With the military preoccupied with the struggle for independence and the national treasury unable to subsidize frontier defense and payments to Indians, much of the northwest became vulnerable to Indian raids that gradually pushed back Mexican settlements along the northern frontier. As the military governor of Sonora, José María Carrasco, reportedly complained to the members of the U.S. boundary commission in 1851, "our territory is enormous, and our Government weak. It cannot extend its protecting arms throughout all portions of the country."[8]

Yet this troublesome territory remained an important source of national hope and pride, both of which were in short supply amid the political upheaval, military violence, and crumbling economy that characterized the first two decades of Mexican independence. If Mexico was weak, its land, many Mexicans believed, would someday make it strong. In 1833 Simón Tadeo Ortiz de Ayala, a prominent proponent of Texas colonization, insisted that Texas alone would someday produce more cotton than the entire United States combined. Even as Mexican political factions contested the class and ethnic boundaries of Mexican nationality, the nation's territory provided a shared source of identification and a reservoir of optimism for future development.[9]

Unfortunately for Mexico, many Americans had also cast their hopes for national advancement on the acquisition of Mexican territory. Territorial expansion had become a part of the American ethos. Many Americans, most notably Thomas Jefferson, believed that the United States' unique experiment in republican government depended on the continued availability of open land. Only by owning their own farms, they argued, could citizens maintain the independence necessary for a virtuous democratic republic. Liberty, then, was dependent on land.

This association provided a logic for the United States' territorial expansion. The incorporation of new western states and the annexation of first Louisiana in 1803 and then Florida in 1819 changed the geographic shape of the United States and contributed to a new way of thinking about national space. In contrast to the emphasis on a historic homeland that would define European nations, Americans embraced the notion that their national boundaries would continue to expand to incorporate ever more land and people under the umbrella of republican government. In the mid-nineteenth century these ideas about expansion and liberty coalesced in the doctrine of "manifest destiny." American continental expansion, believers in this doctrine argued, was not only justifiable but was also preordained.[10]

The concept of manifest destiny justified expansion but did not provide specifics about the methods, direction, or amount of land that this growth would require. These matters, along with their implications for sectional politics and the future of American slavery, were at the center of political debates in the United States. Northern Mexico was not the only area into which the United States could expand. Americans also had designs on Cuba, Yucatán, and large swaths of southern Canada. However, the proximity of Mexico's weakly defended northern territories and the steady flow of American settlers into Texas and traders into New Mexico and California made these territories increasingly desirable. As early as 1825, President John Quincy Adams instructed the U.S. minister to Mexico, Joel Poinsett, to approach the Mexican government about redrawing the border so that Texas, New Mexico, California, and parts of Baja California, Sonora, Coahuila, and Nuevo León would become part of the United States. Ten years later, President Andrew Jackson expressed interest in purchasing a strip of land that would connect the United States to San Francisco Bay. That same year, American settlers in Texas launched a rebellion that would pave the way for the incorporation of Texas into the United States in 1845.[11]

Mexican political leaders repeatedly rejected the United States' offers. While empires traded territory, nation-states, having incorporated land into an inalienable part of the nation, could not do so without undermining their national status and identity. Refusing to sell national territory, Mexican officials demonstrated their commitment to territorial integrity above the opportunity to pay down their substantial national debt. Manuel de Mier y Terán, a Mexican general and patriot who had led a survey of Texas and its boundary with the United States, explained that "Mexico, imitating the conduct of France and Spain, might alienate or cede unproductive lands in Africa or Asia. But how can it be expected to cut itself off from its own soil, give up to a rival power territory advantageously placed in the extremity of its states, which joins some of them and serves as a buffer to all?" "If Mexico should consent to this base act," he concluded, "it would degenerate from the most elevated class of American powers to that of a contemptible mediocrity, reduced to the necessity of buying a precarious existence at the cost of many humiliations."[12]

No matter how poor and wracked by political turmoil, Mexico refused to exchange even its most troublesome national territory for cash.[13]

Mexico's defense of its territorial integrity repudiated the expansionist identity of the United States. This challenge to manifest destiny aggravated American insecurities and left the United States susceptible to territorial challenges. Having won independence from Britain only a half-century before, Americans were well aware that their experiment in nationhood was not completely respected abroad. The United States claimed the Western Hemisphere as the domain of liberty, but few outside the nation's moving borders accepted this claim. Particularly galling to Americans were Great Britain's challenges to the United States' territorial ambitions. In fact, with the British firmly established in Canada and contesting American claims in the Pacific Northwest, it was England, not Mexico, with which American politicians were most preoccupied in the 1840s. In this context the acquisition of Mexican land, and especially California, on which the British were rumored to have designs, became a matter of principle for the United States in which both blocking the British and the future of the nation's manifest destiny hung in the balance.[14]

By the 1840s, having staked its national honor on acquiring territory that Mexico already claimed, the United States was on a collision course with the Mexican Republic. The impending conflict first came to a head in Texas. The formation of the Texas Republic in 1836 had temporarily forestalled the clash between the United States and Mexico and had left the territory in limbo. Up until the United States' annexation of Texas, the Mexican government continued to insist that Texas was not an independent nation but was simply in rebellion. When the United States annexed Texas in 1845, Mexico cut off diplomatic relations. At the same time, another conflict arose over the southern boundary of Texas. While the Texans claimed the Rio Grande (known in Mexico as the Rio Bravo) as the border, Mexico had consistently insisted that the border lay farther north along the Nueces River. Although unable to reclaim all of Texas, Mexico clung to this sliver of territory, known as the Nueces Strip. In 1846 President James Polk ordered U.S. troops into the disputed territory between the Nueces and the Rio Grande. Not long after, the two nations were at war.

The Mexican-American War was a war of U.S. conquest.[15] Polk ran for president on an expansionist platform and, while he would have preferred to buy land from Mexico, he sent troops into the Nueces Strip knowing that Mexico would view it as a provocation. Not long after taking office, Polk had dispatched John Slidell to Mexico City on a secret mission to settle the Texas boundary dispute and negotiate for the purchase of California. Polk, like Adams and Jackson before him, was particularly interested in acquiring San Francisco Bay, but authorized Slidell to offer up to $25 million for New Mexico, Alta California, and the Nueces Strip. The Mexican government refused to even receive Slidell. Meanwhile, U.S. troops under General Zachary Taylor set up camp along the Rio Grande. On April 25, 1846, a Mexican force engaged a U.S. patrol, killing or wounding sixteen U.S. soldiers. On May 11, Polk went before Congress and asked for a declaration of war on the grounds that the Mexican military had shed American blood on American soil. Despite political opposition that denounced annexation by military means and feared the incorporation of new slave states, the United States declared war on Mexico two days later. By May 18, U.S. troops had crossed the Rio Grande and occupied Matamoros.

Within months U.S. forces gained control of New Mexico and California and pushed deep into Mexico. Their success was a signal not just of U.S. military prowess, but also of the power of Indian raiders who had so weakened Mexico's defenses that it was unable to stave off the U.S. incursion.[16] By the summer of 1847 U.S. military victories brought the two nations to the negotiating table. While fighting continued, representatives from both governments met in the Mexican capital to hash out the terms of territorial exchange for which Polk had gone to war. The United States had waged a war of conquest, but just how much land it would claim remained in the hands of these diplomats. It was these men, preoccupied with ending the war and focused on broader territorial concerns, who would create the border.

The peace commissioners did not know much about the territory over which they haggled, and, as a result, their placement of the boundary line would have very little to do with the territory through which the border would pass. Most of northern Mexico was sparsely settled and under the control of Indians. The few maps available were known to contain inaccuracies. The people who knew this country best—Mexican settlers, American traders, and Native inhabitants—were not at the negotiating table. This lack of information would later pose problems for the joint boundary commission, but it did not stand in the way of the peace commissioners. Diplomats made their decision about where to draw the boundary line on the basis of broader territorial concerns. In writing the treaty it was not the line itself but the way that it divided the continent that interested them.

In the absence of detailed information, the negotiators focused on abstract principles and a few highly contested locations. The U.S. peace commissioner, Nicholas Trist, concentrated on acquiring a southern transcontinental railroad route and the ports of San Francisco and San Diego. The Mexican negotiators, former president José Joaquín de Herrera, General Ignacio Mora y Villamil, and two lawyers, Bernardo Couto and Miguel Atristain, operated from a more defensive position. With

Polk's desire for California shored up by its occupation by U.S. forces, Alta California was as good as gone. But the Mexican commissioners managed to draw out negotiations by proposing a series of lesser cessions—just the territory north of 37° N, which would give the United States control of San Francisco Bay, or that above 36° 30′ N, which added Monterey Bay.[17]

The choice of geographic lines, like the 37th parallel, appealed to the negotiators who knew little of northern Mexico's geography. Throughout the negotiations, proposals were most often expressed as lines—37° N, 36° 30′ N, or later the more ambitious U.S. proposals of 32° N, which included San Diego Bay, or 26° N, which cut across the middle of Mexico from near the mouth of the Rio Grande.[18] The fact that each of these lines incorporated hundreds of thousands of square miles of mountains, deserts, and plains, not to mention unknown numbers of inhabitants, only rarely figured into the negotiations.

To the extent that the negotiators took the territories' residents into consideration at all, it was primarily the Mexican commissioners who did so. U.S. politicians expressed racial anxieties about incorporating too many Mexicans and attempted to ingratiate themselves to northern Mexicans by promising to protect them from Indian raids, but they gave little thought to the national preferences of people living in the borderlands. By contrast, the Mexican negotiators tried to fend off U.S. designs on New Mexico by arguing that the Mexicans who lived there did not want to become Americans. They also stressed that the federal government lacked the authority to alienate any part of a sovereign state. Using this logic, they refused to cede any of northern Chihuahua or Sonora, continued to insist on the Nueces River as the traditional boundary of Texas, and attempted to retain San Diego by arguing it was part of Baja, not Alta, California.[19]

With the peace commissioners divided on these critical points, negotiations stalled. Meanwhile, U.S. forces under General Winfield Scott resumed their assault on Mexico City and occupied the capital in September 1847. The occupation of Mexico City shifted the terms of the negotiations. As news of U.S. military victories spread, U.S. expansionists began to demand more territory. For a time it seemed that the Mexican nation was in danger of disappearing as an "all Mexico" movement pushed for annexing the nation in its entirety. Mexican resistance and American concerns about Mexicans' racial difference made this politically unfeasible, but between San Francisco Bay and all of Mexico a wide range of territorial configurations were possible.[20]

Given the many possibilities, the final position of the border was the result of both compromise and chance. The Mexican commissioners ceded Alta California and New Mexico early in the negotiations but pre-

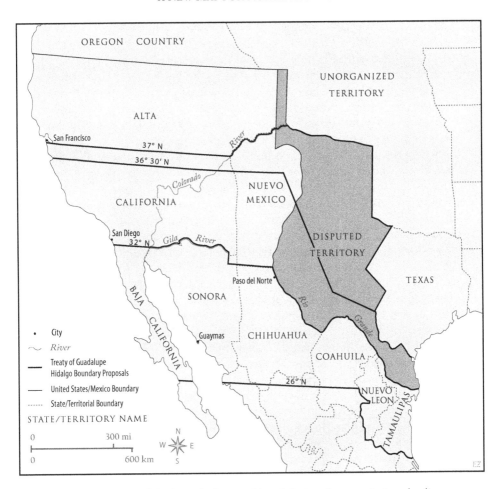

FIGURE 1.1. Some of the boundaries considered during the negotiations leading up to the Treaty of Guadalupe Hidalgo, 1847–48 (map by Ezra Zeitler).

vented the loss of Baja California, Sonora, and Chihuahua. For a time it seemed like Mexico might retain control of the Nueces Strip and San Diego as well. In October 1847, Trist submitted a treaty to his superiors in Washington, DC, which would have established the Nueces River and 33° N as the boundary line. Polk was so outraged by Trist's failure to secure San Diego and the Nueces Strip that he demanded his recall. In opposition to direct orders, Trist stayed in Mexico and met with the Mexican commissioners (with a former foreign minister, Luis Cuevas, replacing Herrera and Mora y Villamil at the negotiating table) to hash out the final treaty in January 1848.[21]

Signed outside of Mexico City on February 2, 1848, the Treaty of Guadalupe Hidalgo remade the map of North America. In exchange for $15 million, the northern half of Mexico became the southwestern third of the United States. As detailed in Article V of the treaty, the final boundary line followed the Rio Grande northwest to the boundary of New Mexico, along the southern boundary of New Mexico, and then north to the Gila River. It then followed the Gila River west to its confluence with the Colorado River and from the Colorado along the boundary line between Alta and Baja California to the Pacific Ocean.

In theory it was simple enough—a patchwork of rivers and already-established boundaries. In reality, even the peace commissioners knew this boundary line was problematic. No one knew exactly where the boundary between New Mexico and Chihuahua or Alta and Baja California lay. Drawing on their limited knowledge and available maps, the commissioners tried to clarify any points of confusion in the treaty itself. New Mexico's southern boundary, they noted, ran north of the town of Paso (which would later become the Mexican town of Ciudad Juárez and the U.S. town of El Paso). The treaty specified that the boundary between the two Californias would begin one marine league south of the Port of San Diego and continue in a straight line to the Colorado River. They also appended two maps to the treaty: J. Disturnell's 1847 map of the United States of Mexico and Don Juan Pantoja's 1782 map of San Diego Harbor. However, despite their efforts to make the treaty as clear as possible, mistakes in both these maps and the peace commissioners' assumptions would result in conflict and confusion in the field.

The final part of Article V provided for the mapping and demarcation of the boundary line. It required that each nation appoint a commissioner and surveyor who would meet at San Diego no less than a year after the treaty went into effect. Together, along with their assistants, these men would make up the Joint United States and Mexican Boundary Commission.[22]

What the treaty did not mention was how difficult it would be for the commission to impose the boundary line and the sovereign authority it represented on the ground. The commission not only needed to mark and map the line but also needed to establish relations with Native peoples, gather scientific data, and explore a region about which neither state knew very much. Each of these tasks put sovereignty to the test. Reeling from its military defeat and persistent economic woes, the Mexican state was eager to demonstrate that its officers could carry out their mapping and surveying responsibilities and operate as equals with the members of the U.S. commission. Already flush with victory, U.S. officials had less to prove but had a no less daunting task in charting the United States' newly acquired territory and seeking to convince its inhabitants, many of whom were Native people who had never acknowledged Mexican authority, to respect U.S. sovereignty.

The treaty did not hint at any of these challenges that awaited the boundary commission. Rather, its confident tone implied that the two nation-states had the power to divide national space and fulfill sovereign responsibilities. It was a document full of aspirations of national strength and authority that neither state could necessarily achieve.

"On land it is not the same": The Challenges of the Joint Boundary Commission

When the Joint United States and Mexican Boundary Commission entered the field in 1849, most Mexicans and Americans believed that after decades of diplomacy and two years of war the most difficult part of creating the border was behind them. However, surveying, mapping, and marking the boundary line would prove to be more of a trial than anyone in either nation had imagined. The boundary survey would last more than seven years, during which seven different boundary commissioners attempted to manage both troubles in the field and the political minefield surrounding the location of the borderline. While the Rio Grande presented a clear, if shifting, landmark, most of the western border existed only in the minds of the treaty makers. Having fought for years against each other for control of the borderlands, the U.S. and Mexican governments now learned that it was not another nation or empire but rather inaccurate information, bad weather, and Native people that would prove the greatest challenges to their authority. As the boundary commission struggled to transcribe the treaty's maps and written descriptions of the boundary line onto the ground, they defined not just the limits of the nation but also the limitations of state sovereignty. While their work established the course of the border, it would be many more years before the nation-states' authority would live up to their expectations of control.

Surveyors, author Wallace Stegner has noted in writing about the U.S.-Canada border, "are not heroic figures."[23] The men who set out to survey the U.S.-Mexico border in 1849 bore out his claim. The Joint United States and Mexican Boundary Commission was made up of scientists, bureaucrats, diplomats, and military personnel. While at times their travails put them in situations that called for brave gestures and a handful of Americans would later write dramatic accounts of their experiences, these were men who, for the most part, spent their days taking measurements and traveling slowly across an unfamiliar landscape.

Although often mundane, the boundary commission's work on the border revealed both the aspirations and limitations of state power and laid the groundwork for much more dramatic transformations to come. In the nineteenth century surveyors were at the center of state-making projects around the world. Both the United States and Mexico dispatched surveying teams throughout their territory to gather information and draw maps that reinforced their claims.[24] Charged with surveying, mapping, and demarcating the boundary line, the joint boundary commission actually had many more responsibilities, ranging from gathering information about flora and fauna to negotiating amicable relationships with Native people. Their mission was twofold—to impose state definitions on the ground and to map what was already there for the knowledge and future use of the state. The boundary survey offered a great opportunity for both governments, and the members of the commission in particular, to demonstrate their scientific prowess and to record the advantages of their respective territories.

Although divided by nationality, the Mexican and American members of the commission shared a commitment to surveying and statecraft. While three of the four U.S. commissioners who served in the field were political appointees with little experience or expertise, many of the commission's members—including not just the Mexican commissioners and both governments' surveyors but also many lower level engineers, assistants, and draftsmen—were trained in surveying, exploration, and cartography. As they worked together to survey and mark the boundary line, their mutual respect and the importance of their work trumped national divisions. It also provided the foundation for a long history in which U.S. and Mexican officials on the border would cooperate in pursuit of shared binational goals.[25]

The boundary survey started out on an optimistic note. Setting out from Mexico City in the spring of 1849, the Mexican members of the commission were upbeat. Rather than dwelling on Mexico's lost territory, surveyor José Salazar Ylarregui reflected on the unsurpassed beauty of the Mexican landscape, which filled him with national pride.[26] Reflecting its own optimism, the U.S. Congress appropriated a mere $50,000 for what would eventually require more than seven years of work and hundreds of thousands of dollars.[27]

However, this confident outlook belied inadequate preparation for the work that lay ahead. Each half of the commission suffered from its own particular set of problems that were indicative of the states' limited ability to efficiently survey the boundary line. The Mexican commission lacked adequate tools, military escorts, and, most importantly, funding. Although the Mexican government had ordered the best possible instruments from Paris, the tools that arrived in Mexico City were of inferior quality. As a result the Mexican commission had to depend on the Americans to perform some measurements until better tools arrived. At times the lack of government funding forced García Conde and Salazar Ylarregui to draw on their personal lines of credit or to suspend operations completely. At others their work was crippled by inadequate military support. In the fall of 1851 assistant engineer Francisco Jiménez led a party across the desert to survey the Gila River with a budget of only 200 pesos and an escort of twenty-one soldiers, nine of whom deserted before they reached Tucson. Jiménez was only able to complete his assignment by drawing on his own credit and securing assistance from Maricopa and Tohono O'odham Indians. By the time he completed his survey in February 1852, he had left a trail of dead mules and abandoned instruments in the desert behind him.[28]

The desert was no kinder to the Americans, but the U.S. commission was better supplied. Although the commission exhausted the initial allocation of $50,000 in just the first few months, Congress authorized additional appropriations to fund the remaining work. This money paid for more precise and varied instruments and a small army of surveyors, engineers, botanists, and artists, as well as the soldiers who accompanied them. While Salazar Ylarregui worked with just four engineers, he noted that the U.S. commission had more than twenty. With its numerous personnel, the U.S. commission gathered extensive information about the people, animals, plants, and land with which they came into contact and produced copious records, ranging from reports to oil paintings.[29]

What American money could not seem to buy was adequate leadership. Of the four U.S. commissioners appointed who served in the field, only one, William H. Emory, had any experience in surveying, diplomacy, or organizing and carrying out a major expedition consisting of large numbers of men, animals, and supplies. As the fifth U.S. commissioner, Emory referred to his predecessors as "persons wholly unused to public affairs, and ignorant of the first principles of the scientific knowledge involved in the questions to be determined by them."[30] While the second commissioner, John C. Frémont, was a renowned explorer, he never served in the field. The others, in keeping with the mid-nineteenth-century U.S. patronage system, were political appointees selected for their party loyalties rather than their preparation for the task at hand. President Polk first appointed John B. Weller, a loyal Democrat and failed gubernatorial candidate from Ohio, as commissioner after Emory, his first choice, refused to resign from the army to take the position. The next U.S. commissioner to serve in the field, John Russell Bartlett, was a former bookseller, amateur ethnologist, and dry goods salesman from Providence, Rhode Island. Another victim of nineteenth-century political patronage, Bartlett had gone to Washington seeking an appointment as U.S. minister to Denmark and come away as the U.S. boundary commissioner instead. Under the leadership of these political appointees, the U.S. commission not only struggled to carry out its mission but also suffered from chronic financial mismanagement and near-constant infighting between the members of the commission. By contrast, García Conde and Salazar Ylarregui possessed excellent credentials and practical experience, but their qualifications alone could not compensate for the fact that the war-weakened Mexican state was unable to provide them with adequate instruments, money, and military support.[31]

Inadequately prepared in these ways, the joint commission set out in 1849 to undertake an arduous task that would have challenged even the most well-equipped nineteenth-century surveyors. Transportation difficulties, unforgiving terrain, extreme weather, inaccurate information, political challenges, and Native people who rejected their sovereign presumptions created an imposing obstacle course for the boundary commission. The problems they confronted would threaten their work and their lives, but perhaps most importantly would prove how little control the United States and Mexico actually exercised over the land they had fought so hard to possess.

The trouble started even before the commission met for the first time. Its members found themselves en route to San Diego just as the California gold rush got underway in the spring of 1849. Traveling via the Isthmus of Panama, the first U.S. commissioner, John B. Weller, became caught up in a swell of forty-niners who strained transportation and lodging facilities and left Weller and his party sweltering in Panama for two months before they were able to book passage to San Diego. The Mexican commission also experienced delays on its two-and-a-half-month journey from Mexico City to San Diego. Despite treaty stipulations requiring the work to commence no later than May 30, 1849, the commission did not even meet in San Diego until early July.[32]

Traveling did not get any easier once the commission reached land. Upon finally beginning work in July, Weller dispatched a surveying party led by Lieutenant Amiel Whipple to survey the confluence of the Gila and Colorado rivers. This stage of the boundary survey took the commission into a landscape of rocky passes, extreme temperatures, and little water. Leaving the coast, the new boundary line between California and Baja California cut through the rugged mountains of the Peninsular Range, reaching heights of more than 3,000 feet before dropping below sea level into the western edge of the Sonoran Desert. As Whipple's company skirted the mountains, following a wagon road used by U.S. troops during the war and now rapidly filling with immigrants en route to the gold fields, they faced flash floods, temperatures over one hundred degrees, and long stretches devoid of water or forage. While in his own account

Whipple was stoic, the commander of the army escort, Lieutenant Cave J. Couts, mocked Whipple's lack of preparation. "[Whipple] finds himself in a terrible stew because I am going to march over the desert by night," he wrote. "Washington City dandies with white kid gloves, etc., don't like roughing it any more than having to get up early in the morning, saying nothing of losing a night's sleep."[33]

Confronted with these environmental challenges, the boundary commissioners scaled back their plans for the demarcation of the line. Weller and García Conde concluded that the arid and mountainous border between California and Baja California could never be settled and thus required no more than seven boundary markers.[34] Yet determining even these few points was not the simple task that the treaty makers had foreseen. Surveyors Gray and Salazar Ylarregui discovered that a discrepancy between Don Juan Pantoja's 1782 map of San Diego Harbor on which the treaty was based and the current shape of the harbor necessitated a lengthy survey of the bay before they could determine the initial point. It was not until five months after arriving in San Diego that they accomplished this task.[35]

As these struggles suggested, the treaty writers' selection of geographic points that they perceived to be both natural and known did not make it easier to locate them on the ground, and in fact posed unexpected challenges to the surveyors. U.S. secretary of state James Buchanan's assumption that "the middle of the Rio Gila, where it unites with the Colorado, being a natural object, there can be but little difficulty in ascertaining this point" proved to be decidedly wrong.[36] Rather than "distinctly marked," the location of the middle, or even the main channel, of the Gila was difficult to determine. The center of the Gila, dependent as it was on the river's flow, was not constant. With the river's banks eroding continuously, Gray explained, "The middle, therefore, to-day, may not be the same as yesterday."[37]

The difficulty in locating these few strategic points was so time consuming that the commission, despite the protests of both surveyors, failed to mark all of the seven designated points before they suspended their work in the spring of 1850. With the U.S. commissioner deeply in debt, having exhausted his $50,000 budget in just a few months, and with both commissioners wary of crossing the desert, Weller and García Conde decided to begin the next stage of the survey from El Paso the following November. When they adjourned, the commission had only completely surveyed and marked the initial point south of San Diego Bay and the confluence of the Gila and Colorado rivers.[38] Far from a boundary, what the joint commission had begun to stake out was a dotted line, a few clearly defined points that suggested, but did not delineate, a legible border.

By the time the boundary commission reconvened in El Paso in 1851, John Russell Bartlett had replaced Weller as the U.S. commissioner. With his background in ethnography, Bartlett brought enthusiasm for the work of the commission but little practical knowledge or experience. Bartlett, noted García Conde, was "a clever fellow, but unqualified for the labors that we must perform."[39] When he first arrived in El Paso, Bartlett could not imagine what lay ahead of him in the desert.

Neither, of course, could García Conde. Although he was already aware of the challenges of boundary making and, as a Sonora native who had previously engaged in mapping Chihuahua, heading into familiar territory, he could not have known that he would not survive to see the survey completed. Nor could he foresee that all of his efforts would be wasted. García Conde and Bartlett's survey would ultimately be a failure that would lead to a renegotiation of the treaty terms and the relocation of the portion of the boundary between El Paso and the Colorado River just two years after García Conde's death. If things had been hard on the California–Baja California border, it was when the commission headed west from El Paso that they really began to fall apart. Confronted with irresolvable inconsistencies between the treaty instructions and borderlands geography and Indians who in word and deed asserted their authority over the region, the boundary commission's experiences revealed the limits of the nation-states' ability to force land and people to conform to their presumptions of sovereignty and divisions of national space.

The second phase of the boundary survey began in much the same way as the first—with trouble figuring out where to start. Upon arriving in the field, the commission discovered that the Rio Grande was two degrees west and El Paso 34 miles south and 130 miles west of where Disturnell's map showed them. Since Disturnell's map, "the town of Paso," and the intersection of the Rio Grande and southern boundary of New Mexico were all explicitly mentioned in the treaty's description of the boundary line, Bartlett and García Conde faced a quandary. Should they draw the boundary from the actual location of El Paso and the Rio Grande or from their positions on Disturnell's map? At stake were thousands of square miles of territory, including Mexican settlements in the Mesilla Valley and copper mines in Santa Rita, New Mexico. Drawing from their actual positions would transfer them to the United States; drawing from the map would keep them in Mexican hands. With each man holding to the interpretation that favored his nation, García Conde and Bartlett decided to compromise. They located the initial point on the "Rio Grande at the latitude given by the map, without any reference to its distance from El Paso."[40] Their agreement moved the boundary line north of El Paso, giving Mexico more land to the north, while the United States

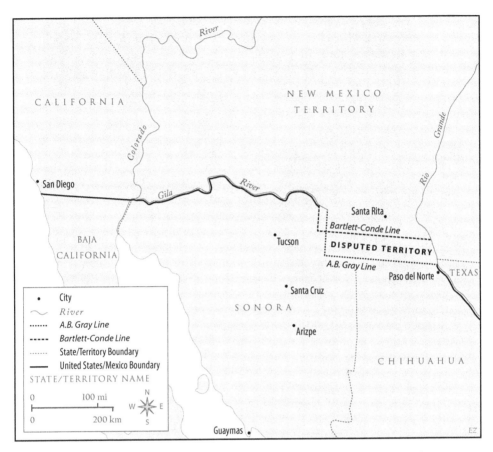

FIGURE 1.2. The disputed portion of the initial boundary line, showing the line agreed to by commissioners John Russell Bartlett and Pedro García Conde, the line favored by surveyor Andrew B. Gray, and the disputed territory between them, 1850–53 (map by Ezra Zeitler).

gained territory to the west as a result of positioning the initial point on the Rio Grande.

Both García Conde and Bartlett walked away from the compromise feeling satisfied. "The most vital question and that of greatest interest in the determination of the dividing line between our Republic and that of the United States, is resolved favorably in the interests of the Nation," wrote García Conde, celebrating Mexico's retention of El Paso and the Mesilla Valley with its two thousand Mexican inhabitants.[41] Bartlett was also confident, believing that in securing the Santa Rita copper mines he had acquired the most valuable part of the contested territory.[42] In light of the cooperative spirit of the commission and the intractable situation they faced, the compromise initially seemed like a successful negotiation of state power. However, as they would begin to learn that September, their compromise ultimately would fail as both surveyor Andrew Gray and many American politicians rejected the negotiated boundary line.

In the meantime, however, the boundary survey began in earnest. After dispatching teams to survey the Rio Grande border, Bartlett and García Conde headed west to oversee the commission's work on the western boundary line. From the initial point on the Rio Grande, the boundary ran west along the 32° 2′ line for three degrees (or approximately 175 miles) and then turned northward to meet the Gila River along which the line continued until its confluence with the Colorado River. This line cut through a desert in which it was difficult to travel and take measurements. The commission worked in temperatures ranging from below freezing in the mountains to over 120 degrees in the desert. The steep and rocky terrain at times forced members of the commission to abandon their wagons and carry their supplies and tools by mule. A Mexican engineer, Juan Bautista Espejo, reported that during a particularly difficult passage through the mountains a horse carrying a sextant and telescope fell and had to be killed. A day later his party endured thirty-eight hours without food and eighteen hours without water as they struggled through deep arroyos and steep mountains through which their mules could not pass and even the soldiers could not carry instruments because they needed their hands free.[43]

These difficult conditions ate away at the optimism with which the commission had begun. "As we toiled across these sterile plains, where no tree offered its friendly shade, the sun glowing fiercely, and the wind hot from the parched earth, cracking the lips and burning the eyes," Bartlett wrote of his journey through New Mexico in May 1851, "the thought would keep suggesting itself, Is this the land we have purchased, and are to survey and keep at such a cost? As far as the eye can reach stretches one unbroken waste, barren, wild, worthless."[44] While holding a no more charitable view of the border's environment, the U.S. commission's secretary, Dr. Thomas Webb, surmised that the bleakness of the landscape suited it to nothing else but a border. Concluding that the Sahara Desert compared favorably to the sandstorms, barrenness, and lack of water he experienced on his journey across the Mojave Desert from the Colorado River to San Diego, he wrote, "Indeed much of this country, that by those residing at a distance is imagined to be a perfect paradise, is a sterile waste, utterly worthless for any purpose than to constitute a barrier or natural line of demarcation between two neighboring nations."[45] Faced with a landscape so unlike the more lush and settled eastern United States, Webb and Bartlett had difficulty imagining how this land could become a productive part of the United States.

Contrary to Bartlett's and Webb's evaluations, this landscape had many uses and a large number of Native inhabitants who had been utilizing it for generations. Although political discourse and treaty language suggested otherwise, the United States and Mexico had exchanged land claimed by Indians. From the Rio Grande to the Pacific Ocean, the western boundary line cut through the homelands of Apache, Tohono O'odham, Pima, Maricopa, Yuma, Cocopah, and Diegueño peoples. Throughout the boundary survey, Native people were a constant presence. They served as guides, provided food and information to the commission, and allowed its members to study them as ethnographic subjects. This was particularly true of the Pimas and Maricopas, of whom the members of the commission thought highly. "They never, on any occasion," wrote the American interpreter, John Cremony, "no matter how much goaded, exhibited any vengeful or adverse spirit toward Americans."[46] Because of this trust and the location of Pima and Maricopa villages at points with forage and water, these places, more than the few Mexican settlements, became rare safe havens for the members of the commission.[47]

These sanctuaries were much needed, not only as sources of food and succor in the desert, but also as a defense against the raids of other Native peoples, most notoriously the Apaches. For generations, a group of distinct bands known collectively as Apaches had raided Pima, Maricopa, Tohono O'odham, and Mexican settlements in a cycle of retributive violence. In the years before the signing of the Treaty of Guadalupe Hidalgo, Apaches nearly drove the Mexicans out of northern Sonora completely. By the time the Americans arrived on the scene, this history of violent conflict had left the border landscape littered with abandoned settlements and barricaded towns and had created a deep sense of mutual hatred and distrust between the Apaches and other borderlands peoples that would persist into the twentieth century.[48]

The threat of attack, by Apaches in Chihuahua, Sonora, and New Mexico Territory, and by Yumas near the Colorado River, was a constant concern of the commission. Although the Mexican members of the commission did not elaborate on the Indian threat in their official reports, which lacked the narrative style and descriptive flourishes of the accounts produced by their American counterparts, they were certainly well aware of the threat they posed. García Conde was a product of the Mexican frontier and would have been steeped in its culture of violence. Arizpe, the town where he was born and would die, had once been the capital of Sonora, but Apache raids had taken their toll, leading the government to relocate the capital to safer territory farther south. If his time away from Sonora had dulled any of his memories of Apache dominance, García Conde would quickly have been brought back to reality when a band of Apaches attacked his party while they were en route to meet with the U.S. commission in September 1851. Despite the presence of more than seventy men, including a military escort, the Apaches were able to get within a quarter mile of the commissioner's tent and drive off his saddle horses.[49]

The experience of the Mexican boundary commission suggested that as far as the Apaches were concerned the outcome of the Mexican-American War was irrelevant to their raiding practices. However, that was not entirely the case. Under Article XI of the Treaty of Guadalupe Hidalgo, the U.S. government had agreed to prevent all Indian raids from U.S. territory into Mexico and to return any Mexicans the Indians had captured.[50] Given that most raids followed a north-to-south trajectory, the U.S. government had in effect promised to do what neither Mexico nor the Spanish empire before it had ever been able to do—to put a stop to Indian raiding in northern Mexico. This treaty provision more than any other would demonstrate just how big the gap was between what the U.S. government believed it could do and what was actually within its power.

Influenced by his paternalistic view of Indians in general and naïveté about the Apaches in particular, Bartlett eagerly embraced the impossible task of enforcing Article XI. As an antislavery Whig, he abhorred the practices of raiding and trading captives that were widespread in the borderlands and saw it as his responsibility as the "nearest and highest representative of the government of the United States" to intervene.[51] His first opportunity to do so came in June of 1851 when a teenage girl named Iñez González arrived with a party of traders at the commission's camp at the Santa Rita copper mines in the mountains to the west of the Rio Grande. An Apache raiding party had captured González near her home in Santa Cruz, Sonora, the previous September and sold her, along with a number of horses and mules, to the traders. Asserting his authority under Article XI, Bartlett ordered the traders to turn González over to his care and began to make plans to take her home. She remained with the commission for three months, enduring the long, rain-soaked trek through the Santa Rita Mountains before Bartlett reunited her with her family in Santa Cruz. The emotional response that greeted González's seemingly miraculous return from captivity filled Bartlett with pride and nearly strained his descriptive abilities. "I have witnessed many scenes on the stage, of the meeting of friends after a long separation, and have read highly wrought narratives of similar interviews," wrote Bartlett, "but none of them approached in pathos the spontaneous burst of feeling exhibited by the mother and daughter on this occasion. Thanks to the Almighty rose above all other sounds, while they remained clasped in each other's arms, for the deliverance from captivity, and the restoration of the beloved daughter to her home and friends."[52] It was Bartlett's proudest moment as boundary commissioner. In rescuing González, Bartlett had for once succeeded in forcing the borderlands to conform to his vision of sovereignty and domesticity. However, Bartlett's romantic redemption narrative lost some of its power when he crossed paths with González again. Less than a year after her reunion with her family, the teenager had left home to live with the military commander of Tubac in present-day Arizona. Although the two would go on to have two sons and eventually marry, Bartlett was disappointed to find his former ward living in what he considered a state of sin.[53]

A more significant challenge to both Bartlett's paternalistic notions and state power came from the Apaches. Few Indians were as willing to surrender their captives as the Mexican and Anglo-American traders who had purchased González. Just a day after González's rescue, two Mexican boys approached John Cremony, the U.S. interpreter, begging for help. The two adolescents, Saverro Aredia and José Trinfan, had been captured by Apaches in northern Sonora and held in captivity for six years. Cremony brought the boys to Bartlett, who in turn delivered them to García Conde who arranged for their return to their families. With the boys gone, Bartlett faced the difficult task of explaining to the Apaches' leaders why he had stolen their captives. The ensuing conversations revealed not just the divide between Bartlett's moral condemnation of captivity and the Apaches' more nuanced economic views but also a profound difference of opinion about who really controlled the borderlands.

Upon hearing of the commission's seizure of the captives, two Apache leaders, Mangas Coloradas and Delgadito, approached Bartlett with what they considered a reasonable suggestion, that he pay the captives' owner for the property he had lost. Unwilling to become complicit in the captive trade, Bartlett initially refused to purchase the boys' freedom. Instead, like the paternalistic figure he imagined himself to be, he attempted to explain the treaty provisions and "the principles of justice and humanity on which it was based" to the Apaches.[54]

This combination of admonishment and explanation was consistent with Bartlett's general approach to Indian relations. Blaming the unprincipled and treacherous acts of Mexican and Euro-American traders, emigrants, and settlers for provoking the Apaches' vengeance, Bartlett was convinced that "kind treatment, a rigid adherence to what is right, and a prompt and invariable fulfillment of all promises, would secure the friendship of the Apaches."[55] While camped at the copper mines, Bartlett attempted to cultivate amicable relations with the Apaches in the vicinity, inviting prominent leaders to dine with him and distributing gifts of clothing, even as he planned to undercut the basis of their economic survival by abolishing raids.

While Mangas Coloradas was happy to accept a broadcloth suit with ornamented buttons from Bartlett, he was not persuaded by Bartlett's lecture on the United States' sovereign obligations and the evils of trading captives. In response to Bartlett's assertions of U.S. jurisdiction, Mangas Coloradas retorted by quickly, and literally, putting him in his place. "You came to our country," he stressed. "You were well received by us. Your lives, your property, your animals, were safe. You passed by ones, by twos, and by threes, through our country; you went and came in peace."[56] Regardless of treaties signed with the Mexicans, the Americans, Mangas Coloradas emphasized, were in Apache country. By the end of the conversation, Bartlett agreed to open the commissary's stores to the Apaches. Giving them $250 in goods in exchange for the captives, he effectively ignored the provision of Article XI that prohibited Americans from purchasing captives. In recounting these events Bartlett explained that he had only resorted to remuneration for fear that angering the Indians would put the entire boundary survey in danger.[57] With this realization, he implicitly recognized who held the balance of power on the border. Despite his statements about American justice and honor, in the end he realized that regardless of what the treaty said, the place where they were was not yet under the control of the United States.

The Apaches hammered this lesson home as the boundary survey continued. Before leaving the copper mines, the commission lost between one hundred and three hundred mules and horses to an Apache raid led by the same chiefs who had negotiated with Bartlett. Lest the Americans misinterpret this blatant act of disrespect, Delgadito, who had only two nights before slept in John Cremony's tent and accepted a shirt and shoes from him as a gift, taunted the Americans who had come to retrieve their animals by, in Cremony's words, "slapping his buttocks and defying us with the most opprobrious language."[58] As the commission moved west, they suffered from additional raids, forcing members of the commission to pass through some of the harshest stretches of the border on foot. At the Santa Rita copper mines, the commission had been encamped with three hundred U.S. soldiers to protect them, but as their work progressed, their surveying duties demanded that they break into small parties with only minimal military escort. Near the confluence of the Gila and Colorado rivers, a small party took a number of prominent Yuma chiefs hostage and traveled at night in order to pass through the territory unharmed.[59] On the border Americans found not only that they were incapable of fulfilling their responsibilities under Article XI, but that they could hardly protect themselves.

At the same time that Indians, the environment, and inaccurate information proved how little control the United States and Mexico exercised
over the new border, political controversy sparked by Gray's opposition
to Bartlett and García Conde's determination of the initial point on the
Rio Grande revealed that the comparatively simple process of delimiting
the boundary line in the treaty was more difficult than it had seemed.

Even as the commission completed its work on the western border in
August 1852, the boundary line began to unravel. On the ground, William Carr Lane, the pro-southern territorial governor of New Mexico,
claimed jurisdiction over the Mesilla Valley in the disputed territory between the line García Conde and Bartlett had drawn and that for which
Gray had argued. Lane threatened to dispatch troops to claim the valley
by force; Governor Ángel Trías of Chihuahua mustered soldiers to repel
them. It was only the U.S. military commander's refusal to take part in
the invasion that prevented violence from erupting along the border.
Meanwhile, in Washington, DC, the controversy over the New Mexico–
Chihuahua boundary line became increasingly enmeshed in sectional
politics as a result of the disputed territory's importance for a potential
southern transcontinental railroad route. Convinced by Gray's argument
that the compromise line left Mexico in control of the passable valleys a
railroad would require, the U.S. Congress rejected García Conde and
Bartlett's compromise line and brought the boundary survey to a halt.[60]

The following May, newly elected President Franklin Pierce, at the urging of his secretary of war, and future Confederate president, Jefferson
Davis, sent James Gadsden to Mexico to renegotiate the southern boundary with the recently returned Mexican president Antonio López de
Santa Anna. Although the onset of new negotiations renewed calls for
extensive territorial cessions, the final settlement secured the smallest
amount of land that Gadsden had hoped to gain—only a thin strip of
territory through which a wagon road and eventually, it was hoped, a
railroad would run. In addition, taking the experience of the boundary
commission into consideration, Gadsden negotiated for Article XI, and
with it the United States' commitment to preventing Indian raids into
Mexico, to be struck from the treaty. In exchange for this additional land
and letting the United States off the hook for Indian raiding, the Mexican
government received $10 million, only a third less than that paid for the
entire territory lost in the Treaty of Guadalupe Hidalgo.[61]

The Gadsden Treaty, or Mesilla Treaty as it was known in Mexico, settled the delimitation of the western boundary line, but it was not without
political consequences. No less than before the Mexican-American War,
the Mexican people believed that the sale of national territory was an insult to national honor and a devastating blow to the nation. Denouncing
Santa Anna for his role in this betrayal, Mexican liberals overthrew him

in 1855. The man who had resuscitated his political career after presiding over the loss of Texas and serving a disastrous stint as president during the Mexican-American War found he could not make a comeback after agreeing to exchange cash for land, no matter how little.[62]

The negotiation of the Gadsden Purchase marked, for a time, the end of political debate about the southern border in the United States. The rapid descent toward civil war left the boundary line behind and dashed southerners' hopes for a southern transcontinental rail line. Decades would pass before the first train would travel through the borderlands. Once again the state's aspirations for the border proved illusive.

The redrawing of the boundary line, however, was more successful. In December 1854 a second joint boundary commission, headed by the former surveyors, William Emory and José Salazar Ylarregui, returned to El Paso to begin resurveying the boundary line. Much was the same—the deserts, mountains, Indian attacks, and, in the Mexican commission, the lack of adequate funding and military support.[63] Along one stretch of the boundary line running southeast from the Colorado River through the heart of the Sonoran Desert to Quitovaquita, the commission faced 125 miles without water. At one point they traveled only seventeen miles in three days as, in Emory's words, "massive rocks and steep precipices constantly impeded the progress of and turned the party out of its course, making the route circuitous as well as hazardous; rough ascents were surmounted, steep ravines followed down, and deep gullies passed; the mules had actually to be dragged along."[64] The Apaches also kept up their assaults. Although Emory bragged that the U.S. commission managed to evade Indian attacks, he noted that "our co-operators on the Mexican commission were twice robbed of every hoof by the Apaches, and extensive losses were sustained by other detachments of United States troops, and by our citizens traversing the region."[65]

However, despite these challenges and thanks in large part to the experience that the commissioners and surveyors now brought to the table, the commission completed its work in the field by October 1855. After following the Rio Grande from the Gulf of Mexico to El Paso, the amended line ran one hundred miles to the west before turning south to the 31° 20′ parallel. It then followed that parallel to the 111th meridian where the boundary angled northwest to connect with the Colorado River twenty miles below its junction with the Gila. Those twenty miles of river formed the final portion of the revised boundary before it connected with the California–Baja California boundary that Weller and García Conde had first surveyed in the summer of 1849.[66] Although the commissioners would have to meet again to approve the final maps, Salazar Ylarregui reported that "the line was completely *surveyed*, *marked*, and *fixed* in all its length."[67] Over the course of the next 150 years, new

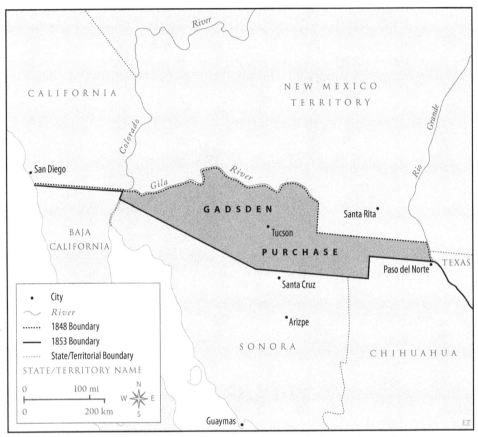

FIGURE 1.3. The western U.S.-Mexico boundary line following the Gadsden, or Mesilla, Treaty, 1853 (map by Ezra Zeitler).

joint boundary commissions would return to the boundary to correct surveying errors, rebuild boundary monuments, and, along the Rio Grande, contend with changes caused by the river's shifting channels.[68] But, for the most part, the boundary line as it exists today was in place.

Of course, no one could have known that at the time. While Salazar Ylarregui and Emory had fixed the boundary line, nothing else was settled in the borderlands. If U.S. and Mexican officials had believed that the Treaty of Guadalupe Hidalgo had ended the struggle for control of North America, the experience of the joint boundary commission had proved just how tenuous their territorial sovereignty was. The signing of the Gadsden Treaty had once again remade maps of the United States and Mexico, but it had done very little to reshape the landscape of power along the border. In the years following the completion of the boundary survey, the struggles for control of the borderlands would continue un-abated along the boundary line. Even as the boundary commission car-ried out its duties, filibusters launched expeditions into Sonora and Baja California and Apaches continued to move back and forth across the boundary line, raiding with impunity. The line was complete, but what it would mean remained to be seen.

Chapter Two

HOLDING THE LINE

Fighting Land Pirates and Apaches on the Border

IN MARCH 1856, as the Joint United States and Mexican Boundary Commission prepared to draft the final maps of the boundary line in Washington, DC, the last Mexican troops pulled out of Tucson. As American settlers raised the U.S. flag, the Mexican soldiers and their families marched south through a storm, headed toward Santa Cruz, just across the new boundary line in Sonora.[1]

The Sonora that they returned to was a state under siege. Apache raiders swept down from the north, attacking cities and outlying settlements. At the same time private armies of French and American adventurers, known as filibusters, plotted to invade the state and usurp Mexican authority. In response Mexican officials repeatedly called on their citizens to rise to the state's defense.

As the attacks on Sonora demonstrated, the delimitation and demarcation of the boundary line had not necessarily created a landscape of national sovereignty in the borderlands, but just a line running through territory that was still very much contested. If the Mexican-American War had been a binational struggle, the fight for control of the borderlands engaged not just the U.S. and Mexican governments, but independent filibusters who imagined they could create new nations on Mexican soil and Apaches who had long dominated the region. The battles for control of the border would continue into the 1880s as settlers, soldiers, filibusters, and Native peoples fought to defend, displace, and defy the boundary line and the sovereign limits it signified.

In order to establish military authority and make the boundary line a meaningful marker of territorial sovereignty, the Mexican and U.S. militaries had to defeat two very different threats—the first from filibusters from outside the region and the second from Apache people who had long lived in the borderlands. The first would pit Mexicans against Europeans and Americans who sought to detach parts of their territory from the Mexican Republic. As they fought off filibusters, the people of northern Mexico not only assured that the boundary line would hold but also solidified their allegiance to the Mexican Republic in opposition to those who would challenge the nation's sovereignty, especially Americans. By contrast, fighting Apaches required Mexicans and Americans to work together across the boundary line. Only by coordinating a binational campaign were the United States and Mexico able to wrest control of the borderlands away from the Apaches in the 1880s and finally claim the territory they had divided over thirty years before in the wake of the Mexican-American War.

While both of these struggles revealed how far the United States and Mexico still had to go before they could claim to fully control the borderlands, they also provided evidence of the subtle ways in which the boundary line had already begun to change the landscape of power in the region. For filibusters, who respected the sovereignty of the United States but not that of Mexico, the boundary line marked the beginning and end of their expeditions. And although Apaches continued to raid back and forth across the border, they increasingly did so strategically, with the knowledge that international law prevented the U.S. and Mexican militaries from following them. Drawing the border did not end the contest for control of the borderlands, but it did alter the rules of the game.

DEFENDING MEXICAN SPACE

Despite the boundary commissioners' claim that the boundary line was complete, in the 1850s it seemed much more likely that it would not hold. It is only with the benefit of hindsight that the Gadsden Purchase has come to mark the end of the United States' acquisition of Mexican territory. In the years following the signing of the Gadsden Treaty, many Americans expected and many Mexicans feared that it would be just the first step as the arc of U.S. manifest destiny swung from west to south. Throughout the 1850s, the U.S. government repeatedly attempted to buy more Mexican territory. At the same time filibusters launched independent expeditions intent on usurping Mexican sovereignty in the borderlands. As pressure increased on the Mexican border, the people of northern Mexico defended themselves again and again. In the process they not only asserted control over the border but also solidified their identity as defenders of the Mexican nation.

The 1850s got off to an ominous start for Mexico. Although Mexico lost only a small amount of land in the Gadsden Treaty, the negotiations leading up to the treaty sent a clear message that the United States' territorial hunger had not been sated. The U.S. envoy, James Gadsden, a South Carolinian with an interest in railroad promotion, had traveled to Mexico with much grander ambitions. In 1853 President Franklin Pierce authorized Gadsden to offer up to $50 million (five times more than the United States eventually paid for the sliver of present-day southern Arizona and New Mexico) for Tamaulipas, Coahuila, Nuevo León, Baja California, and the northern parts of Chihuahua and Sonora. While Gadsden did not achieve all that he had hoped, it was only a matter of time before the United States would try again.[2]

As Mexican troops and settlers reluctantly moved south, the pressure for further U.S. acquisitions mounted in the borderlands. American travelers, military personnel, and mining entrepreneurs began entering the borderlands in the 1850s, adding their voices to the chorus of demands for the United States to push the border farther south into Chihuahua, Sonora, and Baja California. An ex-army lieutenant and mining entrepreneur named Sylvester Mowry was one of the most vocal of this group. After serving at Fort Yuma on the Colorado River, Mowry returned to New Mexico Territory in the late 1850s and purchased a mine near the boundary line in present-day southern Arizona (Arizona Territory was not separated from New Mexico Territory until 1863). As he sought out investors for his mining project, he also campaigned for the United States to annex Sonora. Mimicking earlier arguments about U.S. manifest destiny, Mowry and other expansionists naturalized their calls for annexation. They argued that Arizona and Sonora were part of a shared landscape that the border artificially divided. "The line at present is irregular in its course, and cuts off from our Territory the head of the Santa Cruz River and valley, the Sonoita valley, the San Bernardino valley, the whole course of the Colorado River from a point twenty miles below the mouth of the Gila River," Mowry wrote, "and, worse than all, the control of the head of the Gulf of California, . . . besides a large and extremely valuable silver region, well known to both Mexicans and Americans—the Planchas de la Plata." Nature and economy, according to Mowry, demanded a different boundary line, one that would give the United States control of the port of Guaymas on the Sonoran coast and with it the borderlands' connection to Pacific trade and travel. "The natural outlet for the productions of Arizona must be through a port on the Gulf of California," he argued, "and the acquisition of California necessitates the possession of Sonora."[3]

It did not require much persuasion from Mowry and his compatriots to convince American officials that they should try to acquire more Mexican land. Control of Baja California and a port on the Gulf of California, and with it greater access to Pacific trade, had long been on the United States' wish list of territorial acquisitions. Both items had been on the table during the negotiation of both the Treaty of Guadalupe Hidalgo and the Gadsden Treaty. In 1857, just four years after the signing of the Gadsden Treaty, President James Buchanan made another attempt to push the boundary line southward, authorizing the U.S. minister to Mexico to offer as much as $15 million for northern Chihuahua, most of Sonora, and

Baja California. Reflecting Mowry's justifications for annexation, Buchanan claimed that the transfer of this additional territory would create a more "natural" boundary in which one country, the United States, would control all of the mining districts and the entire course of the Colorado River.[4]

Officials in Mexico City turned down all of the U.S. offers and looked for ways to shore up sovereignty along the border. Despite the drastic reduction in Mexico's defensive perimeter due to the loss of more than half of its territory to the United States, the Mexican Republic continued to struggle to defend itself. Chihuahua, Sonora, and Baja California were still far from Mexico City. Political infighting and economic instability wracked the country and limited the federal government's ability to protect the beleaguered frontier. During the difficult years following the formation of the boundary line, the Mexican government's meager efforts at border security focused on building up a population of loyal citizens and soldiers along the boundary line to defend it. Although Mexico's experiment with colonization in Texas had proved disastrous, the federal government renewed its efforts to attract colonists after the Mexican-American War. Within six months of the signing of the Treaty of Guadalupe Hidalgo, President José Joaquín de Herrera issued a decree establishing colonies along the boundary line. Colonizing the border, Herrera hoped, would help preserve Mexico's "territorial integrity" and defend against Indian incursions.[5] In subsequent years, both local and federal officials supported colonization in Sonora and Baja California. However, although the government offered potential colonists inducements, including land grants and tax exemptions, the discovery of gold in California proved a much more attractive draw, and many Sonorans joined the rush to the California gold fields. This exodus, along with the continuing effects of Apache raids and warfare, caused Sonora, instead of attracting new settlers, to lose population. According to the U.S. consul at Guaymas, the state's population fell from 150,000 in 1840 to 133,300 in 1861.[6]

As the colonies failed to flourish, border defenses were primarily left to state and local governments. In the absence of a strong central government, a few men known as caciques, or caudillos, took hold of state governments and ruled with almost complete autonomy from Mexico City. Drawing on their regional connections and military experience, men like Santiago Vidaurri in Nuevo León, Luis Terrazas in Chihuahua, and Manuel María Gándara and Ignacio Pesqueira in Sonora dominated politics, development, and defense along the border.[7]

Born in Arizpe, Sonora, in 1820, Ignacio Pesqueira grew up in a frontier culture that emphasized honor and defense and prepared him for a long career of fighting political rivals, filibusters, and Apaches. Pesqueira's father was a military officer and his mother was the daughter of a prominent family whose members included the boundary commissioner, Pedro García Conde. When he was a young man, Pesqueira's parents sent him to be educated in Spain and France, but when he returned to the borderlands at the age of eighteen he quickly readjusted to life on the frontier. He became known for his hard drinking and bravery in campaigns against the Apaches. This reputation aided his rapid rise through the military chain of command and contributed to his emergence as a political leader in the early 1850s. In 1856 Pesqueira joined other Sonoran liberals in challenging Manuel María Gándara, the caudillo who had ruled Sonora for twenty years. With Gándara's defeat, Pesqueira became governor. He would remain the most powerful force in Sonoran politics for the next two decades.[8]

Pesqueira was acutely aware of the paradoxical challenges facing Sonora and the rest of the Mexican borderlands. On the one hand the scarcity of settlers and profitable enterprises left the border states vulnerable to Indian raids and filibustering. On the other, due to Mexico's lack of capital and the difficulty of attracting settlers from the south, the means of improving these conditions lay in the hands of foreign capitalists and colonists who also threatened Mexican authority. Officials such as Pesqueira faced the difficult task of deciding which foreign ventures to welcome and which to denounce and drive away. At times Pesqueira worked with Americans to develop mines in the state and to build a railroad between Sonora and the United States. For these efforts he earned the praise of Sylvester Mowry, who called him "honorable, liberal, and especially desirous of forwarding, in every legitimate manner, the wishes and views of Americans whose enterprise has led them to Sonora."[9] However, as Mowry's support for U.S. annexation of Sonora proved, American entrepreneurs could not necessarily be trusted. Throughout his time in power, Pesqueira also worked to build up Sonora's Mexican population while criticizing "Yanqui" imperialists and striking back with military force at foreigners who threatened both his power and Mexican sovereignty.[10]

Among the worst of these threats were a series of filibustering bands that assaulted Sonora and Baja California throughout the 1850s. Derived from a Dutch word meaning *pirate* or *free booty*, the term *filibuster* accurately captured the spirit of the nineteenth-century land pirates who raided northern Mexico hoping to acquire territory for their own aggrandizement. While some of these men imagined themselves as illicit agents of U.S. expansion, neither their background nor their agendas were limited to the United States. Among the leaders of the most significant expeditions against Baja California and Sonora during this period were not only three Americans but also four Frenchmen, a Mexican, and a Venetian-born son of Alsatian and Corsican parents. Drawn to the North American West by the California gold rush, these men launched reckless and arrogant expeditions that reflected the unsettled and opportunistic climate of that time and place more than the imperial ambitions of the United States. Men like Gaston Raousset-Boulbon, the self-proclaimed "Sultan of Sonora," and William Walker, the "Grey-Eyed Man of Destiny," described themselves as state builders and made clumsy attempts to cloak their self-aggrandizing pursuits as Mexican colonization ventures or acts of American expansionism, but they were operating outside the bounds of state authority. During the 1850s this motley group of gold rush refugees, proslavery expansionists, and self-proclaimed visionaries repeatedly assaulted Sonora and Baja California with the intention of carving new nations out of Mexican soil.[11]

The most notorious of the filibusters to invade northern Mexico was William Walker. Walker's invasion of Baja California was only the first step on a filibustering path that would eventually land him in front of a firing squad in Honduras in 1860. Launched from San Francisco in the fall of 1853, Walker's first expedition sailed to the southern part of Baja California and easily captured the capital, La Paz. Walker declared the establishment of the Republic of Lower California and proclaimed himself president before retreating north to Ensenada. There, in an attempt to disguise his retreat as expansion, he changed the name of his new nation to the Republic of Sonora and launched an ill-conceived, overland assault on Sonora. By early 1854 Mexican forces were massing and Walker's men were losing faith. "The conclusion was fast settling upon his and other minds, that the expedition had but one object," reported an anonymous member of the expedition, "viz.: to enrich certain capitalists, and satisfy the ambition of William Walker, Colonel and President."[12] Walker's men proved unwilling to die for his ambition. On May 8, 1854, the filibusters fled north across the border to San Diego.[13]

The effects of filibustering expeditions like Walker's on the border were paradoxical. Filibusters transgressed the boundary line in hopes of creating new national divisions of space in the borderlands, but at the same time, the line limited the spatial parameters of their ventures. Filibusters did not filibuster in U.S. territory. They confined their efforts to territory south of the border, indicating a respect for the U.S. authority embedded in the line, at the same time that they defied Mexican sovereignty. In defining the limits of his new republic, William Walker relied on the existing border, decreeing that the Republic of Sonora would be limited on the north by "the boundary line between the United States and Mexico, as established by the treaty of *Guadalupe Hidalgo*."[14] The border was even more significant in marking the end of Walker's filibuster. In his personal narrative of the expedition, Walker focused not on the origins of his expedition or his march to Sonora, but rather on that moment of defeat when his men marched "from the Tia-Juana country-house to the monument marking the boundary between the United States and Mexico, and there yielded their arms to a military officer of the former power."[15] Even as they violated Mexican territorial sovereignty, filibusters implicitly recognized the authority of the United States and the emerging significance of the boundary line.

If filibusters' respect for the boundary line revealed nascent U.S. sovereignty, resistance to their assaults helped solidify a sense of Mexican national identity along the border. Throughout the 1850s Mexican settlers, Native communities, and civil and military leaders on the frontier joined together despite their differences to defeat filibusters and defend Mexican territorial sovereignty. It was only through their collective efforts that the boundary line stayed in place and a sense of Mexican national identity continued to develop along the border.

Although Sonora had been a part of the Mexican Republic since its founding, internal divisions and distance from Mexico City had inhibited the formation of a strong national identity among its people. Like most of Mexico, Sonora had a heterogeneous population. The state was home to Indians (Yaqui, Mayo, Pima, Opata, Tohono O'odham, and Apache), a growing mestizo population, and Mexican-born Spaniards, or criollos, but it was the "white" criollos who controlled the government and most of its resources. By the 1850s the population had also become politically divided between the supporters of Gándara and those of Pesqueira.[16]

In addition to these internal divisions, Sonorans also had an uneasy relationship with the Mexican central government. Separated from the rest of Mexico by distance and the difficulty of traveling over the Pacific Ocean or the Sierra Madre, Sonora had long been on the periphery of Mexico and its priorities. The inability of the national government to provide adequate funding for frontier defense had strained relations between Mexico City and the frontier. During the height of the Apache raids, conditions were so bad that some Sonoran elites considered seeking annexation to the United States. Cave Couts, a U.S. Army officer who served with the boundary commission, reported that General José María Carrasco, who at the time was the military governor of Sonora, had told him that "in consequence of the neglect of the Govt. he thinks Sonora ought to declare her independence, and apply to the U.S. for annexation."[17] However, if some Sonoran elites saw hope in U.S. annexation, the majority of the state's population was skeptical of American rule, particularly in light of the United States' failure to prevent Apache raids and the growing number of filibustering expeditions that began to invade the state in the 1850s.[18]

While concerns about preserving their territorial integrity pushed Sonorans away from the United States, they did not necessarily draw them to the Mexican federal government. Sonorans were outraged when President Santa Anna signed the Gadsden Treaty in 1853, releasing the United States from its responsibility for preventing Indian raiding and selling off the northern part of the state, which included land owned by some prominent state figures. However, with Santa Anna's removal in the Ayutla Revolt (1854–55), a new liberal regime rose to power in Mexico City that worked to cultivate ties with the regional caudillos, including Pesqueira, and embedded its ideals for liberal governance in the new Mexican constitution of 1857. While most Sonorans did not immediately embrace this government, they were glad to see the last of Santa Anna and optimistic about liberalism and the possibility that the central government would finally offer them support.[19]

A critical step in the formation of a shared national identity among the different segments of Sonora's population and the new national government came in the spring of 1857. In the face of another filibuster assault, representatives of the federal government, state officials, and local people all came together to repulse a filibustering expedition launched by Henry Alexander Crabb. Like many filibusters, Crabb came to Sonora by way of the California gold fields. Born in Tennessee, he had fled Nashville after killing a man and joined the rush to California in 1849. He moved to Stockton, one of the main supply points for the mines, and quickly established himself as a political leader, serving in both the California state senate and assembly. While in California he also reconnected with an old acquaintance from Tennessee, William Walker. Sympathetic to Walker's expansionist agenda, Crabb expressed interest in his plans for a Central American filibuster and testified on his behalf during the 1854 trial in which a proexpansion jury acquitted Walker of violating U.S. neutrality laws when he invaded Baja California. Perhaps it was Walker's influence that caused Crabb, in the wake of a failed reelection bid in 1855, to begin developing his own plan for a filibuster in Sonora.[20]

Crabb's interest in Sonora was not incidental. Shortly after his arrival in California, he had met and married Filomena Ainza, the daughter of a once-prominent Sonoran family, most of which had relocated to California during the gold rush. In 1856 Crabb and his new in-laws began planning to establish a colony in northern Sonora. That spring, Crabb and his brother-in-law, Agustín Ainza, traveled to Hermosillo where they met with state officials and informed them of their colonization plans.

The Sonora in which they arrived was in chaos. Population loss, filibustering attacks, Apache raids, and uprisings among the Yaqui Indians in the southern part of the state had taken their toll. The state was falling into civil war as Pesqueira and his supporters challenged Gándara's control. Crabb and Ainza believed they could take advantage of this instability and the Sonorans' dissatisfaction. In 1856 they approached Pesqueira, promising military and financial assistance in exchange for his authorization of their colony. The terms of this agreement, and whether Pesqueira actually intended to support the undertaking, are unknown. Regardless, in the summer of 1856 Crabb returned to California where he moved ahead with his scheme. As it took shape, Crabb's expedition had many of the traits of a lawful colonization venture that might pose no threat to Mexican sovereignty. After all, while Crabb was an American, his in-laws were native to Sonora. He also enlisted the assistance of a colonial agent, Jesus Islas, who was working to repatriate Mexicans who had gone to the California gold fields. In their communications with Sonoran officials, Crabb and Ainza portrayed themselves as Islas's representatives and stressed that their colonies would serve the poor Mexicans in California and help to protect the Sonoran frontier.[21]

But their filibustering intentions were soon exposed. As Agustín Ainza traveled through Sonora gathering support for the venture in the summer of 1857, he revealed that his ultimate goal was the creation of an independent republic made up of Sonora, Sinaloa, and Baja California. It was rumored that he hoped eventually to seek annexation by the United States. As reports of Ainza and Crabb's plans spread through Sonora, state officials and newspapers responded with a growing sense of distrust and indignation. As early as July, one official noted that the primary purpose of Crabb and Ainza's colonization overtures was to serve as a foundation for "gross machinations." Newspapers from Sonora to Mexico City carried reports that Crabb was planning to invade Sonora.[22]

As these rumors rippled across Sonora a wave of anti-American sentiment rose to meet them. Crabb and the Ainzas had sorely miscalculated Sonorans' antipathy for filibusters, and Americans in particular. Crabb's force represented perhaps the one thing that could bring Sonorans of all stripes together. By the time Crabb and his advance party of eighty-nine men reached the Sonoran border at Sonoita in late March 1857, federal and state officials and communities near the border were aligned and arming against them. From the governor down to the local justices of the peace, national, state, and local officials mustered troops to meet the filibusters. Having defeated Gándara, Pesqueira now turned his attention to Crabb. He ordered detachments from towns all over northern Sonora to prepare to defend against the invaders. José M. Yáñez, the general-in-chief of the forces of the western states of Mexico, called for reinforcements and began marching north from Mazatlán, explaining to his superiors in Mexico City that the "integrity" of Sonoran soil and "the honor and rights of our country" were at risk.[23]

Yáñez's patriotic sentiments were typical of the nationalist rhetoric that accompanied the calls to arms. One official in the small town of Soni reported that although his town was almost completely without arms and ammunition, it was "in the best disposition to shed the last drop of its blood to sustain the government in behalf of union, and not to be sold, like the products of the soil, to foreigners."[24] Captain Hilario Gabilondo convinced a group of Indians to join him by explaining that "we were threatened with a foreign invasion, which endangered our nationality, our families, interests, religion, etc." By invoking this "holy and just cause," Gabilondo informed Pesqueira, he had not only recruited the Indians but had also "succeeded in obliterating the names of Gándara and Pesqueira and made them understand that to obey whoever has the authority, is the duty of every citizen."[25] In the face of American filibusters, elites and villagers, federal and state officials, and whites and Indians came together and put their lives on the line. They not only resisted but at least some also explained their resistance as a patriotic act in defense of Mexican sovereignty.

Even as the forces against him coalesced, Crabb made the critical decision to cross the border with sixty-nine men. Despite Crabb's promise that he would populate his colony with repatriated Mexicans, almost all of these men were Americans. By the time they crossed the border, the party had received word of the defenses being made to meet them. As they headed south toward Caborca, Crabb sent a letter of protest to the local prefect. Claiming that he was leading a legal colonization venture, he denounced the actions being taken against him. "[B]ear this in mind," he wrote, "if blood is to flow, with all its horrors, on your head be it, and not on mine. Yet you may rest assured, while pursuing your hostile preparations, that as regards myself I shall go where I have long intended to go."[26]

The prefect forwarded this letter to Pesqueira, where it evoked a scathing response. Whether Pesqueira was trying to make up for his earlier complicity or was simply venting his patriotic rage, his rejoinder left no doubt that he would treat Crabb and his companions as filibusters:

> Let us fly, then, to chastise with all the fury that can scarcely be restrained in hearts full of hatred of oppression, the savage filibuster, who has dared, in an evil hour, to tread on the national territory, and to provoke—madman!—our anger.
>
> No pity, no generous sentiments for that rabble!
>
> Let them die the death of wild beasts, who, trampling under foot the law of nations, and despising the civil law and all social institutions, are bold enough to invoke as their only guide the natural law, and to ask as their only help the force of brutes!
>
> Let our reconciliation be made sincere, Sonorians, by our common

hatred of that accursed horde of pirates without country, without religion, without honor.

Let the only distinctive mark that protects our foreheads, other than the balls of the enemy, humiliation and insult, be the tri-colored ribbon, the sublime conception of the genius of Iguala. On it we will write those beautiful words, "LIBERTY OR DEATH" . . .

Very soon we shall all return covered with glory, after having assured forever the prosperity of Sonora, and recorded with indelible letters, in scorn of tyranny, this principle: "THE COMMUNITY THAT WISHES TO BE FREE WILL BE SO."

Meanwhile, fellow-citizens, open your hearts and give free vent to the enthusiasm which is swelling in them!

Long live Mexico! Death to the filibusters![27]

Crabb's party finally met the Mexican forces on April 1. As Crabb and his men approached Caborca, the Mexicans opened fire. The Americans fought back, killing a number of the Mexican soldiers and pursuing them as they fell back to Caborca. Inside the village the Mexican troops and townspeople barricaded themselves inside the church while the Americans huddled in houses across the plaza. After the Americans failed to dynamite their way into the church, the fighting settled into a standoff while the Mexicans awaited reinforcements. Within a few days, soldiers and volunteers, including a group of Tohono O'odham Indians under the command of Hilario Gabilondo, surrounded the Americans. The Tohono O'odham shot flaming arrows into the hay roofs of the houses in which the Americans cowered. Faced with a choice between surrendering and making a desperate run for the border, Crabb chose the former. At dawn the next day the Mexican troops executed him and all but one of his men, a boy of sixteen who was left to tell their story.[28]

If there was any doubt about the Sonorans' feelings about the filibusters it was laid to rest in the days and weeks following the executions. Reports filtered back to the United States that the Mexicans had desecrated the filibusters' bodies, leaving them unburied in a field where they became fodder for hogs and coyotes. They cut off Crabb's head and kept it preserved in a jar of vinegar to be shown as a trophy. Meanwhile, Mexican troops pursued the remaining members of Crabb's party who he had left behind at Sonoita. They found sixteen of them en route to Caborca and brought them into the city where they met the same fate as their compatriots. They then captured the final four at Sonoita and killed them as well.[29]

In the following months these events resonated through and beyond the borderlands. Pesqueira cut off all trade with Arizona and people on both sides of the border made threats against one another. "The abrasion was so serious that Americans were not safe over the Mexican boundary," wrote one of the partners in the Sonora Exploring and Mining Company, "and Mexicans were in danger in the boundaries of the United States."[30] The U.S. government, through its minister to Mexico, protested the execution of Crabb and his men. He especially took issue with the Mexican troops' killing of the four men at Sonoita, who a number of witnesses claimed had been on the U.S. side of the line at the time of their capture. Mexican officials, however, were unapologetic. They maintained that Crabb and his men had clearly violated Mexican sovereignty and had received the punishment they deserved.[31]

Perhaps most importantly, Crabb's defeat marked the beginning of the end of filibustering in northern Mexico. Whether the image of Crabb's disembodied head floating in a jar acted as a deterrent or there was simply a shift in the political winds, his expedition was the last filibustering attempt on Sonora in the 1850s. Throughout the remainder of the nineteenth century, reports of filibustering plots would continue to surface from time to time. In the 1860s Mexicans denounced William McKendree Gwin, a former California senator, as a filibuster when he attempted to establish a colony in Sonora with the help of the French. Then in 1889–90, two groups of Californians plotted with English and American capitalists invested in Baja California to launch a filibuster to detach the peninsula from the Mexican Republic. However, neither of these ventures nor any other contemplated expedition ever really got off the ground—or across the border.[32]

Filibusters, for all their efforts, did not move the line. Instead their persistent efforts helped foster a burgeoning sense of Mexican identity among the people of Sonora and cemented the significance of the boundary line as sovereign space that demanded defense. Despite all of the intrigue, filibustering had more of an effect on the psyches of border peoples than the boundaries of border spaces. The western boundary line, as established in the Gadsden Treaty, held.

UNMAKING NATIVE SPACE

The border's significance as a marker of state sovereignty faced another challenge even more serious than filibusters—the presence of large numbers of Native people who did not recognize the authority of either nation-state or the boundary line they had created. The constant threat of Apache raids and the unfettered movement of Indians across the line continued to discourage settlement and called the nation-states' sovereignty into question. As the title of an 1864 travel account of the Arizona-Sonora borderlands emphasized, the region through which the boundary line passed had yet to really become part of the United Stated and Mexico—it was still "Apache Country."[33]

Before the United States and Mexico could claim military authority over the border, they had to constrain Apache movement. For more than thirty years following the creation of the boundary line, both governments tried a variety of methods to confine the Apaches to the north of the border, including establishing reservations, negotiating treaties, and waging a prolonged and bloody war on both sides of the boundary line. Yet despite the best efforts of both states, they could not defeat the Apaches on their own. While the Apaches quickly learned to manipulate the border's power to play Mexicans and Americans against each other, the two states were initially hindered in their pursuit of the Apaches by their inability to follow them across the line. It was only after the United States and Mexico signed a reciprocal crossing agreement in 1882 that the decades-long war to displace the Apaches entered its final stages. In the process the two nation-states learned that sometimes the best way to defend the border was to transcend it.

While many Native peoples inhabited the borderlands, a group of distinct bands known collectively as Apaches posed the most significant challenge to the United States' and Mexico's claims to sovereignty along the western border. Apaches had good reason to consider the borderlands their country. Over hundreds of years of conflict with Spanish and Mexican settlers and troops, the Apaches had established effective control over a large swath of territory centered on the point where the present-day states of Arizona, New Mexico, Sonora, and Chihuahua come together. In the 1830s and 1840s, the Apaches waxed in power, raiding deep into Mexico and driving Mexican settlers to abandon their ranches in northern Sonora. Writing in 1835, one Mexican observer described the destruction of ranches in the San Bernardino Valley through which the boundary line would later run: "Today everything is desolation and ruins! Nothing remains but the memory of the atrocities and the victims sacrificed by the barbarians."[34]

Unlike the United States' conquest of Mexico, the Apaches did not follow up their military domination with the creation of a formal boundary survey. Instead of maps and surveys, place names and patterns of movement demarcated the landscape of Apache authority. "All this country here belonged to us alone," Palmer Valor, a ninety-two-year-old White Mountain Apache, told an ethnographer in Arizona in 1932. "All the mountains around here had names and now they have none. In those days there were lots of us and the trails around through these mountains were well traveled, like roads. Now they are all faded out and hard to see."[35] While successive generations of Spaniards, Mexicans, and Americans incorporated some of the place names of their Tohono O'odham allies (for instance, the place name *Tucson* derived from a mispronunciation of *Chuk Shon*, the O'odham words for "Black Base," which referred to the black mountain that is now marked with an *A* for the University of Arizona), the geography of their Apache enemies did not make it into their maps. It has only been in recent years that Apaches, along with some American scholars and government officials, have begun to systematically collect information about Apache place names and the histories and knowledge of the natural world that they reveal.[36]

Despite Mexicans' and Americans' attempts to wipe the Apaches off the map, their presence was woven into the geography of the borderlands. From bases in what would become the U.S. states of Arizona and New Mexico, Apache raiding parties followed trails to the south where they struck Pima, Tohono O'odham, and Mexican settlements in New Mexico, Sonora, and Chihuahua. In his 1932 interview, Palmer Valor recounted tales of numerous raids he had made into Sonora. "I have been many times to Mexico this way when I was a young man," he explained. "It is almost as if I had grown up in Mexico. From Mexico we always used to bring back lots of horses and cattle, burros and mules."[37] By the mid-nineteenth century, these raids had left their imprint on the borderlands landscape in the form of well-worn trails and abandoned settlements.

The raids also left a deep imprint on borderlands people. Decades of Apache raids and Spanish and Mexican counterattacks created a climate of fear, distrust, and hatred. "Nothing is more noble than the campaign that we have launched," wrote one Sonoran leader in 1883, "that we are fighting against the sworn enemy of civilization, against an avid vampire which draws the blood of humanity on the march of progress."[38] The feeling was mutual. In narrating the history of his life to an American interpreter in 1905 and 1906, Geronimo, the renowned Chiricahua Apache leader, recalled how a Mexican attack in which his mother, wife, and three of his children were killed in Chihuahua in the late 1850s fueled his lifelong desire for vengeance. "It has been a long time since [I last fought the Mexicans]," he narrated as an old man, "but still I have no love for the Mexicans. With me they were always treacherous and malicious. I am old now and shall never go on the warpath again, but if I were young, and followed the warpath, it would lead into Old Mexico."[39]

This mutual hostility informed all aspects of Mexican-Apache relations. Although the Mexican government's official Indian policy called for the peaceful incorporation of Native people into the nation as citizens, their approach to dealing with the Apaches was brutal. With the majority of Apaches unwilling to acknowledge Mexican sovereignty or to integrate themselves into Mexican society, Mexican soldiers and civilian militias set out to remove the Apaches from Mexican soil, if necessary by exterminating them completely. The Sonora and Chihuahua governments also recruited bounty hunters who they paid up to 300 pesos for each Apache scalp they collected. By 1874 the Sonoran government had set aside 9,620 pesos for this expense.[40]

This policy of extermination resonated with many of the Americans who began to arrive in the borderlands in the 1850s. "Treacherous, bloodthirsty, brutal, with an irresistible propensity to steal," a special agent in the Indian Department wrote of the Apaches in 1858, "he has been for years the scourge of Mexico, as the depopulated villages and abandoned fields of Chihuahua and Sonora too faithfully attest, and grave doubts are expressed whether any process short of extermination will suffice to quiet him."[41] "There is only one way to wage war against the Apaches," wrote another American. "A steady, persistent campaign must be made, following them to their haunts—hunting them to the 'fastnesses of the mountains.' They must be surrounded, starved into coming in, surprised or inveigled—by white flags, or any other method, human or divine—and then put to death."[42]

Despite the prevalence of these attitudes, the official U.S. policy regarding the Apaches was not extermination but confinement. Under Article XI of the Treaty of Guadalupe Hidalgo the United States' first responsibility was to confine the Apaches to the north of the boundary line by preventing them from raiding into Mexico. The United States also committed to pay damages for all Apache raids originating in U.S. territory. As U.S. officials in the army and the Bureau of Indian Affairs made their way into the borderlands they attempted to convince Apache leaders to cease their transborder raids. The Apaches, however, were reluctant to abandon raiding patterns that were both an important part of their economic life and rooted in deeply felt antipathy. "Are we to stand by with our arms folded while our women & children are being murdered in cold blood as they were the other day in Sonora?" protested the Chiricahua Apache leader, Mangas Coloradas. "Are we to be victims of such treachery—and not be revenged? Are we not to have the privilege of protecting ourselves?"[43] The U.S. Indian agent's conclusion upon hearing these protests, that "it will be extremely difficult to keep these Indians at peace with the people of Old Mexico," underestimated the Herculean task that faced the Americans.[44] Despite making agreements to the contrary, Apaches would continue to make raids into northern Mexico for decades to come. Within a few years, the U.S. government gave up, negotiating for the revocation of Article XI in the Gadsden Treaty and throwing the responsibility for defending Apache raids back onto the people of Sonora. At the same time, in the newly acquired territory American settlers took to simply buying the Apaches off, signing "calico treaties" in which Apache bands agreed not to attack them in exchange for provisions and a promise not to interfere with their raiding to the south of the border. These agreements only bolstered the Apaches' power and caused them to further focus their attacks on Mexican territory while protecting some but not all Americans.[45]

With the beginning of the U.S. Civil War (1861–65) the United States' tenuous grasp on the borderlands slipped even further. In March 1861 the Butterfield Overland Mail, which had carried mail through New Mexico Territory since 1858, ceased operations in the territory, cutting off the main line of communication between the borderlands and the eastern United States. Shortly after, U.S. troops pulled out of the western part of New Mexico Territory, burning Fort Breckinridge and Fort Buchanan in present-day southern Arizona before they left. "So much for the whites," wrote an American miner in the region in the summer of 1862. "The Apaches, ever taking advantage of a loose state of affairs— the withdrawal of troops and Overland Mail, which they boastingly assert they compelled—become emboldened to kill, steal and make desolate to a miserable degree. During our brief residence here perhaps 100 men have been killed by the Apaches."[46]

Conditions were no better on the Mexican side of the boundary line where the Mexican government was preoccupied with a war of its own. In 1862, seeking reparations for unpaid debts and serving the imperial ambitions of Emperor Napoleon III, French troops invaded Mexico and oversaw the installation of Austrian Archduke Ferdinand Maximilian as the puppet emperor of Mexico. President Benito Juárez was forced to evacuate Mexico City and retreat to Paso del Norte, the Chihuahua border city that now bears his name. For the next five years Juárez struggled to hold the government together and waged a war against the French for control of Mexico—a victory that was finally achieved in 1867 with the withdrawal of French troops and Maximilian's execution. However, in the meantime northern Mexican settlements were left to their own defenses. Between November 1866 and February 1869, Apache raids in Sonora resulted in 106 people killed and 60,000 pesos worth of property loss.[47]

It was not until the 1870s, after the expulsion of the French and the end of the U.S. Civil War, that both nations once again turned their attention to wresting the borderlands from Apache control. As government officials and troops returned to the borderlands, they focused on restricting Apache mobility, removing Apaches from potentially productive spaces, and, most importantly, constraining their ability to conduct raids. While both governments gradually resumed their aggressive military pursuits of Apache bands, on the U.S. side of the line the military strategy was paired with a policy of confining Apaches within reservations in order to prevent raids and to open up land for American settlement. As early as 1850 a U.S. Indian agent reported that "[the Apaches, Comanches, Navajoes, and Utahs (*sic*)] should be compelled to *remain* within certain fixed limits."[48] In 1871 the U.S. government established four reservations for Apaches at Camp Apache, Camp Verde, and Camp Grant in Arizona Territory and in the Tularosa Valley in New Mexico Territory. The following year, Cochise, the leader of the Chiricahua Apaches, met with U.S. General O. O. Howard and agreed "that he could gather in all of his people, protect the roads and preserve the peace, if the Government would allow him the Chiricahua country, where his people have always lived."[49] Located in the southeastern corner of the new Territory of Arizona (which had been separated from New Mexico in 1863), the new Chiricahua Reservation was the only reservation situated immediately on the boundary line in the late nineteenth century.

Reservations, however, were not the havens U.S. officials promised them to be. Complaints like those of Apaches settled at Tularosa, New Mexico, about "sickness and death among the children; the impurity of the water, coldness of the climate, the crops failing from early frost" were common across Arizona and New Mexico. It was little wonder that American officials found these people "generally discontented with their reservation" or that "hundreds had left to get their living in the old nomadic way."[50] By the mid-1870s, although most Apaches had relocated to reservations on the U.S. side of the line, a number of bands continued to view raiding and retreating across the border as an alternative or supplement to life on the reservation. These raids undermined both U.S. and Mexican authority and demonstrated how tenuous their military sovereignty was.

When Apaches launched transborder raids in the second half of the nineteenth century, they followed old trails, but they also engaged in a conscious manipulation of the boundary line that was new to the borderlands. To the Apache raiders the boundary line was not a barrier but a useful tool that they could manipulate to evade capture. While raiding parties thought nothing of crossing the international line with stolen goods, the U.S. and Mexican soldiers who pursued them were more constrained by the jurisdictional boundaries that the border represented. By moving back and forth across the boundary line, Apache raiders played U.S. and Mexican forces against each other, straining U.S.-Mexican relations and underscoring the limits of either country's ability to control its national space.

Although they shared the goal of defeating the Apaches, the spatial division created by the boundary line often left the two nation-states at cross-purposes. Officials on either side of the border blamed their counterparts for failing to control the Apaches within their borders. In 1873,

Governor Pesqueira complained that Cochise and his band, having made peace with the Americans, had turned to "raiding, robbing, and murdering" in Sonora. In response, the U.S. agent for the Chiricahua protested that "all the robbing and murdering in Sonora is not done by Apaches from this side of the line, though, by any means. There are large bands of Apaches living in Sonora who commit the greater portion of the depredations committed there."[51] Seven years later the mutual recriminations continued. In an 1880 letter to the Mexican minister in Washington, DC, the U.S. secretary of state implied that the people of Chihuahua were not only failing to fulfill their responsibility to fight the Apaches, but that they had also provided an Apache band with arms and ammunition that they had used in an attack on U.S. cavalry forces in New Mexico. The indignant minister responded by providing a description of the raids and a map that showed that the direction of the raids had been "from North to South with the exception of a few unimportant evolutions in the interior of the aforesaid territory."[52]

Attacks originating on reservations in the United States were a particular frustration for Mexican officials who complained about "the injuries which we suffer from the Apaches whom the Government of the United States is maintaining on reservations."[53] The Chiricahua Reservation on the boundary line became a hotbed of transborder raids. "On account of the proximity of this reservation to Mexico, it is difficult to prevent raiding incursions into that country," reported the U.S. commissioner of Indian affairs in 1874.[54] In addition to the raids carried out by Chiricahuas, other bands discovered that the reservation made a convenient stopping place for returning raiders. Thomas Jeffords, the agent of the Chiricahua Reservation and a friend of their chief, Cochise, noted, "These parties are generally composed of Indians from several different reservations combined, and this reservation, bordering as it does on the Sonora line, has without doubt been made a kind of a resting-place for these parties."[55]

The tensions between U.S. and Mexican officials, along with the damage done by raiders, made controlling the Apaches' transborder movement a central focus of U.S. and Mexican Indian policy. One U.S. Indian agent pointed out that the best way to do this was not to try to patrol the boundary line itself, but rather to concentrate on cutting off the few points of access. "While there are various passes by which the Indians descend into Arizona and northern Mexico," he explained, "there are, owing to the scarcity of water, but few trails by which they can return with their booty. If these be blocked up by cavalry posts, thieving south of the Gila will be rendered unprofitable, and the Indians will cease to steal cattle, which they cannot drive to their homes. The result would possibly be that the Indians, reduced to a starving condition, would come in, make peace, and settle down on a reservation."[56]

Other officials focused on the need to move the Apaches away from the border. As early as 1850 a U.S. Indian agent concluded that "no Indian tribe should be located nearer than one hundred miles of the line of Mexico."[57] Writing about the Mescalero Apache in New Mexico, a U.S. Army officer complained that "they are so near the Mexican line that they are constantly tempted to commit wrong by the ease with which they can get to foreign soil. . . . Why cannot this tribe be sent to the 'Oklahoma District'?"[58] The problems that arose on the Chiricahua Reservation only further convinced officials that regardless of where they had made their homes in the past, Apaches should not be allowed to live along the border. In 1876, only four years after creating it, the U.S. government closed the Chiricahua Reservation. While the majority of its inhabitants acceded to the will of the Bureau of Indian Affairs and moved north to the San Carlos Reservation, a significant minority led by Naiche and Geronimo retreated into Mexico where they continued to raid and began their long last stand against U.S. and Mexican sovereignty.[59]

As they led their band across the border to escape removal to the San Carlos Reservation, Geronimo and Naiche highlighted the failure of U.S. and Mexican Indian policy. The Chiricahuas' persistent transnationalism proved that neither government could defeat them on their own. The Apaches had realized this early on, but it would take U.S. and Mexican officials years to accept that in order to defeat the Apaches they would have to work together.

This cooperation was made difficult on the national scale by events on the Texas-Chihuahua border. In response to raids across the Rio Grande, in 1877 the U.S. secretary of war issued an ultimatum to the Mexican government: "if the Government of Mexico shall continue to neglect the duty of suppressing these outrages, that duty will devolve upon this government, and will be performed, even if its performance should render necessary the occasional crossing of the border by our troops." Known as the Order of June 1, this decree's unilateral action strained U.S.-Mexican relations and impeded the establishment of an official reciprocal crossing agreement.[60]

With bilateral negotiations stalled on the Rio Grande, civil and military leaders in the west took matters into their own hands and began working out local agreements and temporary exemptions that allowed for limited transborder troop movements and the coordination of U.S. and Mexican maneuvers. The negotiation of these small-scale cooperative agreements outside of official treaty proceedings was both a critical stopgap measure and an example to higher officials of the value of binational cooperation. U.S. military authorities in Arizona and New Mexico secured permission from their counterparts in Sonora and Chihuahua to send army scouts into the Sierra Madre and occasionally to dispatch larger forces across the line. In making these agreements, the Mexicans sometimes found ways to fulfill the letter, if not the spirit, of the laws restricting transborder pursuits. For instance, in April 1882 Lieutenant Colonel George A. Forsyth parted with a Mexican force led by Colonel Lorenzo García with what he described as "cordial good-will" after García had discovered him in Mexican territory, asked him to return to the United States, and provided him with a written pro-test.[61] However, these informal agreements were also insecure. In an-other instance later that spring, a Tucson volunteer corps that had pur-sued an Apache band into Mexico camped with García and General Bernardo Reyes for four days before the Mexicans disarmed them and sent them back to the United States, over 250 miles with nothing but sticks to protect themselves.[62]

Despite the potential for conflict, cooperation between U.S. and Mexi-can forces was more often successful, proving that a binational problem required a binational solution. As diplomatic negotiations continued be-tween Washington, DC, and Mexico City, events in the borderlands con-tinued to demonstrate the strategic importance of coordinating troop movements and allowing for military pursuit across the border.

In 1879 and 1880 local and national arguments about the need for and efficacy of binational cooperation came into focus around the trans-border pursuit of a group of Chiricahua Apache raiders from the Warm Springs Reservation led by the prominent chief Victorio. After a U.S. prosecutor indicted him for horse theft and murder, Victorio and a group of followers fled the Mescalero Reservation in New Mexico Territory and began raiding throughout Arizona and New Mexico, engaging U.S. forces and then ducking back across the border to evade capture.[63]

While many local officials immediately recognized the need for a coor-dinated binational campaign, military officers continued to strain against the constraints of the boundary line. Explaining in December 1879 that a Mexican campaign against Victorio's band would likely drive them back into the United States, the New Mexico governor, Lew Wallace, called for "some concert of action permitted between the military of the two pow-ers." "There is little doubt," he concluded, "that between the forces the enemy could be affectively [sic] disposed of."[64] However, despite Wal-lace's urging, for most of the following year U.S. and Mexican forces persisted in working independently, primarily confining their actions to one side of the boundary line even as the raiders continued to move back and forth across it. By the fall of 1880 officials on both sides of the bor-der had become frustrated. At one point a U.S. Cavalry troop got within fifteen miles of the Apaches before they slipped through their fingers, "going with all speed into Mexico." Noting that "so long as we are pre-vented by the refusal of the Mexican Govt from sending a force into

Mexico to hunt down this band of Indians we are liable to these raids," the commanding U.S. officer asked that "the Mexican Govt be requested to permit us to pursue and break up this band in Mexico."[65]

These complaints, which had become increasingly common along the border, did not go unheard. In order to assist in the campaign against Victorio, the Mexican federal government agreed to temporarily allow U.S. troops to enter Mexico if they were in hot pursuit. In October they got their chance, pursuing Victorio's band into Chihuahua. There a Mexican force led by Joaquín Terrazas briefly joined the Americans in pursuit before assuming control of the operation, noting that he was "grateful for [their] cooperation" and asking them to return to the United States.[66] By October 14, thanks to the combined efforts of the U.S. and Mexican forces, Terrazas and his men were able to corner Victorio's band in the Castillo Mountains. In the ensuing battle, the Mexicans killed eighteen women and children and sixty warriors, including Victorio. "This," U.S. Colonel George P. Buell reported, "is one of the results of our movement into Mexico and virtually ends our war with Victorio."[67] More than a single military victory, the success of the binational campaign against Victorio became an object lesson for U.S. and Mexican officials. With the Mexicans and Americans working together, the Apaches would no longer be able to use the boundary line as an escape hatch.

The success of these local and temporary arrangements and improving U.S.-Mexican relations finally led the national governments to move forward with an official, more permanent reciprocal crossing agreement in the summer of 1882. In July 1882 Matías Romero, the Mexican envoy extraordinaire and minister plenipotentiary, and the U.S. secretary of state, Frederick T. Frelinghuysen, finally signed a treaty establishing that "regular federal troops of the two republics may reciprocally cross the boundary line of the two countries when they are in close pursuit of a band of savage Indians." In order to reduce any possible strains from such incursions, the agreement stipulated that crossings be limited to "unpopulated or desert parts of the boundary line" and that the commanding officer give notice at the time of crossing or before to the nearest civil or military official. It also required that all troops return to their own territory as soon as they finished fighting or lost the Apaches' trail. Although initially enacted for only two years, the United States and Mexico found the reciprocal crossing treaty such an effective tool in suppressing transborder raiding that they reauthorized it repeatedly.[68]

The reciprocal crossing agreement devastated the Apaches' ability to use the border to evade capture. By the 1880s the Sierra Madre Mountains in Mexico had become the final refuge of the independent Apache bands, but with the new agreement the Sierra Madre were open to U.S. military incursions. Aided by Apache scouts from reservations in the

United States, U.S. forces and their Mexican allies began a full-scale assault on the Apache stronghold.

The final campaign against the Apaches came to focus on one man, the outspoken and intimidating Chiricahua spiritual leader, Geronimo.[69] Along with a chief named Naiche, Geronimo led a band of Chiricahuas who repeatedly refused to cease their raids or to submit to either U.S. or Mexican authority. Beginning in 1883 U.S. forces set out to capture Geronimo and put an end to Chiricahua autonomy. With Mexican forces preoccupied with fighting Yaqui Indians in the south, the U.S. military took the lead in this operation. But they could not capture Geronimo on their own. In addition to the authority of the officially authorized reciprocal crossing agreement, General George Crook also relied on local negotiations in which Mexican officials in Chihuahua and Sonora granted him permission to continue operating in Mexican territory beyond the limited timeframe of a hot pursuit. He was also dependent on the knowledge and tracking abilities of Apache scouts who he recruited from reservations in the United States. Thanks to these scouts and after a month of dogged pursuit through the Sierra Madre, Crook was able to find Geronimo and Naiche and persuade them, along with 550 Chiricahuas, to return to the San Carlos Reservation in May 1883.

Crook's victory, however, was short-lived. By May 1885 Geronimo, Naiche, and forty men and one hundred women and children once again fled San Carlos for the Sierra Madre. While exasperated Mexicans dispatched troops to protect border towns and expressed their frustration with the Americans' inability to control the Apaches, U.S. troops geared up for another transborder assault on the Sierra Madre. In November 1885 Captain Emmett Crawford led a force of nearly one hundred Apache scouts deep into Mexico. They were two hundred miles south of the border when they met a group of volunteers from Chihuahua. Either unable or unwilling to recognize the Apache scouts as allies, the Mexican volunteers fired on them, killing Captain Crawford in the attack. This incident not only threatened to derail the binational pursuit of Geronimo's band but also revealed the limitations of the reciprocal crossing agreement. While it may have made it easier for U.S. and Mexican troops to work together, it could do little to change the Mexican troops' deeply rooted distrust of Apaches.

Despite Crawford's death, the U.S. force carried on, now led by First Lieutenant Marion P. Maus. They managed to track Geronimo down and convinced him to come to the border to negotiate again with General Crook. In late March 1886 Geronimo and Naiche met Crook just south of the Chihuahua border. They agreed to surrender on the condition that U.S. authorities would allow them to live as free men on the reservation in Arizona. Although Crook accepted these terms, his superiors did not.

They insisted that Geronimo be exiled from the borderlands completely. Unwilling to be forced from their homeland, Geronimo and Naiche retreated into the Sierra Madre again.

It would take over another year more, but with both Mexicans and Americans in constant pursuit and the band reduced to less than fifty people, Geronimo and Naiche finally surrendered in September 1886. Defying the Mexicans one last time, Geronimo refused to surrender to Mexican officials. Instead he crossed the border and met with U.S. General Nelson A. Miles just north of the Arizona border in Skeleton Canyon. Under the terms of the surrender Geronimo and Naiche agreed to leave the borderlands. On September 8 Geronimo boarded a train bound for Fort Marion, Florida. He would never return to the borderlands.

With the exile of Geronimo and his band to Florida, Apache raiding ceased to be the major concern of military authorities on the border. Two months after Geronimo surrendered, the two governments allowed the reciprocal crossing agreement to lapse.[70] Nearly forty years after the creation of the boundary line, and centuries more since Europeans had first invaded the region, the borderlands were finally conquered. It had taken not only the Mexican-American War but more than three decades of fighting for the United States and Mexico to back up their territorial claims with military might. To the south of the line the people of northern Mexico had fought off filibusters, defending the border and cementing their connection to the Mexican Republic. However, when it came to the Apaches, a people who had lived in the region and vanquished would-be conquerors for generations, neither nation-state could go it alone. Despite their history of conflict, U.S. and Mexican officials needed to negotiate both formal and informal cooperative agreements in order to displace the Apaches and assert their authority over the line. This would not be the last time that the U.S. and Mexican states would have to compromise their aspirations of independent power and inviolable territorial sovereignty and work together to hold the line. Throughout the 1890s small-scale Apache raids would prompt the U.S. and Mexican governments to sign new reciprocal crossing agreements.[71] Beyond these official agreements, in the years ahead, binational cooperation would remain an important part of policing the border.

In retrospect, Geronimo's surrender and exile have come to signify a turning point in the history of not just the border but the United States' conquest of North America as well. In addition to the establishment of military sovereignty along the line, the Apaches' defeat marked, along with the massacre at Wounded Knee, South Dakota, four years later, the end of the United States' Indian wars. But Geronimo's departure did not mark either the end of transborder raiding or the exit of Indians from the stage of border history. While most Apaches lived on reservations located at a distance from the boundary line, small bands and individuals continued to make their presence felt on the border. Throughout the 1880s, the Apache Kid, a former Apache scout who had helped the U.S. Army track down Geronimo, gained notoriety for his raids on both sides of the border. Other Apaches retreated into the Sierra Madre, where they managed to survive and continue raiding Mexican settlements for a few decades more.[72] Even as Americans and Mexicans attempted to relegate Apaches to reservations and increasingly rare rumored sightings of "wild" Apaches in the Sierra Madre, Native people continued to engage in raiding, not as relics of the past, but in response to the emergence of new economic opportunities that capitalism brought to the borderlands in the late nineteenth century.

Despite frequent characterizations of the Tohono O'odham, or Papago, as a peaceful and inoffensive tribe, in the late 1880s Mexican officials complained that a number of Tohono O'odham living along the border in Arizona near Sonoita were raiding Mexican settlements for their livestock and fleeing back across the border to the United States. The Mexican settlers at Sonoita and the nearby mining camp of El Plomo reported losses of seventy head of cattle and expressed concern that the Tohono O'odham had plans for an attack on the customs house at Sasabe. In 1896 a group of Yaqui Indians reversed the typical pattern of transborder raiding, traveling north to attack the customs house at Nogales, Sonora, and then fleeing from Mexican troops into the United States.[73] These expeditions echoed older patterns of borderlands raiding, but at the same time their targets—customs houses in particular—and their self-conscious use of the border reflected the growing importance of the boundary line in their lives.

Neither raiding nor Indians disappeared from the border. Rather, Native people's lives and patterns of raiding became reshaped by the transnational economic development and assertions of national authority that began to define the borderlands in the wake of the Apache defeat. By the late 1880s the boundary line no longer ran through "Apache Country," but between the hinterlands of the United States, Mexico, and an emerging transnational capitalist economy.

Chapter Three

LANDSCAPE OF PROFITS

Cultivating Capitalism across the Border

On October 25, 1882, a crowd gathered on the border approximately seventy miles south of Tucson to celebrate the joining of the Sonora Railway and the Arizona and New Mexico Railroad at the international boundary line. William Raymond Morley, chief location engineer of the Atchison, Topeka and Santa Fe Railroad and general manager of the Sonora Railway, had selected the crossing point in Nogales Pass on the Guaymas-Tucson trade route. His wife drove in a ceremonial spike at the boundary line. As the crowd cheered, two engines, one draped in the red, white, and blue of the United States and the other in the green, red, and white of Mexico, touched cowcatchers. The first transborder rail line was finally complete.[1]

It was a momentous occasion not just for the Morleys and the nascent town of Nogales where the railroads met, but for the entire borderlands. Running from the Gulf of California at Guaymas, Sonora, to Benson, Arizona, where it connected with the main line of the Atchison, Topeka and Santa Fe Railroad, the new rail line linked Sonora, the border, and the burgeoning U.S. rail network. With the arrival of railroads, the borderlands' isolation was shattered. While many people had speculated about the borderlands' potential for mining and ranching, it was only with the railroad that ranchers and miners secured an easy way to move stock and ore to markets. As more people realized this, the borderlands experienced nothing short of a capitalist revolution.

In the railroads' wake, grasslands became ranches, mountains became mines, and the border itself became a site of commerce and communities. U.S. and Mexican military campaigns had made the boundary line a meaningful marker of national space. By providing security they also paved the way for the border to become incorporated into local divisions of property, urban spaces, railroad maps, and communities. This transformation made the border a place that people and corporations owned and called home.

This was a gradual and hard-fought process, and one that was only made possible by the efforts of ranchers, miners, entrepreneurs, and laborers and with the encouragement of both the U.S. and Mexican states. Laying railroad tracks demanded both private capital and government concessions; unearthing copper ore relied on both investment in infrastructure and on the backbreaking work of miners; running a profitable ranch required both herds of cattle and the security of a government-supported private-property regime. Although their motivations were not always the same, capitalists, laborers, and government officials brought capitalism to the border together.

They also assured that that transformation was a shared binational experience. The border was no limit to trade, investment, or labor migration. To the contrary, as the joining of the rails at Nogales in 1882 presaged, the capitalist development of the borderlands would spur the creation of an array of new transborder ties. Railroads built a web of lines that crossed the border, connecting mining camps owned by transnational companies and passing across vast binational ranches. New border towns emerged to serve these businesses and soon became home to binational communities as well. By the early twentieth century the border had become a point of connection and community in the midst of an emerging capitalist economy and the center of a transborder landscape of property and profits.

CREATING CAPITALIST SPACE

Since the first Spanish settlers arrived in northern Mexico in the seventeenth century, people of European descent had been trying to profit from the borderlands' bountiful grasslands and rich veins of ore with little success. It was not just Apache raids that threatened their lives and livelihoods. Rather, an array of environmental, technological, and economic limitations had made it too difficult to get ore out of the ground, cattle to market, crops to grow, and capitalists to invest. It was not until the end of the nineteenth century that entrepreneurs, with the support of U.S. and Mexican government policies, began to overcome these obstacles and integrate borderlands resources and land into an expanding global capitalist economy.

This process began with the construction of railroads into the borderlands in the early 1880s. Providing a direct link to U.S. markets, these rails became the literal and figurative paths that U.S. investment would follow into the region. They connected the borderlands to a broader capitalist economy and created the pathways along which capital, laborers, and consumer goods moved into the borderlands and animals and ore moved out to markets. In the following three decades, U.S. capital funded the emergence of industrial mining, market-oriented ranching, and land speculation on both sides of the border.

While railroads created the initial impetus for this development, the borderlands economic transformation could not have continued without many other legal, economic, and technological innovations, including improvements in mining, smelting, and irrigation and the formation of state-supported private-property regimes and methods of facilitating transnational investment. Together they made possible new uses of borderlands space and resources.

Transportation

Railroads were a prerequisite for the capitalist development of the borderlands. At a time when people primarily relied on animals, water, and their own two feet to move goods, the borderlands' mountains, deserts, and lack of navigable waterways were daunting obstacles to commerce. Before development could go forward, something had to be done about transportation.

The circuitous path to the construction of the first borderlands railroad began outside the region in the 1840s. Even as Mexican settlers retreated in the face of Apache raids, American politicians dreamed of a southern transcontinental railroad that would pass through what was then northern Mexico. While the desire for this prospective railroad led to the Gadsden Purchase in 1853, the intensification of sectional politics in the 1850s made the construction of any transcontinental railroad impossible. As U.S. politicians succumbed to infighting, the borderlands transportation woes were left to the region's local inhabitants and government officials.

By the 1850s there were a growing number of people in the borderlands to whom transportation was critical. During the Mexican-American War, U.S. troops led by Philip St. George Cooke had reopened a wagon road across New Mexico and northern Sonora to San Diego. After the discovery of gold in 1848, thousands of forty-niners followed Cooke's road from the eastern United States and Sonora to the California gold fields. Their movement helped spark an economic resurgence in the Arizona-Sonora borderlands, providing Mexican farmers and merchants in Tucson and Santa Cruz with a new market and enticing a few travelers and military personnel to return to the borderlands and try their hand at mining. Among these men were two army officers who had served at Fort Yuma on the Colorado River, Samuel Peter Heintzelman and Sylvester Mowry. Heintzelman and a mining engineer named Charles Debrille Poston established the Sonora Exploring and Mining Company in 1856 and began developing mines in the Santa Cruz Valley north of the new border near the presidio of Tubac. A few years later Mowry bought another mine, ten miles north of the boundary line, and renamed it after himself.[2]

While Mowry and Heintzelman had little trouble locating old silver mines, getting them up and running and moving the ore to market was another matter. They could buy food from nearby Sonoran farmers, but the more specialized equipment for mining, smelting, and amalgamating had to be ordered and shipped via the Gulf of California and Guaymas. The Sonora Exploring and Mining Company's work was delayed for years as its owners waited for machinery to arrive from San Francisco. The problems did not stop once the ore was out of the mines. The Mowry mine and smelters produced bars of lead and silver that weighed seventy pounds apiece. These had to be transported first by mule or wagon across nearly three hundred miles of Apache-controlled territory to Guaymas, and then by ship down the Pacific coast and across the Atlantic. The cost of transportation, along with any mule or wagon trains lost to Apache raids, cut deeply into profits.[3]

It is no surprise then that Mowry and other entrepreneurs became transportation boosters. Picking up where U.S. politicians had left off, American and Mexican investors sought a concession from the Mexican government to build a railroad across northern Chihuahua and Sonora connecting El Paso with Guaymas. The desire for this railroad brought together American entrepreneurs, like Mowry, with Sonora Governor Ignacio Pesqueira, who first urged the Sonora state legislature to grant the concession and later became a stockholder in the company that had received it.[4] However, despite their enthusiasm for this project, it would not be until the opening of the Nogales-Guaymas route in the 1880s that a railroad finally reached Guaymas.

In the meantime, with plans for the railroad stalled, local people focused on developing freighting and water transportation. Most of their attention focused on the Gulf of California and the port of Guaymas. Located a few hundred miles below the boundary line, Guaymas was the gateway to the western borderlands. The ships that docked there carried everything from wood and nails to furniture and fine liquor, which freighters then transported throughout the region. Pesqueira's government also funded the improvement and construction of wagon roads in Sonora, particularly those leading from Guaymas to northern Sonora and Arizona.[5]

On the American side of the border, the obvious route of transportation was the Colorado River. In November 1852, the *Uncle Sam* became the first steamship to head up the Colorado. For the next twenty-five years, steamships plied the river's shallow and shifting waters, aided by the labor of the Cocopah and Yuma Indians who lived along its banks. However, while these ships transported men and supplies across the border for military and mining ventures, they still relied on wagons and pack animals for transport into the borderlands' interior.[6]

What the borderlands needed was a rail connection, but it would not get it until the 1880s. The resurgence of Apache raiding during the 1860s forced freighters to cease operations and miners to abandon their claims. By 1864 an American journalist traveling through the borderlands reported that the region was more isolated than ever. "At this moment Arizona is, practically, more distant from San Francisco and New York than either of those cities is from China or Norway," wrote J. Ross Browne. "I made the trip from Germany to Iceland and back much more easily, and with much less expense and loss of time, than from San Francisco to Sonora and back."[7]

This began to change when the Southern Pacific Railroad bridged the Colorado River at Yuma in 1877, providing a direct link to coastal California and the U.S. transcontinental rail network. The Southern Pacific immediately superseded the lengthy water route and opened the borderlands to unprecedented economic development. American trade goods that arrived by train and were sent south to Sonora supplanted the northward flow of goods imported through Guaymas. As the railroad gradually built eastward over the following four years, reaching Tucson in 1880 and completing its transcontinental connection with the Atchison, Topeka, and Santa Fe Railroad (AT&SF) at Deming, New Mexico, in 1881, it integrated the borderlands into the U.S. economy and made it possible not only for goods to reach the border but also for American capitalists to more easily extract borderlands resources.[8]

Even as the Southern Pacific laid tracks across Arizona, another railroad appeared on the eastern horizon. Building west from New Mexico, the AT&SF moved into the borderlands in search of a Pacific terminus that would allow it to compete with the Southern Pacific in the west. The Southern Pacific had a monopoly over the California coastline, so the AT&SF settled on Guaymas. In 1879 the AT&SF sent its chief location engineer, William Morley, to survey a route connecting Guaymas with the trunk line at Benson, Arizona.[9] With the joining of the rails at Nogales three years later, the borderlands dream of bringing a railroad to Guaymas was finally achieved.

However, even as it reflected the long-standing importance of Guaymas to borderlands commerce, the new line also represented the leading edge of a transportation revolution that would rapidly reorient the borderlands away from the Gulf of California and toward the U.S. rail network. The

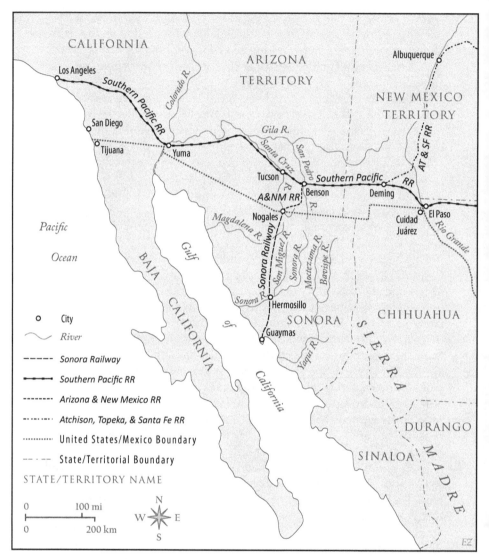

FIGURE 3.1. Borderlands railroads, 1880s (map by Ezra Zeitler).

branch line to Guaymas was the first of a growing number of transborder railroads that snaked across the boundary line in the late nineteenth century. In the years ahead transborder rail lines would bear a southbound traffic of trade goods, tools, and capitalists into Mexico and carry ore, agricultural products, and laborers north to the United States, linking the U.S. and Mexican borderlands in an integrated transborder economy.

These lines were made possible by a combination of private initiative and government support. Although built by private corporations, all of the major U.S. railroads were heavily subsidized by the U.S. government through construction loans and land grants. While the Southern Pacific built its line across Arizona and New Mexico without additional federal subsidies or land grants, the company would not have existed if not for the 7.3 million acres of land and loans of $16,000 to $48,000 per mile provided by the U.S. government to support its construction of the transcontinental Central Pacific Railroad in the 1860s.[10] Similarly, President Porfirio Díaz attracted U.S. railroad companies to build lines throughout Mexico with generous land grants and subsidies. In Sonora he granted a concession to build the railroad from the border to Guaymas and subsidized the construction at a rate of 9,000 pesos per kilometer of track built. Significantly, the recipient of the concession was not the AT&SF, but the Sonora Railway Company, a Mexican subsidiary that the AT&SF incorporated in the spring of 1879 to build and operate the part of the line that ran through Mexican territory. The Sonora Railway Company, which along with the Arizona and New Mexico Railroad (another AT&SF subsidiary) made up the first transborder line, was also the first U.S. railroad to incorporate in Mexico.[11] In the years ahead Mexican incorporation would become increasingly common among Americans who wanted to invest in Mexico, particularly along the boundary line where Mexican law prohibited foreigners from owning land outright.[12] However, at the time of the formation of the Sonora Railway Company, it was a relatively new legal mechanism that mirrored the new economic partnerships between foreign capitalists and the Mexican government.

While American capitalists like Sylvester Mowry had worked with Mexican officials in the past, the scope and scale of these relationships changed dramatically under the administration of Porfirio Díaz. After coming to power in 1876, Díaz worked with foreign investors to develop a nationwide rail system that he hoped would lay the foundation for national economic growth. Following in the path of other Mexican officials, including Ignacio Pesqueira, Díaz granted concessions to U.S. railroad companies to build lines in Mexico. Financed by bondholders in New York, Texas, and California, railroads began to build south toward central Mexico from El Paso and Laredo on the Rio Grande. And to the west of the Sierra Madre on the western boundary line, a series of smaller railroads crisscrossed the border, creating a dense transborder network that fed into the Southern Pacific and AT&SF lines.[13]

By the 1880s, growing numbers of American miners, ranchers, and investors began to follow these rails into the borderlands and across the boundary line. Thanks to improved transportation and the suppression of Apache raiding, these men believed that they would finally be able to profit from borderlands resources. This shift in perception would gradually turn the borderlands' mountains and grasslands into profitable property and bring laborers from all over the world to work on the line.

Mountains into Mines

The significance of the railroads' arrival was nowhere more apparent than in the boom in borderlands mining. As the U.S. and Mexican militaries began pushing the Apaches onto reservations and into the Sierra Madre, miners traveled to the region in pursuit of mineral wealth. In 1877 a prospector named Edward Schieffelin discovered silver in southeastern Arizona. In recognition of the still-insecure landscape, he dubbed his new claims Graveyard and Tombstone. Although the area, as these ominous names suggested, was not entirely safe from Apache attacks, Schieffelin's discovery unleashed a boom by the beginning of the 1880s. In the next few years, eastern capital and western characters like Wyatt Earp and Doc Holliday poured into Tombstone, taking advantage of the Southern Pacific Railroad that ran fifty miles to the north of the mining camp. "For awhile," remembered one early resident, "all roads led to Tombstone." By 1883 its population had swelled to between ten and fourteen thousand.[14]

Even as miners struggled to uncover silver at Tombstone and other mining camps, the ore that would eventually become most significant to the borderlands remained buried in the earth awaiting technological innovations. That all-important metal was copper. Abundant deposits were located throughout the mountain ranges running across the border from northern Chihuahua and Sonora into New Mexico and Arizona. In 1877, around the same time that Schieffelin struck silver at Tombstone, a government scout named Jack Dunn discovered an outcropping of copper in the mountains approximately twenty miles to the south at a location that would soon become the city of Bisbee.

Not much farther south, but across the boundary line in Sonora, mining engineers also identified copper deposits at old mines at Nacozari and Cananea. In the 1860s Ignacio Pesqueira turned his attention to the Cananea mines that were near to his family's ranchlands. Rebuilding an abandoned smelter, Pesqueira began producing gold- and silver-bearing copper at Cananea and soon found himself engaged in the ongoing borderlands struggle to get his ore to market.[15]

The arrival of the railroads helped solve this transportation dilemma, but other technological innovations were equally important to the development of copper mining in the borderlands. The copper industry owed its expansion to innovations in both the production and use of copper. Initially less attractive than silver or gold, copper was an industrial metal.

The electrification of the United States created a surging demand for pure copper and also made possible an electrolytic refining process that could efficiently remove impurities from the metal. By the end of the nineteenth century, the technologies of production, transportation, and use all came together to create a borderlands copper boom.[16]

Among the most important engines of industrial growth was the New York–based import-export firm, Phelps, Dodge, and Company (Phelps Dodge). In the late nineteenth century the company began investing in borderlands copper mines. Phelps Dodge first bought into the Bisbee mines in southern Arizona in the early 1880s. By the end of the century it had consolidated control over Bisbee and expanded into Sonora with the acquisition of the Pilares mine at Nacozari in 1896.[17]

That same year, William Cornell Greene, a small-time rancher and miner who had worked in Arizona since 1877, acquired an interest in the Cananea mines from Ignacio Pesqueira's heirs. In August, Greene boarded a train from Arizona to New York City to look for investors. He returned a month later with the financial backing that would launch him on what one biographer has called the "copper skyrocket." With American financing and the support of Mexican officials, the Cananea Consolidated Copper Company—the Mexican corporation Greene founded—transformed Cananea into a dynamic industrial city. Laborers poured in from Mexico and the United States to work in the mines. By 1901 the company had four thousand people on its payroll.[18]

As the transborder economy grew, so did the need for labor. While miners and ranchers began by hiring Mexicans and Indians from the region, by the turn of the century large numbers of Mexicans, Anglo-Americans, and European and Asian immigrants were making their way to the border to find jobs. Border mines, smelters, ranches, and other businesses spurred unprecedented population growth along the border. Between 1900 and 1910 the population of Cochise County, located in the heart of the copper country along the border in southwestern Arizona, exploded from 9,251 people to 34,591. Although the population growth was less dramatic in border counties where ranching was the primary economic activity, such as Arizona's Santa Cruz County and New Mexico's Grant, Luna, Doña Ana, and Otero counties, these too experienced significant growth. While the big copper mines at Cananea, Nacozari, and Bisbee were the biggest employers, many men and women also went to work right on the boundary line. By 1913 the Calumet and Arizona and Copper Queen smelters at the new border town of Douglas employed seven hundred and more than one thousand men, respectively.[19]

The borderlands labor market was segmented by race. While Mexi-

can bankers, ranchers, and shareholders reaped economic rewards on a
par with those of their American peers, working-class ethnic Mexicans
who labored as cowboys, miners, and smelter workers earned lower
wages and were denied better-paying jobs in favor of Anglo-Americans
and European immigrants.[20] In the Bisbee mines, ethnic Mexicans were
restricted to lower-paying jobs as assistants, helpers, surface workers,
and smelter workers, while higher-paying underground work and the
highest level jobs as foremen, engineers, and mechanics were almost exclusively reserved for whites. In addition to this occupational segregation, mining companies also embraced a dual-wage system in which
they established separate pay scales for Mexicans and whites and Americans. In 1917, mining engineer J. C. Ryan openly acknowledged that
miners' wages in Bisbee depended on "whether they were Mexicans or
white men." "Mexicans," he explained, "were paid a lower rate."[21] As a
result of both the dual-wage scale and occupational segregation, ethnic
Mexican workers on both sides of the border earned less than their
white counterparts. In 1910, wages for Mexican and Mexican American
miners in Bisbee averaged only $1.25 per day compared to $3.50 for
native-born whites and northern and western European immigrants.
Similar discrepancies prevailed in the Sonoran mines. In 1906 miners at
Cananea went on strike complaining that Mexican workers were not
promoted on the basis of their aptitude and that, while both Mexicans
and Americans earned $3.00 a day, the company paid Mexicans in sil-
ver, while Americans received more valuable gold currency. "The foreigners occupied decorous residences, reached a high level of life and
had large amounts of money that they brought to the neighboring country," noted one Mexican worker at Cananea, "while the aspect of the
Mexican population and its economic condition offered a pathetic contrast." "Thus," he concluded, "was imposed the racial foreign hegemony
over all of the enterprise, on our own soil, at the expense of national
interests, at the expense of the sacrifice of the wage-earning Mexican
and of national dignity and of the most elemental principles of justice
and national honor."[22]

The tensions within the racially stratified workforce were manifested
in workplace conflicts throughout the borderlands. As early as the 1860s,
with racial divisions exacerbated by lingering resentment over the Crabb
filibuster, Mexican employees of the Sonora Exploring and Mining Company murdered Charles Poston's brother and forced Poston and a mining
engineer to flee to Yuma. With the industrialization of borderlands mining, Mexican laborers more often turned to strikes to express their dissatisfaction with unequal wages and hiring practices, but these too could
end in violence. When Mexican workers struck at the Black Diamond

smelter near Tombstone in 1904, their white co-workers responded by forming a posse to suppress them.[23]

The worst incidence of labor-related violence occurred at Cananea in 1906. Mexican workers at the Cananea Consolidated Copper Company went on strike demanding a pay raise, reduced hours, and access to the higher-ranking jobs reserved for Americans. While the workers' representatives negotiated with management, the strikers took to the streets shouting, "Viva Mexico; $5.00 and 8 hours of work!"[24] At the company lumberyard, the manager, George Metcalf, met the marchers with rifles and a fire hose. Turning the hose on the crowd, Metcalf triggered a riot. Gunfire erupted and people fell dead in the street. Chaos ensued as Mexicans and Americans clashed throughout the city and company management and local officials began to send panicked pleas for armed assistance.[25] This clash, as I will discuss further in the next chapter, sent shockwaves through Mexico and across the border, threatening both the borderlands' capitalist economy and the binational networks that sustained it.

As much as the industrial production of metal, the divisive racial hierarchies and potential for violent strikes signaled the incorporation of borderlands copper mines into a transnational mining economy. Like other mines in Butte, Montana; Bingham, Utah; and Ludlow, Colorado, borderlands mines took form from an amalgamation of natural resources, investment capital, technological innovation, and immigrant labor.[26] Together they remade the borderlands into an industrial capitalist landscape.

Ranges into Ranches

Rangelands along the border were also caught up in the transborder boom. As with mining, Apache raids and distance from markets had long frustrated the ambitions of borderlands ranchers. The suppression of raiding and the arrival of railroads allowed those ambitions to be realized. At the same time that capitalists invested in borderlands mines, ranchers started stocking the ranges with cattle and buying property on both sides of the border. In the process they transformed large stretches of the borderlands into a transborder landscape of privately owned and productive ranches that were tied to the U.S. economy and were largely under the control of American capitalists.

Both longtime borderlands residents and newcomers from Europe and the eastern United States participated in the emerging ranching economy. Among the first were descendants of Spanish colonists who had acquired land grants in exchange for their military service. These included the members of the extended Elías family who claimed vast tracts of land in

Arizona and Sonora, including the Los Nogales de Elías, Agua Prieta, and San Pedro Palominas ranches on the border. While many of the Elíases returned to ranching after the suppression of the Apaches, other land grant recipients chose to sell their land rights to newcomers from the eastern United States and Europe.[27]

Among the new arrivals was a Texas cattleman named John Slaughter. Drawn west by the availability of land and the opening of new markets, Slaughter came to Arizona in the late 1870s. In 1884 he acquired the San Bernardino Ranch. This 65,000-acre ranch spanned the eastern Arizona-Sonora boundary line in the San Bernardino Valley. Its title stemmed from an 1822 land grant made by the short-lived Mexican Empire to First Lieutenant Ignacio Pérez, a member of the extended Elías family, in exchange for his military service. In 1853 the Gadsden Treaty had drawn the international boundary line through the ranch, leaving one-third in Arizona and the remaining two-thirds in Sonora. Slaughter established his headquarters right on the boundary line and began operating a transnational ranch. Not only did his cattle graze back and forth across the boundary line within the boundaries of the San Bernardino Land Grant, but the ranch also became a way station through which cattle passed as Slaughter bought them from Sonoran ranchers and then sold them to both local and far-off American consumers.[28]

By the end of the nineteenth century, the animals that moved through Slaughter's ranch joined hundreds of thousands of cattle that grazed on both sides of the border. Ranchers then loaded them onto Southern Pacific and AT&SF railroad cars and sent them to markets throughout the United States. In 1887, just one ranch, the San Rafael operated by brothers Colin and Brewster Cameron just east of Nogales, ran a herd of more than 17,000 cattle. Raised on borderlands grasses, these cattle were sent to markets as far away as California, Colorado, Kansas, Missouri, and Montana.[29]

The emergence of capitalist-oriented ranching in the borderlands was as much about land as cattle. As they bought and sold ranches, ranchers like John Slaughter and the Elías family helped to integrate land along both sides of the border into a landscape of private property and a market in real estate. While the Elíases used some of their land for ranching, they also profited from selling other tracts to new arrivals. Slaughter, for instance, acquired title to the San Bernardino Ranch in 1884 from a Mexican land speculator named Guillermo Andrade who was also heavily invested in Baja California real estate.[30]

Government policies conditioned the real estate market in which individuals like Andrade, Slaughter, and the Elíases engaged. Committed to the idea that putting land into private hands would help promote economic development, both governments adopted nationwide programs to transfer public lands, or *terrenos baldíos*, to private individuals. The United States dispatched government surveyors and passed the 1862 Homestead Act and 1877 Desert Land Act to facilitate the distribution of public land. The Mexican government contracted private surveying companies, which received large tracts of land in exchange for their surveys.[31]

These policies privatized huge amounts of land but were also characterized by inaccuracy, inconsistency, and inequity, leading to the appropriation of millions of acres of land that were inhabited, used, or claimed by Indians and other borderlands people. Throughout Mexico and the U.S. southwest many communities that had held land in common found their claims challenged by U.S. government surveyors and the private surveyors subcontracted by the Mexican government. Native peoples were particularly hard hit. As surveyors marched into the Yaqui River Valley in southern Sonora, they contributed their efforts to the Sonoran government's long war to remove the Yaquis from their land and helped to push many Yaquis to relocate across the border in Arizona.[32]

The Tohono O'odham, or, as they were known by contemporary Americans and Mexicans, the Papago, also saw their claims to lands they had inhabited for years erased in the governments' push to create private property. Despite the Tohono O'odhams' history of cooperation in fighting the Apaches, the U.S. government did not even acknowledge them in adjudicating competing claims to Arizona's Upper Santa Cruz Valley where they had lived for generations. Without title to the most desirable parts of their homeland, the Tohono O'odham continued to live in Tucson and the more isolated stretches of the desert on both sides of the Arizona-Sonora border. By the twentieth century, many Americans seemed unaware that the Tohono O'odham had even been dispossessed. "It has been the good fortune of the Papagoes to live in a country which the white man as yet has not found it profitable to exploit by cattle raising or, still less, by dry farming," wrote traveler Karl Lumholtz in 1912. "Therefore, they have so far been left alone in their native country."[33] However, to the contrary, as Mexicans and Americans expanded ranching operations along the western Arizona-Sonora border, scattered conflicts erupted between ranchers and Tohono O'odham over access to scarce water and grazing resources. Faced at times with land invasion and the potential for violent reprisals in Sonora, many Sonoran Tohono O'odham migrated across the line to the United States. Some Tohono O'odham, in both Arizona and Sonora, took jobs as cowboys with Mexican and American ranching outfits and became integrated as wage earners into the lower rungs of the transborder economy, but the broad picture was one of land loss.[34]

The shift to private property not only hurt Native peoples but also negatively affected some Mexican and American landowners who lost land in the governments' rush to redefine and sell the public domain. The large and vaguely defined land grants that had once been the only form of private property in the borderlands did not hold up well in the new capitalist regime. Early surveys, like that done for the San Bernardino Ranch in 1821, relied on natural landmarks such as "the little spring on a timber covered hillock" or "a tableland covered with scrub oaks, at the edge of a deep creek, which is in front of the place known as the Potreritos."[35] These descriptions, no matter how vivid a portrayal of the landscape they provided, lacked the legal precision that later courts expected. With the growing demand for border real estate, the absence of exact property boundaries made it difficult for many landowners to clearly assert their claims. While some well-connected landowners managed to manipulate land grant titles to their advantage elsewhere in the U.S. southwest, when it came to ranches right along the boundary line, these titles were liabilities. In the 1880s and 1890s private land surveyors contracted by the Mexican government rejected the broad claims of grant holders like the Elíases and redefined large swaths of their Sonoran ranchlands as public domain. Despite protests from some family members, large chunks of their property were soon on the market where American investors were eager to buy surveyed lands with secure titles.[36]

Property titles derived from Spanish and Mexican land grants were even less secure on the U.S. side of the line, despite provisions of the Treaty of Guadalupe Hidalgo that obligated the U.S. government to respect them. American surveyors and settlers challenged land grant titles throughout the southwest. Although brothers Colin and Brewster Cameron had acquired the San Rafael de la Zanja Land Grant and begun ranching there in 1882, between fifteen and twenty Mexican and American families also claimed portions of the property. These settlers were soon engaged in a range war with the Camerons. For the next two decades the brothers waged a two-front war to keep settlers off their property and the U.S. government from classifying their land as part of the public domain, with Colin handling day-to-day operations on the ranch and Brewster, a lawyer and Justice Department agent, managing the political machinations. Meanwhile, the settlers in the valley ran cattle, cut fences and trees, and even burned the Camerons in effigy.[37]

In order to defend their claims, the Camerons and other land grant owners went to court. By 1891 the conflict over land grants prompted the U.S. Congress to establish a special Court of Private Land Claims to adjudicate contested claims. Land grant claimants were at a disadvantage in this court, which pitted ranchers who derived their title from Mexican and Spanish grants against U.S. attorneys who sought to enlarge the public domain. Government attorneys and surveyors researched title documents, surveyed the land, and evaluated claims. The claimants had no choice but to enter into expensive court proceedings or lose their land. "The land grant fight and costs were terrible," recalled John Slaughter's wife, Viola, of their defense of the San Bernardino Grant. "We had all our papers clear back to the grant itself, but the U.S. government sent out surveyors and lawyers and all sorts of people to take it away from us. It went on for years. . . . There were court and suit costs. It was terrible."[38]

The Slaughters' case, like other claimants', required them not only to demonstrate their chain of title, but also with more difficulty, to explain unfamiliar provisions of Spanish and Mexican land law to a skeptical U.S. court. The Slaughters first had to convince the court that the Intendente of Sonora and Sinaloa had maintained its authority to make land grants after Mexican Independence. Then they had to undertake an extensive search in the Sonoran archives to produce a record of the grant. Although the Slaughters provided an authentic chain of title, the court narrowly interpreted the grant as only entitling them to a portion of the property. While the Slaughters' surveyors determined that the grant contained 13,746 acres north of the boundary line in the United States, the government only approved their title to 2,383 acres. Fortunately for the Slaughters, the Mexican government took a more generous view of their title, allowing them to retain title to 38,000 acres on the Mexican side of the line.[39]

The U.S. court rejected or reduced land grant claims all along the border. Partners Frederick Maish and Thomas Driscoll lost 11,621 of the 17,354 acres of the Yerba Buena, or Buenavista, Ranch. Although the Elías and Camou families retained property elsewhere in the borderlands, the courts denied their claims to the Agua Prieta and the Los Nogales de Elías grants in Arizona completely. As for the Camerons, after years of fighting in the courts and with settlers in the San Rafael Valley, they saw their claim in the San Rafael de la Zanja grant dramatically reduced from 152,980 acres to just 17,352 acres. The U.S. Supreme Court's confirmation of this ruling in 1902 brought an end to the Camerons' dreams of creating a ranching "principality" on the border.[40]

However, even as the Camerons' dreams faded, others took their place with the confidence that the newly adjudicated property titles would provide a more secure basis for economic development. Following a series of severe droughts and economic downturns that drove many ranchers out of business in the 1890s, a wave of new investment flowed into the borderlands. While some longtime ranchers, like John Slaughter, managed to keep their ranches afloat, others, like the Cameron brothers, sold out. In 1903 mining magnate William Cornell Greene bought the San Rafael de la Zanja Ranch from the Camerons for $1,500,000. Investing the proceeds from his mining ventures in rangeland, Greene accumulated vast acreage on both sides of the border, including the Elíases' San Pedro Palominas Ranch near Naco. Extending from his original homestead in the San Pedro Valley seven miles north of the border all the way to Cananea, Greene created a transborder ranching realm alongside his mining empire. To the east, another group of Americans formed the Palomas Land and Cattle Company and bought two million acres of ranchland in Chihuahua. With its northern border extending for 140 miles from boundary monument 5 to monument 64, the company controlled the entire border with New Mexico.[41]

By the late nineteenth century, U.S. investment had also extended to the California–Baja California border, this time driven by advances in irrigation. With little water and few mineral resources, this stretch of the border had remained isolated and sparsely populated throughout the nineteenth century. However, in the final years of the century, after years of false starts, a group of engineers and entrepreneurs finally developed a viable irrigation scheme by which they brought Colorado River water to the desert basin known as the Salton Sink. A transborder venture operated as the Colorado Development Company on the U.S. side of the border and the Sociedad de Terrenos y Irrigación de la Baja California in Mexico dug a canal that extended from a cut in the Colorado River just north of the border, in a southward loop through Mexican territory, and back into the newly christened Imperial Valley.

Even before this canal brought water into the valley in the early summer of 1901, a land boom began. The first wave consisted of boosters and surveyors who laid out farm sites and plotted towns, including Calexico on the boundary line. Settlers followed just behind. Taking advantage of the provisions of the 1877 Desert Land Act, which allowed an individual to file a claim on 320 acres of desert lands, and the 1862 Homestead Act with its smaller allotment of 160 acres, settlers established farms and waited for the irrigation companies to deliver water.[42]

Seeing the intensive development underway north of the border, a group of Los Angeles businessmen bought up the adjoining land on the Mexican side of the line. Led by *Los Angeles Times* chieftain Harrison Gray Otis and his son-in-law Harry Chandler, this syndicate organized as the Colorado River Land Company, SA, and bought up over 860,000 acres extending south from the boundary line through the Colorado River Delta. Although they initially stocked their property with cattle and sheep, their intention was to develop it for irrigated agriculture.[43]

As elsewhere in the borderlands, private investment and land development along the California–Baja California border came at the expense of Native people, in this case the Cocopah, or Cucupá. A small tribe, numbered at less than two thousand by American reports, the Cocopah had had little contact with Mexican officials but had maintained a good rapport with local American settlers and government officials during the mid-nineteenth century. However, as American investors became interested in land along the eastern California–Baja California border at the end of the century, both Mexicans and Americans began to see the Cocopah as obstacles to development. Mexican officials displayed little regard for the Cocopah, who one local official described as living in misery and resisting civilization.[44] Locals on the U.S. side of the line at the new border town of Calexico shared this condescending opinion, characterizing the Indians as drunkards. In 1901 a local Mexican judge ordered soldiers to remove some Cocopah who he determined were squatting on the property of an American-owned development syndicate. Finally, in 1917 Woodrow Wilson established a tract of land lying thirteen miles south of Yuma along the eastern edge of the Colorado River as a reservation for the Cocopah.[45]

As the twentieth century began, the landscape of private property that had gotten its start with the displacement of Native people and the emergence of market-oriented ranching was rapidly being incorporated into a broader economy of land speculation and development. Shored up by government-sponsored surveys and adjudicated land titles, the commodification of border lands made it easy for American investors who were unfamiliar with the particular conditions of the borderlands to see the region as a good place to invest. By the beginning of the twentieth century, American capitalists would own most of the land along both sides of the boundary line.

The Politics of American Investment in Mexico

American economic dominance of the border was quite an achievement given that it was made difficult by Mexican law. Americans gained control of vast acreages abutting the border in Mexico, despite an 1856 Mexican federal law that prohibited foreigners from owning land within twenty leagues (approximately sixty miles) of the nation's borders. This seeming paradox, or at least legal infraction, provides another window into the politics of transborder investment. As the official restriction on foreign ownership suggested, Mexicans had long been worried that American economic involvement would pave the way for more intrusive forms of intervention or even annexation. However, at the same time most Mexican government officials, most notably President Porfirio Díaz and his closest economic advisors, realized that the nation desperately needed to attract capital. During the period from 1876 to 1910 in which Porfirio Díaz was in power, known as the Porfiriato, the Mexican government made attracting foreign investment a priority.[46]

Prior to the development of irrigated agriculture in Baja California, the Mexican government decided, despite Mexico's troubled history of colonization in the borderlands, to grant colonization contracts for the most isolated border regions. Both foreign and Mexican colonization companies (although the latter were often financed with foreign capital) gained control of vast swaths of Baja California on the condition that they would settle the land with colonists. Developer Guillermo Andrade and a group of American investors contracted to settle colonists in the Colorado River Delta. The Connecticut-based International Company of Mexico launched an even more ambitious colonization project, signing a contract for 5,394,989 hectares, virtually the entire northern half of Baja California stretching from the border to the 28th parallel. Altogether, by 1887, 60 percent of Baja California had been granted through colonization concessions.[47]

Despite their large-scale ambitions, these ventures struggled from the outset. The International Company of Mexico succumbed to financial problems and in 1889 sold out to a British concern after only three years. Andrade struggled for two decades to find enough colonists to fulfill his contract. He sent agents as far as Germany to look for colonists, but even had difficulty establishing the twenty Cocopah families that the Mexican government had stipulated should be settled on the property.[48]

The experiments with colonization were not much more successful for the Mexican government. Although the contracts had provisions that were meant to prevent a repetition of the disastrous earlier experiments with colonization, including a prohibition on foreign ownership along the border, a requirement that a certain percentage of colonists be Mexican nationals, and incentives for settling repatriated Mexicans, they continued to provoke controversy. In 1890 officials in the Mexican Land and Colonization Company—the successor to the International Company— were implicated in a filibuster attempt in northern Baja California.[49] Rather than securing the nation's borders, colonization ventures continued to be seen as a threat to national sovereignty.

In light of the problems with colonization, many Americans opted for other methods of acquiring land south of the border. Some signed long-term leases or secured permits from the Mexican government. These were particularly attractive methods for ranchers who had no interest in settling their lands with colonists. John Slaughter gained control of the majority of the San Bernardino Ranch on the Mexican side of the boundary line through a ninety-nine-year lease. Brewster Cameron claimed that he could secure an even longer lease for 999 years, which was "about the same [as owning land.]"[50] Ranchers also paid the Mexican government for special permits that allowed them to own land within the prohibited zone. In 1890 the Cameron brothers secured one such permit for $500.[51]

Since Mexican citizens were not subject to the restrictions on owning land along the border, foreign capitalists could also access citizenship rights by partnering with Mexican nationals, becoming naturalized Mexican citizens, or forming Mexican corporations. Andrade contributed his Mexican citizenship to a number of partnerships with Americans interested in developing the Colorado River Delta. One of Andrade's competitors, William Denton, took a different tack, becoming a naturalized Mexican citizen himself. Originally from England, Denton had arrived in California during the gold rush, married Elena Cano de los Rios of Mulege, Baja California, in 1860, and settled with his family in San Diego in 1874. However, it was not until he began investing in Baja California property at the end of the century that he switched citizenship. By the time of his death in 1907, Denton's estate included two ranches near the boundary line and a number of mines in northern Baja California.[52]

Naturalization made sense for someone like Denton whose life and business ventures were confined to the California–Baja California border, but it was not a realistic option for the growing number of American capitalists, like Harrison Gray Otis or William Cornell Greene, who viewed their activity south of the border as just one part of a wide-reaching investment portfolio. For these men, becoming a Mexican citizen would have closed more doors than it opened. What they needed was a way to access all the economic advantages of Mexican citizenship without giving up their identity and status as individual U.S. citizens. They found the perfect solution in corporate nationality. Under Mexican law, any company incorporated under the laws of Mexico carried all the rights of citizenship, save voting. By forming a Mexican corporation, or *sociedad anónima*, American capitalists legally transcended the limitations of their U.S. citizenship. While Otis and Greene remained Americans—and as such were prohibited from owning land immediately adjacent to the boundary line—the Colorado River Land Company and Cananea Cattle Company were Mexican corporate nationals fully capable of doing so. Operated in conjunction with U.S. corporations of different names, but identical objectives and personnel, American-owned Mexican corporations became the linchpins in the transborder economy. By the beginning of the Mexican Revolution in 1910, these corporations dominated mining, ranching, irrigation, and real estate speculation along the boundary line.[53]

They also spurred the creation of a dense economic support system on the border. Railroads were the most important part of that network and they too were controlled by Americans. American mining companies built railroads across the border to carry copper ore from the mines to the smelters and onto the U.S. market. In 1900 William Cornell Greene obtained a concession to build a railroad between Cananea and Naco on the border. A few years later trains also began carrying raw ore from the Nacozari mines to Phelps Dodge's smelters in the new border town of Douglas. When the Southern Pacific refused to build a branch line to Douglas, Phelps Dodge, under the auspices of the El Paso and Southwestern Railroad, built yet another railroad to connect Douglas to the border transportation hub of El Paso. Meanwhile, the Southern Pacific was busy building other lines. In 1897 it negotiated a deal with the AT&SF to acquire the Benson-to-Guaymas line that passed through Nogales and began consolidating its control of traffic across the western border. Five years later the Southern Pacific (SP) began work on the Inter-California Railroad, a branch line from their main line to the Baja California border at Calexico. At Mexicali, the railroad became the Ferrocarril Inter-California, looping through Mexican territory and recrossing the border at Algodones on its way to reconnecting with the SP main line at Yuma. In 1902 the Southern Pacific also bought Greene's Cananea line. These Mexican railroads were consolidated in 1909 as a Mexican corporation, the Ferrocarril Sud-Pacífico de México, or SP de Mex.[54] Knitting the Mexican borderlands more tightly to American markets, these transborder rail lines made borderlands investments more attractive to American capitalists.

In addition to railroads, transborder businesses relied on a binational network of government officials, investors, and professionals. The support of Mexican officials was critical to Americans' ability to invest and build businesses across the boundary line. In addition to the Díaz administration, state officials, like Luis Terrazas and Enrique Creel in Chihuahua and Luis E. Torres, Rafael Izábal, and Ramón Corral in Sonora, courted potential investors, offering exemptions from customs and land laws and subsidies and concessions for railroads, mines, and irrigation projects. Americans and other foreign investors came to rely on these officials not just for their initial generosity, but to help them maintain and grow their businesses and negotiate political and economic hurdles.[55]

As American investment in Mexico increased, a growing number of American capitalists became experts in purchasing land, securing title, and transacting business across the border. Investors were also assisted by specialized professionals, including attorneys, customs brokers, and title investigators, who facilitated transborder trade and helped guide them through the unfamiliar provisions of Mexican law. The largest companies, like the Colorado River Land Company, maintained lawyers in California, Baja California, and Mexico City. The New Mexico attorney, and future United States senator, Albert Bacon Fall, assisted with William Greene's legal work and took a leadership role in some of his Mexican enterprises. Smaller businesses could rely on border-town law practices that specialized in transborder business. The firm of Gregg and

Viesca in Douglas was one of these. "Established for the practice of Mexican law," their advertisement claimed, "we examine and obtain for persons or companies Mining Titles, Land Titles, Water Rights, Surface Rights, Patent Rights, Trade Marks, Railroad, Banking and Industrial Concessions, Registration and Organization of Companies, Corporation and Commercial Concessions, etc."[56] Local bankers and customs brokers also facilitated transborder business. Jesus Barcenas, attorney of Mexican law, R. S. Barbachano, legal and commercial translator, and F. Aldrete, customshouse broker, of San Diego and Tijuana summed up the range of these activities in an advertisement that announced their services as "Agentes Aduanales y de Negocios Judiciales Comisionistas/Mexican Law, Translating, and Brokerage Bureau/Legal Claims, Collections, Petitions and Law Suits in Mexican Courts/Search and Abstracts of Mexican Titles/Bonding and Clearing of Autos, Hunting Parties and General Merchandise into Mexico/Mexican Lands for Sale or Lease in Five Acre Lots and Up/Mexican Mines/Hunting Preserves."[57]

These businesses, along with investors, ranchers, laborers, and government officials, were critical to the functioning of the transborder economy. But more than mere cogs in that economy, these individuals became part of binational communities as well. The focal points of both community and economy were border towns.

FORGING BINATIONAL COMMUNITIES

Before the 1880s, one of the most distinctive differences between the desert and Rio Grande halves of the border was the absence of permanent settlements along the western half of the boundary line. While towns like El Paso and Laredo had long histories of settlement that predated the creation of the U.S.-Mexico boundary line, the twin towns of the desert border were a product of the boundary line itself.[58] The founding of those towns after 1880 reflected the growing importance of the border in the emerging transborder economy. The boundary line ran right through the middle of an increasingly productive landscape of copper mines, ranches, and irrigated agriculture. All of these businesses required customs facilities, rail connections, supplies, business support, and other services for their owners and employees. Border towns became home to all of these. But more than that they also became homes to border people. By the early twentieth century, twin border cities were both the economic and social hubs of binational borderlands communities.

The bifurcated towns of Nogales, Arizona, and Nogales, Sonora—known collectively as Ambos Nogales (Both Nogales)—were the first of the major twin cities to emerge on the border as a result of the linking of

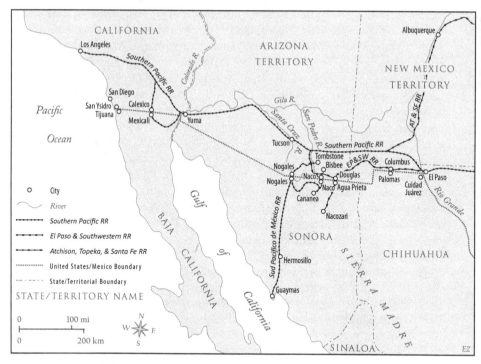

FIGURE 3.2. Western U.S.-Mexico borderlands, ca. 1910 (map by Ezra Zeitler).

the New Mexico and Arizona Railroad and the Sonora Railway in 1882. Two decades later, two new sets of border towns grew up at the points where the Mexican and American railroad branches running from the mines connected at the boundary line—Naco, Arizona–Naco, Sonora, on the rail line from Cananea, and Douglas, Arizona–Agua Prieta, Sonora, on the line from Nacozari, Sonora. Both were in many ways mining company towns.[59] The businessmen, organized as the International Land and Improvement Company, who staked out the Douglas town site in 1900, acted on rumors that Phelps Dodge was planning to build a smelter there. The town eventually hosted two smelters—the Calumet and Arizona was first "blown in" on November 15, 1902, followed by Phelps Dodge's Copper Queen smelter in March 1904. By 1903 six Sonoran mining companies had made Douglas their headquarters. The smaller town of Naco, Arizona, with the railhead from Cananea, was home to a Cananea Consolidated Copper Company forwarding agency and company store. Even the Mexican and U.S. customs officials and U.S. immigration inspectors operated out of buildings built and owned by the mining companies. Railroads, with their shops, stations, and switching yards, rounded out the industrial landscape of border towns and connected the borderlands region in an intricate economic web.[60]

Border towns also emerged to serve transborder ranching and land development ventures at Columbus, New Mexico–Palomas, Chihuahua; Calexico, California–Mexicali, Baja California; and San Ysidro, California–Tijuana, Baja California. Calexico was a product of the Imperial Land Company's master plan for the Imperial Valley. Just across the border, Mexicali became home to the Colorado River Land Company and many other binational business ventures. The Palomas Land and Cattle Company set up its headquarters on the border in Columbus, New Mexico.[61]

The boundary line ensured that the boundaries and governance of twin border cities remained divided into their Mexican and American parts, but the frequency of transborder movement and the integration of social and economic life meant that each border city was simply one half of a binational whole. In 1908 representatives of transborder companies with operations in Calexico and Mexicali noted that "like Nogales, Mexicali is divided by the boundary line between Mexico and the United States, there being a town, Calexico, on the American side, and Mexicali on the Mexican side. Geographically these towns are one."[62] Binationalism was embedded in the emerging urban landscape of border towns. Business and place names reflected the binational spirit of town boosters. The blended names of Calexico and Mexicali, as well as the double names of Naco, Sonora–Naco, Arizona and Ambos Nogales underscored the unity of border towns. Visitors to Mexicali could get a room at the Hotel Internacional, while those visiting Douglas might stay at the International Hotel. Residents of Nogales lived, worked, and shopped on International Street, saved their money in the International Bank, and spent it in the International Drug Store or La Internacional.[63]

The communities that took form in these urbanizing spaces and many of the activities in which they engaged were also binational. Shortly after its founding, Naco, Sonora, according to an 1899 registry, was home to fifty-eight households. Forty-one of these were listed as Mexican, eight American, and nine French. By 1910 Douglas had a population of 6,437—approximately 43 percent native white of native-born parentage, 19 percent native white of mixed or foreign parentage, and 35 percent foreign-born white, which included most Mexicans, as well as European immigrants. Nogales, Arizona, had an even larger percentage of foreign-born or native-born with mixed or foreign parentage. Of 3,514 inhabitants, approximately 24 percent were native white of native-born parentage, 27 percent native white of mixed or foreign parentage, and 47 percent foreign-born white. Because people of Mexican descent were considered white by the census, the majority of those labeled as "foreign-born white" and "native-born white of mixed or foreign parentage" were in fact Mexican.[64] Even without crossing the line, border residents lived and interacted with ethnically and nationally defined others on a daily basis.

At the same time the prevalence of transborder movement in daily life also increased the opportunities for binational interaction and the ability of border town residents to imagine themselves as belonging to a binational community. As a result of tariff duties and the relative scarcity of different goods in the United States and Mexico, shops on either side of the border developed distinct specialties that drew customers from both sides of the line. While shops on the U.S. side offered goods and tools produced in the United States, those on the Mexican side specialized in local agricultural products and European imports that the U.S. government taxed heavily. Luxury stores such as La Moda in Nogales, Sonora; Donnadieu Hermanos in Agua Prieta; and Jaussaud y Labourdette and Expectación Carrillo in Mexicali advertised opulent wares, including French liquors and silk, Mexican cigars and cigarettes, and ornamental fabrics.[65] Other border people crossed the line to make more mundane purchases. Luis Escalada, whose family ran the Escalada Brothers general merchandise store in Nogales, Arizona, remembered that most of his family's customers came from Mexico. A woman who moved to Nogales, Arizona, from Indiana in 1914 recalled regularly crossing the border to attend the market across the line. "[T]o see all these booths with all different kinds of vegetables and fish in barrels, oysters," she wrote, "it was an education in itself just going across the line and seeing things like that and at that time, there was practically no produce on this side of the line so everybody shopped in Nogales, Sonora."[66] More than just an expression of economic agency, transborder shopping promoted cultural interaction, albeit selective and often segmented by class, among Americans and Mexicans along the border.

Social as well as commercial activity provided opportunities for the formation of binational associations in border towns. Many Mexican and American children grew up playing and going to school together. In 1904 prominent American and Mexican residents of Naco celebrated the groundbreaking for a new school on the Sonoran side with champagne, speeches, and a tableau performed by two little girls, one American and one Mexican. Administered by the Sonora public schools department, but conducted on the plan of the "graded American school," the new school was a binational institution. The *Douglas Daily Dispatch* noted that the school would "doubtless attract many Mexican families of means who want their children to enjoy its advantages. It will also attract many American pupils of the vicinity who may wish to learn the Spanish language in order to fit themselves for business pursuits in Mexico."[67] Many Mexican students also attended American schools. One of these was Abelardo Rodríguez, who would go on to serve as governor of the Northern District of Baja California and interim president of Mexico.[68]

Adults incorporated the same spirit of binational inclusion and cooperation in a variety of voluntary organizations. Masonic lodges, athletic clubs, and women's societies often included citizens of both nations in their membership and sponsored transborder events. Ada Ekey Jones recalled that the Nogales of her girlhood accommodated a bustling social life, including athletic club, dances, dramatic club, young ladies mandolin club, and social club and that many of the members were "Mexican girls too." [69] Local newspapers carried frequent accounts of benefits, dances, and celebrations that drew citizens from both sides of the line.[70]

As American and Mexican business and government elites worked and lived together they increasingly formed a transborder social network. Viola Slaughter remembered hosting Colonel Emilio Kosterlitzky of the Mexican customs police and other Mexican officials at the Slaughter ranch. "I liked Kosterlitzky," she told an interviewer in the 1930s, "he was entertaining and intelligent and very handsome. He was often at the ranch." The interviewer followed this by noting that "Slaughter had many friends among the finest families of Sonora where homes were always open to him."[71] In a few cases these transborder friendships took the more intimate form of marriage. As in the case of Captain James L. Mix, a building contractor and mayor of Nogales, Arizona, who married the sister-in-law of the leading Sonoran politician Ramón Corral, the bonds of marriage could further contribute to the ties of friendship, economics, and diplomacy that bound transborder elites together.[72]

While Americans occupied a position of privilege on both sides of the border, class, more than nationality or citizenship, determined Mexicans' position within the borderlands. "Mexican" was both a neutral term used to refer to Mexican nationals and a pejorative term for racialized, lower-class ethnic Mexicans living on both sides of the border. While Viola Slaughter recalled that her husband was good friends with many "Mexican officials and men of importance," a number of whom they entertained at the ranch, it can be assumed that these men dined with the Slaughters, not in the "Mexican" dining room that was set aside for the cowboys who were "usually pretty dirty."[73] The *Douglas Daily Dispatch* reflected a similar dualism, praising Mexican officials while disparaging unnamed ethnic Mexicans whom it held responsible for numerous drunken brawls and petty crimes.[74] Along the border, being Mexican did not condemn every person to racial prejudices and a lower wage scale. But when paired with lower-class status, Mexicanness was often racialized, relegating working-class ethnic Mexicans to a subordinate position. In the binational context of border towns, society was divided by neither national citizenship nor the boundary line, but by class and racial-ethnic categories that took their meaning from the context in which they were used.

These divisions were on display during a Cinco de Mayo celebration in Douglas in 1905. In honor of the Mexican national holiday, the Mexican vice consul hosted a ball for Mexican and American elites, and the Junta Patriotica put on a dance for the "Mexican colony in Douglas" and visitors from Agua Prieta. While Mexicans organized both events, the *Douglas Daily Dispatch* noted that in contrast to the vice consul's elegant upper-class affair, the Junta's dance was a more raucous and segregated celebration where "the attendance was more suggestive of the country whose holiday it was than at the former place. Here they danced until daylight and most of them seemed good for several hours more."[75] Racialized "Mexican" and national "Mexican" operated as overlapping yet distinct categories—categories that were largely defined not by physical characteristics or national boundaries, but by class.[76]

The dual meaning of "Mexican," like many features of border society, was a product of the transborder economy. As the border became a site of commercial exchange and international investment, class and capital took precedence over preexisting categories of national difference. While their shared commitment to a capitalist economy forged some Mexicans and Americans into a binational community of mutual respect and common goals, that same economic system led to the subordination of other Mexicans. As they emerged along the boundary line, border towns became home to both and sites where the tensions between sympathy and distrust and unity and difference were negotiated on a daily basis in the context of the booming transborder economy.

In February 1896, a crowd once again gathered on the international boundary line at Nogales, this time to celebrate George Washington's birthday. The Nogales Fire Department, accompanied by a company of the Arizona National Guard, marched down Morley Avenue to the international line. As they crossed the line, the militiamen halted and a company of the Mexican Gendarmería Fiscal, or customs guard, led by Colonel Emilio Kosterlitzky, took up the firemen's escort. Together they paraded through the streets of Nogales, Sonora, stopping to salute both Mexican government officials and the American consulate. Meanwhile, the Arizona National Guard troops paraded north of the line, presented arms at the Mexican consulate, and then rejoined the firemen as they recrossed the border. Later that evening both companies, along with Colonel Kosterlitzky, Colonel Juan Fenochio, and Lieutenant Jose de la Rosa of the Gendarmería Fiscal, capped off the celebration with dinner, speeches, and songs.[77]

Fourteen years after the celebration of the joining of the Sonora Railway and the Arizona and New Mexico Railroad, the capitalist transformation that the railroads had ushered in had transformed the boundary line from an isolated outpost to a site of binational celebration. By the early twentieth century, Americans and Mexicans celebrated national holidays together in twin towns all along the border. Washington's Birthday, Mexican Independence Day, Cinco de Mayo, and the Fourth of July were all commemorated with enthusiasm and pageantry that blended national traditions.[78] "The union of Americans and Mexicans at Nogales in the observance of the Sixteenth of September was as fitting as it was handsome," wrote the Nogales *Oasis* of an 1895 celebration of Mexico's Independence Day. "The two nations have much in common, and the glories celebrated on their respective natal days belong to both. The names of Washington and Hidalgo, Lincoln and Juárez, Grant and Porfirio Díaz belong singly to no race, to no nation. They are the heritage of humanity. True lovers of liberty, everywhere, revere and honor them."[79]

These transborder commemorations were emblematic of the way in which Mexicans and Americans had begun to create a sense of a shared binational future on the border—a future committed to the continued development of transnational capitalism. The transborder flow of railroad cars, cattle, and investment capital had brought the U.S. and Mexican halves of the borderlands closer together and had forged a new and dynamic society that spanned the border. For some people at some times, this society became a source of pride and real binational identity. But life on the border was not one big parade, and nations were more than patriotic symbols. Even as the inertia of transnational capitalism seemed to threaten to blur the boundary between the United States and Mexico to the point of obliterating it, U.S. and Mexican officials arrived on the border intent on carving out a space for state power.

Chapter Four

THE SPACE BETWEEN

Policing the Border

BY THE 1890s John Brickwood's saloon was among the many buildings that crowded the boundary line between Nogales, Arizona, and Nogales, Sonora. Brickwood's saloon straddled the border on the aptly named International Street, which ran along the boundary line, its northern edge in U.S. territory and the rest of the road in Mexico. On the sidewalk piled against the building was a mound of stones, the remainder of the boundary monument that marked the border where Brickwood built his business.

Brickwood's saloon was strategically positioned to take advantage of the border. The saloon could sell both Mexican cigars and American liquor duty free—the cigars from a stand in front of the saloon on the Mexican side of the boundary and the liquor from the bar on the U.S. side of the line. Brickwood was not alone in this manipulation of the boundary line. As officials of the new International Boundary Commission reported in 1896, this was simply one example of the "open, yet lawful, evasions of customs duties" that went on along International Street.[1]

By the 1890s the forces of transnational capitalism had crowded the border, creating a landscape in which the division between U.S. and Mexican space was not always obvious. Yet with the growth of settlement, trade, and development it also became increasingly important for the U.S. and Mexican governments to make sure that national distinctions were clear. As the threat of Apaches and filibusters faded, the border shifted from a site where the state proved its power through military defense of its territory to one in which sovereignty was measured in customs collected, immigrants rejected, and bandits arrested. All of these responsibilities demanded that U.S. and Mexican officials not only knew where the border was but also attempted to control who and what crossed it. Customs agents needed to be able to tell when goods entered the country, immigration inspectors required a clear sense of whether an immigrant was in Mexico or the United States, and law enforcement officers had to be aware of where their authority ended.

In order to make this possible, the U.S. and Mexican governments resurveyed the boundary line and established new ports of entry along it. They also dispatched a growing force of customs, immigration, and law enforcement officers to the border to enforce a growing number of conditional restrictions on who and what could cross the line and where they could do so. With these efforts the nation-states increased their presence in everyday life along the border and laid the foundation for the modern border control apparatus.

However, while a burgeoning force of government agents represented the nation-states' interests on the border, they did not shape sovereignty by themselves. Policing the border was a surprisingly collaborative undertaking in which state representatives and local people negotiated how crossing regulations were implemented, and U.S. and Mexican officials adopted binational law enforcement strategies. Although not without conflict and occasional eruptions of nationalist antipathy, these negotiations enabled the nation-states to monitor and profit from transborder traffic and build binational ties that helped bring law and order to the border.

Clarifying the Boundary Line

John Brickwood's saloon was not the only place where poor demarcation facilitated smuggling operations or led to conflicts over property boundaries. The years since the completion of the first boundary surveys had been hard on the western boundary line. Many of the original boundary monuments had been damaged or destroyed. Visitors had chipped away at the boundary marker on the Pacific coast, leaving its edges ragged and its inscription illegible. At the other end of the boundary line in El Paso, bullet holes pocked the initial monument. Along the line between the two, many of the monuments had disappeared completely.[2]

In response to these conditions, in July 1882 the United States and Mexico formed a new International Boundary Commission and charged it with resurveying and remapping the border, replacing monuments that had been displaced or destroyed, and adding monuments so that they would be no more than 8,000 meters apart in even the most isolated stretches of the border and closer in areas "inhabited or capable of habitation."[3] A combination of repair and improvement, the commission's work would leave behind a more clearly marked and permanent boundary.

Upon taking the field in 1892 the commission commented on the sorry state of the border. "The boundary," the U.S. team reported, "originally marked with an inadequate number of monuments, many of them unsubstantial and without distinctive features, had become almost obliterated."[4] Between the Colorado River and the 111th meridian (the point just to the west of Nogales where the Arizona-Sonora boundary begins to cut diagonally toward Yuma), the U.S. team could only locate eleven of nineteen markers, and even these were merely piles of stones. One American traveler attributed the markers' disappearance to "wandering bands of Sonoranians" who "in their hatred of everything American, had doubtless mutilated it as an expression of national antipathy."[5] With fifteen or twenty, and at one point one hundred, miles between markers, it was difficult to determine the exact location of the boundary line. This ambiguity, noted the commissioners, was "giving rise to many disputes between miners, farmers, and herders, and permitting every facility and encouragement for smuggling."[6] Fernando Ortiz, a rancher near Sasabe, got a rude surprise when a U.S. surveyor determined that part of his ranch was in the United States in 1887. Although Ortiz had been paying taxes in Sonora, U.S. officials demanded taxes amounting to 1,000 pesos, and when Ortiz could not pay, arrested him.[7]

To make the boundary line more legible, the commission replaced the irregular and eroding markers with standardized stone or iron monuments at intervals of no less than 8,000 meters. Each monument was at least six feet high and had a hole in which a flag could be inserted to make it more visible. Three monuments located near cities were enclosed in iron picket fences "better to preserve the monuments from injury by trespassers or animals." A warning that "The destruction or displacement of this monument is a misdemeanor, punishable by the United States or Mexico" was inscribed in both English and Spanish on the monument, literally imprinting the authority of the United States and Mexico on the line.[8]

The work of this boundary commission was an improvement over earlier efforts, but far from perfect. Although they discovered inaccuracies in the first survey that had resulted in territorial losses that "fell most heavily upon Mexico," the new commission lacked treaty authority to correct the mistakes by altering the boundary.[9] Like their predecessors, the boundary commission also compromised its work because of the intense desert heat and lack of water. Temperatures reached 150°F in the sun. "At times the breeze which had swept over the scorching sands to the south," wrote the U.S. commission, "was so hot as to wither vegetation and burn the skin as would the heat from a furnace, rendering it necessary, even when in the shade, to screen the face from its scorching heat."[10] Despite discrepancies between some of the U.S. and Mexican measurements on the Arizona-Sonora border, the commission decided, "As both of these cases occurred on the desert, where water was difficult to obtain, and where remeasurements would have caused serious delay, and as they exceeded the limit but slightly, it was considered best, in the interests of

FIGURE 4.1. Boundary monument 255 near Tijuana on the California–Baja California border, ca. 1894. The boundary commission constructed the iron fence around the monument to protect it from vandalism. Album of Photographs of Old Monuments and Other Views along the Mexican-American Border, 1892–94, Records of the Office of the Chief of Engineers, RG 77, National Archives and Records Administration, College Park, Maryland.

the work, to accept these discrepancies rather than to attempt remeasurements under such adverse conditions."[11] Similarly, between the Pozo Verde Mountains near Nogales and the Colorado River, a distance of more than 323 kilometers described by the commissioners as "difficult of access, remote from railroads, is practically uninhabited, and is a true desert, containing but five badly spaced permanent watering places in the entire distance," the commission agreed to reduce the mapping and surveying of the adjacent land from the requisite two and a half kilometers on either side of the border to just one.[12]

Border towns, where border-straddling buildings and binational activity made it difficult to distinguish between U.S. and Mexican space, posed another set of problems for the boundary commission. By the time the commission reached Nogales, it had become a transborder community of 3,500 people clustered around International Street on the boundary line. On the U.S. side of the line, buildings including Brickwood's saloon teetered on the edge of U.S. territory. These buildings facilitated "open, yet lawful, evasions of customs duties" and made it difficult for customs and law enforcement officers to apprehend smugglers. "The grasping and

FIGURE 4.2. Boundary monument 122 in Nogales, ca. 1894. This new monument, located alongside Brickwood's saloon, replaced the crumbled stone monument that the boundary commission had found piled on the sidewalk outside the saloon. Album of Photographs of Old Monuments and Other Views along the Mexican-American Border, 1892–94, Records of the Office of the Chief of Engineers, RG 77, National Archives and Records Administration, College Park, Maryland.

overreaching actions of the United States settlers in building right up to the boundary line," noted the U.S. commission, "results in many inconveniences to the customs officials and peace officers of the United States, who, in order to patrol this important street, must rely for permission to do so upon the kindness and courtesy of the Mexican officials."[13]

Hoping to carve out a space dedicated to state surveillance, the boundary commission recommended that both governments prohibit building within a reserve strip of at least fifty feet along both sides of the boundary line. They suggested that "the erection of buildings on either side of the line, within these limits, be prohibited by law; provided, however, that such reservations may be used for public streets or highways."[14] Following this recommendation, on June 25, 1897, President William McKinley issued a proclamation setting aside a sixty-foot reserve strip along the border in Nogales from a point one mile east of newly num-

FIGURE 4.3. The cleared strip along the boundary line between Nogales, Arizona, and Nogales, Sonora, ca. 1900. The creation of the cleared strip made it easier for government officials to monitor transborder movement and prevent smuggling within Nogales and other border towns. Still Pictures, Records of Boundary and Claims Commissions and Arbitrations, Record Group 76, National Archives and Records Administration, College Park, Maryland.

bered monument 122—relocated at the expense of a portion of the south wall of Brickwood's saloon—to a point one mile to its west. This clarification of the border for the purpose of state control imposed significantly on local life in Nogales where many homes and businesses had been built close to the line. In addition to Brickwood's saloon, residences, businesses, barns, fences, and a railroad depot had to be relocated from the newly designated cleared strip. Their owners were given ninety days to vacate.[15]

The need to clear a space for state control spread with the emergence of each new town along the border. Land immediately adjacent to the boundary line was prime real estate, offering access to both sides of the line and the resulting opportunities for smuggling. The governor of the Northern District of Baja California noted that some of the best property in the new town of Mexicali lay within the designated restricted zone.[16] In Columbus, New Mexico, the U.S. boundary commissioner reported that plans were afoot to "obtain ground on both sides and abutting on the boundary, for the purpose of erecting buildings that shall be located partly in each country." Alluding to smuggling, he concluded, "It is quite evident for what purpose buildings so erected are to be used."[17] In Douglas a number of Mexican families disregarded restrictions and "pitched their tents and built their cabins right on the line." By obscuring the line, the *Douglas Daily Dispatch* reported, this colony posed a problem, because "the officer who goes down there at night finds it impossible to tell where the line is and whether he is arresting a man in the United States or in Mexico." According to a local deputy, this was exactly the intention of some of the Mexicans who were "acquainted with the conditions existing and [took] advantage of it."[18] In light of the continued disputes arising over access to the cleared strip, President Theodore Roosevelt issued a proclamation on May 27, 1907, extending the sixty-foot reserve to the entire border within the states of California and the territories of Arizona and New Mexico.[19]

With the resurveying of the boundary line and the creation of the cleared strip, the nation-states reclaimed the border as a space of state surveillance. However, as they sent growing numbers of agents to police that space, they would discover that the boundary line did not belong to the United States or Mexico alone, but to both nation-states and the people who lived along and moved across it. While government officials could clear the boundary line of buildings, dealing with people required a more nuanced strategy.

CHANNELING, RESTRICTING, AND TAXING TRANSBORDER MOVEMENT

The calls for a cleared strip along the boundary line revealed how much had changed on the border. Not only were town builders busily transforming the desert landscape, but a new group of government officials also followed them to the border intent on enforcing national customs, and later immigration, laws. By the end of the nineteenth century, thanks to the suppression of filibusters and Indian raiders and the growth of transborder trade, customs enforcement replaced military security as the primary concern of the U.S. and Mexican governments on the western boundary line.

The arrival of U.S. and Mexican customs officers ushered in a new era of state control that changed the way people crossed the border, channeling them through ports of entry and requiring them to submit to bureaucratic procedures. These new state priorities also brought local representatives of the nation-states into dialogue with border people who resisted inconvenient crossing requirements and expensive customs duties. Sometimes these conversations broke down into bitter recriminations, but more often they led to negotiation and compromise as government officials and private citizens worked out together what national sovereignty would look like on the border.

The first crossing regulations stemmed from both nation-states' desires to collect taxes on the growing stream of transborder commerce. In the nineteenth century tariffs were a critical source of revenue for both governments. Exactly how much these duties would be and which items were taxed were matters of national politics. Heated debates raged in the United States and Mexico over how each country should tax the goods and commodities that moved into and out of its territory. The determination of tariff rates required each government to choose a balance point between accruing tax revenue, protecting domestic producers, and promoting international trade. In the late nineteenth century, the United States and Mexico developed divergent trade policies. While there were political debates and variations within each nation, for the most part the United States kept tariffs high to protect its expanding industrial and agricultural producers from foreign competition, while Mexico kept its tariffs comparatively low to encourage trade with the United States and Europe in hopes of bolstering its weak economy.

Trade was particularly important along the border. In 1884, believing that high tariffs were hindering the economic development of the northern frontier, the Mexican government established a free trade zone, or *zona libre*, along the entire length of the border. The decision to create the free zone came after a fierce debate about the role of U.S. trade in Mexican economic growth and national security. Although some officials worried that the pull of U.S. markets would loosen the weak national ties binding the border to Mexico, politicians gradually embraced the *zona libre*. Established first on the Texas-Tamaulipas border in 1858 and then along the entire boundary in 1884, the *zona libre* was a narrow, twenty-kilometer-wide strip adjacent to the boundary line in which American goods could be imported duty free. Subsequent legislation imposed reduced tariffs at a fraction of regular duties, but the free zone—if in fact a misnomer—remained a distinct border zone in which transborder trade trumped nationwide tariff laws.

The free zone was a boon for local commerce, but it crippled the development of industry along the border. Reduced import duties made it cheap to move goods into the *zona libre*, but with export duties applying to goods moving both back across the border to the United States and into the interior of Mexico, exportation was prohibitively expensive. As investment increased within the zone, this double export tax became increasingly impractical. On July 1, 1905, President Díaz abolished the *zona libre*, hoping to make the border less dependent on imports and to promote agricultural and industrial development. Thereafter, the Mexican government relied on selective exemptions to lessen the burden of import duties without hampering the flow of goods between the border and the interior.[20]

While the Mexican government crafted the *zona libre* with the particular conditions of the border in mind, the U.S. government gave less thought to the Mexican border or how the trade laws they made would affect it. Still, the laws they passed had a profound effect on transborder trade. Tariffs increased the price, and thus reduced the flow, of a wide range of items, from cigars and liquor to cattle and copper ore. Ranching and mining, the two major industries of the Mexican borderlands, depended on the ability to export cattle and copper to the United States. While U.S. lawmakers added copper to the free list in 1894, thus allowing the transborder copper trade to thrive, regulations on the importation of cattle strained the northern Mexican cattle industry. In 1890 the U.S. Congress passed the highly protectionist McKinley Tariff Act, which raised import duties on most manufactured goods and farm products—including Mexican beef. Under this act the U.S. government collected ten dollars per head for cattle over a year old and two dollars per head on those under a year. By making access to the American markets prohibitively expensive, the tariff sent the Sonoran cattle industry into a steep decline.[21]

While tariffs cut off transborder trade in some cases, they more often had a more subtle but no less important effect on the movement of commodities, goods, and animals across the line. The goal of customs officers was not to stop transborder movement, but to channel crossings into designated ports of entry where they could monitor, restrict, and, most importantly, tax them. Both governments established new ports of entry on the boundary line and staffed them with customs officers who became the first nonmilitary personnel assigned to patrol the border. As early as 1880 the Mexican government established new customs stations on the line at Quitovaquita, Sasabe, Palominas, and Nogales. By 1892 the boundary commission noted that the customs receipts at Nogales were "very large, as Nogales is situated on the railway which runs from Benson, Ariz., to Guaymas, on the Gulf of California, and is the only railway entering Mexico between the Rio Grande and the Pacific."[22] As railroads crossed the border and new towns sprang up along the line, both governments created customs houses to accommodate them. In 1902 the United States established a customs office in Calexico. Three years later Mexican customs officials moved into offices across the line in Mexicali. By 1910 two more customs houses were added to serve the Imperial-Mexicali valleys at Los Algodones and between monuments 203 and 204.[23]

The channeling of goods, animals, and other commodities through ports of entry helped both nation-states create a more rational and manageable economic landscape for their agents to oversee, but it also interfered with the existing landscape of transborder commerce. By designating a few points on the boundary line as ports of entry, the U.S. and Mexican governments officially closed the remainder of the line to traffic. Although neither government built fences along the border until the early twentieth century, the requirement that trade pass through official ports of entry made most of the border legally off limits. Located at all railroad crossings and a number of other designated points on the border, ports of entry were a convenient stopping point for some shippers but an unwelcome detour for others. While most shipments coming in and out of the mining districts moved by rail through official ports of entry, ranchers were more likely to simply drive their stock across the line at the nearest point. This could work to the advantage of ranchers who happened to own land near a port of entry. The Elías family, for instance, hosted an annual roundup at one of their ranches near the San Pedro customs house.[24] But for others, traveling to an out-of-the-way entry point was a matter of considerable time and expense. The Nogales *Oasis* complained in 1895 that requiring cattle coming out of Sonora to cross at Nogales "adds greatly to the cost, besides working a great loss in shrinkage of the animals. And it works a hardship on the cattlemen here, for the cattle from afar eat up the feed on the hills about Nogales, which is needed to sustain the animals who find their natural crossing place at this point."[25] This cost and inconvenience frustrated ranchers like the Cameron brothers who complained that crossing through designated ports of entry "would accomplish no good whatever to the government but would result in the destruction of the cattle business on the border."[26]

In their attempts to divide the border between closed stretches and open ports of entry, customs officers conceived of the boundary line as a clear point of division between the United States and Mexico. In so doing they initially failed to accommodate or understand businesses like Brickwood's saloon or John Slaughter's ranch, where dutiable goods and animals moved back and forth across the boundary line, not through import and export but by walking out on the porch or straying to better pastures. When an American named William Sturges bought a boundary-straddling ranch near Sasabe from Fernando Ortiz, he discovered that not only did he have to pay property taxes in both countries, but also that he would have to pay customs duties on any goods that he brought from one side of his property to the other.[27]

Customs officers' attempts to collect duties on cattle that ranged freely back and forth across the border proved particularly problematic for transborder ranchers. "In the absence of any natural or other barrier at the international boundary line, and during stormy and cooler portions of the year, when all stock move southward," wrote a group of Arizona ranchers, "it is practically impossible to prevent our cattle and horses from straying into the State of Sonora."[28] As the cattle were bound at roundup to be returned to U.S. territory, ranchers thought little of this practice, but customs agents saw the situation differently. The deputy collector at Lochiel, Arizona, in the San Rafael Valley, explained to the Cameron brothers that if their cattle that strayed into Mexico "are not reported for inspection they in my opinion are seizable as it is impossible for me to tell the length of their stay in Mex. or whether the same are contraband."[29] Another group of American ranchers complained that the Mexican collector of customs at Nogales would not allow them to cross the line to retrieve their strays. These were not insignificant matters. Stock loss and customs duties were expensive. In 1908 one Calexico rancher found himself facing duties amounting to $5,000 when he brought a flock of his sheep back across the line from their pasturage in Mexico.[30]

The protests and appeals against these costly and inconvenient regulations did not fall on deaf ears. Despite what politicians had decided in Mexico City and Washington, DC, the customs officers on the border maintained a great deal of discretion in enforcing customs regulations on the boundary line. State power operated on a variety of scales in which local officials' decisions about enforcement made laws more flexible in practice than they were on paper. Stationed in close-knit border towns where they worked closely with businesspeople engaged in transborder commerce, many local officials proved willing to bend the rules. In 1891 John Slaughter met with Colonel Juan Fenochio of the Gendarmería Fiscal and worked out an agreement allowing Arizona ranchers to cross the border in pursuit of strays. In another case in the late 1880s, Arizona territorial judges found in favor of the Cameron brothers and other border ranchers who argued that they should not have to pay duties on cattle that had simply strayed across the line. Praising one of these decisions, the editors of the *Arizona Daily Star* noted that "it is not possible to drive every animal that steps over an imaginary line past the custom house, nor is that necessary to protect the revenues."[31] According to Brewster Cameron, the local customs collector agreed. "The absurdity of requesting a man whose cattle merely graze across an imaginary line to drive them twenty-five miles or more away from their own range to be inspected by an officer of customs," Cameron wrote, "was so apparent to Collector Magoffin that he said it would be an outrage upon citizens which he would not countenance."[32]

Beyond adjusting their enforcement of federal laws to accommodate transborder business, some local government officials also used their influence with higher-ups to try to change some of those laws. Consular officials were particularly active in lobbying for measures that would ease transborder movement. Prior to the passage of the McKinley Tariff, the U.S. consul in Nogales, Delos H. Smith, wrote to his superiors warning that high tariffs would strike a blow to U.S.-Mexican relations. "We are now as a nation making every effort to cultivate friendly commercial relations with our Sister Republics of the two continents," he wrote, "and consequently the propriety of taxing these ores and cattle to the extent proposed by this bill is a matter of grave doubt with many."[33] When the McKinley Tariff went into effect despite his pleas, Smith continued to negotiate with U.S. and Mexican customs officials on behalf of ranchers who sought to enter Mexico to round up their stray cattle and return them to the United States without paying the new duties. Over time, calls for policy changes did make their way to Washington, DC, where federal officials made adjustments in customs laws to accommodate transborder businesses. In 1897 the U.S. Congress included a special provision in the new Dingley Tariff Act that relieved pressure on border ranchers by allowing for the duty-free reentry of stock that had been pastured in Mexico for periods of less than six months.[34]

Despite these exceptions, the existence of customs duties and crossing regulations continued to make it neither cheap nor easy to move a wide range of goods, commodities, and animals across the boundary line. In response to these policies, some people turned to smuggling, which took the form of both trade in prohibited or stolen items and the movement of legally admissible goods without inspections or duties. All along the border people participated in petty smuggling, bringing a gallon or two of mescal, a box of cigars, or a couple of mules or horses across the line without declaring their merchandise to the customs inspectors. Cattle that strayed across the boundary line could even be said to smuggle themselves. Smuggling legal goods was not just a matter of money, but of convenience. For ranchers in particular, customs and quarantine regulations that required out of the way trips to official ports of entry could easily be evaded by "smuggling" stock across the open border.[35]

In addition to these more innocent acts of evasion, an illicit trade in outlawed or stolen goods and animals also developed along the border. While tariffs and crossing regulations made the movement of some goods across the border prohibitively expensive and inconvenient, other laws prohibited the importation of goods outright. In 1909 the U.S. Congress passed the Act to Prohibit the Importation and Use of Opium for Other Than Medicinal Purposes, followed by the Harrison Narcotics Law in 1914. These laws gave birth to drug smuggling on the border. However, at the turn of the century most illegal trade was in stolen stock. Cross-border cattle rustling fell particularly hard on Mexican ranchers who were hard-pressed to track their stolen stock across the border before it disappeared into the American market. In the early 1880s a gang of American rustlers known as "Cowboys" (who became notorious as the black-hatted villains who faced off against Wyatt Earp at the O.K. Corral in Tombstone in 1881) plundered ranches on both sides of the Arizona-Sonora border. In 1900 the Mexican consul in Nogales wrote to his superiors in Hermosillo calling for stricter laws to curtail the prevalent horse and cattle thieving that was hamstringing ranching operations along the border.[36]

By the 1880s the pervasive smuggling led both nation-states to establish forces of roaming customs agents to patrol the border. On the U.S. side of the line, the Treasury Department augmented the customs officers stationed at ports of entry with a handful of mounted inspectors. The Arizona Rangers, a territorial police force first organized in 1901, also pursued cattle rustlers, but they never numbered more than twenty-six and were phased out in 1909.[37] South of the border, customs enforcement was in the hands of a larger and more martial force—the Gendarmería Fiscal. Established by Porfirio Díaz in 1885, the Gendarmería Fiscal operated under the authority of the Ministry of Finance but became synonymous with not just customs enforcement but law and order in general along Mexico's northern border. The officers of the Gendarmería, most notably the well-known "Indian fighter," Emilio Kosterlitzky, came from the ranks of the border military elite, while the men under their command more often belonged to the lower ranks of society. In order to subsidize their meager pay, these enlisted gendarmes divided seized contraband among themselves. Well armed and quick to dispense justice, the Gendarmería Fiscal gained a reputation in local lore for their ruthless patrol of the border. C. E. Wiswall, the longtime manager of the Cananea Cattle Company, remembered that a particular cottonwood tree on the company's property gained notoriety as the place where Kosterlitzky hung cattle thieves. According to one of Slaughter's biographers, Kosterlitzky entertained other guests at the Slaughters' dinner table with "stories too gory to believe. Each course brought half a dozen more oral killings."[38]

Whether through dramatic pursuits of cross-border cattle rustlers or more mundane inspections of ore-filled railroad cars at ports of entry, customs officers helped transform the boundary line into a landscape of state surveillance and regulation. Other government representatives would follow in rapid succession, augmenting the nation-states' presence and adding layers of bureaucracy to the act of crossing the boundary line. Along with tariffs, quarantines on imported stock also had the power to disrupt transborder ranching by restricting the entry of Mexican cattle. In 1887 the governor of Arizona threatened to order a ninety-day quarantine on all cattle coming out of Sonora to prevent them from spreading disease to Arizona herds. Desperate Sonoran officials resorted to diplomatic channels to get the U.S. federal government to pressure the governor to change his mind.[39]

However, rather than blanket quarantines, the U.S. Bureau of Animal Industry more often relied on inspectors to weed out infected animals and ensure that cattle were dipped in petroleum to kill off any disease-carrying ticks as they crossed the border. These inspectors were particularly concerned about Texas fever, a disease spread by ticks that ravaged North American herds in the late nineteenth century. By the turn of the century the Bureau of Animal Industry had eradicated Texas fever in most of the United States but continued to struggle along the border in Southern California where ranchers complained that dipping and quarantining their animals would accomplish nothing as long they continued to come into contact with tick-infested Mexican herds. In 1909 officials in the Bureau of Animal Industry concluded that the only solution was to build a fence along the border. Completed in 1911, this range fence along the California–Baja California border became the first federally built fence along the U.S.-Mexico boundary line.[40]

The early twentieth century also saw the initiation of another important first in the history of border control—the first U.S. patrols charged with preventing the entry of unauthorized immigrants along the boundary line. While Mexicans and Americans moved freely back and forth across the boundary line, by the late nineteenth century a series of new U.S. laws restricted a growing number of immigrants from crossing the border. The U.S. Congress passed the first law restricting immigration—specifically that of convicts and prostitutes—in 1875. By 1910 new legislation had added Chinese immigrants, lunatics, people likely to become public charges, contract laborers, polygamists, anarchists, and others deemed undesirable to the list of excluded groups.[41] This legislation turned what had been an innocent movement of people into illegal immigration.

While most immigrants entered the United States through seaports, by the turn of the century heightened restrictions and intensified enforcement led many excluded immigrants to attempt entry across the more laxly controlled Mexican and Canadian borders. This backdoor traffic, primarily made up of Chinese immigrants denied entry after the United States passed the first Chinese Exclusion Act in 1882, joined the heavy stream of admissible immigrants of many races and nationalities who were finding their way across the border to join the borderlands labor force. These first unauthorized immigrants ushered in an emphasis on controlling the entry of undocumented immigrants that would eventually dominate debates about the U.S.-Mexican border in the second half of the twentieth century.[42]

Customs officers on the border initially took responsibility for preventing the entry of restricted immigrants. But by the turn of the century concerns about unauthorized immigration prompted the creation of the

Bureau of Immigration in Washington, DC, and the appointment of specifically designated immigration inspectors to monitor the boundary line.
By 1904 eighteen men, under the leadership of immigration inspector
George W. Webb in Tucson, were assigned to the New Mexico and Arizona borders. These inspectors were responsible for prohibiting the entry
of or deporting restricted immigrants as well as collecting head taxes on
those who were legally admissible, but they spent most of their time trying to stem the tide of excluded Chinese immigrants. As a result they became commonly known as "Chinese inspectors." One of the first of these
inspectors was Charles Connell. Originally from Iowa, Connell relocated
to Arizona in 1879 where he worked as a trader on the San Carlos Reservation, a deputy marshal for southern Arizona, the superintendent of a
mine, and the Tucson city recorder before becoming an immigration inspector in 1903. Although officially assigned to Douglas, Connell's work
took him all over the borderlands to Tombstone, Naco, Cananea, and
other Arizona and Sonora towns.[43]

Immigration inspectors like Connell faced the difficult work of weeding out large numbers of unidentifiable unauthorized immigrants, most
of whom tried to hide whatever part of their past marked them as excluded. Newspapers were filled with stories of battles of wit between inspectors and "wily" Chinese immigrants. Replete with racial and cultural
stereotypes, these accounts presented Chinese people as easily identifiable outsiders, but not everyone who was racially or ethnically Chinese
was deportable and not every excluded Chinese immigrant was easily
identifiable. Chinese immigrants who had immigrated before exclusion
and carried a certificate of registration, known as a "chok chee," were
allowed to reside within the United States. Other Chinese immigrants
had intermarried, became incorporated into Mexican communities, and
acquired Mexican citizenship that enabled some of them to cross the
border. While legislation was clear about who was and was not allowed
to enter the United States, Chinese immigrants did not openly display the
characteristics that marked them as either admissible or excluded. Other
restricted immigrants, including prostitutes and contract laborers, carried even fewer visual markers.[44]

It is unlikely that immigration officials could have excluded all the immigrants targeted by federal legislation even if they had lined up single
file at monitored ports of entry. Of course, immigrants—especially those
who knew they were liable to be denied entry—did not line up, opting to
cross at unguarded points on the boundary line. As of 1906 there were
only five immigrant stations on the western border. "There are, however,"
a U.S. report noted a year later, "row boats, carriage roads, pathways,
and mountain trails, throughout this broad expanse of imaginary line, all
passable and all being used for surreptitious entry into the United States.

However vigilant the border inspectors may be, a mere handful of them can accomplish next to nothing."[45]

In response the U.S. government created a new position of mounted Chinese inspector, or "line rider," to patrol outlying areas of the border in 1904. Jeff Milton, a former mounted customs inspector, took the first of these jobs and went back to the border, this time to look for illegal immigrants. Traveling alone with a string of horses through the most isolated desert stretches of the border between Nogales and Yuma, he would earn the nickname "the one-man Border Patrol." However, despite this reputation Milton often worked with Charles Connell and other immigration officers based at ports of entry. He was merely one part of the United States' developing immigration control apparatus that combined borderline inspections with wide-ranging pursuits and deportation efforts and formed the foundation for the future Border Patrol that the U.S. government would establish in 1924.[46]

To counter state efforts, sophisticated immigrant smuggling operations emerged on the border. In 1908 the U.S. secretary of labor noted that "a profitable industry has grown up in the promotion of immigration, by methods seldom more than colorably legal and often simply illegal." "Immigrant bureaus" specializing in illegal entry and doctors claiming expertise in removing "the signs of disease" set up shop in Mexican border towns.[47] Some of the agents charged with preventing entry got in on the business, collecting bribes to facilitate entry or to look the other way. Smugglers charged up to $100 to transport Chinese immigrants from Mexican seaports through Mexico and across the border. While some immigrants simply walked across the line, others concealed themselves in railroad cars. One immigration inspector remembered that "Chinese attempting to reach inland cities undetected hid in every conceivable place on trains: in box cars loaded with freight, under the tenders of the locomotives, in the space above the entryway in the old passenger cars, in staterooms rented for them by accomplices, and even in the four-foot-wide ice vents across each end of the insulated Pacific Fruit Express refrigerated cars, iced or not."[48]

The cat-and-mouse games between immigrants and U.S. immigration inspectors contributed to a consolidation of racial stereotypes and the association of Chinese race and ethnicity with outsider status within the United States. Meanwhile, to the south of the border, although the Mexican government enacted laws that restricted the entry of immigrants on the basis of health, age, politics, and morality, it also actively encouraged Chinese immigration to promote population growth and economic development in northern Mexico. By the turn of the century, Chinese immigrants had become a significant presence in Chihuahua, Sonora, and Baja California where they established small businesses and worked as cooks, launderers, household servants, and farmers. However, while their produce, products, and profits could cross the border into the United States, most of them could not. In Mexico, Chinese could immigrate, become citizens, establish businesses, and form families (either with other Chinese or through intermarriage with other ethnic and racial groups), but crossing the boundary line instantaneously transformed all but a handful of merchants into outlaws who were subject to arrest and deportation.[49]

If caught, the best-case scenario was that they would be sent back to Mexico. "Aliens rejected at the ports, or deported after unlawful entry, are simply turned back or sent across the border, and are then free to apply for admission again and again," noted a 1908 report. "It is not an unusual instance for an alien to be arrested in the United States after surreptitious entry and deported to Mexico three and four times within as many months."[50] Other Chinese immigrants, particularly those who had not established Mexican citizenship, were not just sent back across the border, but were deported to China. In October 1906, Inspector M. H. Jones arrested two Chinese immigrants—Ah Sam and Ah Lee—when they crossed the line at Nogales. The men testified that they had left China three months earlier and had not intended to enter the United States. "I was looking for work," testified Ah Lee, "did not know where the line was." Ah Sam concurred: "I did not want to come into the U.S. I do not want to go to China. I want to go back to Mex. If returned to Mex I will remain there." Despite their protests, U.S. immigration officials deported both men to China the following January. They were not alone. For many Chinese immigrants, simply stepping across the boundary line brought an end to their long journey to North America.[51]

Although hardly a happy ending, these stories had a far better conclusion than many. In another case, an employee of the Southern Pacific Railroad sealed a group of Chinese immigrants into a boxcar en route to California. When they were discovered in Yuma, they had long since exhausted the small amount of water with which they had started. One immigrant died shortly after he was taken from the car. Jeff Milton discovered the bodies of another group of sixteen Chinese immigrants in a canyon to the west of Nogales where their smugglers had killed them after collecting a $100 smuggling fee from each.[52] As these Chinese immigrants learned, the enforcement of sovereignty on the border could have lethal consequences.

But not all Chinese became victims of the border; some learned to use it to their advantage. Ah Sing, a forty-nine-year-old Chinese man, apprehended by Jeff Milton near Nogales, confessed that he had crossed the border in hopes of being deported to China. After eight months spent

DYING OF THIRST IN THE DESERT.

FIGURE 4.4. "Dying of Thirst in the Desert," 1891. This image from an 1891 exposé about Chinese immigration across both the U.S.-Mexican and U.S.-Canadian borders highlighted the dangers faced by Chinese immigrants who attempted to evade U.S. officials by crossing the desert border. Reprinted from *Harper's New Monthly Magazine*, March 1891.

looking for work in Mexico, he testified that "I like to go back to China—have no money to pay expenses can not make a living in Mexico."[53] For another immigrant, who did not want to return to China, crossing the border in the opposite direction allowed him to stay in the borderlands. Under suspicion for having violated the provisions of his certificate of U.S. residency by traveling to Cananea, Ah Fung chose to "voluntarily deport" himself to Mexico to avoid forced deportation to China. With Charles Connell on his tail, he raced to Cananea. "Me don't wanna go back to China," Ah Fung reportedly told Connell. "You no catchee me. Me stay Cananea now."[54] While Ah Fung could not stay in the United States, he could at least continue to live in the transborder community of which he had become a part.

Thanks to state policing efforts, pursuits like this became increasingly common on the border. Where troops had once tracked Apache raiders, customs agents and immigration inspectors now tailed smugglers and immigrants who attempted to evade border-crossing restrictions. But while these chases were dramatic, they were a relatively minor part of the states' overall plan for regulating immigration and trade on the border. Government officials spent most of their days not in hot pursuit but sitting at ports of entry filling out paperwork. While they made enemies of many Chinese immigrants and cattle rustlers and annoyed more than a few ranchers with their restrictions on transborder movement, most of the people these agents policed submitted to their oversight and even came to rely on them to help navigate inconvenient laws. While both nation-states had supported the use of military force to defeat the Apaches, collecting customs and controlling immigration required a more subtle assertion of sovereignty. In order to achieve their goals the U.S. and Mexican states strategically employed local agents and spatial controls; and, on the border, they also learned to work together.

BINATIONAL COOPERATION AND ITS LIMITS

As Ah Fung's story suggests, the boundary line could not contain immigrants or the state officials who pursued them. The same transborder networks and patterns of movement that allowed immigrants to evade deportation and rustlers to smuggle cattle across the boundary line required immigration inspectors, customs agents, and law enforcement officers to develop binational strategies to stop them. The U.S. and Mexican governments had resorted to reciprocal crossing treaties to defeat the Apaches in the 1880s, but in the years that followed, local officials developed more ad hoc forms of binational cooperation to deal with the challenges of immigration, customs, and law enforcement on the boundary line. Although local U.S. and Mexican officials did not always trust each other and transborder pursuits occasionally provoked conflict, binational cooperation was critical to the nation-states' early efforts to police the border.

On the local level U.S. immigration inspectors extended their operations across the border to ferret out smuggling rings based in Mexican towns, including Cananea, which was on Charles Connell's regular circuit. It was there in June 1904 that Connell and Jeff Milton, with the assistance of local Mexican law enforcement, uncovered the roots of a vast smuggling ring with operations on both the Mexican and Canadian borders. A report in the *San Francisco Bulletin* mistakenly formalized the informal arrangements that allowed American inspectors to travel into Mexico, stating that Milton was "now a roving inspector in Mexico, stationed there with the consent of the Mexican Government."[55]

Binational cooperation in immigration control was so successful at the local level that officials in Washington, DC, approached the Mexican government about establishing a formal transborder arrangement to control immigration. In 1907 the U.S. secretary of commerce and labor asked the Mexican government to allow U.S. immigration inspectors to be stationed at Mexican seaports and other major transportation centers to turn back immigrants before they reached the border. Based on a similar arrangement in effect between the United States and Canada since 1901, this agreement would have transferred enforcement of U.S. immigration restrictions away from the boundary line in order to preserve the fluidity of transborder movement. "If an arrangement cannot be made by which the immigration laws can be effectively administered along the Mexican border," explained the secretary of labor and commerce, the United States would be forced to adopt alternate measures that might interfere with "the conditions which have hitherto prevailed whereby the citizens of each country have been allowed to pass freely to and fro, notwithstanding any obstructions which may be placed thereby in the way of travel and personal intercourse, and in spite of any damage which may be done to the business of legitimate transportation."[56] Although the Mexican federal government refused to sign on to this agreement, on the local level officials continued to allow U.S. inspectors to cross the border to track down immigrants.

Customs officers also pursued smugglers across the border. Years before he began looking for immigrants, Jeff Milton got his start in border enforcement when he went to work for the Customs Service in 1887 as a mounted inspector. Assigned to the border between Nogales and the Gulf of California, Milton moved his headquarters from Tucson south of the border, first to Altar, Sonora, and then to the Aguirre Ranch, located just south of the line near Sasabe. Later he was reassigned to the eastern Arizona-Sonora border. At that time, before the founding of Naco or Douglas or the resurveying of the boundary line, the border was barely marked on the open range, making it difficult to be sure of its location. At one point Milton and his partner, C. B. Kelton, caught a group of Mexicans and saw them convicted of smuggling and sent to the penitentiary only to discover that they had made the arrest not in the United States but in Mexico. Since the men had never left Mexican territory, they not only could not have smuggled, but Milton and Kelton also could have been charged with kidnapping for having forcibly brought the men across the border.[57] Even after the boundary line was re-marked and cleared of buildings, parts of the border remained blurry and enforcing customs regulations required flexibility.

Law enforcement efforts often required a similar jurisdictional flexibility. Thanks in no small part to the belief that criminals could evade capture by simply stepping foot across the boundary line, the border gained a reputation for lawlessness and violence. Concerned about his investments in the Mexicali Valley, Harrison Gray Otis wrote to Porfirio Díaz in July 1908 bemoaning "the fact that all border towns are used as a rendezvous by unlawful characters from both sides of the International Line."[58] The border town of Douglas, according to former Arizona Ranger Captain Thomas H. Rynning's 1932 memoir, was "the toughest proposition then on the whole American border." He recalled that "cattle thieves, murderers, all the worst hombres of the United States and Mexico made their headquarters there."[59]

This unruly reputation impeded the efforts of transborder boosters and created a demand for cooperative law enforcement efforts. Each state spawned its own host of crime fighters, including sheriffs, marshals, soldiers, and Rangers on the U.S. side of the line and town police forces, rural police (Rurales), soldiers, National Guard troops, and the Gendarmería Fiscal in Mexico. While each of these forces had its own set of responsibilities, the nuances between them disappeared as they worked together to capture bandits and maintain law and order on the boundary line. By contrast, the national distinctions were clear. Americans may have occasionally confused Emilio Kosterlitzky's Gendarmería Fiscal with Rurales and Mexicans might not have always been able to tell sheriffs and Rangers apart, but no one mistook Rurales for Rangers.[60]

Yet despite these clear national divisions, U.S. and Mexican forces shared a sense of purpose that led them to work together. In place of the official reciprocal crossing agreements that had facilitated the Apache campaigns in the late nineteenth century, local law enforcement officials negotiated off-the-record agreements that allowed them to pursue criminals across the boundary line. Transborder law enforcement efforts operated according to an informal protocol that masked the ways they challenged sovereign boundaries. Joint patrols, captive exchanges, and leaves of absence in which Rangers temporarily resigned their posts in order to act as private individuals when across the line all helped to disguise the extent to which law enforcement officers overstepped their jurisdictional authority by crossing the boundary line in pursuit of criminals.[61]

Two of the most notorious of these outlaws were Burt Alvord and Billy Stiles. Around the turn of the century, Alvord and Stiles led a binational gang of rustlers, thieves, and train robbers in a transborder crime spree that eluded both U.S. and Mexican officials. Originally a deputy sheriff, Alvord began his criminal career as a cattle rustler before masterminding a train heist with Billy Stiles and an outlaw gang in September 1899. The following February, members of the Alvord-Stiles gang held up Jeff Milton, who was at the time loading freight cars at Benson in between stints with the customs and immigration services. After Stiles turned state's evidence, Alvord and their coconspirator, Bravo Juan Yoas, were imprisoned, but soon after Stiles broke both men out of jail. In December 1903 Alvord and Stiles again landed in jail and again managed to break out. Two months later the *Douglas Daily Dispatch* reported that the Alvord-Stiles gang was continuing its depredations with impunity. "This feeling of security," suggested the *Dispatch*, "is perhaps, due to the fact that the Mexican populations on the other side of the frontier line, where they now are, are in sympathy with the defiant highwaymen, warning them whenever the officers of the law are in their vicinity." Government and business elites were, however, far from sympathetic. Mexican and U.S. officers redoubled their efforts, and William Greene offered a $10,000 reward for the capture of the two men dead or alive.[62]

Alvord and Stiles's transborder crimes required a binational strategy to stop them. In February 1904 the *Dispatch* reported that Mexican authorities had deputized American residents of Sonora to drive Stiles and Alvord from their hiding place in the San Jose Mountains.[63] Captain Thomas Rynning and three Rangers also crossed into Sonora in pursuit of the outlaws where they joined forces with Captain Cayetano Molina and six Rurales. Rynning's account of this transborder pursuit, although recorded nearly thirty years later in an often-embellished memoir, provides insight into the many small negotiations of national difference and jurisdiction that shaped binational law enforcement efforts. Rynning recalled that when their pursuit took them into a narrow box canyon, Molina and his men opted for a less dangerous detour. "Didn't blame him much for deciding not to go through it," he wrote. "Alvord and Stiles might lay for us in there. And they wasn't noways his outlaws, belonging on our side of the line—if we could get them."[64] As far as Rynning was concerned, the identity of Stiles and Alvord as American citizens left them jurisdictionally, if not physically, within the bounds of U.S. law enforcement.

The Rangers failed to catch Alvord and Stiles. Instead the outlaws cornered them in the canyon and forced them to give up their pursuit, suggesting that Molina's decision to avoid the canyon was not just diplomatic, but strategic. According to his account, Rynning compensated for Alvord's and Stiles's escape by single-handedly capturing a Mexican bandit named Andreas during his retreat. Rynning took full credit for the capture, but evaded responsibility for the harsh sentence that followed. Although Andreas had stolen American stock in his possession and Ranger Jeff Kidder recognized him as the murderer of a Bisbee barber, the Rangers turned Andreas over to Molina. Claiming that he "couldn't do anything, as we were in their country and they had charge of the proceedings," Rynning stood by as Molina's men forced Andreas to dig his own grave, stood him at its end, and shot him.[65] Although this account echoed borderlands tropes of Rangers' heroism and Rurales' mercilessness, it also suggested that while binational cooperation operated on a basis of mutual respect and deference, it also opened up opportunities to deflect responsibility and blame.

Not long after Rynning and Molina's joint pursuit, another group of American sheriffs and Rangers finally managed to capture Alvord at the Young Ranch, one mile west of Naco on the Mexican side of the line.

Burt Stiles and Bravo Juan Yoas, however, escaped. The two men retreated into the San Jose Mountains just south of the border where they
were rumored to have stashed $8,000 that they had recently stolen from
a Magdalena merchant. Despite reports of his imminent surrender, Stiles
was reported a month later to be living on the Mexican side of the line,
frequenting the outskirts of Naco by night and benefiting from his "many
friends among the Mexicans, who afford him every assistance and keep
him in good concealment."[66] In April, Stiles and Yoas were credited with
the "daring robbery" of $2,500 from the Aguirre Mercantile Company
Store in Naco, Sonora. "The robbery was a particularly bold one," noted
the *Dispatch*, "the store being adjacent to the Mexican guard house
where the customs officers and border guards are stationed."[67] During
the following year reports drifted back from Mexico that Stiles and his
binational gang were plotting to rob the Klondyke Mine near Magdalena
and the Mexican customs house at Agua Prieta. One *Dispatch* report even
named Stiles as the leader of a group of Yaqui Indians accused of murdering some Americans in Sonora. Although the Rangers and Rurales remained vigilant, Stiles continued to evade them. He finally died in January 1908 in Nevada, far from the border and the binational officials he
had frustrated.[68]

Despite such failures cooperative law enforcement efforts did help to
make transborder businesses safer. Economic development depended on
investment security, and investment security depended heavily on the
maintenance of law and order. A few big outfits, like the Cananea Cattle
Company and John Slaughter, offered rewards for the capture of outlaws
and hired private men to protect against bandits and rustlers, but most
borderlands ranches, railroads, mines, banks, and businesses relied on binational law enforcement efforts to defend their interests. In 1905 the
Douglas Daily Dispatch credited effective law enforcement with keeping
Arizona's insurance rates on bank safes lower than those in New York.
With the growth of labor tensions in mining camps after the turn of the
century, law enforcement agents were also mobilized to suppress strikes at
Globe in 1902; Clifton, Morenci, and Metcalf in 1903; and most notoriously, Cananea in 1906.[69] However, while binational law enforcement
had been effective in suppressing banditry, it nearly provoked an international crisis at Cananea.

The violence that erupted at Cananea in 1906 evoked one of the largest binational responses that the borderlands would witness. Yet as
Americans rushed to William Greene's defense they also revealed the limitations of the informal arrangements that made such operations possible. The protocol of transborder law enforcement could temporarily
mask but not erase jurisdictional boundaries. If law enforcement officers

ignored its protocols or overstepped their authority, national divisions and distrust could, and did at Cananea, reemerge with a vengeance.

The Cananea strike began as a fairly commonplace dispute over wages and hours. On June 1, Mexican workers walked off the job at the Cananea Consolidated Copper Company's Oversight Mine, asking for an eight-hour day and to be promoted and compensated on a par with Americans. The strikers marched to the company lumberyard where the manager, George Metcalf, turned a fire hose on the crowd. Someone (each side would later blame the other) opened fire. Soon men on both sides lay dead and the lumberyard was in flames. As the violence spread through Cananea, William Greene desperately called for American arms and reinforcements and telegrammed Mexican officials demanding military support.[70]

With smoke rising above Cananea and word of the riots spreading through Sonora and across the border, hundreds of armed American volunteers massed at Naco, where the Mexican customs guards refused to allow them to cross the boundary line. The next morning, Governor Rafael Izábal arrived in Naco en route to Cananea (due to the configuration of borderlands railroads, Izábal had traveled north to Nogales, crossed the border, and then traveled east through U.S. territory to Naco where he recrossed the border and would continue south to Cananea). Ranger Captain Thomas Rynning, who had led men across the border many times, approached Izábal to seek permission for the Americans to cross the boundary line. Izábal, however, was wary. While he was desperate to restore order in Cananea, he recognized that the entry of an armed U.S. force of this size would strain the limits of binational cooperation and violate Mexican sovereignty. Even so, the bleakness of the situation prompted Izábal to allow the Americans to cross the border. Described by Rynning, who led them across the line, as "cowpunchers, miners who'd seen service in Cuba and the Philippines, some of my rangers, and the usual scattering of outlaws you'd always find round that range," the ragged and heavily armed crowd crossed into Mexico where Izábal swore them into the Sonora militia.[71]

This transgression outraged many Mexicans and only increased the tensions in Cananea. Although Izábal insisted that the Americans were not "a military force, but only of individuals who did not belong to the army nor to the American militias" and that they agreed to "be exclusively under my orders and in consequence under the authority of the laws of Mexico," news quickly spread that a U.S. force had invaded Mexican territory.[72] While some borderlands elites may have been willing to compromise sovereignty for the benefit of transborder security and development, Mexican workers rejected U.S. economic dominance and

FIGURE 4.5. Rangers and gendarmes posing after the Cananea strike, 1906. Although the Rangers' intervention at Cananea was not successful, this image reflected the continued importance of cooperation between U.S. and Mexican law enforcement officers in the borderlands. Among the men pictured are Emilio Kosterlitzky (center, on the white horse) and Thomas Rynning (center, to the left of the yucca plant). Courtesy of the Arizona Historical Society/Tucson, AHS Photograph #4362.

military intervention. At Cananea, William Greene, Rafael Izábal, and other elites quickly learned that they did not hold a monopoly on determining when national divisions mattered and when they should be compromised. With the armed Americans behind them, Izábal and Greene attempted to calm the strikers, but to little effect. Only the arrival of Emilio Kosterlitzky brought an end to the conflict. Riding into town at the head of a body of gendarmes, Kosterlitzky reasserted the control of the Mexican government, putting an end to both the riots and the American "invasion." He asked his American colleagues to go back across the border and forcibly restored order. In the following months, Kosterlitzky would remain in Cananea at the head of a force of gendarmes whose presence helped to discourage future strikes.[73]

As the events at Cananea made clear, when law enforcement officers crossed the boundary line, they walked a fine line between binational cooperation and territorial encroachment. The rioting and military intervention that these tensions provoked were extraordinary, but the resentment was not. All along the border, national distrust, discrimination, and discontent remained undercurrents that periodically ruffled the waters of binational communities and economies.

Frequent collaboration did not completely erase the boundaries of state sovereignty or the jealousies over jurisdictional authority. Mexican authorities often complained that U.S. officials crossed the border in pursuit of criminals without proper authorization. In early 1907, Ranger Harry Wheeler, Yuma Constable Julio Martinez, and their guide, Ygnacio Carbajal, followed Raymundo Garza across the border. They ambushed Garza at Colonia Lerdo in Sonora and in the fight that followed shot his wife, Beatriz, twice. Mexican officials were livid. The Mexican consul at Tucson called the incident an "outrage" and a "great dishonor for Mexicans." The Mexican minister of foreign relations considered trying to extradite Wheeler and Martinez to Mexico on charges of kidnapping.[74]

Incidents that occurred right on the boundary line were less clear cut but could also strain binational relations. Bar brawls were rarely the purview of the U.S. State Department and the Mexican Department of Foreign Relations, but when one of these fights led to a boundary-line arrest in 1893, jurisdictional questions forced the matter onto the desks of diplomatic officials. On July 23, 1893, Jesús García and another Mexican national got into a fight in a Nogales, Arizona, saloon. When Deputy Sheriff John Roberts attempted to arrest them, García made a break for the boundary line. He had barely reached the border when Roberts, with the help of another U.S. citizen, caught him and took him into custody. The problem was that an investigation by Reuben A. George, the U.S. vice consul in Nogales, Sonora, discovered that the arrest had only been possible because an American passerby had pushed García back across the line. George advised the American sheriffs that they should turn García over to Mexican authorities. García meanwhile lodged a complaint with C. Fernandez Pasalagua, the Mexican consul in Nogales, Arizona. Fernandez Pasalagua reported the incident to the Mexican ambassador who in turn filed a protest with the U.S. State Department. The issue was only laid to rest three years later when an investigation by a new U.S. consul at Nogales determined that both sides were in the right—when the American had tackled García he had fallen down on the line—his head and shoulders were in Mexico, the rest of his body lay in the United States.[75]

While cooperative efforts and informal crossing agreements sometimes made it seem as though the border did not really matter, it did. Depending on who was involved and whether they followed protocol, a few inches could be either completely insignificant or a matter of freedom or imprisonment or life and death. And while U.S. and Mexican officers and officials often worked together, they did not always like or trust each other.

Jeff Kidder, an Arizona Ranger who was killed by Mexican police in

1908, learned this lesson in the hardest of all ways. In April 1908, Kidder had just finished a five-year stint with the Rangers and had returned to Naco, Arizona, to reenlist. While waiting for his captain to arrive, Kidder crossed the border and entered a dance hall. He danced, drank, and then went into a back room with a prostitute. After, in Kidder's words, "fooling around," he and the woman got into an altercation. He claimed she had stolen a dollar from his pants pocket and when confronted had punched him, but other witnesses reported that Kidder had slapped her first, causing her to call the police. Whatever the cause, two Mexican policemen soon arrived on the scene. A gun battle ensued in which all three men were shot. Seriously wounded, Kidder left the dance hall and began crawling toward the boundary line. Under fire from Mexican officers patrolling the line, Kidder nearly made it across the border before he ran out of ammunition and the Mexican officers arrested him. American doctors examined him, but there was little they could do. The following morning, after spending the night suffering from intestinal wounds, Kidder died in the Mexican jail at Naco.[76]

Kidder's death reverberated along the border. Rumors spread among Americans that the Mexican policemen who shot Kidder had planned in advance to ambush him. Mexican officials blamed the incident on Kidder, reporting that the police had only intervened after Kidder insulted or assaulted someone at the dance hall. Delays in getting Kidder's body and personal effects back across the border caused by international restrictions and regulations made the situation worse. For a time more violence seemed imminent. The return of Kidder's body, gun, and Ranger badge temporarily averted violence, but tempers continued to simmer. Two weeks later Sonoran officials replaced all of the police and line riders in Naco and closed the town's fifteen saloons. Billy Olds, Kidder's friend and fellow Ranger, resigned his commission and set off for Mexico to avenge Kidder's death.[77]

But what does this one man's death reveal about international relations and national identities on the border? After all, despite the glowing reports of his behavior that followed his death stressing his upright, brave, and "manly" qualities, Kidder's activities on the night of his death and his history in the Rangers suggested he was less than virtuous. A number of shooting deaths were attributed to him, and his record was marred by accusations that he was a "hot-headed man" who used unnecessary violence. It is possible that Kidder had many enemies, Mexican and American alike. However, it was not Americans who killed Kidder, but Mexicans—specifically, Mexican law enforcement officers who were reported to resent Kidder because of past run-ins.[78] On the border, national antipathies and divisions channeled personal grudges, class conflicts, and racial prejudices. The men who shot Kidder may have hated him for past wrongs or they may have simply been doing their job, but they were also Mexicans and Kidder was an American, and those facts nearly precipitated Kidder's death into an international crisis. And it was Kidder's awareness of the importance of these national divisions that caused him to use his last bullets and some of his last breaths to try to fight his way back across the boundary line.

The image of Kidder dragging his bullet-riddled body toward the boundary line in 1908 contrasts markedly with the 1896 celebration of George Washington's birthday in Nogales with which the last chapter concluded. Yet both stories turned on the same act of crossing the border. These crossings were only two among hundreds of thousands that took place in the context of the transborder economic boom and the growth of border towns. Most crossings were much more mundane—a herd of cattle being driven to market, local people going to the store, a shipment of ore en route to the smelter. Yet though they lacked the drama of Kidder's last stand or a transborder parade, each of these crossings marked a moment in which border people negotiated sovereign space.

By crossing the boundary line, people, goods, and animals by definition moved from one sovereign space into another. Yet how, when, where, and for whom this national transition mattered varied widely. In constructing sovereign space, the United States and Mexico had begun to create not an absolute division but an assortment of regulations that made the border fluid for some and unyielding for others. While U.S. immigration inspectors sought to make the border an increasingly intractable barrier to Chinese immigrants seeking to enter the United States, U.S. and Mexican officials opened up loopholes to allow ranchers, investors, and law enforcement agents to move easily back and forth across the line. Border crossings grew ever more frequent at the same time that customs and immigration regulations complicated the process. The growing government presence both established state authority on the line and demonstrated how sovereign principles could be compromised with local needs.

Operating on the border required a careful balancing act. Government officials weighed sovereign prerogatives against the practical difficulties of enforcement and the potential profits of leniency. American economic interests walked the tightrope between investment and encroachment, relying on the stabilizing force of the promise of transborder economic growth. Local communities seesawed between the unity of binational celebrations of national holidays and the discord of violent conflicts and class and racial strife. Despite persistent tensions and periodic outbursts of violence, the binational balance remained remarkably stable through the first years of the twentieth century. However, unbeknownst to the investors who continued to buy up land along the boundary line or the citizens of the United States and Mexico who lived together in border towns, events loomed on the horizon that would send shockwaves throughout the borderlands and reinscribe national difference in the boundary line with violent clarity.

Chapter Five

BREAKING TIES, BUILDING FENCES

Making War on the Border

JUST AFTER 4 P.M. ON AUGUST 27, 1918, an unknown man approached the boundary line in Nogales, Arizona. Suspecting that the man was smuggling something, U.S. Customs Inspector A. G. Barber ordered him to halt, but the man continued walking toward Mexican territory where Mexican guards waved him on. Drawing his gun, Barber, a Nogales resident who had left his job as an electrician to become a customs inspector only six months before, repeated his order to halt. Two U.S. soldiers posted nearby also raised their rifles. Across the line, Mexican customs and immigration officers mustered their weapons as well. One fired, hitting a U.S. sentry in the face. The other American soldier returned fire. Within moments the two halves of the town were at war. Government officials, soldiers, and civilians joined the fray. For more than two hours, bullets rained back and forth across the boundary line. U.S. soldiers moved into Mexico and took up positions. By the time civilian and military officials managed to restore order many people had been wounded and at least twelve, including the *presidente municipal* of Nogales, Sonora, lay dead.

After the battle few people were entirely clear on what had brought the two halves of Nogales to blows. Government investigations and news reports focused on the unknown man who had attempted to cross the line and disputed who had fired the first shot.[1] But the roots of the conflict ran much deeper. Since the beginning of the Mexican Revolution eight years earlier, violence, diplomatic disputes, and economic instability had disrupted the transborder economy, brought underlying national antipathies and suspicions to the surface, and strained the binational bonds between the Mexicans and Americans who lived and worked together along the border. As Mexican anxieties about U.S. territorial encroachment and economic dominance mixed with American fears about Mexican insurgents and political intrigue on the border, the national divisions that border people had successfully blurred reemerged with stark clarity.

These changes did not occur all at once but developed gradually over a decade scarred by war. Beginning with the Mexican Revolution's first battles in 1910, the 1910s witnessed the devolution of that revolution into civil war and saw the United States' entry into the First World War in 1917. It is helpful to think about the decade in three periods—the early years of the war between 1910 and 1913 when both Mexicans and Americans held out hope that the revolution would be a short-term conflict after which conditions would return to normal; the middle period between 1913 and 1917, which saw some of the greatest violence and destruction as the Mexican Revolution devolved into civil war and the United States and Mexico nearly went to war; and the final years of the decade during which the United States' engagement in World War I led to the creation of new border-crossing regulations.

What happened in Nogales in 1918 could not have happened earlier. While two other battles had been fought in Nogales, first in 1913 and again in 1915, neither had seen the two halves of the community turn against each other as they did in 1918. Rather, these three battles of Nogales stand out as signposts of the gradual decline in conditions on the border. While the struggle between Mexican factions in the First Battle of Nogales in 1913 proved that the binational border town could not escape the ravages of the revolution, it also held out hope that the violence and destruction could be contained by the boundary line. The Second Battle of Nogales in late 1915, a transborder skirmish between U.S. and Mexican troops, reflected the growing hostility between Mexicans and Americans. However, it was not until the Third Battle of Nogales in 1918, in the context of new World War I crossing restrictions and after years of strife had disrupted transborder ties and inflamed local tensions, that Ambos Nogales imploded.

The events of that August afternoon marked the end of the era of fluid transborder movement and peaceful binational communities that had peaked in the first decade of the twentieth century. As concerns about national security and military victory trumped the importance of transborder commerce and communities, both countries called for tighter controls on transborder movement and stepped up their presence on the line. Finally, in the wake of the Third Battle of Nogales, U.S. and Mexican officials agreed to build a fence along the border through the center of Nogales. By the end of the decade, the boundary line had been transformed from Nogales's binational main street to a militarized buffer between two nations at war.

During the war years U.S. and Mexican officials began to replace the landscape of binational cooperation and conditional controls that had been developed with the countries' customs, immigration, and law enforcement needs in mind with stricter regulations on who and what could cross the border and armed men and physical barriers to enforce them. These measures, along with years of violence and bloodshed, took their toll on the social and economic ties that had bound border communities together. Underlying national tensions had never disappeared, as moments such as the aftermath of the Cananea strike and Jeff Kidder's death made clear. But until war came to the border, binational elites had effectively suppressed them. War brought these tensions to the surface and kept them there for years at a time, changing the border from a point of interaction and cooperation to one of conflict and division. By 1918 the events at Nogales and the resulting fence that divided the town were emblematic of the boundary's metamorphosis. The border had become a divide.

Holding the Line in the Midst of Chaos, 1910–13

The Mexican Revolution began in the fall of 1910 when Francisco Madero issued the Plan de San Luis Potosí, calling on Mexicans to rise up and overthrow Porfirio Díaz's rule. This revolutionary call to arms (which despite being named for a Mexican town was written in San Antonio, Texas, where Madero was then living in exile) marked the culmination of liberal political critiques that had been mounting over the course of Díaz's administration. Since coming to power in 1876, Díaz had brought capitalist development to Mexico, but not without political and social costs. Policies that supported the privatization of land and capitalist production had pushed rural Mexicans off their land and made them increasingly dependent on wage labor. The strike at Cananea in 1906 was only one example of the resulting class conflict that was rife throughout Mexico. At the same time, political and judicial corruption and Díaz's unwillingness to cede power provoked political critiques from liberal elites. Facing political pressure, Díaz briefly agreed not to seek reelection in 1910, but then changed his mind. The ensuing election was marked by corruption and coercion as Díaz suppressed and imprisoned his rivals, including Madero, the European- and American-educated son of a wealthy Coahuila family, who had mounted a campaign for the presidency. When Díaz was declared the victor it marked the end of liberal hopes for a peaceful political transition of power. Within months Madero fled Mexico for the United States and called on his countrymen to overthrow Díaz and restore democratic rule. No one, least of all Madero who embraced a plan of limited political reforms, could know that this revolt would begin a decade-long struggle that would tear Mexico apart and remake its political system and national identity. Nor could they anticipate how this conflict would erode transborder ties and binational communities along the boundary line.[2]

The early years of the Mexican Revolution brought violence, economic instability, political intrigue, and anxiety about border security to the boundary line, but most people believed they would be temporary. As rebel armies across Mexico rose up in response to Madero's call to arms and warfare began to disrupt transborder business, U.S. and Mexican officials initiated stopgap measures to prevent insurgents, arms smugglers, and stray bullets from crossing the line and waited for the revolutionary storm to pass. At the same time Mexicans and Americans began to learn how different the experience of war would be for people on either side of the boundary line.

The Mexican Revolution's transformation of the boundary line was not incidental. As transportation hubs, customs houses, and access points to the United States, border towns were strategically important. Over the course of the revolution, the Mexican armies' desire to control these important border gateways turned Tijuana, Mexicali, Nogales, Naco, Agua Prieta, Columbus, and Ciudad Juárez into battlefields, in some cases repeatedly.[3]

With the beginning of warfare, customs control took on an entirely new significance. Mexican officials depended on duties collected at border ports of entry to fund military operations and relied on customs agents to prevent arms and ammunition from being shipped across the border to their enemies. U.S. customs officers also worked to prevent violations of neutrality laws and enforce arms embargoes, restricting the entry of not only ammunition and weapons but also of food, shoes, uniforms, airplanes, and even Harley Davidson motorcycles. The U.S. collector of customs also stepped up scrutiny of routine shipments of explosives to northern Mexican mines.[4]

In response to these restrictions and the demand for arms and other wartime necessities, smuggling boomed along the border with everyone from local residents to revolutionary generals getting in on the action. Three Mexican soldiers stationed in Agua Prieta were arrested for smuggling when they tried to walk back across the border with one hundred rounds of 38-caliber Winchester cartridges that their sergeant had sent them to buy at the Copper Queen Store in Douglas. Outside Columbus, a group of men moved a load of arms by buggy and burro across the border into Mexico.[5]

Yaqui Indians, who had prior experience with evading capture and moving arms across the boundary line, also became involved in arms trading along the border. Throughout the nineteenth century, the Yaqui had resisted Mexican efforts to remove them from their homeland along the Yaqui River in southern Sonora. Facing violent repression and forced removal, many Yaqui had fled north of the border to Arizona Territory where they became integrated into the Arizona economy as wage laborers and continued to funnel guns and ammunition south to the Yaqui resistance. By the time of the Mexican Revolution, they were experienced arms smugglers. In 1912 Emilio Kosterlitzky apprehended eleven Yaquis loaded down with arms and ammunition outside Nogales. By 1919 an American observer claimed that Yaquis smuggled between $80,000 and $100,000 worth of ammunition across the border each year. "They are allowed to buy only 100 rounds at a time; but there is no limit to the number of times an individual may buy a hundred rounds," he explained. "All the large general stores along the border carry heavy stocks of arms and ammunition, so it is a very simple matter to pick up a supply, if one has a little patience."[6]

While arms were in particularly high demand, they were not the only merchandise brought across the border illegally. Along with the persistent smuggling of cattle, narcotics, and Chinese immigrants, the revolution spawned traffic in seized and stolen goods. Military officers operating near the border, including General Francisco "Pancho" Villa, engaged in a transborder trade of confiscated cattle for arms. Jewels and bullion also illicitly passed across the boundary line as Mexican revolutionaries sought to raise funds for their war efforts.[7]

Government officials kept a close eye on not only what but also who crossed the boundary line. Under Díaz's repressive political regime, many opposition leaders had moved across the border to operate from within the relative security of the United States. As Díaz began to lose control, many of these political dissidents traveled to the border and began plotting to return to Mexico and join the revolution. In 1912 American consular officials reported that Mexican revolutionaries were operating out of the Gadsden Hotel in Douglas and the National Hotel in Nogales. "Refugees representing the interests now in open revolt against the constituted authorities of Mexico speak openly and seditiously against a friendly nation," wrote some Nogales residents, "claiming that shortly an army of filibusters will, from the United States, invade Nogales, Mexico, adjoining Nogales, Arizona, take that Port of Entry and from there overrun Sonora as the revolutionists formerly over-ran Chihuahua."[8]

In response to these threats, the U.S. government dispatched troops to the border to help enforce neutrality laws. Along with the large number of government agents already stationed on the line, these soldiers worked to ensure that revolutionaries did not access American arms or launch invasions from U.S. soil. In contrast to the nineteenth century when the U.S. government had failed to prevent filibusters and Apaches from assailing Mexican territory, by the beginning of the Mexican Revolution the U.S. government could rely on soldiers and customs agents to thwart revolutionaries' plans for transborder attacks. In deference to neutrality agreements, U.S. officials monitored and arrested conspirators and attempted to prevent armed bands from crossing the border. Despite their efforts, however, U.S. border towns continued to be hotbeds of intrigue and arms smuggling throughout the war.[9]

One of the most serious threats came from the followers of the Mexican political dissidents Ricardo and Enrique Flores Magón. In 1900 the brothers began publishing a newspaper, *Regeneración*, in which they criticized Díaz and other Mexican officials. After their political critiques repeatedly landed them in prison, the Flores Magón brothers moved first to San Antonio, Texas, in 1904 and then to St. Louis, Missouri, in 1905, from where they continued to challenge the Díaz administration, forming an oppositional party, the Partido Liberal Mexicano, and publishing increasingly radical critiques of the Mexican political and economic system in *Regeneración*. While Madero at one time expressed sympathy with the Flores Magón brothers, by the time the revolution began they had moved far to the left, establishing a sense of common cause with socialists, anarchists, and labor organizers. Not long after Madero launched the Mexican Revolution in late 1910, the Flores Magón brothers' followers, known as Magonistas, embarked on their own assault on the Díaz regime, crossing the California border and invading Baja California in early 1911. An international band of Mexican exiles, radical unionists, and soldiers of fortune, the Magonistas captured Mexicali at the end of January.[10]

The Magonista invasion spread fear along the border and sent American tourists scrambling back across the boundary line from Tijuana. However, once back on U.S. soil most Americans assumed they were out of danger. Although there was no physical barrier on the border to prevent battles from spilling into U.S. territory, Americans seemed to take for granted that respect for U.S. sovereignty and the few U.S. soldiers stationed on the boundary line would prevent Mexican combatants from crossing the border. Displaying this confidence in the legal and psychological power of the boundary line, many Americans crowded at the border to catch a glimpse of the war during the Battle of Tijuana in June 1911. A photograph shows the crowd not cowering in fear but arrayed beside the boundary line as if seated in a grandstand. After successfully occupying the city, the Magonistas turned the American curiosity to profit, charging each person twenty-five cents to view the battle site. An American woman who was present reported, "We were advised not to snap our cameras nor to comment on the breastworks thrown up nor to make laughing criticism of anything we should see." Although she noted that "this last warning was most unnecessary, for no one with a ray of humanity could have felt anything but sympathy for the band of federals and *rurales* prepared to fight for their homes," the inclusion of this warning suggested that not everyone viewed the battle scene with such a sympathetic eye.[11]

FIGURE 5.1. Crowd watching the battle of Tijuana from the boundary line, June 22, 1911. Courtesy of San Diego History Center.

While the Magonistas entertained some Americans, the majority of people who lived and owned property in Baja California were not amused. Both Mexicans and Americans took refuge in the United States while Magonistas seized stock and supplies from ranches below the border. Fearing for the security of their investment, the owners of the Colorado River Land Company lobbied for the formation of a joint U.S.-Mexican military force to defeat the Magonistas. This suggestion, which had the potential to provoke a hostile response much like the response that met the American volunteers at Cananea in 1906, revealed American capitalists' lack of confidence in Díaz's ability to regain control. The anxiety provoked by the possibility that Baja California might remain under Magonista control even led some Americans to call for the United States to annex the peninsula.[12] The reemergence of this annexationist threat was an ominous sign of how U.S.-Mexican relations would decline as the revolution wore on.

Díaz could not restore order in Baja California, but Madero's forces did. Following a series of Maderista military victories, culminating in their capture of Ciudad Juárez in May 1911, Díaz resigned. A month later, on June 22, Maderista forces defeated the Magonistas at Tijuana. These decisive events brought an end to the revolutionary battles in Baja

California. By the summer of 1913, a Mexican observer confidently stated that "the revolution in Mexico will not, in any affect any property in Lower California or any where else, principally when there is no revolution in the Peninsula."[13]

While Madero's victory improved conditions in Baja California, it brought only a temporary respite to the rest of Mexico. Although Madero was easily elected president in a nationwide election in October 1911, his revolution had unleashed demands for an array of political and economic reforms that Madero was not necessarily willing or able to deliver. He was in office for only a month before his former allies began to turn on him, destabilizing the entire nation. Conservatives within the Mexican government, with the support of U.S. Ambassador Henry Lane Wilson, launched a military coup in February 1913 that resulted in the assassination of Madero and elevated General Victoriano Huerta to the presidency. Almost immediately, anti-Huerta forces led by Emiliano Zapata in Morelos, Venustiano Carranza in Coahuila, Francisco "Pancho" Villa in Chihuahua, and Álvaro Obregón in Sonora began to organize to resist his regime. In March, Carranza, Villa, and Obregón formed the Constitutionalist Army and selected Carranza as its leader. Soon the entire country descended into war again.[14]

One of the first battles between the Huertistas and the Constitutionalists came in March 1913 at Nogales, the first of the three revolutionary battles that would be fought there. Led by Obregón, who would go on to become one of the most prominent leaders of the revolutionary era, the Constitutionalists met federal forces under the command of the legendary border peacekeeper, Emilio Kosterlitzky. Before the battle began, refugees, including approximately two hundred otherwise excluded Chinese, crossed the border. As the armies prepared for battle, U.S. officers warned them to keep the conflict on the Mexican side of the line. Relying on this restriction, American spectators clustered near the border in Nogales, Arizona. As the battle heated up, bullets began to whiz around them. In the confusion a few disoriented Mexican soldiers found themselves on the wrong side of the line. This was unacceptable to the Americans. Training their guns on the Mexican troops, the U.S. commanders ordered a cease-fire. Besieged from all sides with his back against the border, Kosterlitzky was forced to surrender, not to Obregón but to the U.S. Army. Marching across the line, the federal troops laid down their weapons and passed into the protective custody of the U.S. military. Not only would they withhold their surrendered arms from Obregón, but after a period of internment many would also return to Mexico to fight another day.[15]

Given his position as a figurehead of the cooperative binational order, Kosterlitzky's departure was symbolic of the beginning of a steep decline in stability, security, and U.S.-Mexican relations. In subsequent years U.S. citizens would watch battles across the boundary line with an increasingly wary eye as Mexico fell into civil war and violence ravaged the nation. The ensuing chaos would cause both Mexicans and Americans to lose confidence in the transborder economy and bring the two nations to the brink of war.

The Depths of War, 1913–17

The Constitutionalist challenge to Huerta marked the beginning of the bloodiest and most destructive phase of the Mexican Revolution. Four months after Kosterlitzky's surrender, the Constitutionalists forced Huerta's resignation. But Huerta had hardly gone into exile before the Constitutionalist coalition fell apart. Despite their shared hatred of Huerta, Carranza, Villa, and Zapata could not agree on who should rule Mexico or what direction the revolution should take. As the coalition's members turned on one another, the revolution imploded into a series of brutal civil wars. In Washington, DC, the U.S. government wavered between proclamations of neutrality and a variety of diplomatic, financial, and military interventions. Meanwhile, on the border the effects of the war became inescapable as refugees fled to the border, raiders attacked American-owned ranches on both sides of the line, and a growing number of battles sent bullets flying across the boundary line. The border had become a battleground.

As the Mexican Revolution dragged on, its violence and destruction ravaged Mexico. Scholars have estimated that between 1.5 and 2 million Mexicans died between 1910 and 1920. As the loosely controlled armies raged across the countryside, looting towns and tearing up railroad tracks, they left a path of death and destruction in their wake. Ranches along the boundary line, as elsewhere in Mexico, suffered from the seizure and destruction of stock, supplies, and infrastructure. Between January 1, 1911, and December 31, 1917, the Cananea Cattle Company's losses amounted to 394,792.46 pesos. In the peak years between 1913 and 1915, American rancher, Burdett A. Packard, lost more than $45,000 worth of stock from his ranch on the border at Douglas–Agua Prieta.[16]

Since the beginning of the Mexican Revolution, people of all nationalities who lived in Mexico had sought refuge across the boundary line in U.S. territory. In advance of battles in border towns, many people secured money, possessions, and family members across the line.[17] As the war dragged on, however, its effects spread through Mexico, prompting hundreds of thousands of people to cross the border not just to wait out a battle but to find a new life. Impoverished workers and farmers, upper-class political dissidents, American ranchers and mining engineers, and persecuted Chinese immigrants—refugees came from all levels of Mexican society. According to the official records of the U.S. Commissioner General of Immigration, 890,371 people legally entered the United States from Mexico between July 1910 and July 1920. Adding estimates of uncounted refugees and immigrants the numbers surge to nearly 1.5 million. While Mexicans had been migrating across the border since its creation, the revolution marked the beginning of a prolonged upward trend in Mexican immigration to the United States that would continue through the twentieth century.[18]

Northern Mexico's Chinese communities were particularly hard-hit. A rising wave of xenophobia targeted these recently arrived and relatively prosperous immigrants with forced loans, discriminatory legislation, and mob violence. In the worst of these attacks, a mob of lower-class Mexicans turned on the Chinese community in Torreón, Coahuila, killing more than three hundred Chinese and causing approximately $850,000 in property damage. In the face of these attacks, many Chinese fled. While some moved to China or relocated to Baja California where anti-Chinese measures had yet to be enacted, others chose to cross the border where they joined tens of thousands of refugees and migrants.[19]

The flood of refugees strained resources on both sides of the boundary line. Recalling the stream of refugees during a battle in Naco, one eyewitness commented that "when the Mexicans retreated across the line, they didn't come across like a regular army. Here come men, women, children, dogs, goats; all come [sic] their own walking across the wall."[20] While some refugees joined family or friends, many others found themselves in an unfamiliar area with little money or food and no place to stay. Some border town residents provided the refugees with shelter, sustenance, and other assistance. One longtime Nogales resident recalled how a former Mexican ambassador and his family moved into her home after they were forced to flee the revolution.[21]

When private efforts proved insufficient, government officials intervened. To provide for refugees and prevent violations of immigration regulations, U.S. immigration and military officers set up refugee camps near the border. During the Battle of Agua Prieta in November 1915, a battalion of U.S. soldiers posted in Douglas escorted refugees from the border to a fenced enclosure measuring two hundred by three hundred yards. By November 3 this camp housed 2,700 refugees, mostly women and children. While U.S. officials released "well-to-do" refugees, they continued to detain thousands of restricted immigrants such as indigent refugees and Chinese immigrants barred by U.S. immigration laws. At Douglas the U.S. soldiers segregated the Chinese and kept them under guard. Not surprisingly, many continued to enter the United States illegally.[22]

Refugees were not the only people who crossed the border and brought the Mexican Revolution to U.S. soil. Mexican soldiers and bandits turned to the old borderlands practice of transborder raiding, targeting ranches on the U.S. side of the line. In Texas these raids coincided with reports of the Plan de San Diego, a 1915 manifesto calling for Mexicans, blacks, and Indians to kill all white men over the age of sixteen and take control of Texas, Colorado, New Mexico, Arizona, and California. As rumors of the plan spread, Anglo-Americans violently targeted ethnic Mexicans along the Rio Grande border. Watching events in Texas with a wary eye, some Americans along the western border also expressed fears that violence would ensue if American soldiers were not able to put a stop to transborder raids.[23]

Despite these fears, the western boundary line did not experience the same widespread interracial violence that marred the Rio Grande border. Even so, a handful of Americans were casualties of stray bullets that crossed the boundary line during battles in Mexican border towns. "We were out and we could hear 'em zipping around every once in a while," John Hutchison Darling remembered of being in Douglas during the Battle of Agua Prieta in 1915. "There was stray bullets hit all over Douglas. Hit different places round here all over Douglas."[24] Some of these bullets hit Americans. Among those killed by Mexican bullets were two U.S. soldiers, Harry J. Jones and Stephen D. Little. U.S. officials later renamed military posts outside Douglas and Nogales after these two fallen soldiers, embedding these two moments of unintended conflict between the United States and Mexico in the border's geography as constant reminders of the potential danger the Mexican Revolution posed to Americans.[25]

These tragic accidents also caused many Americans to begin to question the power of the boundary line to protect them. "The [boundary] monument was a symbol. How small a material thing it takes to guard our safety, our lives!" a resident of Naco, Arizona, remembered years later. "How massive a meaning can be crammed into a miniature wall. 'Thus far shall thou go and no farther,' meant the monument which marked the International Line. As a child I thought of The Line as a material line; first a heavy chalk line, then a cord line such as my father used in construction work; then a long, long fence like those dividing farms. But The Line is simply a monument here and there along the miles."[26]

As Americans living along the border became more concerned about the revolution spilling over the line, they increasingly turned to the U.S. government with demands that the government intervene to prevent raids and ensure that border battles remain restricted to Mexican territory. President Taft had sent U.S. troops to the border as early as 1911, but as the effects of the Mexican Revolution rippled across the boundary

FIGURE 5.2. U.S. soldier on picket on the border at Douglas, Arizona, near Agua Prieta, Mexico, ca. 1915. The labeled post marking the boundary line was not an official boundary monument but rather a temporary marker erected during the Mexican Revolution. Postcard in author's collection.

line local officials and citizens asked for additional troops. In April 1914 the citizens of Columbus, New Mexico, wrote to New Mexico Senator Albert Fall demanding that as many as five hundred troops be sent to the border to maintain a strict patrol as the town was "in danger every minute" from transborder raids.[27] In response to these concerns and the escalation of border violence, the War Department gradually increased the number of U.S. troops on the Mexican border. These troops patrolled the line and marked parts of the border with flags, fences, and wooden posts to more clearly signal the division between U.S. and Mexican territory. During the Battle of Naco (Sonora) in 1914 U.S. troops marked the boundary line with U.S. flags to prevent combatants from crossing into the United States.[28]

In Mexico the thin line between the two countries also became increasingly problematic as the threat of U.S. intervention loomed ever larger. Woodrow Wilson, influenced both by his desire to support democratic governments and the lobbying of Americans who had investments in Mexico, had a hard time making up his mind about what to do about the Mexican Revolution. Although officially neutral the U.S. government sought to influence events in Mexico through diplomatic maneuvering, arms embargoes, and selectively allowing Mexican troops to travel between ports on the border by crossing U.S. territory.[29]

The United States, however, could not seem to decide whose side it was on. Although Ambassador Henry Lane Wilson had conspired with Huerta to overthrow Madero, President Woodrow Wilson openly opposed Huerta, who he believed was a dictator. In February 1914 Wilson threw his support to the Constitutionalists by lifting the arms embargo that had cut off their access to U.S. arms. But in April when Wilson ordered the U.S. Navy to occupy the port of Veracruz to prevent Huerta from receiving a shipment of German arms, he went a step too far. Facing resistance from Mexican soldiers, U.S. marines and sailors were able to gain control of the city, but only after U.S. warships bombarded the Mexicans' positions. As U.S. forces inflicted hundreds of casualties on both Huerta's soldiers and noncombatants, Huertistas and Constitutionalists alike reacted angrily to the United States' blatant violation of Mexican sovereignty. Protesters filled the streets of Mexican cities, denouncing the United States, attacking American businesses, and desecrating the U.S. flag. For practical reasons the Constitutionalists continued to court Wilson's support, but the Veracruz incident left a deep rift between Mexican leaders and the U.S. government. Once the Constitutionalist coalition fell apart, Wilson waffled between support for Villa and Carranza, succeeding in only further complicating the struggle for power in Mexico and rapidly pushing Mexico and the United States to the brink of war.[30]

In the midst of this worsening situation, some American politicians and business leaders began to more aggressively call for U.S. annexation of Mexican territory. In the summer of 1916 the U.S. Congress considered sending a commission to Mexico to negotiate for the purchase of parts of northern Mexico, including Baja California. Fortunately for U.S.-Mexican relations, cooler heads in the State Department advised against this move as it might have had "an unfortunate effect upon Mexican public sentiment," and nothing came of the resolution.[31] However, for the remainder of the war, public outcry and political pressure would continue to raise the possibility of annexation, stoking Mexican fears and destabilizing binational relations.[32]

In Mexico, U.S. intervention and the threat of annexation were cause for serious concern. Although factional leaders courted the U.S. government to secure American arms and military and diplomatic support, they were wary of appearing to pander to or be controlled by the Americans. The possibility of a U.S. invasion provoked fear, anger, and a strong nationalist response. In language that echoed Ignacio Pesqueira's call to arms against the filibusters half a century before, officials of all factions insisted that they would not succumb to American conquest. "[Officials in the Sonoran government] claim that Americans do not understand Mexican patriotism and honor, and that any attempt at intervention would call for the utmost resistance in their power," a U.S. military intelligence briefing reported in 1915, "and while they would ultimately be defeated by the overwhelming forces America could send against them the cost to America would be far greater than is contemplated, for the warring factions would unite against the foreign invader and offer a resistance far beyond American conceptions of the power of Mexican patriotism."[33] The governor of the Northern District of Baja California, Esteban Cantú, shared these sentiments, even as he continued to cultivate relationships with American investors. "Intervention is shortly coming," Cantú proclaimed in October 1919, "and when it does, every patriotic Mexican is expected to seize a rifle and drive the gringoes from Mexican soil."[34] Much as Pesqueira had done before him, Cantú recognized the political necessity of drawing a clear line in public between encouraging U.S. investment and rejecting American violations of Mexican territorial sovereignty. Resisting the United States' imperialist tendencies remained a cause that could bring Mexicans together in the defense of their nation.

No one better illustrated the complicated relationship between Mexican leaders and the United States than Francisco "Pancho" Villa. The leader of a rebel faction based in Chihuahua and the commander of the famed División del Norte, Villa helped the Constitutionalists defeat Huerta and then emerged as the dominant rival to Carranza, his former ally. Early on, a range of U.S. interests, from liberals and radicals to big business and the Wilson administration, favored Villa as the future president for varied and sometimes contradictory reasons. Access to U.S. markets and the friendship of American investors contributed significantly to Villa's rise to power. However, by mid-1915, after Villa suffered a series of military defeats and Carranza promised to protect American property, Wilson abandoned Villa and moved toward recognizing Carranza's government instead.[35]

Unprepared for the change in U.S. policy, Villa began a fateful march on Sonora in the fall of 1915. After a series of disastrous defeats, Villa decided to attack Carranza's forces in Sonora, hoping that a victory there would boost his weakened army's morale. His primary target was the Carrancista garrison at Agua Prieta, which he believed was cut off from reinforcements. However, even as the División del Norte began its laborious trek from Chihuahua to Sonora over the Sierra Madre, Carrancista troops boarded trains in El Paso en route to Douglas–Agua Prieta. Unbeknownst to Villa, on October 9 the Wilson administration had officially recognized Carranza and given him permission to send reinforcements by rail through the United States. By the time Villa arrived, thousands of Carrancista soldiers were entrenched in Agua Prieta. Expecting to attack a small garrison under the cover of darkness, Villa instead found the town well defended and, at a crucial point in the fight, illuminated by a spotlight, said by some to have been located in the United States. "Poor unsuspecting Pancho, believing that a garrison of but 1,200 defended the town, ordered an immediate charge, first cautioning his soldiers not to shoot toward the American side," wrote an American journalist. "Three hours later his was a bleeding army, crushed, tired, helpless."[36] Outside Agua Prieta, the Villistas "swarmed in to the [Slaughter] ranch," remembered Viola Slaughter, "needing clothing, begging food."[37] U.S. soldiers threw their canteens across the boundary line to share water with the Mexican troops. When complaints from the Carrancista commanders forced them to stop, local people took their place, filling canteens and passing them out to the weary Mexican soldiers.[38]

Despite local Americans' offers of aid to his troops, Villa vented his frustration with Wilson on all Americans. Villa, remembered one American who was present at the battle, "did have it in for the American government because they let Carranza ship his troops by rail over the road here into Agua Prieta."[39] Following the battle Villa threatened to shoot two American doctors who had crossed over to attend to the wounded, telling them that "from this moment on, I will devote my life to the killing of every Gringo I can get my hands on and the destruction of all Gringo property."[40] In the following months, Villa began to make good on his threat, targeting vulnerable U.S. citizens both in Mexico and across the border.

The frustration of Villa and his men was evident in late November in the days leading up to the second battle fought at Nogales. Following their defeat at Agua Prieta, the Villistas moved west to Nogales where they attempted to regroup. But with the Carrancistas closing in, Villa decided to abandon the town, ordering his men to carry what they could with them and destroy the rest. As the Mexican half of Nogales descended into chaos, five companies of the U.S. 12th Cavalry took up positions on the boundary line. On November 24, Villista troops, venting their fury with the United States, rode up to the border brandishing their guns and threatening American soldiers and civilians. A few even crossed the line and began menacing people in the streets of Nogales, Arizona. The next day, U.S. intelligence received reports that Villa had informed his men that the "United States Government was to blame for his present predicament and that he was going to get even by waging a guerilla war against [the] Arizona border."[41] On November 26, a Villista soldier deliberately took aim at the U.S. troops in Nogales. They returned fire, killing the shooter and sparking a chaotic scramble for control of Nogales. Even as the Villistas fought with the Americans and rushed to complete their retreat, Carrancista troops marched into town and entered the fray. Mistaking a company of Americans for Villistas, the Carrancistas engaged the U.S. troops, killing Private Stephen D. Little. Before the end of the battle, an estimated fifty Villistas also lay dead. While Obregón and the U.S. commander agreed that this had been no more than a mistake, it presaged both the dangers of Villa's anger and the trouble that U.S. officials and Carranza would have in cooperating to defeat him.[42]

Following their retreat from Sonora during the winter of 1915/16, the Villistas lashed out at Americans in Chihuahua. In January they attacked a train carrying a group of American mining engineers outside Santa Ysabel, Chihuahua, and killed them. Beyond his anger with the U.S. government, Villa had become convinced that he needed to foment a split between Carranza and Wilson. In pursuit of this goal and fueled by a desire for revenge, Villa began plotting an assault on U.S. soil. He considered attacking Presidio, Texas, and Naco, Arizona, but decided on Columbus, a small customs outpost on the New Mexico border.[43]

In the early morning hours of March 9, 1916, Villa led his forces across the border into Columbus. They attacked the military garrison at Camp Furlong and rode through town, raiding the local bank and stores and shooting civilians. Hours later the Villistas' retreat into Mexico marked the end of what, in military terms, was a failed mission. Over one hundred Villistas had lost their lives and, despite attacks on Columbus's garrison, bank, and stores, had failed to secure any arms, money, or supplies. Villa's forces were beaten back with minimal American casualties (seventeen Americans, most of them civilians, were killed), but the attack traumatized Columbus's residents. "The town was a holocaust," remembered Mary Means Scott, who had been a child at the time of the attack, "and many were said to have been murdered in their beds—military and civilian alike." "Main Street was in chaos," she continued. "Men were frantically digging in the smoldering ruins for bodies. Others looked distractedly at yesterday's places of business, now blackened junk."[44]

These images of chaos and horror roiling across the boundary were splashed across the front pages of newspapers across the United States. William F. "Buffalo Bill" Cody rapidly incorporated Villa's raid into his Wild West Show. From across the United States men volunteered to go south to protect U.S. territory. President Wilson sent thousands of troops to the border, mobilizing army regulars and calling out the National

Guard. With men streaming in from all over the country, the attack on Columbus both brought the border to the attention of Americans and also brought growing numbers of Americans to the border.[45]

It also, for the first time during the Mexican Revolution, brought U.S. troops across the border. On March 15, General John "Black Jack" Pershing led the American Punitive Expedition into Chihuahua in pursuit of Pancho Villa. Mary Means Scott remembered the patriotic fervor as the expedition crossed the border near Columbus:

> And then the day arrived when General Pershing planned to enter Mexico! Men, horses, field artillery, trucks, supplies, repair units, all poised for the start. As usual, the townspeople were caught up in the great moment—at last—retribution was at hand. It would be the culminating show.
>
> Early, at the border, marked by a barbed-wire fence, families began to gather. . . . We watched for hours, it seemed, as the horses and riders passed in a giant parade: flags and guidons flying; pistols at the waist, sabres at the saddle, all enveloped in a canopy of dust. There was applause, whistles, waves, and shouts of "goodbye" as friends came into view. Then men and boys volunteered much advice on what to do with Pancho Villa when caught.
>
> It was a great exodus—an historic hour. The might of the United States army departing on a punitive mission to right a wrong visited upon an unsuspecting border town—the cavalry to the rescue! It was a thrilling sight to us.[46]

Although there was no declaration, the United States seemed to be going to war.

As flag-waving U.S. troops marched across the border, U.S.-Mexican relations nose-dived. Positioning himself as the leader of the Mexican resistance against the U.S. incursion and complicit Carranza government, Villa experienced a brief resurgence. In late 1916 he issued a nationalist manifesto in which he called for a prohibition on all American and Chinese land ownership in Mexico and for cutting all railroads, telegraph lines, and trade ties connecting Mexico and the United States. While revolutionaries had cut rail and telegraph lines for strategic reasons and the transborder economy had suffered collateral damage since the revolution began, Villa's manifesto made them a specific target both to punish the United States and to cut Mexico off from its influence.[47]

The United States' unilateral action infuriated Carrancistas as well. Carranza had attempted to appease the Americans, proposing a reciprocal agreement like the agreement that had helped defeat the Apaches in the 1880s, but the U.S. government's decision to act on its own turned their pursuit of Villa into an assault on Mexican sovereignty. Secretary of

State Robert Lansing informed the Carranza government that if it was "unwilling or unable to give this protection by preventing its territory from being the rendezvous and refuge of murderers and plunderers, that does not relieve this Government from its duty to take all the steps necessary to safeguard American citizens on American soil."[48] If Carranza could not fulfill Mexico's sovereign obligations by securing the border, he warned, the U.S. government would not respect that sovereignty.

Many believed war between the United States and Mexico was imminent. Writing to a representative of an American copper company in Sonora, army chief of staff General Hugh Lenox Scott explained, "we are shoving in the National Guard on the border just as fast as we can get hold of them, with the hope of holding the border with them and using the Regular Army to go across the whole line in case Pershing is attacked."[49] These deployments only intensified Mexican fears of invasion and annexation. Meeting with Americans in El Paso, Obregón noted "that men did not usually take a cannon to kill birds with and that people did not usually take artillery and infantry to hunt outlaws and that it looked suspicious to them and as if it meant a permanent occupation or a means to scare their people."[50] Many Mexicans remained convinced that Pershing's expedition was only the opening salvo of another U.S. war of conquest. According to Secretary of State Lansing, the Mexican secretary of foreign relations implied as much. "Your Government intimates . . . that the intention of the United States in sending its troops into Mexico is to extend its sovereignty over Mexican territory, and not merely for the purpose of pursuing marauders and preventing further raids across the border," Lansing noted in his response. "The *de facto* Government charges by implication which admits of but one interpretation, that this Government has as its object territorial aggrandizement even at the expense of a war of aggression against a neighbor weakened by years of civil strife."[51] In this climate of mutual suspicion, with emotions running high and national pride on the line, diplomatic negotiations dragged out over ten months. It was only in January 1917, with Pershing having failed to capture Villa and tensions with Germany growing, that Wilson backed down and ordered unconditional withdrawal.

Pershing's retreat marked a triumph for Carranza and Mexican sovereignty, but it did not restore trust between the nations. Even after the last U.S. troops left Mexico on February 5, 1917, resentment and suspicion of Americans remained high and Mexican forces continued to fear another U.S. incursion. As late as 1919, U.S. Army intelligence on the border reported that troop emplacements in Nogales, Sonora, were thought to be "constructed as much for defense from the Mexican as from the United States also."[52]

It was in the midst of this climate of burgeoning anti-American sentiment that Mexican politicians met at Querétaro in 1916 and 1917 to draft a new Mexican constitution. The document they produced addressed many of the long-standing critiques of the Díaz administration, including the extent to which foreigners, and Americans in particular, had come to control the nation's land and resources. Under Article 27 of the Constitution of 1917, all privately owned lands, waters, and resources became subject to appropriation or nationalization as necessary for the public interest. It also strictly prohibited foreign ownership within a zone of one hundred kilometers along the border, requiring that foreign stockholders in Mexican corporations revoke their right to invoke the protection of the country of their citizenship and closing the loophole of corporate nationality.[53]

Following the adoption of the Constitution of 1917, Mexican citizens began to move onto the vast American-owned properties abutting the boundary line in anticipation that the Mexican government would revoke American titles. Although widespread nationalization would not take off until the mid-1920s, climaxing under the Cárdenas administration in the 1930s, the seeds of nationalization sown during the Mexican Revolution undermined the security of American ownership. So-called squatters had already been a problem for many companies, but anti-American sentiment and the force of Article 27 gave them new license. In Baja California, stockholders in the American-owned San Ysidro Company discovered that not only local settlers but also a military camp under the authority of Governor Esteban Cantú occupied portions of their property east of Tijuana. With Mexican citizens unwilling to testify on behalf of Americans and judges appointed by Cantú, local courts provided little help. In Chihuahua the Palomas Land and Cattle Company not only faced hundreds of squatters but also received notice from the Mexican secretary of agriculture that their entire property, approximately 2 million acres and worth $5 million, was subject to nationalization.[54]

Panicking at the looming loss of their investments, many American investors turned to the U.S. government. Americans capitalists, including such influential transborder businessmen as Walter Douglas, president of the Moctezuma Copper Company; C. F. Kelley, vice president of the Greene-Cananea Copper Company; the Slaughter Land and Cattle Company; and the California-Mexico Land and Cattle Company (the American partner company of the Colorado River Land Company), joined together to form the National Association for the Protection of American Rights in Mexico. Adding credence to Mexicans' accusations, this organization dedicated itself to lobbying for U.S. intervention.[55]

With American investors pressing for government intervention, Mexicans outraged by U.S. interference, and the memories of Villa's raid and

Pershing's expedition still fresh, U.S.-Mexican relations reached a low point. The transborder economic connections that had helped foster binational cooperation before the war now exacerbated the already existing tensions between the two governments. In early 1917 it seemed that the United States and Mexico would soon be at war.

Making the Border a Divide, 1917–20

Indeed, war was to come to the United States that year, but not with Mexico. As Carranza continued to try to stamp out his opposition in Mexico, the United States declared war against Germany on April 2, 1917. This made war with Mexico much less likely but did not put an end to troubles on the U.S.-Mexico border. New concerns about U.S. national security in the midst of World War I were added to the cumulative effects of the Mexican Revolution, continuing to wear away at the ties that had bound transborder communities together. Although the Mexican battlefront shifted away from the boundary line in the final years of the revolution, the ongoing political and economic instability and the continued presence of armed men and wartime regulations left the border on edge. As the presence of soldiers, binational suspicions, and restrictions on transborder movement began to seem like permanent conditions, both governments moved to institutionalize once-temporary border controls. Although peace returned to the border at the end of the decade with the signing of the Treaty of Versailles in 1919 and Obregón's ascendancy to the Mexican presidency in 1920, many of the wartime changes in the border would remain.[56]

As the United States moved toward entering World War I, concerns about international espionage joined Americans' worries about upholding neutrality laws, repelling raiders, and dodging stray bullets along the boundary line. "If the people of Los Angeles knew what was happening on our border, they would not sleep at night," reported the *Los Angeles Times* in April 1917. "Sedition, conspiracy, plots and intrigue are in the very air. The telegraph lines are tapped, operators have been seduced with gold and spies come and go at will. Men who are known all over Europe hob-nob with Mexican bandits, Japanese secret service agents and renegades from this country."[57] It was rumored that Mexican leaders, including Carranza and Baja California Governor Cantú, were in cahoots with the Germans. A decoded telegram from the German foreign secretary, Arthur Zimmerman, offering Mexico support to "reconquer its former territories in Texas, New Mexico, and Arizona" in exchange for an alliance against the United States only fueled these fears. As news of the Zimmerman telegram spread in February 1917 many Americans worried about the vulnerability of the border.[58] "In the event of war, which now seems certain," the *Los Angeles Times* wrote, "the long Mexican border will prove the cancer that must be cut out if the United States is to survive."[59]

While the *Los Angeles Times* undoubtedly reflected the bias of its owner, Harry Chandler, and his growing desire for U.S. intervention in Mexico to protect his investments there, this editorial was far from the only place where American fears were given voice. A letter in the *North American Review*, "America's Unguarded Gateway," suggested that it was only a matter of time before "some German emissary furnishes the money to some pirate in Mexico" to launch an attack on New Mexico from Mexico.[60] U.S. intelligence reports also detailed the daily activity of Germans operating near the border. While some were clearly aiding the Mexican forces or acting as government agents, others, including the German wife of Governor Cantú, fell under suspicion simply for being German. The U.S. government also stepped up security on the border and issued orders for soldiers to be on the lookout for German operatives.[61]

Responding to concerns that enemy agents might slip across the border undetected, the U.S. government effectively closed the boundary line to all but local traffic in 1918. The wartime Passport Control Act, in effect from 1918 to 1921, required that all aliens obtain a visa before entering the United States. "No one can cross the border without a regular passport, accompanied by photographs, etc," explained one American who owned property on the border near Tijuana. "These passports are issued in Washington and it takes several weeks to obtain them after application has been made."[62]

These new laws disrupted the fluid transborder movement to which border people had been accustomed before the war. Passport regulations did not initially include exceptions for local people who regularly crossed the border for business or pleasure. In the face of local complaints, the U.S. Immigration Service began issuing border-crossing cards to locals, but even these were initially tightly regulated. In Nogales, the U.S. consul used "food cards" and passports to restrict the ability of the residents of the Mexican half of the town to shop or work across the line. Although he allowed Mexicans who worked in the United States to cross daily, he reported that "nearly all of the balance, however, of the people living on the Sonora side of the servant class have been cut down to one day a week, both for passport privileges as well as food card." Under the provisions of this law, one hotel employee had to bribe the U.S. consul so that he could cross the line to retrieve some items for the hotel's customers.[63]

The U.S. government also stepped up customs enforcement. Agents

were instructed to inspect all motion pictures to ensure that those showing the German side of the war were not exported to Mexico. American
soldiers stationed on the line helped perform searches, monitor the movement of goods, and prevent illegal crossings. At designated points of
entry, soldiers "hefted" trunks and searched railroad cars and automobiles. While the government recognized that it was "not possible to station detachments at every road crossing the international boundary
along the whole border," patrols were instructed to "stop and search
every vehicle which attempts, or which, though not actually attempting,
is believed destined, to enter Mexico at isolated points."[64] As with passport laws, customs enforcement made crossing the border ever more difficult. "When one had a permit for years to enter Mexico at any time and
at any place, without Custom House formalities," wrote one American
who owned land in Baja California, "it is hard to submit to the red tape
of the present day. We sometimes sigh for the good old days under Díaz
but they are gone forever."[65]

Customs agents, immigration inspectors, and soldiers stood out as
representatives of the federal government and acted as physical obstacles to transborder movement along the line. During the Mexican Revolution, new regulations required that U.S. line riders stationed at Nogales, who had previously spent most of their time in outlying areas,
also patrol the line within the city. At the same time inspectors received
instructions to extend their hours of patrol and inspection, bringing
them out of the guardhouse and into the streets more often. Personal
interaction with customs and immigration officers, as well as the paperwork their bureaucratized operations demanded, presented border people with at least a minor annoyance and often an imposing obstacle to
transborder movement.[66]

Armed soldiers made an even stronger impression. The influx of soldiers over the course of the war represented an unprecedented population increase along both sides of the sparsely settled border. The addition
of 12,000 U.S. servicemen at its wartime peak more than quadrupled the
1910 population of Nogales, Arizona.[67] Recalling how the arrival of
troops transformed her childhood home of Columbus, Mary Means
Scott wrote:

> The town ballooned and there was commotion and confusion. From
> a quiet, backward, out-of-the-way border town, Columbus became
> a bustling small city. Each train that arrived from the east or west
> was filled with soldiers. They overflowed onto the freight trains and I
> was fascinated with the flat cars that arrived bristling with uniformed
> men. Stores filled with milling bodies were unable to serve all their
> wants and needs. At the grocery store, I retreated behind the show
> case to save being trampled upon, but peeped out admiringly at the

sea of uniforms. To me it was a mammoth circus with only the big tent missing.

But there were tents. A city of tents grew up south of the railroad tracks and south of town. It was a dry, dusty, rock strewn area supporting only unfriendly prickly pear cactus and torn-armoured mesquites.[68]

Rather than blending in with the local population, soldiers were outsiders and representatives of the U.S. government or the Mexican faction for which they fought. They were unfamiliar with the binationalism of border communities and were more likely to focus on national differences. Along with their guns, they brought suspicions and stereotypes of the people on the other side of the border. Writing more than twenty years later, one Arizona woman described the misplaced "enthusiasm" expressed by a company of California militiamen as they arrived on the border, "'There's a Mexican!' shouted one as he jumped from the train. 'There's another! Another!' cried the American boys; and as they charged down the street, every dark-faced man in sight fled across the Line—no matter on which side of it he had been born."[69]

These soldiers became a human wall along the boundary line. While the sixty-foot reserve had marked the space between the two nations, the positioning of military sentries on the line created not just a distinction but also a barrier. This transformation is readily apparent in wartime photographs showing Mexican and American soldiers standing beside each other on the boundary line. As one woman wrote below an out-of-focus photograph she took of the border: "Patrolling the International Line—not a necessity until the Revolution of 1910—A continuous performance since."[70] In the absence of a permanent physical barrier marking the line, armed soldiers performed the border.

Locals' responses to the United States' militarization of the border were mixed. The presence of U.S. forces created a protective bulwark against raids and revolutionary overflow but also restricted the freedom of transborder movement and brought unwanted government interference. "The troops was all along the border, we had to contend with them all the time," complained cowboy John Henry Eicks. "They was more trouble to us than anything else . . . they would hold us up all the time, wanting to know what we was doing on the road right at that time."[71] In addition to being meddlesome, soldiers could also be dangerous. In the year before the Third Battle of Nogales in August of 1918, U.S. soldiers killed two Mexicans, one of whom was a Mexican customs officer, as they crossed the line at Nogales. A similar incident occurred in 1919 on the border between Calexico and Mexicali, where a U.S. sentinel disemboweled a man named Alfredo Valenzuela.[72] With the combination of young, newly trained recruits and heightened border insecurities, minor offenses and miscommunications became matters of life and death.

FIGURE 5.3. U.S. soldier and Mexican revolutionary, battle of Agua Prieta, 1915.
The image in this picture postcard highlighted the distinction between U.S. and
Mexican space and how soldiers maintained that division along the border during the war years. Note that all of the writing, including that on the post that
identifies the boundary line, was added to the negative after the photograph was
taken. Courtesy of the Arizona Historical Society/Tucson, AHS Photograph
#58732.

FIGURE 5.4. U.S. and Mexican sentries patrolling the line at Nogales, ca. 1913. Note that the United States is on the left and Mexico is on the right, not the opposite as the printing on the postcard indicates. Courtesy of the Arizona Historical Society/Tucson, AHS Photograph #PC42_70611.

All of these tensions came together when violence erupted in Nogales on August 27, 1918. By the summer of 1918 the unknown man whose approach to the border initiated the conflict there had to run a gauntlet of government agents. In addition to A. G. Barber, the U.S. customs inspector who ordered him to stop, there were Mexican and U.S. immigration officials who checked passports, Mexican customs officers who searched for smuggled arms, and heavily armed U.S. and Mexican soldiers who patrolled the line. Any of these officials might have asked the man to halt for any number of reasons. Barber later said that he believed the man was a smuggler, but a U.S. sentry who was shot said he thought the man was a German spy. Most importantly, there were many reasons why, when the man refused to stop, so many people raised their weapons. Fear, distrust, aggression, anger, defense, and duty, all of these had become part of the border during the long years of war. Once the first shot was fired, they all rushed to the surface.[73]

In the wake of the Third Battle of Nogales, with twelve people dead, U.S. and Mexican officials tried to piece together what had occurred and find a way to prevent it from happening again. But rather than disarm their soldiers or rethink their efforts to restrict transborder movement, they looked for ways to control that movement even more. They decided

FIGURE 5.5. Nogales showing the border fence erected in the middle of the cleared strip along the boundary line, ca. 1920s. Built in 1918 in response to wartime conditions, this fence would become a lasting part of the Nogales landscape and a symbol of division. Courtesy of Pimería Alta Historical Society.

to build a fence. Range fences had marked the line in some areas outside border towns, and both governments had built temporary fences in Nogales and at other points on the border during the war. But this new fence was to be a permanent and impressive feature of the border dividing Ambos Nogales.[74]

Before the battle the *presidente municipal* of Nogales, Sonora, who would himself be killed in the battle, had ordered the construction of a six-foot wire fence extending a short distance through town and encouraged U.S. officials to do the same. He hoped the fences would cut down on conflict by channeling all transborder movement through two designated crossing points where government agents could more easily monitor it. After the battle the U.S. government followed through with his plans. Less than a year later the U.S. State Department reported that "the building of a fence at Nogales is said to have put a stop to firing by patrols upon pedestrians who attempted to cross the border at points near that town. At the present time it is understood that all persons going into Sonora by way of Nogales pass through the gateway near the customs house."[75]

Following in Nogales's footsteps, the U.S. government also built a fence on the border between Calexico and Mexicali after the shooting of Alfredo Valenzuela in 1919. In investigating where the U.S. soldiers had shot Valenzuela, the U.S. consul in Mexicali, Walter Boyle, and a number of U.S. military and immigration officers discovered that "none of these officials including myself could accurately fix the international boundary line."[76] To determine if Valenzuela was shot on U.S. soil they had to call in an engineer to determine the location of the boundary. Noting the need to clearly demarcate the boundary line given the heightened border controls, Governor Cantú suggested that the U.S. government build a fence to assure that its soldiers knew which side someone was on before they shot. Boyle agreed. A fence was necessary, he explained, because the military patrol was both overly severe in its propensity to shoot "petty line runners" and, at the same time, not large enough to effectively patrol the length of the border since "a person who is willing to walk ten or fifteen miles and is of the Caucasian or Mexican race finds little difficulty in crossing or being apprehended." As he saw it, there were only two options—either "softening the harsh border control measures" or "fencing the populated part of the border and the establishment of a neutral zone or dead line beyond which persons must not pass or sentinels shoot thus eliminating possibility of shooting persons in Mexico if it is still considered expedient to maintain severe control at present exercised."[77]

Rather than being envisioned as antagonistic structures, fences were intended to be cooperative measures that both governments embraced in hopes of ameliorating the dangers of wartime crossings. "Border fences," Boyle noted, "are to be desired wherever possible along the line."[78] By the 1920s fences would divide all or part of most major border towns.[79]

Regardless of government officials' hopes that good fences would make good neighbors, however, the border fences they built would become some of the most lasting and poignant symbols of the divisions between the two nations. In his request for the fence, Boyle suggested that it "should be of heavy woven wire, paddocktype six feet high surmounted by three strands barbed wire"—hardly a symbol of transborder unity.[80] Only two miles long, the fence did not completely restrict border crossings, but it was a physically distinctive and visually imposing landmark that cut through the heart of Calexico-Mexicali. In contrast to mapping, marking, and clearing the border, these new fences divided border towns in a way that was more alienating to their residents. Pointing to both the fence and the soldiers patrolling the line outside Tijuana, where a barbed wire fence had already been erected in 1911, one observer noted: "This border line, by the way, is no imaginary one these days."[81]

As one of the most notable features of the local landscape, fences signified the fact that the border was not just where two nations met, but where two nations were divided. While the violence and tensions that first made them necessary faded with the end of World War I in 1919 and

Mexico's gradual return to political stability, the fences would remain as permanent, physical barriers between border communities and unavoidable markers of difference. They would become not only the most powerful visual representation of the twentieth-century border, but would also increasingly be seen as symbols of the decline in transborder relations and the increasing sense of disparity and distrust between the United States and Mexico.[82] As border towns and transborder trade expanded in the calm following the war years, these fences and the sense of difference they signified would become distinctive features of the meeting of the United States and Mexico and their respective populations.

Sixty years after the Third Battle of Nogales, longtime Nogales residents remembered it as an anomalous moment in the peaceful history of their unified transborder community. Their memories, recorded in a series of oral histories in 1989, made sense of the event by incorporating it into a wartime narrative. "Well it was revolution," explained John Jund, "it was revolution people. It was an awful time, that time."[83] Or, in the words of Lincoln Canfield, "This was in the First World War, remember; the First World War was still going on."[84] While not everyone was as explicit as these men, each person's memories reflected his or her awareness of the ways war had changed the border, emphasizing heightened restrictions, armed soldiers, and outsiders.[85]

What these eyewitnesses did not discuss was how the battle had also revealed their community's internalization of the development of distinct and sometimes hostile national divisions. They nostalgically recalled a unified past, characterizing the battle as an aberration rather than a culmination of building resentment. Blaming outsiders, including government officials, soldiers, and even German spies, they disguised the fact that many participants in the battle were local people, some of whom happened to be employed as customs or immigration inspectors. In their stories, their community was the victim of, rather than an active agent in, the development of binational violence.

In these memories the Third Battle of Nogales became a watershed moment in which outside divisions were imposed on their town and became symbolized by the border fence. Although some respondents acknowledged that some kind of limited fence had been built before the battle, most cited the absence of a fence as a hallmark of the transborder spirit of the time. "[Ambos Nogales] was closer together because you practically didn't have any fence or any thing," Charley Fowler explained. "You just walked back and forth."[86] Recalling the openness of the line, Louis Escalada and Frank Arcadia told stories of how they had played on the line as boys in the years before the battle. In contrast, writing in the 1970s, two Nogales historians noted that the border fence was a "reminder of this low-point in Arizona-Sonora friendship" during the Mexican Revolution.[87]

The fence became a souvenir from a time that most of the people of Ambos Nogales would rather have forgotten. However, while the violence that erupted on that afternoon in 1918 only lasted for the equivalent of a historical moment, the fence would become a permanent feature of the border landscape and their lives. In years to come, government officials would find new uses for the fences, uses that testified to the nation-states' expanding power and once again transformed the meaning of the boundary line.

Chapter Six

LIKE NIGHT AND DAY

Regulating Morality with the Border

ON JANUARY 30, 1926, Thomas and Carrie Peteet and their two daughters, twenty-six-year-old Clyde and nineteen-year-old Audrey, left their home in San Diego for a week's vacation in Tijuana. They passed through the border gate at San Ysidro near the spot where only fifteen years before Americans had gathered to watch the Magonista invasion. But like the thousands of American tourists who regularly visited Tijuana's bars, brothels, casinos, and racetracks in the 1920s, the Peteets were seeking a different kind of thrill. Thoughts of war would have been far from their minds as they drank and gambled, enjoying their vacation from Prohibition and other U.S. morality laws.

But then on February 3 their vacation began to go horribly awry. That evening Carrie Peteet stayed behind at the hotel while her husband and daughters went out on the town. At the Oakland Bar, they met Luis Amador, the bar's owner, and the Tijuana chief of police, Zenaido Llanos. Together they drank and danced. And then the details of the night become unclear. According to the Peteets, Llanos and Amador slipped something into their drinks. In a "drugged stupor," the Peteets were unable to resist as Llanos and Amador took Audrey and Clyde to a hotel and raped them. Afterward, Llanos returned Audrey to her parents' hotel. Clyde rejoined the family the following morning when her father, with the help of Tijuana police, found her in Amador's hotel room. Others, however, told a different version of the night's events. Both men denied drugging and raping the women. Amador asserted that he and Clyde had had consensual sex, while Llanos, despite evidence that later led the San Diego coroner to conclude that Audrey had been raped, denied having had sex with her at all. A number of other witnesses denounced the whole family as habitual drunks and accused Clyde and Audrey of sexual promiscuity.

While it is impossible to know exactly what happened that night, there is a clear historical record of what followed. On the morning of February 4, after locating Clyde, the Peteet family recrossed the border. They spent most of the day meeting with U.S. immigration officials and the mayor of Tijuana, issuing statements about the previous night's events. By nightfall the Peteets were back on the road to San Diego, where the police pulled them over and, discovering that Thomas, Carrie, and Clyde were drunk, impounded the car, arrested Thomas, and sent the three women home in a taxi. Following his release the next morning, Thomas returned home. Not long after, the entire family lay down on their kitchen floor while Thomas, gun in hand, turned on the gas on the kitchen stove. On February 6, San Diego police discovered Thomas, Carrie, and Audrey dead. Clyde, who was still clinging to life when the police broke the windows and released the gas from the house, died a few days later.[1]

In the days that followed, news of the Peteet "Shame Suicides" was splashed across the pages of regional and national newspapers. The press published portions of their suicide note, pieced together the narrative of their last days, and covered the ensuing investigation and arrest of Llanos and Amador.[2] The tragic and scandalous story captured the public imagination and helped reignite a smoldering debate about the dangers of the Tijuana vice districts, the U.S. and Mexican governments' responsibility for regulating moral behavior, and border control.

Even as the newspapers and Mexican courts tried to determine who was to blame for the Peteets' demise, a vocal group of indignant Americans shifted their attention away from the specifics of the case to focus on the border and the tens of thousands of Americans who, like the Peteets, crossed it each year. In the hands of American reformers, the Peteets' story became a parable of the dangers of the vice districts that had emerged along the boundary line in response to American antivice laws. Shock about the events that were reported to have taken place at the Oakland Bar turned to outrage about the very existence of that bar and the ease with which Americans could visit it. Suspicions about police chief Llanos grew into an indictment of all Mexican officials. And calls for justice became demands for a border-crossing curfew. Just two weeks after the Peteets' deaths, the U.S. Treasury Department acceded to reformers' calls for action. At 5:45 p.m. on February 18, 1926, a rush of cars began driving from Tijuana's tourist district toward the San Ysidro port of entry. For fifteen minutes U.S. customs and immigration inspectors hurriedly processed the heavy traffic across the line. And then, at 6 p.m., they closed the gates. A few stray cars rolled up to the border; U.S. officials turned them away. The border was closed for the night. It would not open until the following morning at 8 a.m.[3]

The closing of the border gates on February 18 was not an entirely new phenomenon. By the time of the Peteets' deaths, border closures and the fences, gates, and government officials that made their enforcement possible had become part of the border control apparatus. What was new in the 1920s was not that U.S. officials were closing the border, but why and when they did so. By convincing the Treasury Department to establish early closing hours, American reformers successfully harnessed the power of border control to enforce moral regulations. Over time the U.S. and Mexican governments had established ports of entry to facilitate customs collection and built fences to prevent the violence of the Mexican Revolution and World War I from overtaking border towns. But by the 1920s both Americans and Mexicans had become aware that the border control apparatus that the states had erected on the border for national defense and customs enforcement could also be used for new state prerogatives, including morality regulation.

Like other border controls, early closing hours established conditions on border crossing. The boundary line was not completely closed; most of the line remained open. Desperate drinkers could have walked a few miles to the east or west and railroads continued to roll all night long along the tracks of the San Diego and Arizona Railroad carrying agricultural products from American-owned farms in Baja California to markets in the United States. But even these conditional controls raised questions about who had the right to regulate the boundary line and on what basis they should be allowed to enforce that control. While American reformers lauded the establishment of early closing hours, many business people, bureaucrats, and Mexican nationalists challenged the U.S. government's authority to unilaterally use the boundary line for the purposes of enforcing moral standards. The U.S. experiment with early closing hours revealed both the power of border controls and the difficulty of untangling the social, political, and economic spaces that overlapped and intersected at the border.

THE RISE OF BORDER VICE DISTRICTS AND THEIR CRITICS

The border vice districts that American moral reformers targeted with early closing hours in the 1920s were a product of those reformers' earlier successes in the United States. In the early twentieth century, American antivice crusaders convinced local, state, and federal authorities to pass laws defining alcohol, narcotics, prostitution, gambling, and a number of other activities of questionable morality as "vices" and restricting access to them. Throughout the United States, businesses that catered to these activities shut down or went underground. In the southwest, vice migrated across the boundary line as saloon owners, casino operators, prostitutes, and race and fight promoters relocated to the more permissive Mexican legal climate just across the border.

The movement of U.S. vice to Mexican soil was the result of the legal significance of the boundary line. Although reformers in Mexico and the United States had similar concerns about drinking, gambling, drug use, and prostitution, their governments adopted different strategies for regulating these vices. The Mexican government chose to register and tax vice purveyors, while U.S. officials completely outlawed gambling, prostitution, and the sale of drugs and alcohol. These U.S. laws restricted the supply of vice, but they did not reduce demand. With the enactment of local "dry" laws in California, statewide prohibition in Arizona in 1914, and World War I restrictions on the manufacture and sale of alcohol, Mexican towns became the easiest places to get a drink along the border. Each new law restricting gambling, prostitution, and prize fighting spurred the growth of border vice districts as well.[4]

Vice districts developed in every border city, but Tijuana became the exemplar of border vice. American morality legislation transformed Tijuana from a dusty customs outpost to a mecca for American tourists and thrill seekers. In 1900 less than four hundred people lived in the vicinity of Tijuana where a few merchants and tourism promoters catered to local ranchers and American sightseers who wanted to see the border. In 1907 Porfirio Díaz legalized gambling in Baja California and opened the way for Mexican and American entrepreneurs to receive concessions to operate casinos and racetracks. The federal government restricted horse racing and gambling in 1909, but with the beginning of the Mexican Revolution the following year local authorities reinstated both activities in hopes of profiting from the lucrative concessions. As battles raged elsewhere on the border, Governor Esteban Cantú maintained relative peace in Baja California and presided over the dramatic growth of the Tijuana and Mexicali vice districts. Cantú granted concessions and licenses to vice promoters who, with the passage of the Walker-Otis Anti-Race Track Gambling Bill of 1909, the Red Light Abatement Act of 1913, and a California law outlawing prizefighting in 1916, needed a new place to do business. In 1915 Antonio Elosúa, a Mexican citizen, secured a gaming permit that enabled him to include boxing, gambling, and races in his "Typical Mexican Fair." The same year, Cantú granted the American-owned Lower California Jockey Club a concession for another racetrack that soon eclipsed Elosúa's operations. Under the direction of Los Angeles race promoter Baron Long and San Francisco boxing promoter "Sunny Jim" Coffroth the Lower California Jockey Club became a major draw for American tourists. Thousands of Americans attended the inaugural horse race at the club on January 1, 1916.[5]

Wartime restrictions on border crossing forced the races to close temporarily, but with the end of the First World War and the beginning of nationwide Prohibition in the United States in 1920, Tijuana boomed. During the 1920s Tijuana developed a substantial and diversified vice economy. Racing began again on January 1, 1920. Between 1920 and 1924, the number of saloons in Tijuana doubled from thirty to sixty. By

FIGURE 6.1. Automobiles parked in front of the Blue Fox Café and ABC Bar in Tijuana, December 1928. By the 1920s Tijuana was home to dozens of bars, as well as gambling halls, brothels, and racetracks, that catered to Americans' demands for products and activities that had been outlawed in the United States. Courtesy of San Diego History Center.

the time of their ill-fated visit in 1926, the Peteets would have had many bars besides Luis Amador's Oakland Bar to choose from—Miguel Calette Anaya's Blue Fox Café; Herman Cohen's San Francisco Bar; M. Escobedo's Tijuana Bar and Café; and Marvin Allen, Frank "Booze" Beyer, and Carl Withington's Tivoli Bar, to name a few. Even the American heavyweight boxer, Jack Johnson, operated two Tijuana nightclubs, although one, which catered exclusively to African Americans, would have been off limits to the Peteets. Over the course of the decade, Tijuana saw dramatic changes in the quality, as well as quantity, of these establishments. The vice industry achieved a new pinnacle with the opening of the Agua Caliente resort and casino in 1928. Built by a group of American investors at a cost of $10 million on land leased from Governor Abelardo Rodríguez, Agua Caliente consisted of a five-hundred-room hotel, casino, spa, swimming pool, golf course, gardens, private radio station, airport, and both greyhound and horse racing tracks. Benefiting from proximity to the booming populations in San Diego and Los Angeles, Tijuana was popular with both average Americans, like the Peteets, and celebrities and mobsters, including Buster Keaton, Gloria Swanson, Clark Gable, Charlie Chaplin, Jack Dempsey, Bugsy Siegel, and Al Capone.[6]

No other border town matched Tijuana's opulence, but border vice districts emerged along the length of the boundary line from Texas to California. With the onset of Prohibition, Ciudad Juárez, just across the Rio Grande from El Paso and the largest of the Mexican border cities, developed a thriving vice district with bars, brothels, gambling halls, and other businesses that catered to Americans from the southern, southwestern, and midwestern United States. Mexicali got its start in 1901 when the founding of Calexico as a dry town created a demand for liquor just across the boundary line. According to local tradition, Mexicali's first business was a plank beneath a mesquite tree from which laborers bought mescal and tequila.[7] Over the next two decades, thanks to the same restrictive California laws and permissive Baja California policies that influenced Tijuana's growth, Mexicali became a popular nightspot for the predominantly middle- and working-class residents of the Imperial Valley and the salesmen and investors who visited there. By 1924 one critical American visitor counted no less than thirty-six cabarets and twelve "crib houses" (houses of prostitution) on his tour of Mexicali. "Literally throngs of men and women," he noted, "—some through idle curiosity, others to engage in the unbridled vice and debauchery that is permitted to hug our American border—cross daily back and forth between America and Mexico at this point."[8] Home to numerous brothels, saloons, and opium dens, Mexicali's Chinatown in particular became associated with vice.[9]

Vice also flourished along the Sonora-Arizona border, though to a lesser extent. The onset of statewide prohibition in Arizona on December 31, 1914, pushed the saloons that had proliferated on both sides of the border south of the boundary line. Sonoran state and municipal governments issued special concessions for gambling and liquor sales to capitalize on the new demand. The Donnadieu brothers, who ran a store specializing in French liquor and Mexican cigars in Agua Prieta, opened up La Caverna saloon and restaurant in a cave on Elías Street in Nogales. Another Nogales establishment, a casino and dance hall called the Southern Club, was operated by a group of Americans who ran a club of the same name in Mexicali.[10]

As the border vice districts grew in popularity and profitability, they also came under attack from reformers on both sides of the boundary line. According to their critics, the problems of the border vice districts were twofold. First, there was the problem of vice; second, there was the problem of the border. The critique of vice was not surprising. Like moral reformers around the world, these reformers believed that gambling, drinking, and having sex with prostitutes was morally wrong and destructive to individuals, families, and communities. These were the same arguments that had led to laws regulating these practices in Mexico and outlawing them in the United States. However, along with the familiar refrain of antivice crusaders, these reformers' assaults also reflected a series of concerns about national image and state sovereignty that were specific to the border. On the one hand, American reformers expressed frustration that their compatriots could take advantage of the boundary line to evade U.S. morality laws. Mexicans, on the other hand, faced the challenge of managing both the flood of Americans who crossed the border and the presumptions of economic and political influence that they brought with them. These concerns about the border would come to dominate the debates about border vice districts, leading to calls for new border controls and creating tensions between Mexicans and Americans along the border.

Although they would grow to encompass questions of national identity and state sovereignty, the critiques of the border vice districts began as well-intentioned and fairly commonplace attacks on vice. The reform impulse that resulted in Prohibition and other so-called morality laws in the United States and Mexico was part of a broader transnational movement that swept across Europe and North America around the turn of the century. Along the boundary line, Mexicans and Americans denounced the border vice districts as threats to the moral and physical health of individuals, families, and communities. In 1909 a group of men who identified themselves as the "fathers and family heads and residents" of Mexicali petitioned President Díaz, bemoaning the fact that their town had become a "frightful center of vice and depravation." They expressed outrage that even as bars and brothels flourished, the Mexicali school, which flooding had destroyed in 1907, had yet to be rebuilt.[11]

Most reformers, like these self-proclaimed fathers and family heads, saw the border vice districts as a particular threat to young people and families. A frustrated member of the Men's Federated Bible Class of Douglas, Arizona, complained that not only did many Americans go over, get drunk, "often leaving their families in need," but "still worse is the fact that a number of young people, some boys and girls of High School age, go over and are some times ruined by those trips."[12] An officer of the Women's Christian Temperance Union at Calexico reported that in one year she had "detained and kept from crossing the line more than 4,000 young boys and girls."[13] In addition to the more obvious dangers of drink, drugs, gambling, and prostitution, the availability of quick divorces and marriages in Mexican border districts represented yet another assault on American family values.[14]

Embedded in these critiques was a characterization of the border vice districts as sites of sexual promiscuity and perversion. This was most apparent in the references to the proliferation of prostitution in Mexican border towns. The fathers and family heads of Mexicali complained that prostitutes plied their trade in the center of town where neither visiting Americans nor virtuous Mexicans could avoid them.[15] For many Americans the border vice districts seemed particularly dangerous because of the possibilities for interracial sex. Border brothels defied the racial barriers of the Jim Crow–era United States. Despite the predominance of Americans among both prostitutes and their clientele, the racial and ethnic diversity of the border brothels offered many opportunities for sex across the color line. "These women place themselves at the disposition of any man that presents himself, without distinction of race, color or cleanliness," reported the U.S. consul in Mexicali. He described the Black Cat, a well-known Mexicali brothel, as "crowded by Chinese laborers, Mexicans, Japanese, negroes and white men in all stages of intoxication, any of whom will be 'entertained' by the women of the resort if they are willing to pay the price." "It would be difficult," he concluded, "to conceive of a dive more repulsive than this, or of conditions more appalling than can be witnessed in it."[16]

According to reformers this climate of interracial activity and sexual promiscuity affected not just prostitutes and their clients, but innocent young women like Audrey and Clyde Peteet. The Peteets were not the first women to report that they had been drugged and raped. In 1919 a San Diego pastor warned that in Tijuana "girls were doped and used as 'common property' of American, Mexican and Chinaman alike."[17] This undercurrent of sexual and racial danger infected even the most innocent movements of people in border towns. "The decent American," U.S. Consul William C. Burdett noted, "blushes with shame when he sees the unholy mob of drunken debauchees of both sexes and all colors reeling through the town, and realizes that they are his fellow countrymen."[18]

Concerns about moral and physical health were linked in reformers' descriptions of border vice districts.[19] One San Diego pastor complained that Tijuana was a " 'moral sink hole,' and a constant source of disease and disgrace."[20] Other American observers referred to Mexicali as a "plague-hole" and its brothels as "festering sores."[21] In 1924, the U.S. secretary of state, Charles Evans Hughes, opined that conditions at Tijuana and Mexicali represented a "grave menace to the health and welfare of American communities."[22] The debates centering on prostitution in particular blurred the line between the dangers of moral corruption and those of venereal disease. According to one reformer, "Fake medical examinations are resorted to in these dives to instill into the patrons a certain sense of false security from disease."[23] American reformers worried that young American soldiers stationed near the border were at risk from border red light districts. While World War I crossing restrictions limited the ability of servicemen to visit the border vice districts, at the end of the war, reformers renewed their calls for protective measures. "[I]n view of the warfare of Army and Navy against vice among enlisted men, and the desire of fathers and mothers to have a respectable environment for their sons," a San Diego pastor wrote that he hoped the secretary of war would oppose, "the planned orgies of disgrace and lawlessness upon our borders."[24]

While these criticisms echoed the concerns of like-minded people throughout the United States and Mexico, the binational dynamics of the border vice districts added another dimension to reformers' arguments. Their critiques not only raised questions about morality but also about national sovereignty, responsibility, and character. Beyond the damage done to their citizens and communities, many Mexicans worried about the effect of the border vice districts on their national reputation. In their 1909 petition to Porfirio Díaz, the Mexicali fathers and family heads stressed that they were writing as good citizens who strove to maintain "the good name of our country and its government." Contrasting Calexico's schools, stores, and hotels with the bordellos and bars of Mexicali, they expressed their concerns that conditions in Mexicali were making their American neighbors reluctant to cross the line.[25] An official in the Mexican department of Gobernación agreed with them, noting that Mexicali was a "very sad and very unfavorable example of our towns." "The importance, then, of this subject is not only in respect to morality," he emphasized, "but also because it significantly affects the good name of our country."[26]

Ironically, while Mexican national honor was at stake, Americans were largely to blame for conditions on the border. Although located on Mexican soil, border vice districts were filled with Americans. In Nogales the U.S. consul noted that Americans owned most of the larger saloons and that "the clientele is largely American."[27] In 1922 H. C. von Struve, the U.S. consul at Mexicali, reported the "humiliating" fact that "the gambling resorts openly operated in the past have been entirely American owned, and that from 75% to 80% of the prostitutes and procurers plying their trade here and in Tijuana have been of American nationality."[28] During one two- to three-year period, seven hundred American women reportedly relocated to brothels in Tijuana and Mexicali. An American reformer, Edwin Grant, reported that in one Mexicali brothel, all but three of a hundred prostitutes were Americans, some of whom he recognized from his antivice work in California.[29] While Mexicans and Asian and European immigrants also operated bars and brothels, American transplants dominated the border vice districts, especially the big resorts, racetracks, and casinos. Among the largest operators on the border was Carl Withington, who first relocated from Bakersfield to Mexicali in 1914. There he partnered with Marvin Allen and Frank "Booze" Beyer to form the A.B.W. syndicate. Beginning with The Owl (El Tecolote) bar and brothel in Mexicali, the trio eventually ran a number of well-known vice establishments, including the Tivoli Bar and Sunset Inn casino in Tijuana, and expanded into brewing, liquor importing, gambling, and racing. Another group of Americans, Wirt Bowman, James Crofton, and Baron Long, who the Southern California press would dub the "border barons" because of their entrepreneurial activities south of the line, built and operated the Agua Caliente Casino.[30]

Americans were even more heavily represented among the consumers of vice. Border vice districts were entirely dependent on Americans who crossed the boundary line to visit saloons, casinos, brothels, and racetracks. A U.S. State Department report noted in 1929 that 95 percent of the money spent in such resorts came from the United States. "Thousands of Americans cross the border daily at Tijuana, and on holidays and Sundays the crowds are unbelievably large. On Labor Day, 1927, it is said that 16,000 American motor cars entered Mexico through the gateway of Tijuana."[31] In 1931, the first year in which the U.S. government kept official statistics of border crossings at the San Ysidro port of entry, nearly five and half million people, 90 percent of whom were Americans, crossed through that port of entry alone. Reformers and officials alike were forced to assume, as Consul von Struve did, that "without American exploitation and support local vice conditions would undoubtedly be much less deplorable than they have been in the past and still are."[32]

All of these Americans left their imprint on Mexican border towns. Many of the bars and casinos bore English names like the Blue Fox Café and Sunset Inn. Reformer Edwin Grant complained that "flaring electric signs" faced the American border, luring customers to the "debauch emporiums." While signs advertising "legitimate Mexican enterprises are usually in Spanish," he added, "the vice and booze signs are in the English language." According to Grant, the Americanization of Tijuana was complete. "At Tia Juana [sic]," he wrote, "these Mexicans find on their side of the line, an American town, run by American capital, harboring American underworld women and American white slavers, the medium of exchange being American money, and all this unbridled debauchery being accomplished through the medium of the American language."[33] Although advertisements for Tijuana in San Diego newspapers continued to urge tourists to "Visit this quaint Mexican village and send a post card from a foreign land," another American consul concluded that with the exception of the presence of Mexican government officials, "There is little Mexican about the village."[34]

The predominance of Americans in the border vice districts complicated the debates about what, if anything, should be done about them and who was responsible for doing it. The combination of American people and Mexican places made the border vice districts hybrid, binational spaces that reformers and state officials on both sides of the boundary line had a stake in controlling. However, while Mexican and American reformers worked to convince their respective governments that they shared the same interests in stomping out vice along the border, they did not meet with the same response.

Government Regulation and the Establishment of Early Closing Hours on the Border

When it came to the border vice districts, the U.S. and Mexican governments had different perspectives and priorities. While the districts caused U.S. officials nothing but trouble, for Mexicans they were also a source of economic growth and power. As officials from each nation responded to reformers' complaints they not only had to consider the protests' merits but also whether they had the power to take action and how their response might affect the nation-state's interests. These questions transformed local concerns about border vice into a series of binational debates about morality regulation, national integrity, and the power and purpose of border controls.

From the perspective of many moral reformers, the easiest solution to the problem of the border vice districts was for Mexico to establish the same prohibitory laws as the United States. Phil D. Swing, the U.S. congressman for San Diego and Imperial counties, spearheaded a movement to persuade the Mexican government to create a fifty-mile-wide vice-free zone along the boundary line. "Such a zone," volunteered a group of Yuma, Arizona, citizens, "would reduce friction between the two countries to a minimum and would be of mutual advantage."[35] However, while reformers stressed the binational benefits of a border "dry" zone, they primarily intended the policy to protect Americans. In effect what these reformers wanted was an extension of U.S. antivice legislation into Mexican territory so that vice would be out of reach of American consumers. "[President] Obregon," wrote one angry San Diegan, "should move the hell holes fifty miles from the border."[36]

Although the Mexican government briefly considered the establishment of a border "dry zone," the vice districts along the boundary line continued to thrive.[37] While many Americans believed there was a clear solution to the dilemma of border vice districts, Mexican officials did not even agree on the nature of the problem, let alone the solution. In contrast to American reformers' focus on cutting off Americans' access to gambling, prostitution, and liquor, Mexican officials wanted to balance the economic benefits of the border vice districts with the maintenance of their national image and authority. As a result of these different priorities, Mexican authorities had very little interest in shutting down the vice districts completely. Rather, embracing the regulatory approach that characterized moral reform throughout Mexico, Mexican state, territorial, and federal officials adopted a series of measures that sought to maximize the state's ability to profit from vice while minimizing its negative effects.

Vice brought a lot of money across the border. Licensing fees and taxes poured into government coffers and funded public works. Throughout the 1910s and 1920s, prostitution, gaming, and alcohol made up between 9 and 48 percent of the revenue coming into the municipal government of Mexicali. One brothel alone paid the government between $13,000 and $15,000 each month. At 5,000 pesos a month, Sonoran gambling concessions also brought in much-needed funds to that state's treasury. In addition to basic operating expenses, these fees made possible public works projects that mediated the negative effects of the vice districts in the eyes of the Mexican residents of border towns. Governor Esteban Cantú channeled income from the vice districts into the construction of improved roads and a new high school in Mexicali. In 1919 the Sonoran government authorized beer and wine sales in municipal saloons in Nogales, Naco, Agua Prieta, and other Sonoran towns with the profits specifically designated for support of an Industrial School in Hermosillo. When the capitol building in Mexicali burned down, gambling concessions financed its reconstruction. In the 1920s, Governor Abelardo Rodríguez used funds derived from vice taxes and concessions to finance such progressive public works as a theater and library in Mexicali as well.[38]

These men also profited personally from the proliferation of vice, leading to charges of corruption. Under-the-table kickbacks and payoffs were pervasive, and some local officials doubled as smugglers. In 1922 the U.S. consul at Mexicali reported that two high-ranking military officials and the *presidente municipal* of Mexicali were not only heavily invested in local gambling establishments but were also involved in smuggling drugs and alcohol across the border into the United States. Esteban Cantú's cozy relationship with U.S. railroad companies, agricultural interests, and vice promoters like Marvin Allen, Frank "Booze" Beyer, and Carl Withington, led his critics to denounce him as an unethical sellout. Abelardo Rodríguez also came under attack for his close associations with American vice purveyors. He not only owned the land on which Agua Caliente Casino was built and received rent from its owners, but his brother also oversaw the construction of the hotel and casino, using materials that Rodríguez arranged to be imported duty-free by claiming they would be used to build a government-funded dam. Reformers on both sides of the border protested against these abuses of government power and demanded federal intervention.[39]

However, while these officials' behavior was far from beyond reproach, personal greed was not the only reason they encouraged the development of the border vice districts. Many government officials believed that they could use the taxes and fees collected from vice establishments to benefit the people of Baja California. Cantú's construction of the new Mexicali school was emblematic of the potential benefits of border vice. In 1909 the Mexicali fathers and family heads had paired their demands for reform of the vice districts with complaints about the failure of local officials to rebuild the Mexicali school destroyed by floods in 1907. Lamenting the fact that their children had no option but to attend schools on the U.S. side of the line, they wrote, "At least, if the previously mentioned vices were tolerated in order to acquire the means for the promotion of instruction and the construction of a decent school, it would be somewhat excusable." Cantú did exactly this, using vice revenue to build a school that attracted both Mexican and American children. No longer did the people of Mexicali need to worry that their children would have to attend school in a foreign country, "to study a language that is not their own" in sight of "a flag that is not their parents."[40] The Mexicali school gave the town's Mexican residents something to be proud of.

It also assuaged some of their fears that Mexican authority, identity, and culture would be lost in the onslaught of Americans. Many Mexicans were justifiably concerned about the Americanization of the border. As early as 1912, General Manuel Gordillo Escudero issued a decree requiring that all employees speak Spanish and commercial signs be written in Spanish. Despite his efforts this short-lived policy had been forgotten by the 1920s. English-language signs filled the border vice districts where they could be read by both American tourists and many English-speaking, American workers. Former police officer and labor organizer, Julio Dunn Legaspy, recalled that Americans "controlled all the activities," including the "authorities who gave them protection." It was "as if Tijuana was an American city," he explained, adding, "the Mexicans did not have the right to work, not even in the vice dens. It felt as if we were in a foreign country."[41] In response to these conditions, Mexican nationalists and labor organizers, like Legaspy, demanded that territorial officials close American vice establishments or at least require them to hire Mexicans. In 1925 a Baja California court ruled that all companies would be required to employ Mexican nationals as at least 50 percent of their workforce. Thanks to this law and continued pressure by local unions, by the late 1920s large numbers of Mexicans worked in casinos and bars. The Agua Caliente Resort drew the vast majority of its workforce from local ethnic Mexican populations, as indicated by the fact that more than 90 percent of its workers had Hispanic surnames.[42]

By requiring vice establishments to hire Mexican workers and pay taxes to support public works, Baja California officials maximized the economic benefits of the border vice districts. But this did not mean that they simply let vice run wild. Mexican officials gradually established a regulatory regime. In addition to providing income, the fees on gambling, prostitution, narcotics, and alcohol limited what was available and who could sell it. As in other parts of Mexico, territorial officials required prostitutes to register with local governments, pay licensing fees, and submit to health tests. Mexican immigration officials also deported unwanted foreign prostitutes. After coming to power in 1915, Cantú instituted a plan of heavy taxation in order to eliminate all "vicious vices" and to clean up and raise the level of border vice to draw more middle- and upper-class tourists.[43]

In addition to regulating vice, many of these reforms were intended as political statements. During times of political instability, Mexican officials cracked down on border vice as a show of state power. In 1912, in the wake of the Magonista rebellion, General Manuel Gordillo Escudero temporarily enacted a series of harsh regulations to restore order in Mexicali by banning prostitution and games of chance, closing dance halls, and shuttering cafés and saloons at 10 p.m. Another crackdown on border vice accompanied President Álvaro Obregón's deposal of Cantú and reestablishment of federal authority over Baja California in 1920. Finally, following the Peteets' suicides in 1926, Baja California officials moved quickly to try to limit American outrage. Within days the Tijuana police arrested Llanos, Amador, and five others and charged them with complicity in the Peteets' deaths. Mexican President Plutarco Elías Calles, Governor Abelardo Rodríguez, and the mayor of Tijuana announced plans to clean up the city by deporting "undesirables" and closing fifty-two saloons. The eighteen bars that remained were restricted to a confined area and required to pay a $10,000 security bond and $1,500 a month in licensing fees. Responding to concerns about women's vulnerability, Governor Rodríguez issued an order forbidding women from entering saloons without an escort.[44]

Despite these measures American reformers remained dissatisfied with the proliferation of vice along the border. Faced with the fact that they had different priorities than Mexican officials, they turned to the U.S. government and border controls instead. In order to convince U.S. officials that they should use the border control apparatus to keep Americans out of Mexican vice districts, American reformers had to change the

way they framed the problem of border vice. Stressing the preponderance
of Americans and their active evasion of U.S. law, reformers tried to convince U.S. officials that they should think about the United States' sovereign responsibilities not in terms of geography but in terms of population. The fact that the border districts made it possible, in the words of
the U.S. consul at Mexicali, "for the nearby residents of the United States
to step across the border and there to enjoy certain privileges and perform certain acts which are illegal in the country and state of their actual
residence," represented a challenge to the sovereignty of the U.S. state.[45]
Border vice was not a Mexican problem, but, in the words of reformer
Edwin Grant, "a conspiracy of outlawed Americans who have expatri-
ated themselves for the clear purpose of evading American laws and
reaping a fortune just outside the protection of the American flag by
preying on American victims."[46]

In addition to framing border vice districts as threats to U.S. sovereignty and American morality, American reformers also pointed out that
even if Americans' indulgence in vice was restricted to Mexican territory,
the effects of their behavior were not. In 1924, U.S. Secretary of State
Hughes opined that conditions at Tijuana and Mexicali represented a
"grave menace to the health and welfare of American communities."[47]
Returning to the United States from the Mexican vice districts, Americans carried the dangers of depravity with them. Writing to President
Calvin Coolidge in 1923, the Men's Federated Bible Class of Douglas,
Arizona, noted that "a great many Americans go over and bring back the
booze inside of them, often leaving their families in need."[48] Drunk drivers returning from Mexico threatened the innocent Americans with
whom they shared the roads. "Along the highway to San Diego," one reformer noted, "as these stages and private machines make their mad rush
from the Mexican Border, the roads are often strewn with wrecks,
drunken drivers and petting parties."[49] Locals dubbed the road from Tijuana to San Diego the "Graveyard Highway."[50] Drug addicts also men-
aced U.S. border communities. In 1923 the warden of the Arizona state
penitentiary complained that "the whole border is seething with dope
fiends from one end to the other. They have collected from all parts of the
country and are committing crimes almost every day in an effort to pro-
cure money to keep their cravings for dope satisfied."[51]

Drug and liquor smuggling were also associated with the vice districts.
Beginning with the 1909 Act to Prohibit the Importation and Use of
Opium for Other Than Medicinal Purposes and the 1914 Harrison Narcotics Law in the United States and the Mexican federal government's
prohibition on the importation of opium in 1916 followed by all narcotics in 1923, drug smuggling was born on the border. With the onset of

Prohibition, liquor joined the illegal flow across the line. The illicit trade in outlawed drugs and alcohol quickly became very profitable. In 1924 an ounce of morphine that sold for $35 in Mexicali was worth $100 in Los Angeles. At times piggybacking on the already established channels for smuggling Chinese immigrants, drug traffickers and rumrunners found numerous ways to get their goods across the line. From his post in Mexicali, Consul von Struve reported that "all imaginable means of transportation from carrying on the person of the smuggler to conveyance by airoplane [sic] [are] being employed."[52] One man fitted his shoes with special heels to carry narcotics. Two others cut a hole in the inner tube of their spare tire, inserted cans of narcotics, patched up the hole, and pumped up the spare again to disguise their handiwork. In Calexico a customs inspector seized a truck that had been outfitted with a metal tank extending the entire length of the vehicle to carry a "large quantity of foreign liquor."[53] While these methods betrayed a level of expertise and experience, many other smugglers simply concealed contraband on their person and walked or drove across the line.[54]

It primarily fell to U.S. customs officers to stop cross-border drug and alcohol smuggling. With liquor and opium completely outlawed in the United States, but in wide supply in Baja California (despite official bans on opium), the dynamics of supply and demand dictated that most drug and alcohol smuggling moved from south to north. By the beginning of Prohibition, customs officers were old-timers on the border, well versed in exercising sovereignty and enforcing state regulations within the local transborder context. Rather than create a new force to tackle the growing traffic in narcotics and alcohol, the U.S. Treasury Department simply dispatched more customs officers to the line. Between 1925 and 1930 the number of customs officers stationed on the U.S.-Mexico border increased from 111 to 723. These new officers were instructed in the particulars of weeding out drug and liquor smugglers from the stream of tipsy tourists and legitimate businesspeople. "[E]ach person should be questioned as to whether he has in his possession or in his baggage or conveyance any intoxicating liquors," explained a 1925 customs circular. "If intoxicating liquors are declared they should be seized and forfeited . . . but no fine should be imposed. If no liquors are declared and are found on the person, in the baggage, or conveyance, they should be seized . . . and a fine of $5.00 should be imposed for each bottle of distilled liquor or wine and $2.00 for each bottle of beer."[55] With standardized directives like this issued from Washington, DC, the Customs Service became a more regular and professional presence on the line. One circular encouraged customs officers to be "courteous, tactful, and diplomatic when dealing with and searching the baggage of difficult travelers."[56] An-

FIGURE 6.2. U.S. officers dumping confiscated alcohol at the border near Tijuana, 1920s. As Prohibition created a burgeoning demand for illicit liquor in the United States, officers like these stepped up their efforts to prevent smuggling across the boundary line. Courtesy of San Diego History Center.

other specified that all customs officers, aside from office employees and mounted inspectors, be in uniform of olive drab cloth and have their badges displayed.[57]

These new measures also changed the way that tourists experienced the boundary line as they increasingly found themselves subjected to intrusive and time-consuming searches. In a 1920 article the *New York Times* warned potential visitors to Tijuana that U.S. customs agents would stop and search them at the border on their return to the United States. While one official "deftly runs his hands over your clothing, perhaps lifting your hat for you if it happens to have a high crown," another "opens up the hood of the car, sounds the radiator, studies the tires, peeps into the horn, removes cushions, investigates the tool box and even examines the spark plugs, sometimes, or peers under the rubber matting in search of opium."[58] Not surprisingly, given these lengthy investigations, traffic often backed up at the border.

Despite these new measures, customs officials could not stop all of the drug smugglers and rumrunners, and many American reformers remained dissatisfied. "Unfortunately," Consul von Struve noted, "the number of American customs officers guarding the boundary line is entirely inadequate to meet the difficulties imposed by an extended open boundary that can be crossed almost anywhere from the Colorado River at Yuma to the Pacific Ocean at Tia Juana [*sic*], and by the resourceful-ness of the expert criminal minds that are attracted to the traffic by the large gains it offers."[59] Another observer noted that the rush of automobile traffic across the border at Tijuana made customs inspection there a "veritable farce" in which "the degree of effectiveness of search is largely spasmodic."[60]

Although imperfect, antismuggling efforts provided a reminder of the power of the border control apparatus—a power that reformers wanted to put to work to limit Americans' access to the border vice districts. The U.S. government did not have the power to legislate morality in Mexico, but it could, reformers argued, make it more difficult for Americans to move back and forth across the border. Thanks to the governments' success in channeling the majority of crossings into a few designated ports of entry, officials had the ability to stymie transborder traffic simply by shutting the customs offices and locking the border gates. Of course, no one, not reformers and the U.S. state even less, had any interest in completely closing the border. The key, as it had been in the past, was to develop a system of conditional controls that would obstruct the movement of vice tourists without interfering with other forms of transborder trade and travel. The solution American reformers struck upon were early closing hours.

The origins of nighttime closures lay with the association of vice with the thriving border nightlife. Vice establishments, explained Consul von Struve, were dependent on "the patronage of transient Americans who visit Tijuana and Mexicali from nearby American territory at night after the close of ordinary business and return to American territory almost invariably the same night." He concluded that if the ports were closed at night that they would "be deprived of at least seventy five per cent of their profitable patronage and would therefore no longer be able to pay sufficient legitimate or illegitimate revenues to enable their further existence except on a very small scale."[61] Following this logic, reformers argued that closing the border at night would cut off Americans' access to nighttime vice and ultimately remove the danger by driving the vice industry out of business. Letters urging the federal government to establish a border-crossing curfew poured into Washington, DC, from towns all along the border. Early border closing, concluded a letter from the Men's Federated Bible Class of Douglas to President Calvin Coolidge, was "for the good of the American people."[62]

Despite these pleas, many U.S. officials were reluctant to use the border to enforce moral standards. While most authorities believed the U.S. government clearly had the right and responsibility to prevent the entry of smuggled drugs and alcohol, when it came to using the border control apparatus to regulate the movement of Americans to and from the border vice districts, the government's role was not as clear. U.S. State Department officials, who had to manage the diplomatic fallout that would follow the imposition of early closing hours, were particularly troubled by these proposals. Secretary of State Robert Lansing concluded in 1920 that the State Department should not "attempt to control the morals of its citizens in a foreign country through passport regulations," as "the Department does not wish to constitute itself as a censor of morals."[63] Based on similar concerns, both the State Department and the Labor Department concluded that they lacked the authority to take action in response to a 1923 petition from the Calexico Rotary Club asking that they prevent minors from entering Mexico without a guardian at night.[64] The question of whether the U.S. government, and if so which department, had the authority to regulate Americans' ability to travel to Mexico continued to vex government officials throughout the 1920s. A 1924 State Department memo noted that the department had been considering the issue "for a great many years without any effective method having been found to correct the abuses," and that "there appears to be much confusion as to which Department of this Government, if any, has authority to deal with the situation effectively." After a review of the "voluminous" pertinent correspondence, the author concluded that "the question of mitigating the evil being protested against is a difficult one under the present law, and that no one Department has the machinery of preventing entirely the crossing of Americans over the Border."[65]

Yet even as officials in Washington, DC, pondered questions of jurisdictional authority and state power, a number of U.S. customs offices on the boundary line began closing ports of entry at night. In the early 1920s, following the relaxation of wartime border-crossing restrictions, individual customs offices established a variety of closing times in response to local conditions and demands. For a time during the early 1920s, customs and immigration officials at Douglas and Naco put a stop to gambling by closing the line at 6 p.m.[66] In 1924 the U.S. State Department notified the Mexican government that due to the "flagrant immoralities" at Tijuana and Mexicali, the California–Baja California border would be closed after 9 p.m.[67] In response, the Mexican federal government ordered Mexican immigration officials at both towns to respect the early closing hour as well. Finally, in the wake of the Peteet suicides, reformers succeeded in pushing the U.S. government to close the Tijuana port of entry at 6 p.m.[68]

By 1929 ports of entry along the U.S.-Mexico border had a hodgepodge of closing hours. All ports in Arizona, New Mexico, and Texas, with the exception of El Paso and San Luis, closed at midnight. The line closed at 9 p.m. in El Paso and Calexico, 7 p.m. in San Luis, and 6 p.m.

in Andrade and Tijuana. Early closing hours had an immediate effect on border vice districts. Following the establishment of a 9 p.m. closing time on the California border in 1924, Consul von Struve reported that drinking, gambling, and prostitution fell off by 50 to 90 percent in Tijuana and that arrests and drunk driving had decreased in Mexicali and Calexico. In response, vice promoters began planning new hotels to cater to overnight guests.[69]

While many reformers applauded these developments, the overall response across the border region was far from universally enthusiastic. Many Mexicans, who both understood and rejected Americans' characterization of Mexican vice districts as depraved and dangerous places from which Americans needed to be protected, were indignant. Mexico City's *Excelsior* newspaper opined that early closing hours were "an insult" to "national honor" and that they discriminated "against Mexico because of the absence of similar early closing regulations on the Canadian border."[70] The Mexicali and Tijuana chambers of commerce, comprised of both Mexican and American nationals who did business in the border towns, also condemned the closing hours as discriminatory. The Mexicali chamber denounced the reformers as "a craven political organization" that was slandering Mexicans and "engendering hatred between the two nations."[71] "[W]e do not consider ourselves an inferior race whose contact means danger at night hours nor as a body afflicted with an infectious plague," wrote representatives of the Tijuana Chamber of Commerce to President Herbert Hoover in 1929, "and consequently request equal consideration and the same treatment accorded other peoples."[72]

Governor Abelardo Rodríguez spearheaded retaliation in response to both the 1924 9 p.m. closing time and the 1926 6 p.m. closing time. His frustration with the United States' unilateral action was at least partly personal. Rodríguez had worked his way up to become part of the transborder elite. As a child he had lived in Nogales, Sonora, and attended school on the U.S. side of the line. He rose to prominence within Sonoran political circles and was appointed Governor of the Northern District of Baja California in 1923. The new restrictions on transborder movement not only threatened Baja California's tax base and Rodríguez's personal income, but also ran counter to the binational pattern of Rodríguez's life. Particularly egregious was an incident in which a U.S. customs inspector forced Rodríguez and his family to get out of their car and submit to a search during a routine crossing at Calexico. Although State Department officials later chastised the customs officers and ordered them to accord Rodríguez the "courtesies to which he was entitled," the damage had been done.[73]

In the face of the United States' insults to his honor and that of the

Mexican nation, Rodríguez responded to the American early closing hours by establishing his own border-crossing regulations. After U.S. officials began closing the Baja California ports of entry at 9 p.m. in 1924, Rodríguez ordered that all Americans entering Baja California submit to a registration process as well. While Rodríguez argued that he was simply trying to do his part to reform the vice districts, the U.S. consul at Mexicali interpreted the order as a form of retaliation. "The officials making the registration are apparently making no attempt to expedite it," wrote Consul von Struve, "but on the contrary seem to endeavor to draw out the work as much as possible."[74] Rodríguez's officials made exceptions for the owner and some of the employees of a Mexicali brothel, but most Americans were kept waiting for two to three-and-a-half hours. However, if Rodríguez hoped that the added inconvenience would convince the U.S. government to drop its regulations, he was disappointed. The U.S. government would continue to close the border at night for almost another decade, while the Mexican federal government ordered Rodríguez to halt the registrations in order to appease transborder businessmen after just sixteen days.[75]

Five years later Rodríguez made another attempt to pressure U.S. officials to abandon early closing hours and to assert his authority over border control. Unable to keep the border open, he once again adopted a policy that he hoped would so disrupt transborder commerce that U.S. authorities would have to revoke the early closing order. The U.S. border curfew only applied to foot and automobile traffic. Railroads—the major conduit of transborder commerce—however, continued to move across the boundary line throughout the night. Rodríguez decided to change that. "As the American authorities have limited the international traffic at Tijuana, Tecate, Mexicali, and Algodones, to certain hours of the day, and they only allow the traffic of the trains at any other hour," wrote Rodríguez to the general manager of the Tijuana and Tecate Railroad, "it has been considered that such an exception is discriminatory to other carriers." As a result, "taking in consideration that there should be no time restrictions for the traffic between both countries," Rodríguez ordered that all traffic would be "subject to the time restrictions imposed by the authorities of the neighbor country," and that trains would only be allowed to cross the border "within the hours of free international traffic."[76] Either everyone could cross at night, or no one would.

This announcement quickly got Rodríguez the attention he was looking for. Although Congressman Phil Swing wrote it off as an ill-conceived bluff, the managers of transborder rail lines were less dismissive. "It is imperative that we are permitted as in the past at all times," the president of the San Diego and Arizona Railroad wrote to the U.S. State Department, "to have our trains engaged in this transcontinental business cross and recross the international line between Mexico and the United States at all hours day or night."[77] When it came to shipping perishable goods, time was money, and the San Diego and Arizona Railroad had a $22 million investment at stake. Desperate for government intervention, the railroad companies not only turned to Washington, DC, but also approached officials in Mexico City, initiated court proceedings in Baja California courts, and engaged Juan Brittingham Jr., a well-connected binational businessman, to approach Governor Rodríguez. Their legal approach proved most successful. On August 14, the Federal Court at Tijuana issued an order preventing Rodríguez's restriction on rail movement from going into effect.[78]

The protests against early closing hours were not limited to the Mexican side of the border. Less puritanically inclined Americans complained that early closing hours caused traffic jams, disrupted transborder business, and violated their right to freedom of movement. The only people who supported the early closing hours, insisted one San Diego resident, "are some fanatics who seem to think that by closing this gate at 6 o'clock they are preventing people from drinking. It does not prevent one person from going over there. It only causes a bigger crowd on Sundays and a jam at 6 o'clock, endangering life and keeping people in line from 1 to 2 hours."[79] Others saw this less as an inconvenience and more as an attack on basic freedoms and an intervention in the "natural" connections between the United States and Mexico. Thousands of San Diegans signed a petition requesting that "restrictions upon travel be removed and our rights restored, in order that we may have freedom to join our Mexican neighbors in building up the great domain south of our border, which is the natural field for expansion of San Diego's trade, commerce and industry."[80] In 1924 Frank "Booze" Beyer demonstrated his frustration with the early closing time, which threatened his diverse range of vice establishments, by stepping over the chain that customs officers drew across the border at 9 p.m.[81]

While U.S. officials did not lament any damage they might have done to "Booze" Beyer's business interests, they were concerned about the effects of the early closing hours on other transborder businesses. The growth of the border vice districts in the 1920s coincided with a period of renewed vigor in transborder trade and investment. Throughout the 1920s Americans continued to invest in agriculture, ranching, mining, transportation, and limited industrial development along Mexico's northern border.[82] The border-crossing curfew and the resultant strains in international relations took their toll on transborder commerce. While reformers insisted that nighttime closures had no impact on legitimate business, the opposition of many border business leaders suggested otherwise. The Mexicali and Tijuana chambers of commerce and

FIGURE 6.3. U.S. Customs closing the line at 9 p.m. at Tijuana, 1920s. Nighttime closures appeased some moral reformers but also disrupted transborder movement, raised questions about the government's authority to restrict border crossings, and angered many people. Courtesy of San Diego History Center.

the Union of Merchants and Manufacturers of Tijuana wrote to the U.S. State Department protesting that early closing hours disrupted the economic and social links between the United States and Mexico. One businessman with interests in mining, water power, and irrigation in Baja California complained that it was so difficult for his laborers to drive between San Diego and his properties south of the border within the hours the border was open as to make it "impossible for successful and profitable business operations." Denouncing Congressman Swing and his allies as "fanatics," he requested that the government establish the more liberal closing hours "necessary for the proper conduct of business by American citizens in Mexico, and to promote friendship between these two great Republics."[83]

Despite their differences, the vice industry and so-called legitimate businesses shared both the economic space of the border and the need to maintain the favor of Baja California officials. Pleading with the State Department to keep the border open until at least 11 p.m., the president of the Calexico Chamber of Commerce noted that he spoke for "legitimate commercial interests." "Mexicali is [the] capital," he continued, "where [the] governor resides and friendly intercourse is essential to [the] progress of this community."[84] While agricultural interests did not profit directly from vice, they did benefit from the low tax rates made possible by the vice industry's assumption of the majority of the tax burden. "Any regulation that operates in the interests of the tourist business will also presumably continue to assure comparative tax exemption for the non-tourist interests," explained Frank Bohr, the new U.S. consul at Mexicali. "While on the other hand anything that would harm the tourist interests would also undoubtedly result in increased taxes to the non-tourist interests."[85]

As the sense of moral crisis that had fueled both the nationwide turn to Prohibition and the calls for early closing hours ebbed in the late 1920s, growing numbers of inconvenienced Americans and U.S. officials called for the repeal of the early closing policy. Although government agencies continued to receive letters from church groups and other reform organizations in support of the border-crossing curfews, they were increasingly accompanied by others asking for special exemptions to the prohibition on nighttime crossings. In November 1928 authorities and business interests in Tijuana requested that the international boundary line be kept open until 9 p.m. to accommodate the tourist traffic from the Masonic Convention of the American Legion to be held over the Armistice Day weekend in San Diego. Although a Treasury Department official recognized that the only reason for keeping the line open was to "afford the members of the Convention an opportunity to get drunk," he agreed to make an exception to departmental policy.[86] In the following month the Treasury Department granted additional exceptions to the early closing policy, issuing orders to keep the San Ysidro port of entry open until 9 p.m. on Christmas and New Year's Eve. However, they drew the line at 9 p.m., denying similar requests that they keep the San Ysidro, Calexico, and Andrade ports of entry open until 12 a.m. during the holidays.[87]

As more calls for exceptions to the 6 p.m. closing hour—for horse races, concerts, and holiday celebrations—poured in over the next few years, the establishment of a uniform closing hour for all border ports of entry became increasingly attractive to U.S. officials who favored efficient and standardized enforcement measures. "It would be in the interest of efficient administration," noted one U.S. State Department official, "to maintain a uniform hour."[88] Assistant Secretary of the Treasury Seymour Lowman suggested that all ports in Texas, New Mexico, and Arizona close at midnight, with all California ports closing at 9 p.m. More than just a matter of expediency, Lowman's discomfort with the border curfews reflected his uneasiness about the inequity caused by the variations in closing hours along both borders. Meeting in the spring of 1929, State Department officials concluded that keeping the border open twenty-four hours a day—as was done on the Canadian border—would reduce smuggling, encourage commerce, and promote "friendly international relations."[89]

Perhaps most importantly, these officials doubted whether the U.S. government had the power to "regulate the morals of American citizens" in this way.[90] As the American reform crusade lost steam in the late 1920s, officials became increasingly dismissive of reformers' concerns. Answering a query from Congressman Phil Swing, Arthur Bliss Lane, the chief of the State Department's Mexican Division, explained in 1929 that he "questioned the right of the United States Government in keeping Americans out of the United States." Backed into a corner, Swing made the ludicrous argument that "the closing of the Border did not exclude them. It was quite possible for an American citizen to climb over the fence. He would then be detained until the officials came on duty the next morning, but he would be within the United States." Lane pointed out that with an eight- to ten-foot fence in Tijuana he "would not be able personally to duplicate this feat nor would American citizens in general be able to do so."[91]

Despite assertions like Swing's, which bordered on the ridiculous, and the accumulation of arguments against the early closing hours, the U.S. government did not immediately reopen the border at night. Consultation with members of the California congressional delegation revealed that President Herbert Hoover would face negative political fallout if the federal government reduced border controls. However, within the year the Great Depression would completely transform the political landscape. As morality ceased to be a major political preoccupation, legalized vice reemerged in the United States. With these developments the significance of nighttime closing regulations on the border faded. In December 1933, following the repeal of Prohibition in the United States, U.S. officials informed Abelardo Rodríguez, now the interim president of Mexico, that with the exception of El Paso all ports of entry on the Mexican border would remain open twenty-four hours a day.[92]

With nighttime border closures the U.S. government attempted to establish a particular form of relational space that would allow the passage of legitimate trade and traffic, but bar that deemed illicit or morally reprehensible. With the ever more sophisticated and standardized systems of border gates, fences, and enforcement officers, both governments gained a greater ability to segregate streams of traffic and regulate movement across the border. In putting this elaborate border control apparatus to work in service of the United States' antivice campaigns, U.S. officials demonstrated how dramatically both the power and priorities of the U.S. government had shifted by the 1920s. Meanwhile, although Mexican officials undertook their own moral reforms within Mexican territory, the inability of Abelardo Rodríguez to manipulate border controls to force a change in U.S. policies was indicative of the imbalance of power that characterized the border.

The enforcement of unilateral U.S. crossing regulations reinforced national distinctions on the border and infused them with moral judgments. During the 1910s the boundary line had come to mark a divide between the danger and economic insecurity of the Mexican Revolution and the safety and security of the United States. With the fading of border violence, the concerns with safety and security did not disappear. Instead they shifted to an emphasis on other more intangible threats—the dangers posed to American morality by the Mexican vice districts and the trade in drugs and alcohol.

With the beginning of the Great Depression, the emphasis would shift once again. In the face of mounting economic problems, protecting American morality became less of a government priority. In 1933 the United States repealed Prohibition and horses began racing in California again. The border vice districts lost their competitive advantage. The following year, Lázaro Cárdenas became president of Mexico, ushering in a period of heightened morality regulations and sweeping nationalist reforms in Mexico. In 1935 Cárdenas ordered all Mexican casinos to close. Not long after the Mexican government appropriated the lavish Agua Caliente resort and transformed it into an industrial trade school.[93]

While neither vice nor the vice districts disappeared completely, new issues rose to prominence on the border. As the Depression created a sudden surplus of labor across North America, both Mexicans and Americans turned on the immigrants in their midst and began to expel them across the boundary line. By the early 1930s immigration control would begin to take its place as the central concern of state policy along the border.

Chapter Seven

INSIDERS/OUTSIDERS

Managing Immigration at the Border

IN JULY 1925, while tourists rushed into Tijuana, Charles Geck, a seventy-three-year-old U.S. citizen who had been living and mining in Sonora for sixteen years, filed an angry complaint with the U.S. Bureau of Immigration. Geck was furious with the chief of the Naco, Arizona, immigration office, Nick D. Collear, who he claimed had detained respectable Mexican women, subjected them to "vulgar and indecent" questioning, and prevented them from crossing the border. When Geck intervened on behalf of one of these women, Collear demanded he produce documents to prove he was a U.S. citizen. When he could not, Collear denied him entry as well. Collear, Geck concluded, was a "pot-bellied swell-headed fool" who was "more of an autocrat than the Czar of Russia, or the sultan of Turkey ever was."[1]

Like most border people, Geck was accustomed to crossing the border without the interference of immigration officers. At the time of his run-in with Collear he "had been crossing the line now for the last 16 or 18 years, and had crossed at almost every port along the line," without officials asking for proof of citizenship. While Geck acknowledged that he had "had a passport when we were at war, when everyone was required to carry a passport," he no longer carried it. Geck conceded that Collear had the authority to ask for documents and detain immigrants, but insisted that such strict enforcement was both contrary to the intended purpose of immigration laws and out of step with local practice on the border. To prove it, he cited examples of the discretionary power shown by customs and immigration officials in other contexts and at other ports of entry. "While the strict letter of the law has not been complied with," wrote Geck, "still the object and intention of the law has been fulfilled, And that is what I call useing [*sic*] good common horse sence [*sic*] or in other words useing [*sic*] your head."[2]

The files of the U.S. Bureau of Immigration are filled with similar, if more restrained, complaints from businesspeople and other border crossers frustrated by the enforcement of immigration laws, along with the responses of equally aggravated immigration officers. Their letters echoed concerns about the effects of national laws on transborder traffic that government agents had been hearing for at least a half-century. These grumblings were an integral part of the process of complaint and accommodation by which government officials and private citizens negotiated sovereignty along the border. As growing numbers of immigration inspectors took their place on the boundary line in the first three decades of the twentieth century, they were increasingly incorporated into this process of negotiation.

An important part of that process was the ability of the government's representatives to use their discretion in interpreting and implementing immigration law. Federal immigration laws reflected aspirations of a conditional immigration barrier—a border that would exclude undesirable immigrants but let in citizens, local crossers, and much-needed immigrant laborers. The effectiveness of this conditional border relied on the ability of individual immigration officers to distinguish insiders from outsiders even as the official definitions of those categories changed.

Deciding who could cross the border in the early twentieth century was not a simple matter. Since the U.S. government enacted the first federal immigration law restricting the entry of convicts and prostitutes in 1875, both the United States and Mexico gradually added laws that made crossing the border increasingly complicated. Much as treaties established territorial limits, immigration laws delimited categories of people (citizens, local crossers, contract laborers, Chinese, prostitutes, anarchists, and many more) and dictated which taxes, inspections, literacy tests, and exclusions would apply to them. It was up to the immigration inspectors on the line to try to determine who belonged in each category and how to enforce the laws. Inspectors' discretion, rather than undermining federal immigration laws, was integral to their enforcement. Ideally, inspectors could use their discretion to adapt federal laws to local conditions and changing circumstances and to reduce conflict between state officials and the people they policed. Collear's inflexibility was the exception that proved the rule. In carrying out their duties, immigration officers not only depended on statutes but also on their personal knowledge of local people, their assumptions about race and class, and their interpretation of the intent of the laws. Immigration enforcement on the border, as Geck noted, was as much a matter of common sense as of federal law.

Common sense, however, is not historically consistent. Immigration officials' discretionary power not only reflected their sensitivity to local conditions but also shifting national circumstances. Changes in the law, economic conditions, the demographics of transborder immigration, and the officers' assumptions determined how immigrants and other border crossers moved across the boundary line at any given time.

Of particular importance during this time period was the changing status of Mexicans within the United States. While immigration controls first emerged in the late nineteenth century, these early laws had little effect on most people living on the border. Early U.S. immigration restrictions targeted Asian and European immigrants; Mexicans were explicitly exempted from the most restrictive measures. The Mexican government also enacted immigration restrictions, but these laws had a minimal effect on transborder traffic. Laws prohibiting the entry of prostitutes, vagrants, and other groups affected some Americans and Mexicans, and passport laws and nighttime closing hours inconvenienced Americans and Mexicans alike. But the majority of U.S. and Mexican citizens, like Geck and the Mexican women whose stories he related, expected to cross the border without anyone standing in their way.

Beginning in the 1910s, however, as hundreds of thousands of Mexicans fled north from the Mexican Revolution, new U.S. immigration laws made Mexican immigrants subject to inspections, fees, and restrictions for reasons ranging from disease and poverty to illiteracy and immorality. These new laws made it possible for U.S. officials to restrict Mexican immigration across the border, but did not lead to immediate wholesale change. Rather, for the majority of the 1910s and 1920s, Americans' demand for Mexican migrant laborers prompted immigration officials to interpret these laws loosely. It was only with the onset of the Great Depression that both Americans and Mexicans cracked down on immigrants in response to the economic crisis, restricting immigration in an attempt to reduce competition for jobs and limit the number of people making claims on government relief. While Mexicans once again targeted Chinese immigrants in northern Mexico, anti-immigrant sentiment in the United States focused on Mexicans. Using the already existing laws and state apparatus to severely restrict Mexican immigration and expel many ethnic Mexicans living in the United States, U.S. officials demonstrated the power they had at their discretion and, consequently, the vulnerability of ethnic Mexicans within U.S. society. Many Mexicans, who had always been insiders, if not the equals of Anglo-Americans, on the border, suddenly became outsiders in the eyes of immigration officials. While the U.S. government's willingness to admit Mexican immigrants would ebb and flow in response to labor demands for the remainder of the twentieth century, Mexican immigration would remain subject to immigration controls that were not always enforced, but could be at any time.

THE CREATION OF AN IMMIGRATION CONTROL
APPARATUS ON THE BORDER

Many readers may find it hard to imagine that restricting Mexican immigration has not always been the central feature of state control on the U.S.-Mexico border. But in fact, as the previous chapters have shown, immigration was only one arena—and a fairly late developing one at that—of state control along the boundary line. It was not until the turn of the twentieth century that both nation-states gradually began to restrict the entry of immigrants on the border. When they finally did so they both brought new, transnational ideas about the need to control migration to the local context of the border and borrowed from already-established methods of controlling movement and negotiating sovereignty along the boundary line.

The changes in immigration enforcement along the border were tied to the expansion of global migration that swept across the globe in the late nineteenth and early twentieth centuries. The far-reaching forces that brought capitalists to the borderlands to develop railroads, mines, and ranches in the late nineteenth century also set migrants in motion around the world. The men and women who crossed the border in the early twentieth century came from both nearby Sonoran towns and far-away cities and villages in Europe and Asia. In December 1906, for instance, Florencio Silva, a thirty-two-year-old laborer from Querétaro, Mexico, crossed the border in transit from Magdalena, Sonora, to Mowry, Arizona. A few weeks later Ilia Popovich, a twenty-four-year-old miner who was originally from the small town of Virpazar, Montenegro, made a similar trip from Cananea to Bisbee through the Naco port of entry. On Christmas day a group of Japanese immigrant laborers crossed at Naco en route to Los Angeles. While they came from different places and had different destinations, these immigrants were part of a shared experience of global migration that began to transform the border in the early twentieth century.[3]

This global flow of migrants confronted a phalanx of newly empowered states intent on protecting capitalist development and public health. As they raised barriers to immigration, many states revealed their view of immigrants as no more than laborers whose supply they had to regulate and bodies that carried germs, behaviors, and ideas against which they had to protect their citizens. Characterized as racially inferior and unfree "coolie" laborers, Chinese immigrants were among the first to face restrictive laws not only in the United States but also in Australia, New Zealand, Canada, and Hawai'i as well. Along with the restrictions on Chinese immigration established in the Chinese Exclusion Acts beginning in 1882, the U.S. Congress gradually expanded immigration restrictions to a long list of undesirable immigrants including prostitutes, convicts, polygamists, anarchists, and contract laborers. These U.S. immigration laws focused on regulating the labor force and creating a physically and politically healthy workforce to labor in the fields and factories of the United States' booming capitalist economy. The Mexican government, although notably more welcoming of Asian immigrants, also enacted immigration laws to bar those who it believed were ill-suited for work and citizenship. The Mexican Immigration Act of 1908 prohibited the entry of prostitutes, anarchists, beggars, criminals, and any foreigners who were too young, too old, too disabled, or too sick to work.[4]

The western U.S.-Mexico border was initially at the periphery of this transformation in immigration laws. Most immigrants arrived in the United States and Mexico by sea, so early immigration enforcement concentrated on ocean ports. As I discussed in chapter four, it was only after excluded Chinese immigrants turned to the border to evade restrictions at Pacific ports of entry that U.S. officials began to monitor immigration across the western boundary line. Even then, the Department of Commerce and Labor, which oversaw immigration, was slow to adjust to the new conditions. As of 1906 inspectors at ports of entry on the western U.S.-Mexico border used immigrant manifest forms that included spaces for the name of the ship on which each immigrant had arrived and from where it had sailed. Along with other entrants at Arizona ports of entry, Florencio Silva, the Mexican miner who walked across the border at Nogales in 1906, was recorded as traveling via the "S.S. foot sailing from Mexico."[5]

After the turn of the twentieth century, as more Chinese immigrants attempted to cross the border, the U.S. Bureau of Immigration dispatched immigration inspectors first to man border ports of entry and then to patrol outlying areas on horseback. These efforts to restrict Chinese immigration across the border created the foundation of a state apparatus of immigration control along the boundary line, but the handful of so-called Chinese inspectors were unconcerned with the vast majority of border crossings. Local Mexicans, Americans, and Native peoples moved back and forth across the boundary line along with investors from New York and Los Angeles and immigrant laborers from Europe and the Mexican interior. Within the diverse and fluid transborder communities that flourished along the boundary line in the years before the Mexican Revolution, Chinese immigrants were among the few people who could not cross the border free from the interference of immigration officials.

It was not until the 1910s that this situation began to change as a result of the combined effects of new U.S. immigration restrictions and an increase in Mexican migration. Beginning in 1910 the violence and economic instability of the Mexican Revolution prompted unprecedented numbers of Mexicans to migrate to the United States. Although incomplete U.S. immigration records make it impossible to determine exactly how many Mexicans crossed the border, historians have estimated that nearly 1.5 million Mexicans relocated to the United States at some time between 1910 and 1920.[6] At the same time that the Mexican Revolution unleashed this wave of migrants, the U.S. Congress passed a new comprehensive Immigration Act over President Woodrow Wilson's veto in 1917. Influenced by anti-immigration agitation and concerns about wartime security, the Immigration Act of 1917 imposed a literacy test and eight-dollar head tax on immigrants and reasserted the prohibition against contract laborers. Although mainly intended to restrict immigration from southern and eastern Europe, this act for the first time applied to Mexican migrants as well.[7]

These new restrictions and the growing numbers of Mexican migrants, many of them made destitute by the revolution, transformed the dynamics of immigration and the states' attempts to regulate it on the border. Mexican migration in itself was nothing new. Although statistics are impossible to compile because the U.S. government did not systematically record Mexican land entries until 1908, Mexicans had immigrated across the border as long as the boundary line had existed. The first mass migrations of Mexicans to the United States dated from the California gold rush when many Sonorans fled their unstable state and flocked north to the mines. By the late nineteenth century, Mexican migration had begun to increase as the same capitalist forces that transformed the borderlands consolidated landholding in Mexico and created a burgeoning population of landless laborers who were drawn north to work in the fields, mines, and railroad camps of the United States.[8] What was new was not Mexican immigration but the scale of that movement and the U.S. government's growing desire to regulate it.

Following the enactment of the Immigration Act of 1917, Mexican migrants who had historically been able to cross the border freely became subject to registration, literacy tests, head taxes, and health inspections. Immigrants who could not afford the eight-dollar head tax crowded into Mexican border cities. To prevent overcrowding, Sonoran state officials published the U.S. immigration requirements in hopes that Mexican workers who were unable to fulfill them would stay away from the border.[9]

Wartime passport laws further complicated the process of crossing the border. In April 1917, President Wilson authorized a set of new regulations requiring both aliens and U.S. citizens to carry passports for the duration of the war. With the Passport Control Act of 1918 Congress added its legislative stamp of approval to these laws, giving the president sweeping powers to restrict both aliens and U.S. citizens from entering or departing from U.S. territory. Since the Mexican government placed few restrictions on the entry of Americans, the Passport Control Act, which remained in effect until 1921, was the first law to substantially limit Americans' ability to cross the boundary line in either direction.

The new regulations inconvenienced border crossers and government officials alike. "Every day there are two lines of people in front of the consulate.... These lines begin to form by six in the morning and at times there are two to three hundred people in front of the office," wrote the U.S. Consul at Nogales. "I have had to employ a guard especially to keep them in order, so great is their desire to secure a passport visa.... I have had to put on three typists, girls, to take care of the applications. I have not been to bed a night this week before midnight and more than one time have still been in the office at one in the morning." "I am sure," he concluded, "that there are ten or twelve thousand 'crossings' daily, what with the recrossings, the hundreds of automobiles of electric light, telephone and ice men, of the several railroad and switch engine crews, of delivery boys from the stores, of people who cross over to Mexico to the restaurants and to the municipal markets, etc., etc."[10]

Seeking a solution to the bureaucratic back-ups and growing frustration, immigration officials adjusted enforcement to accommodate local conditions. On an official level, the Immigration Service seized on a provision of the 1917 immigration law that allowed for the issuance of border-crossing cards to local people. While these cards, like passports, were government documents bearing the names and photographs of their holders, they were much easier to obtain. Unlike passports, which could only be issued by State Department officials, border-crossing cards were dispensed by immigration officers to Americans and Mexicans who desired to cross the border for "legitimate" purposes.[11]

In addition to issuing border-crossing cards, immigration officials also adjusted their enforcement to accommodate local traffic. Immigration officers on the border relied on their familiarity with border people to limit the extent to which they inconvenienced local crossers. When a Nogales dentist appealed a local inspector's decision, the commissioner general of immigration deferred to his inspectors. "The Bureau replied that it would not undertake to consider here in Washington, many miles distant from the Mexican border ports, appeals from decisions rendered by the immigration officers," the commissioner general explained. "The immigration officers on the ground are in position to render prompt and just decisions."[12] However, not all higher officials were as understanding of local accommodations. In early 1918, A. A. Musgrave, an immigration inspector at Calexico, received a letter from his supervisor in El Paso criticizing him for failing to check passports. Musgrave defended his job performance. The people in question, Musgrave explained, "not only cross every day, but most of them many times each day, and the officers really do know them at a glance." "To a person unaccustomed to the traffic and to the population," he continued, "it would seem as if the line were 'Wide Open.' This, however, is far from the fact."[13] By 1918 the border was certainly not "wide open," but neither was it "closed," despite passport controls and the growing list of immigration restrictions. Even during periods characterized by crackdowns on border crossings, local government officials used their discretion to make the border a conditional barrier that enabled locals to cross more easily than outsiders.

In addition to the need to accommodate local crossers, regional labor demands also created pressure for local and federal immigration officials to ease the movement of migrant laborers across the border as well. Policy makers not only relied on immigration officers to use their discretion on the line but also adjusted the laws governing immigration to fulfill the economic demand for immigrant laborers without angering anti-immigrant political factions. Almost immediately after Congress passed the 1917 Immigration Act in May, wartime labor demands led the U.S. secretary of labor to waive the contract labor clause, literacy test, and head tax. With the war cutting off the supply of European immigrants, employers in the U.S. Southwest desperately needed Mexican migrants to build railroads and perform agricultural labor. They employed labor contractors to recruit workers along the border and send them north to fields and railroad camps. Contractors created such a drain on Mexican labor in Sonora that state officials instructed municipal authorities to bar them from operating in national territory and to try to prevent local laborers from leaving for the United States.[14]

The conclusion of the First World War brought an end to the immediate labor crisis but ultimately did little to slow the flow of Mexican migrants across the boundary line. In response to the political pressure of southwestern employers who demanded a steady supply of Mexican migrant laborers, the U.S. Congress crafted immigration laws that allowed for immigration from countries within the Western Hemisphere and led to increases in immigration across the country's land borders.

The continued growth in Mexican immigration occurred at the same time that the U.S. government severely restricted immigration from almost every other part of the world. Following World War I, the postwar economic downturn and the specter of the renewal of unchecked immigration prompted public protest and legislative action. The U.S. Congress responded first by enacting the Immigration Act of 1921, an emergency measure that capped total immigration at 387,803 and restricted immigration from any European country to 3 percent of the number of foreign-born from that nation living in the United States in 1910. Three years later, under the Johnson-Reed Immigration Act of 1924, Congress further lowered the number of admissible immigrants to 186,437 and limited immigration from every nation in the world, with the exception of those in the Western Hemisphere (including Mexico), to 2 percent of the population of that nationality that had been residing in the United States in 1890. Influenced by Progressive Era notions of racial and ethnic differences, these acts established a formula that sharply reduced the

number of immigrants from southern and eastern Europe and marked
the culmination of restrictionist pressures that had been building since
the U.S. Congress first began to restrict immigration in the 1870s.[15]

Although Mexican immigrants were exempt from the quotas, it was
not because lawmakers or employers believed they should be welcomed
as equals into U.S. society. To the contrary, Mexican Americans and
Mexican immigrants alike were subject to racist attacks and racial subordination both on the floor of Congress and in cities, towns, mines,
fields, and factories across the United States. Although the Treaty of
Guadalupe Hidalgo had guaranteed citizenship rights to Mexicans living in the United States, few Anglo-Americans treated Mexicans as their
equals. In the half-century after the Mexican-American War, Anglo-
Americans used law, coercion, and violence to wrest land, resources,
and political and economic power away from the ethnic Mexican inhabitants of the southwestern United States. Class and local conditions
lessened the effects of racism for some wealthier and better-connected
ethnic Mexicans, particularly in binational border communities. But as
more Mexican immigrants arrived in the United States in the 1910s and
1920s, they not only became incorporated into this racial hierarchy, but
also reinforced Americans' characterizations of Mexicans as poor, un-
educated, unsanitary, and racially inferior. People of Mexican descent
were relegated to low-wage, unskilled jobs and substandard housing
and government services.[16]

In some cases prejudice against ethnic Mexicans took violent forms.
During the Mexican Revolution, events in Texas nearly devolved into a
race war as transborder raiding and rumors of the 1915 Plan de San
Diego, a plot calling for Mexicans on both sides of the border to conquer
Texas, spurred Anglo-Americans to violently lash out at ethnic Mexicans, resulting in hundreds of deaths in the lower Rio Grande Valley.[17]
The Ku Klux Klan also targeted ethnic Mexicans throughout southwestern communities with activities ranging from restricting Mexicans from
professional careers and politics to torture and murder. In San Diego a
woman remembered seeing Klansmen drag, lynch, whip, and burn Mexican laborers. Former Klansman Wayne Kenaston Jr. noted that "their
main zeal was in 'chasing the wetbacks across the border.'"[18] These attacks, like so much of the hostility directed at ethnic Mexicans, blurred
the lines between nativism and racism, targeting people of Mexican descent sometimes on the basis of their race, sometimes because of their
immigration status, but more often than not because of some combination of the two.

Yet for all the ways that Anglo-Americans' racism shaped ethnic Mexicans' lives, it initially had little effect on how Mexican immigrants
crossed the border. It was not until the 1920s that politicians began to

incorporate anti-Mexican sentiments into a concerted movement to restrict immigration from Mexico. In Congress, Texas Democrat John C.
Box led a faction that called for the inclusion of Mexicans within the
quota system, arguing that Mexican immigrants would undermine the
U.S. free labor system and degrade the racial purity of white America.
"Mexican labor is not free; it is not well paid; its standard of living is
low," wrote Box. "The yearly admission of several scores of thousands
from just across the Mexican border tends constantly to lower the wages
and conditions of men and women of America who labor with their
hands in industry, in transportation, and in agriculture." Noting that immigration laws were intended to protect "American racial stock from
further degradation or change through mongrelization," Box went on to
describe Mexican immigrants as a "blend of low-grade Spaniard, pe-
onized Indian, and negro slave."[19]

Despite these arguments, the forces that favored unrestricted Mexican
immigration won out throughout the better part of the 1920s as employers of Mexican migrants lobbied effectively to insure that their labor supply was not curtailed. Yet even as politicians and employers insisted that
Mexican laborers did not pose a threat to free labor and white racial
purity, they embraced strikingly similar ideas about Mexicans' race.
Much like their political opponents, supporters of unrestricted Mexican
immigration conflated race and class in their characterization of Mexican immigrants as racially inferior peons who were predisposed to mi-
gratory labor. Rather than refuting the racist characterizations of Mexicans, lawmakers and employers simply deployed racialized notions of
Mexican inferiority to demonstrate that they posed no threat to U.S. society. They argued that Mexicans' innate submissiveness, willingness to
work for low wages, and clannishness made them ideal laborers who
would stick to themselves and return to Mexico once their work was
done. The proximity of the border and ease with which Mexicans could
return to Mexico contributed to characterizations of Mexicans as unthreatening "birds of passage."[20]

Thanks to these arguments and the continued demand for migrant laborers, lawmakers left Mexicans, along with all Western Hemisphere immigrants, outside the quota system. While the quota acts barred the entry
of hundreds of thousands of immigrants, only general restrictions and
the new requirement that all immigrants pay $10 to attain an immigra-
tion visa prior to entry applied to Mexican immigrants. Between 1920
and 1928, U.S. immigration officials recorded the entry of nearly half a
million immigrants from Mexico.[21]

Even as they crossed the border, these migrants entered the United
States under the shadow of widespread assumptions about their racial
inferiority and within the context of a burgeoning immigration control

apparatus along the border. The same racialized arguments that made Mexican migrant laborers seem unthreatening also began to change the way all ethnic Mexicans experienced the border. In making the case for allowing the entry of Mexican laborers, employers and lawmakers naturalized the association of Mexican immigrants with unskilled, low-paying, manual labor. As hundreds of thousands of Mexican migrants crossed the border, both the majority of Americans and a growing number of immigration officials on the boundary line increasingly perceived Mexicans not as familiar and unthreatening members of a broadly defined transborder community but as subordinate foreigners whose passage across the line was contingent on their labor.

This changing perception was apparent in the way immigration inspectors treated Mexican migrants on the border. Although immigration officials did not have a congressional mandate to restrict Mexican immigration, concerns that immigrants would spread disease or become public burdens led U.S. officials to begin subjecting Mexican migrants to increasingly invasive interrogations and health inspections as early as the 1910s. Mexican immigrants and local crossers alike complained that inspectors' attempts to determine whether they were morally, physically, and economically eligible for entry were intrusive and offensive. Beyond the required literacy tests, immigration inspectors pried into crossers' work, family, and sexual histories. The most vocal criticism was reserved for the health inspections begun in 1917 by the U.S. Public Health Service at border ports of entry. With the goal of preventing the spread of typhus, U.S. Public Health officials required Mexican border crossers to surrender their baggage and clothing for sterilization, strip naked, and endure intrusive examinations and disinfection processes.[22]

Facing inspections, head taxes, and visa charges, many Mexican migrants chose to cross the border outside of legal channels. Unauthorized immigration became an increasingly attractive and practical option for Mexican migrants confronting long waits, examinations, and crossing fees at authorized ports of entry. The supervisor of the El Paso district admitted that "it is oftentimes necessary for hundreds, even thousands, of [immigrants] to wait for days and weeks before their turn at immigration inspection arrives," and as a result they exhausted their "slender resources" and "though willing to stand inspection and pay head tax, they are forced to resort to illegal entry in order to avoid starvation."[23] According to the commissioner general of immigration the enforcement of the literacy test and head tax "naturally stimulated illegal immigration to such an extent that, as already stated, it is not possible even to estimate the number of Mexicans who enter the country without inspection over the long and largely unguarded stretches of border that lie between stations of our service."[24] Along the Arizona-Sonora border, a U.S. intelligence agent reported that tens of thousands of "penniless and thinly clad" Mexicans were crossing the border surreptitiously, causing a serious problem "in all border cities where they have become objects of charity and public charge."[25]

Mexicans were not the only immigrants crossing the border illegally. The quota laws, like the Chinese Exclusion Acts before them, prompted many European and Asian immigrants barred from legally entering the United States to continue to turn to the border as an alternative to legal entry through U.S. seaports. Following the enactment of the Immigration Act of 1921, the U.S. commissioner general of immigration reported that immigrants who could not obtain visas or wanted to evade the quota restrictions "have proceeded to both Canada and Mexico in large numbers," where they attempted "to gain admission by stealth, usually with the aid of hired smugglers."[26] With each new measure more immigrants turned to illegal entry—and many of them chose to do so across the Mexican border. While most European immigrants initially sought access across the more proximate eastern half of the boundary, fear of detection gradually induced them to attempt entry as far west as California. In 1925 the head of the Los Angeles Immigration District explained, "as has been the case in all immigration experience, each added restrictive measure increased the incentive to illegal entry and to smuggling; so with the act of 1924 we find that smuggling activities and efforts of individuals to evade immigration examination have advanced apace."[27]

In the face of this influx many immigration officials expressed serious doubts about their ability to control immigration at the border. Noting that the few immigration inspectors were "wholly—pitifully—insufficient even to discourage the rush of proscribed aliens," the supervisor of the El Paso immigration district opined in 1923 that "for the hundreds arrested after illegal entry thousands entered the country from Mexico without being detected and safely reached interior points."[28] A year later he explained that "it would require a large-sized army to effectively patrol the border line of approximately 1,000 miles so as to prevent illegal entries of aliens, and it would be useless to station a handful of immigration officers on the line expecting them to prevent illegal entries or even to apprehend aliens in the act of entering without inspection."[29] Given the length of the line and the impossibility of preventing every unauthorized entry at the border, some agents shifted their attention to the transportation links that connected the border to cities and towns throughout the United States. "It is not hard for aliens to cross the international boundary line," concluded the supervisor of the El Paso district. "The difficulty lies in getting away from the border towns on the American side, as the aliens must do sooner or later, since those places have little or no employment to offer them."[30] Even as immigration officials shifted some of their enforcement efforts from seaports to the boundary line, they were forced to acknowledge the strategic limitations of policing the border.

By the mid-1920s the work of tracking down immigrants who crossed the border outside of legal channels increasingly fell to the newly created Border Patrol. In conjunction with the Johnson-Reed Immigration Act of 1924, the U.S. Congress appropriated $1 million to employ 472 men to patrol both the U.S.-Mexico and U.S.-Canada borders. This was a substantial increase in the border immigration force that prior to that time had never numbered more than seventy-five. To organize the new force, the Immigration Service chose Clifford Alan Perkins, who had been working as a Chinese inspector on the U.S.-Mexico border since 1911. Expanding on the mounted guards who patrolled the Mexican border, the Border Patrol supplemented the immigration inspectors at ports of entry by patrolling both the line itself and interior areas. While immigration inspectors were still the only officials authorized to determine the admissibility of aliens, border patrolmen could detain anyone they expected of smuggling or entering the country outside of legal channels. This expansive role, as well as a preference for recruits with a law enforcement background, meant that the patrolmen acted less like bureaucrats and more like police. "While the primary duty of this force is to prevent the unlawful entry of aliens," explained the commissioner general of immigration in 1925, "the very nature of the work of the officers comprising it throws them into contact with the lawless element which infests the borders."[31] The Border Patrol quickly became a symbol of national authority and border enforcement along the boundary line.

Border Patrol agents, like other government officials on the border, also quickly learned that enforcing national laws was rarely the clear-cut matter they expected. For instance, in the winter of 1925-26 Border Patrol agents headquartered at El Centro in the Imperial Valley began raiding ranches in the vicinity, picking up immigrants found to be illegally in the country and sending them back across the border. While there is no record of how the Mexican workers, many of whom had been living in the United States for some time, felt about being rounded up and returned to Mexico, immigration officials did document the displeasure of local ranchers who were left without their laborers. The local immigration officers' responses to the ranchers' objections provides a telling example of how economic demands and local negotiations continued to influence immigration enforcement on the border. Reporting on the situation to his superior in Washington, DC, I. F. Wixon, the inspector in charge at Calexico, explained how local conditions made the current enforcement measures ineffective. "It is physically impossible with the means at our disposal to prevent Mexicans from seeping across the line," wrote Wixon, "nor is any material result accomplished by placing such aliens back across the line . . . as the aliens are back at their employment, often times, almost as soon as the officer has returned to his official station." Rather than have Border Patrol agents and immigrants continue to engage in this "'hide and seek' proposition," Wixon developed a plan with the cooperation of local ranchers that would allow Mexican immigrants already in the country, with the help of their employers, to register with immigration officials and set up an installment plan to compensate for their unpaid visa fees and head taxes. "While the plan is not all that could be desired, since it contemplates a lack of immediate action upon the part of our service in dispossessing aliens found to be unlawfully in the country," Wixon explained, "it is the best, nevertheless, that has suggested itself to me. . . . [I]t is one, however, which I believe eventually will operate to the good of our service and to the enforcement of immigration laws."[32] As a local representative of the nation-state, Wixon used his discretion to adopt a plan that both appeased local ranchers and held true to the spirit of U.S. immigration laws that had been developed to tax, but not halt, the movement of Mexican migrant laborers.

Arrangements like these reflected the continued importance of local negotiations in border enforcement, but also revealed the growing concern with controlling the movement of Mexican migrants. The battles over immigration on the border had begun as multinational affairs pitting U.S. patrolmen against immigrants from Asia and Europe. But by the late 1920s, with the success of campaigns to enforce immigration quotas and the simultaneous increase in Mexican migration, the border dynamic took on an increasingly binational character. By 1928 almost 99 percent of the recorded entries across the U.S.-Mexico border were Mexicans.[33]

In 1929, on the eve of the Great Depression, more than forty thousand immigrants crossed the border from Mexico and joined the hundreds of thousands of their compatriots who were already living and working in the United States.[34] They did so within the context of immigration laws, Border Patrol agents, and the racist assumptions of Anglo-Americans that threatened to bar their entry at any moment. Before the year was out that gate came crashing down.

DEPRESSION AND DEPORTATIONS

With the collapse of the U.S. economy in 1929, the appetite for Mexican migrant laborers, and with it the justifications for facilitating Mexican immigration, evaporated in the United States. Opponents of Mexican immigration renewed their calls for restriction, and government officials began to look on the Mexican migrant population as little more than surplus labor and a drain on already overtaxed public services. The U.S. government quickly mustered existing border controls to prevent new entries. There was no need for new laws or structures. Much like the fences dividing border towns, immigration laws, once enacted, became part of the border control apparatus that government officials could use strategically. U.S. officials had used their discretion to facilitate the flow of Mexican migrant laborers in the 1920s, but, in the context of an economic crisis, they demonstrated that they could just as easily use their judgment to make transborder movement more difficult. Stepping up their enforcement of existing laws as they applied to Mexican migrants, government officials not only made it more difficult for new migrants to cross the border but also criminalized Mexicans as "illegal aliens" and encouraged, coerced, and forced hundreds of thousands of Mexican nationals and U.S. citizens of Mexican descent to move to Mexico.

For its part, while the Mexican government worked to accommodate the repatriated migrants it did not extend the same assistance to its own immigrant populations. Like the United States, Mexico increased immigration restrictions and lashed out at northern Mexico's vulnerable ethnic Chinese population. Before long, unwanted immigrants crowded both sides of the border, testifying by their presence to the limits of national inclusion and inscribing the border as a more meaningful boundary of national citizenship.

As the demand for Mexican immigrant workers disappeared with the beginning of the Great Depression, many Americans, who had only grudgingly accepted Mexican immigrants because of their labor value, argued that they had no place in an economy struggling with unemployment. Viewed as expendable labor and barred from many government support and work programs that were limited to citizens, Mexican immigrants felt the effects of the Depression disproportionately. Rather than sympathizing, many Anglo-Americans blamed Mexican immigrants for taking work from U.S. citizens and lashed out at both Mexican nationals and U.S. citizens of Mexican descent.[35]

This hostility was apparent in many border towns. In Douglas, a group of men sent a protest to Secretary of Labor Frances Perkins when they heard that Phelps Dodge was delivering flour to the Mexican consul's office "to feed alien Mexicans, imported to [be] peon American labor" while American laborers were being cut off.[36] In Nogales, where large numbers of Mexican nationals resided on the Mexican side of the boundary line but crossed the border to work, the Nogales Labor Protective Association pressured government officials to use visa regulations to deny Mexican workers access to jobs. Expressing solidarity with the association, the governor of Arizona, George Hunt, asserted that "the immigration restrictions should be strictly enforced to prevent foreign labor crossing the line to compete with citizen labor. . . . Local citizens, regardless of their race or color, should receive every protection by the Immigration Department to insure their having preference in what little work is available."[37]

In response to these attitudes and with the intention of limiting the number of people on public support, the U.S. government restricted Mexican immigration. State Department officials began to strictly enforce the requirements that every immigrant pay a visa fee and pass a literacy test. Embracing the long-standing provision of U.S. immigration law that denied the entry of anyone likely to become a public charge, U.S. consuls turned visa seekers away, in the words of the commissioner general of immigration, "in light of the reduced opportunities for self-supporting employment in the United States."[38] Facing these restrictions and the likelihood that they would no longer be able to find work in the United States, far fewer Mexicans chose to cross the border. Between 1928 and 1932 the number of Mexicans who immigrated to the United States fell from 61,622 to 2,058.[39]

As they had in the past, some border-town Americans complained about the heightened crossing restrictions. Despite the economic downturn—in fact, in some cases because of it—many Americans living and doing business in border towns remained dependent on transborder commerce. Businessmen in Nogales, Arizona, protested that "the presence of the immigration officers in the center of the city retards trade as thousands of people fear to cross the border from the west coast of Mexico to make their purchases in local business establishments."[40] With the Depression already taking a toll on many borderlands businesses, merchants were particularly concerned that immigration enforcement would further impede transborder trade. "We are at this time really feeling the depression," wrote one Nogales booster, "mines are closed, cattle no value, our high tariff which our government has put on followed by a Mexican tariff to retaliate and the immigration restrictions have absolutely put us on the bum." Like earlier antirestriction campaigns, this plea emphasized the economic contribution made by Mexican border crossers. However, it also drew a clear class distinction between Mexican shoppers who the immigrant inspectors should allow to enter and Mexican workers who they should turn away. This was no defense of Mexican immigrants. "I don't mean to allow the Mexicans to enter and reside in our country, but to let them come into our border towns and do their purchasing without having to go thru a lot of red tape," he explained. "We do not care whether they are physically fit or can read and write in order that they may cross the border for a few hours to do their shopping and spend their money."[41] Yet immigration officials remained unconvinced. "The purchasing power of the average Mexican has dwindled to the barest necessities of life," explained the El Paso Immigration District's acting director in 1931. "[M]ost of the peon class of Mexicans are barely able to earn a living, and the plain facts are that they have no money to buy anything and consequently no reason to cross to the American side."[42]

More than charity cases, many of these Mexican immigrants were also denounced as criminals. Although labor demands during the mid-1920s had led many Americans to make allowances for Mexican migrants who had crossed the border outside of legal channels, with the retraction of the labor market, U.S. officials increasingly looked upon them as illegal aliens who were subject to arrest and deportation and who often were treated as criminals. Central to this process was a law Congress passed in March 1929 that made it a felony for immigrants who had been deported to attempt to reenter the United States. In crossing the boundary line outside of official channels or without the proper paperwork a person was transformed into a criminal—an illegal immigrant.[43]

If caught in the act of illegal entry or found to be living in the United States without having entered through official channels, immigrants faced the option of "voluntary" return or deportation. Seeking to cut relief rolls and competition for jobs, U.S. immigration officials raided immigrant communities and initiated deportation proceedings against thousands of Mexicans. Fear of deportation spread throughout ethnic Mexican communities. A San Diego social worker reported that "the young Mexican-Americans in San Diego are afraid of the Border Patrol uniform and run when they see it. Many make a practice of carrying their birth certificates."[44] The total number of immigrants deported nearly doubled from 9,495 in 1925 to 18,412 in 1931. While Mexicans made up only 18 percent of deportees in 1925, by 1931 they represented almost 46 percent. In addition to those immigrants officially deported, many immigrants when faced with deportation opted instead to "voluntarily" return to Mexico.[45]

In addition to official deportation proceedings, Americans used a variety of methods to encourage and coerce hundreds of thousands of ethnic Mexicans living in the United States to relocate to Mexico. Cities, counties, and charitable organizations across the United States organized transportation, refused welfare, and threatened deportation in order to repatriate both Mexican immigrants and some U.S.-born Mexican Americans. While some Mexican immigrants willingly chose to return to Mexico because of the lack of work in the United States, others were scared into leaving by the growing discrimination and government campaigns targeting undocumented immigrants. After losing his job at the Copper Queen smelter in Douglas in 1931, Isidro Romero took advantage of Phelps Dodge's offer to pay for his family to repatriate to the small village of San Pedro de la Cueva, Sonora, his hometown, where he still owned some farmland.[46] Many other ethnic Mexicans, however, were given very little choice. Throughout the early 1930s immigration officials and law enforcement officers conducted immigration sweeps that rounded up undocumented immigrants and spread fear through ethnic Mexican communities. In February 1931 officials targeted the Plaza in the heart of Los Angeles's Mexican American community, detaining over four hundred people and requiring them to show proof of legal entry and residency. Although only seventeen people were taken into custody, this raid, like others throughout the United States, spread fear of harassment and deportation through the ethnic Mexican population.[47] In Yuma, cotton growers complained that the Border Patrol had taken to "descending on a ranch with trucks, revolvers and handcuffs, making a wholesale seizure of Mexican laborers and sending them over the border." In the Imperial Valley, the Border Patrol agents reportedly "stopped Mexicans indiscriminately and questioned them and, if not satisfied, took them to jail without warrants." Both the Mexican consul and chief of immigration at Mexicali complained that these agents were "rough" and "abusive," employing "swearing, slapping and striking; as well as verbal intimidation, in order to secure 'voluntary departures' or confessions."[48]

Mexican officials protested against the persecution of their nationals and considered boycotting American trade, replacing American workers with Mexicans, or deporting and confiscating the property of Americans doing business in Mexico, but there was little they could do.[49] Despite the fact that many Mexican migrants had established families and communities in the United States, many Americans viewed them primarily as alien laborers who threatened the economic well-being of U.S. citizens and thus needed to be removed. "The alleged hardship to the alien ordered deported, or to his family, is often pleaded as a reason for avoiding removal," explained the commissioner general of immigration, "but there is no comment upon the hardships inflicted upon the American citizen and lawfully resident and law-abiding alien in their exposure to the competition in employment opportunities of the bootlegged aliens—who comprise a large proportion of deportees—to the detriment of American standards and the lowering of wage scales."[50] Between 1929 and 1939, hundreds of thousands of ethnic Mexicans—including U.S.-born children who were U.S. citizens—left the United States for Mexico.[51]

Repatriation and deportation resulted in the mass movement of ethnic Mexicans from throughout the United States to Mexico, where they severely strained the already limited resources of Mexican border towns. The U.S. district director of immigration in charge of the California–Baja California border noted that Mexicans deported to Baja California found themselves "in a portion of Mexico where it is unlikely that they can make a living, and from which travel to their homes in other parts of Mexico is next to impossible without involving travel through the United States." "As these deportees are seldom in possession of any considerable funds," he continued, "they must either revert to pauperism or smuggle back into the United States."[52] The unemployment situation was so severe along the Baja California border that the governor of the Northern District of Baja California asked U.S. officials to divert deportations to the Texas border.[53]

In order to alleviate the hardship on their nationals, Mexican officials tried to facilitate the entry and reincorporation of the repatriates back into Mexico. The Mexican government exempted repatriates from processing fees and allowed the duty-free entry of their possessions, sparing them considerable expense. Hoping to alleviate overcrowding on the border and reduce the welfare responsibilities of border towns, officials also provided free transportation from the boundary line to the Mexican interior. The Mexican Migration Service, after 1932, the National Repatriation Committee, and, after 1934, the National Repatriation Board, spearheaded Mexican efforts to raise money and establish colonies for the repatriates. In 1932 the Mexican Migration Service resolved to develop a program to establish agricultural colonies and provide for the assimilation of the Americanized children who repatriated. However, despite government efforts, the experience of repatriated Mexicans, especially those American-born children for whom Mexico was a foreign country, was often one of social dislocation, difficult adjustments, and economic hardship in depression-stricken Mexico. Some tried to return to the United States but were turned back at the border by U.S. officials who rejected anyone who had been repatriated by the government or a charitable organization.[54]

At the same time that Mexican officials facilitated the return migration of Mexicans from the United States, they also, like the United States, restricted the entry of other immigrants who might compete with their citizens for jobs. In 1931 the Mexican government prohibited the entry of immigrant workers. A year later the U.S. consul general reported that Mexico had adopted "a system of enforcement similar to that now being carried out by American Consuls under the 'public charge' clause. Workers who might replace Mexicans will be rigidly excluded; on the other hand, persons with capital need worry only to the extent that they will have to contribute more than previously to the national revenue."[55] By 1934 immigrants to Mexico were also required to pay a ten-dollar registration fee. To enforce these measures the Mexican government established a Border Defense force that worked in conjunction with migration officials at ports of entry. The enforcement of these restrictive measures was sufficient to cause U.S. immigration officials along the border to ask the Immigration Bureau to better publicize the restrictions to prevent hold-ups on the border.[56]

While these measures targeted laborers in general, they also concentrated on particular national and ethnic groups. As early as 1927 Mexico suspended in "an absolute manner the admission of 'laborer-immigrants' of Syrian, Libanese [sic], Armenian, Palestinian, and Turk origin."[57] Throughout northwestern Mexico, most xenophobia focused on the significant and relatively successful ethnic Chinese communities. The Chinese had first become targets of xenophobia and racism during the Mexican Revolution when Mexican mobs assaulted Chinese and attacked Chinese-owned businesses. While instances of outright violence declined with the subsidence of revolutionary warfare, anti-Chinese sentiment remained rife throughout the northern Mexican borderlands. Throughout the 1920s anti-Chinese committees were active in many northern Mexican cities, calling for immigration restrictions, deportations, sanitary regulations, bans on intermarriage between Chinese and Mexicans, taxes on Chinese-owned businesses, and laws limiting the number of Chinese employees that businesses could hire. Much like the attacks on Mexican immigrants north of the border, anti-Chinese activists espoused racialized notions of Chinese immigrants as threats to public health and competition for Mexican workers. For instance, in 1924 the president of the Nogales Anti-Chinese Committee wrote to the president of the republic complaining that Chinese crossing the border were not subject to sufficient sanitary monitoring and asking that he remove the sanitary agent at the Nogales port of entry who he perceived to be sympathetic to the "yellow elements."[58] In response to these attacks, the Chinese government attempted to intercede on behalf of the Chinese in Mexico. Protesting against a proposed law that would restrict Chinese to certain areas within the state of Sonora, the Chinese president, Sun Yat Sen, wrote to President Álvaro Obregón in 1924 to ask that he "protect treaty rights of Chinese citizens and bring about nullification of [this] harsh law."[59] However, neither the Chinese government nor the Chinese residents in Mexico had much leverage in the face of the powerful strains of xenophobia that were manifested in both Mexican nationalist politics and the burgeoning Mexican labor movement.[60]

With the onset of the Great Depression and the arrival of Mexican repatriates, anti-Chinese sentiment reached a new peak in northern Mexico. Leading Sonoran politicians reinstated discriminatory legislation and demanded that Chinese be expelled to open up jobs for unemployed Mexicans. In Baja California, which had once been a relative refuge for the Chinese, unions, nationalist groups, and anti-Chinese committees also began to call for the strict enforcement of sanitation laws and the expulsion of Chinese. In the face of this persecution, many Chinese de-

FIGURE 7.1. Chinese aliens crossing the border at Nogales, 1931. Courtesy of
the Arizona Historical Society/Tucson, Earl Fallis Photograph Collection, AHS
Photograph #42945.

cided to leave Mexico. In August 1931 members of the Sonoran Chinese
community announced their plans to abandon the state and began liqui-
dating their property.[61]

Some of these fleeing Chinese found themselves in the improbable position of turning to the United States for assistance. Although officially
inadmissible, Chinese opted for arrest and deportation in the United
States rather than persecution in Mexico. Thousands of Chinese fled
across the border and into the custody of U.S. immigration officials. Between October 1931 and February 1932 the U.S. District Court of Arizona at Nogales alone filed arrest proceedings against hundreds of
Chinese individuals for illegal entry.[62] In 1931 the flood of Chinese "practically forced out of Lower California by lack of work and sustenance"
into California caused what the commissioner general of immigration,
Harry Hull, called a "vexatious problem."[63] The crux of the dilemma was
that once these immigrants were taken into American custody, the U.S.
Bureau of Immigration became responsible for their deportation—to
China. Hull elaborated in his report for 1932: "Some of this expelled
class have been able to pay their own transportation to China and so
have legally applied for admission. . . . All the illegal entrants had to be
deported at the expense of this service." Noting that the Mexicans were
responsible for driving the Chinese out and leaving the majority of them
destitute, Hull added, "Of course, those responsible for their expulsion

FIGURE 7.2. Processing Chinese aliens at Nogales, 1931. Courtesy of the Arizona Historical Society/Tucson, Earl Fallis Photograph Collection, AHS Photograph #42947.

from Mexico were fully aware that these orientals would be arrested on this side of the line, and testimony obtained shows that many were brought to points on the border where their apprehension would be certain."[64] While Mexican officials could do little to prevent the United States from repatriating Mexicans, they could use the boundary line to force the U.S. government to help fund the deportation of Mexico's Chinese population.

A photograph taken in 1931 shows a group of Chinese immigrants from Mexico squeezing underneath the chain-link border fence into Nogales, Arizona. Another shot, taken shortly thereafter, shows U.S. immigration officers processing them and taking them into custody. These photographs can tell a number of stories. Focusing on the Chinese immigrants, the story is tragic, a tale of people whose persecution at the hands of Mexicans forced them to abandon their homes for jail and eventual deportation. From the perspective of the U.S. state, these photographs were an illustration of sovereign order. The sequence of events displayed in these photographs portrayed the border as a controlled space in which illegal entry led directly to arrest. In contrast to the rocky, uneven landscape and huddled Chinese, both the fences and immigration officers appear upright and orderly. The authority of the U.S. state was embedded in these spatial controls and, through them, in the border itself.

However, an awareness of the history outside the photographer's lens provides a more complicated story than either of these two interpretations would suggest. While the history of the Chinese in Sonora was indeed tragic, in crossing the border they not only fled their persecutors in Mexico but also forced the U.S. government to fund their deportation to China. Although they had only a limited range of options and none of them were good, the Chinese in Mexico, like the Apaches a half century before them, understood the power of the boundary line and used it in the only way they could. In doing so they proved that state officers did not hold a monopoly on the ability to manipulate the meaning of the boundary line.

The border had become a powerful tool of the states, but its power could also be used to the states' disadvantage. This was the subtext of the orderly narrative of state control depicted in the photographs. Every unauthorized immigrant that the immigration officers took into custody had the potential to cost the U.S. government the significant expense of returning that person to China. Although they did not approach the boundary line with the same power, both uniformed officials who represented the state and the impoverished immigrants who they sought to exclude had to work within the structures, laws, and spaces of the border.

This power had been accumulating on the border since the late nineteenth century. As boundary commissioners, soldiers, customs officers, immigration agents, and fence builders made their mark on the line, both governments gained the power to control transborder movement. By the 1920s the border had become not an absolute barrier but a complicated system of relational space in which spatial controls responded flexibly to a variety of government directives. Based on state prerogatives the border could either be fluid or firm. With the structures already in place, it could shift quickly from allowing Mexicans to cross with ease during times when migrant labor was needed to barring their entries in response to economic anxieties and xenophobia.

This is not, of course, to say that either the United States or Mexico exerted complete control over the border or migration across it. Even further outside the photographer's lens, unauthorized immigrants and local people who did not want to be inconvenienced by the immigration bureaucracy surely crossed the line outside official channels and the scrutiny of the states. The persistence of undocumented immigrants, along with other people who went under, over, through, and around the states' fences, testified to the constant challenges to the states' authority to define the meaning of the border and control who and what crossed it. However, while the states did not run the table, they did determine the rules on the border. Even evasions of national laws implicitly recognized their power. Immigrant smugglers studied the movement of Border Patrolmen in order to evade them. As the Mexican Chinese squeezed under the border fence they knew that it was likely to lead to arrest and deportation. By the 1930s, state control, if never complete, had become the defining feature of spatial organization along the border. The relational spaces of the border shifted with changes in government policy but were always a reflection of those laws. The border then became shaped primarily not by those who lived along and moved across it, but more often by distant politicians and national ideas of racial and national differences. It fell to border communities and businesses to live and work within the confines of these state spaces and to continue a transborder existence that would increasingly be overshadowed by concerns with national border controls.

Conclusion

In 2006 the U.S. Congress passed "an Act to establish operational control over the international land and maritime borders of the United States"—an act better known as the Secure Fence Act of 2006. The latest in the U.S. state's efforts to assert authority over the U.S.-Mexico boundary line, the Secure Fence Act defined "operational control" as "the prevention of all unlawful entries into the United States, including entries by terrorists, other unlawful aliens, instruments of terrorism, narcotics, and other contraband."[1] It was one piece of a broader government agenda that focused on bulking up national security and increasing border enforcement after the September 11, 2001 attacks. Along with the Secure Fence Act, Congress provided for more Border Patrol agents and immigration and customs enforcement officers as well as a new requirement that Americans show proof of citizenship to reenter the United States from Mexico or Canada.[2]

But the focus of the law, as well as the political discourse and public attention surrounding it, was the fence. The debates about the Secure Fence Act raised evocative and politically resonant comparisons—the Great Wall of China, the Berlin Wall, the demilitarized zone between North Korea and South Korea, and the barrier between Israel and the West Bank. Texas congressman Lloyd Doggett even built a speech around Humpty Dumpty and the wall from which he had had his great fall.[3] In 2006, in the months leading up to the vote on the Secure Fence Act, supporters of the bill sent bricks to their congressional representatives and members of the Minutemen Civil Defense Corps, a political organization committed to cracking down on undocumented immigration, began erecting their own fences along the border in hopes of pressuring the U.S. government to do the same.[4] Critics of the fence also made their voices heard, pointing out that building fences would not only be expensive but would also disrupt transborder trade and communities, negatively affect the environment, be an affront to Mexicans, and ultimately be ineffective.[5] Mexican president Vicente Fox called the Secure Fence Act "shameful." His successor, President Felipe Calderón, noted that "humanity committed a grave mistake in building the Berlin Wall. I'm sure that the United States is committing a grave mistake in building this fence."[6]

These various perspectives were echoed on the floor of the U.S. Congress where representatives and senators debated the significance of border fencing. "So we need to have a fence and a wall on this border," insisted Republican congressman Steve King of Iowa, "and we are also watching today as 4 million illegals cross this border a year, that's 11,000 a night. Santa Ana's [sic] army was 6,000 strong. Twice that number every night is coming into America. You can't sit on the border in the dark like I have and listen to that infiltration and believe that you can do it with something called virtual. It has got to be a physical barrier."[7] Another Republican, Arizona congressman J. D. Hayworth agreed:

The graffiti is strewn on the wall at our international border in Nogales. "Borders are scars upon the earth," it reads. No, Mr. Speaker and my colleagues, borders are not scars upon the earth. They are reasonable and necessary lines of political demarcation between nation states to ensure the sovereignty and security of those nation states in the post-9/11 world.

It is absolutely necessary that we move to secure our borders. And as the poet wrote, "good fences make good neighbors."[8]

On the other side of the aisle, some Democrats provided contrasting views of the meanings of borders and fences. "The solution to our problems with immigration will take more than concrete. You cannot build a wall high enough or long enough," Texas Democrat Lloyd Doggett insisted. "History and Humpty-Dumpty teach us that great walls are not the answer."[9] His Texas colleague, Sheila Jackson Lee, agreed, noting that "building walls and fences is not a panacea." Citing the U.S. Customs and Border Protection commissioner, W. Ralph Basham, she explained, "Stemming the flow of illegal immigration and drug trafficking requires a combination of manpower, technology, and infrastructure, not just barriers."[10]

While most opponents of the bill emphasized the need for a more economically efficient and comprehensive response to border control, their protests also revealed a discomfort with the divisive character of fences. Speaking in opposition to the bill, Senator Patrick Leahy cautioned, "Once this fence is built, it will be very difficult to go back, and we will have taken a step down a road that I do not think a civilized and enlightened nation should travel." Arguing in support of a more technologically sophisticated and nuanced approach to controlling transborder movement, Leahy concluded: "Long after the political and cultural storms over immigration pass, this cobbled-together fence will remain an ugly scar, and will serve as a reminder of a very poor decision made out of fear rather than reason."[11]

Despite these protests, the Secure Fence Act easily passed both houses of Congress. Soon after its passage the U.S. Department of Homeland Security began installing barriers along the boundary line. Estimated by some to ultimately cost more than five times the $1.2 billion Congress initially authorized for it, the new border "fence" is in fact a patchwork of physical and technological barriers. It includes parallel lines of steel-mesh walls, concertina wire-topped cyclone fences, vehicle bollards, and an array of surveillance technologies that create a "virtual fence."[12]

As these new barriers go up along many stretches of the border they underscore how much has changed along the western U.S.-Mexico boundary line since its creation in the mid-nineteenth century. While heat and aridity continue to take the lives of hundreds of immigrants each year as they attempt to evade capture by crossing through the desert, most people's experience of the border region is now tempered by irrigation and air conditioning. The transportation woes that once plagued Sylvester Mowry and Ignacio Pesqueira are no longer relevant to the millions of people who traverse the border by car and plane every day. While ranching continues along many parts of the border, not even the most ambitious nineteenth-century border boosters could have imagined the border assembly plants, vast irrigated fields, and burgeoning cities that now cluster along much of the border. As of 2010 the U.S. Bureau of Customs and Border Protection operated official ports of entry in twelve cities on the western U.S.-Mexico border. The long lines of cars and trucks that stretch away from most of them testify to the growth in transborder travel and commerce as well as the expansion of the nation-states' border control apparatus.[13]

These striking contrasts reflect the many social, economic, political, and technological changes that took place over the border's history, changes that have transformed the region and the boundary line itself. The dotted line that the Joint United States and Mexican Boundary Commission first marked across the western half of North America in the 1850s has become a powerful tool with which the U.S. and Mexican governments attempt to regulate who and what enters each nation and how they do so.

This transformation did not happen quickly or predictably. At the conclusion of the Mexican-American War, both the United States and Mexico were young nation-states that lacked the power to authoritatively define, let alone control, their new border. The first role of the boundary line was simply to divide the continent between these two adolescent republics. However, while they claimed extensive territorial boundaries, neither nation-state could assert its sovereignty over their new boundary line or the Native people who lived and raided across it. It took another forty years before they were able to shore up their territorial claims with military sovereignty through the suppression of filibustering expeditions and the confinement of Apaches. During this period the erstwhile enemies realized that their common goals demanded binational cooperation. Despite their history of competition and conflict, U.S. and Mexican officials embraced first informal cooperative arrangements and then official reciprocal crossing agreements that allowed them to defeat the Apaches and establish military sovereignty over the line in the 1880s.

Both as models for future cooperation and because of their practical effect in defeating the Apaches, reciprocal crossing agreements, along with railroads, ushered in an era of cooperation and capitalist development on the border that lasted until the Mexican Revolution. In the late nineteenth and early twentieth centuries, ranchers, miners, investors, laborers, and railroad builders integrated the borderlands lands and resources into a capitalist economy and established binational communities along the border. At the same time U.S. and Mexican officials began to arrive on the line intent on making it a meaningful customs and immigration checkpoint. Together U.S. and Mexican officials and local people negotiated state sovereignty along the border, balancing local and national and U.S. and Mexican agendas and shaping the flow of transborder movement.

In the 1910s the tensions stemming from the Mexican Revolution and the First World War undermined the spirit of binational unity and cooperation that had been fostered along the border. With border battles sending stray bullets across the line and both nations wary of transborder invasion, U.S.-Mexican relations declined and both Mexicans and Americans sought ways to make the border a protective barrier. Soldiers, heightened crossing restrictions, and finally fences filled this wartime demand, but also left a lasting legacy of division along the boundary line. By the 1920s both governments could call on a range of crossing regulations, physical structures, and border enforcement agents to restrict transborder traffic. While the Mexican government used border controls to collect customs and expel Chinese immigrants, it was the U.S. government that most aggressively deployed the border control apparatus, attempting to restrict Americans' access to border vice districts and to regulate Mexican immigration. These measures, along with the fences that bisected border towns, highlighted the divisive qualities of the border.

Despite the persistence of transborder communities and commerce, this sense of the boundary line as a stark divide dominated much of the discourse about the twentieth-century border. "The border," Gloria Anzaldúa famously wrote in her 1987 book, *Borderlands/La Frontera: The New Mestiza*, "is *una herida abierta* [an open wound] where the Third World grates against the First and bleeds."[14] The asymmetries in wealth and power between the United States and Mexico that were already evident in the 1930s escalated over the remainder of the twentieth century as the United States consolidated its position as a global power. Even as the U.S.

and Mexican economies became increasingly integrated, culminating with the liberalization of trade regulations under the General Agreement on Tariffs and Trade (GATT) in 1986 and the North American Free Trade Agreement (NAFTA) in 1994, economic inequalities persisted.

The power imbalance between the United States and Mexico has been reflected in the politics of border control. While the history I related in the preceding pages closed with the emergence of the modern border control apparatus in the 1920s and 1930s, both nation-states continued to build on that foundation for the remainder of the twentieth century. Although U.S. and Mexican officials continued to negotiate bilateral border agreements and cooperative enforcement measures, the twentieth-century border was most influenced by the United States' political and economic agendas as well as the persistent challenges to those goals. From the 1930s through the end of the twentieth century U.S. border policy primarily focused on encouraging the flow of transborder trade, while regulating the movement of Mexican immigrants and stemming the stream of illegal drugs across the boundary line.[15]

From its beginnings with the rumrunners and opium smugglers of the 1910s and 1920s, the smuggling of illegal substances emerged as one of the most significant contemporary border control issues. In the second half of the twentieth century drug smuggling expanded along the U.S.-Mexico border in response to American consumers' growing demand for illegal drugs and the success of antismuggling efforts in other locations. Efforts by both the U.S. and Mexican governments to crack down on drug production and smuggling in the 1970s and 1980s led to some short-term successes, but ultimately prompted the development of increasingly sophisticated and violent drug cartels that channeled drugs from South America through Mexico to the United States. With the advent of NAFTA in 1994, both governments once again moved to escalate antidrug enforcement efforts to quell fears that free trade would facilitate drug smuggling. However, despite increasing drug seizures, they failed to stem the transborder drug traffic. By the early twenty-first century, the continued traffic in drugs and the escalating cartel violence had created a crisis on the border.[16]

The U.S. government was not much more successful in its attempts to apply conditional controls to Mexican immigration over the course of the twentieth century. Beginning with the flexible enforcement of immigration restrictions in the 1920s and the subsequent crackdown on Mexican immigration in the 1930s, the U.S. government consistently demonstrated its desire to strategically use immigration laws and the border control apparatus to ease the flow of Mexican migrant laborers during times when labor was in demand and to stymie it during periods of low employment. Following the repatriation campaigns of the Depression years, the U.S. government embraced more liberal immigration policies in the 1940s in response to wartime demands for labor. Beginning with World War II, the U.S. and Mexican governments established the Bracero Program to bring Mexican workers to the United States as contract laborers. At the same time, however, many Mexicans chose to cross the border outside legal channels, spurring U.S. and Mexican officials to work together to identify and deport undocumented Mexican migrants. In the final third of the twentieth century, undocumented Mexican immigration emerged as an increasingly contentious issue along the border as both U.S. policies and conditions in Mexico caused a growing number of Mexicans to cross the border outside of legal channels. The end of the Bracero Program in 1964 coincided with a new U.S. immigration act that made it more difficult for Mexicans to secure legal entry into the United States. Imposing a quota on Western Hemisphere immigrants for the first time, the Immigration Act of 1965 set the annual limit for the entire Western Hemisphere at 120,000. At the same time political and economic instability pushed many Mexicans, and increasingly Central Americans as well, to seek work and refuge in the United States. Most had no choice but to wait many years for a visa or to turn to illegal entry. Between 1960 and 1978 border apprehensions increased dramatically from 71,000 to over a million. By the 1980s and 1990s, as the conditional control of the boundary line that the United States desired remained out of reach, the flow of undocumented immigrants continued and the border became a focal point of political debates about immigration control.[17]

While the scale of undocumented immigration and drug smuggling increased over the course of the twentieth century, neither those problems nor the U.S. government's persistent attempts to use physical barriers and border patrols to stop them were new to the border. State agents had been present on the border since the first boundary surveyors, soldiers, and customs officers arrived there in the nineteenth century. Fences, which first appeared on the boundary line in 1909, proliferated on the border over the course of the twentieth century. The United States' escalation of drug and immigration enforcement along the border during the twentieth century was accompanied by a gradual expansion of fence building that culminated in the Secure Fence Act of 2006. The first government fence built on the border was the range fence the Bureau of Animal Industry built in 1909 on the California–Baja California border to stop the movement of fever tick-infested cattle. In the following decade fence building increased dramatically as U.S. and Mexican officials began building fences between border towns to limit the violence stemming from wartime crossing restrictions. Throughout the remainder of the century, government officials built a range of barriers along different parts of the border to enhance their ability to prevent some unwanted crossings, while channeling movement into ports of entry where state agents could better oversee and restrict it. Beginning in 1935, the U.S. section of the International Boundary and Water Commission oversaw the erection of barbed-wire fences to control the movement of cattle across the line (though by the 1950s they had abandoned their maintenance to local ranchers). Meanwhile, U.S. officials continued to erect more substantial chain-link fences to channel human movement in more heavily populated areas. In the 1940s Border Patrol officials in Calexico erected a chain-link fence, salvaged from a Japanese American internment camp, along 5.8 miles of the boundary line to prevent illegal immigrant entries. By the 1980s, although immigrants and smugglers cut holes in the chain link and most fences consisted of only a few strands of barbed wire meant to keep out nothing more than cattle, fences marked much of the border.[18]

The early 1990s brought another wave of fence building. On October 1, 1994, the Immigration and Naturalization Service (INS), responding to mounting concerns about undocumented immigration amid free-trade negotiations, launched Operation Gatekeeper at the western end of the boundary line. Under Gatekeeper, by June 1998 the total length of border fences and walls within the San Diego sector increased from nineteen to over forty-five miles, the number of Border Patrol agents rose from 980 to 2,264, 766 underground sensors were installed, and the number of infrared scopes in use increased from twelve to fifty-nine. A ten-foot-high metal wall replaced the chain-link fence along the boundary line between San Ysidro and Tijuana. By the late 1990s, not only San Diego but also large stretches of the border (including El Paso, home to another border enforcement escalation known as Operation Hold-the-Line) featured what one author has called "blockade-style operations" and high-tech militarization typical of "low-intensity conflict" doctrine.[19]

The Secure Fence Act was the direct descendant of these efforts; the new government barriers that are rising on the border today echo those earlier fences and their aspirations of state control. While the technology of the fences, the cities they separate, and the demographics of immigration have all changed dramatically in the last hundred years, the idea that the enforcement of national laws requires a physical barrier to transborder movement has its origins in the early twentieth century. We are living today with the legacy of those ideas about the border and state control as well as the constant reminders that they are imperfect and incomplete.

In many ways the Department of Homeland Security's new border fences seem like the high modernist culmination of the nation-state's long-standing aspirations of authority over the border. Since the U.S. and Mexican governments began trying to contain the Apaches in the mid-nineteenth century, they have sought ways to monitor and regulate the movement of people, goods, and animals across the boundary line. While in early years there was nothing but border crossers' respect for the law to assure that they paid customs duties and entered through ports of entry, the states gradually dispatched agents to the boundary line to enforce a growing range of crossing regulations. By the early twentieth century, physical barriers helped channel that movement as well. These agents and structures carved out spaces of state surveillance on the border that have reached a new level in the early twenty-first century. In contrast to the irregular barbed-wire fences that blend into the ranchlands through which they run, the parallel lines of steel-mesh fencing that now run along portions of the boundary line are unmistakably state structures. And, while collapsing, cut-up chain-link fences had become symbols of the border's vulnerability in the 1980s, the new border walls evoke permanence. Although some stretches of the border are still marked by no more than barbed wire, these new barriers, combined with motion detectors, observation towers, searchlights, airplane surveillance, and ever-increasing numbers of Border Patrol agents, customs and immigration officers, and even National Guard troops are at the center of an unprecedented level of state surveillance.

While there is no doubt that fences have become formidable parts of the border landscape, critical components in the United States' border control apparatus, and the dominant metaphors, symbols, and physical markers of the western U.S.-Mexico border, they also continue to provoke great debate. Supporters of the fences credit them with significantly impeding unauthorized entries. Between 2006 and 2007, the Border Patrol's apprehensions of undocumented immigrants on the U.S.-Mexican border dropped by 20 percent, falling from 1,072,018 in 2006 to just 858,722 a year later. In the Yuma sector apprehensions plummeted from 5,571 in March 2007 to 751 in March 2008 after the Department of Homeland Security built a triple-layer barrier—a twenty-foot-high reinforced steel fence, a steel mesh fence, and a wire-topped cyclone fence—on the border between San Luis Rio Colorado, Sonora, and San Luis, Arizona. "A lot of people have the misconception that it is a waste of time and money," noted Michael Bernacke, a Border Patrol agent stationed in the Yuma sector, "but the numbers of apprehensions show that it works."[20] Reading these statistics and thinking back on how much has changed since the Joint United States and Mexican Boundary Commission first struggled to mark the boundary line in the 1850s, it is easy to imagine the fence as a monument to state power.

However, in many ways this monument and the state power it represents are just a mirage. Although politically powerful symbols, fences are not the most effective way to deal with the problems of drug trafficking and undocumented immigration which extend far beyond the border. Smugglers and undocumented immigrants continue to find ways to enter the United States. "History shows that even the most substantial walls can be breached," Congresswoman Sheila Jackson Lee stressed. "In California, the border fence has been circumvented by tunneling (20 tunnels have been discovered) and by going around both ends of the fence."[21] As Arizona governor Janet Napolitano said, "You show me a 50-foot wall and I'll show you a 51-foot ladder."[22] Evaluating the United States' 1990s border enforcement escalations, including Operations Gatekeeper and Hold-the-Line and the building of walls along some stretches of the boundary line, political scientist Peter Andreas concluded that the build-up was a "politically successful policy failure"—a policy that satisfied the public without doing much to address undocumented immigration or drug smuggling.[23] With the passage of the Secure Fence Act in 2006, the U.S. Congress continued down this same path, adopting a politically popular, but not necessarily effective, response to concerns about drug smuggling and undocumented immigration. Even as the border fencing continues, there is ample evidence that the border is not the best place to prevent violations of U.S. immigration laws considering that approximately half of undocumented immigrants in the United States did not cross the border illegally, but rather overstayed their visas.[24] For these people a fence is irrelevant.

Furthermore, whether or not they successfully reduce the number of unauthorized entries by immigrants and smugglers, fences are a failure of relational power. As some of the least flexible of border enforcement measures, fences threaten to interfere with the nation-states' goal of creating a conditional border that will allow the easy movement of some people while restricting that of others. Border Patrol officers can distinguish among different categories of people and use their discretion to adjust for extenuating circumstances, but a wall cannot. Due to this lack of flexibility, border fences have many negative social, economic, and environmental side effects. By making it more difficult for all people to cross the border no matter how legitimate their reasons, fencing disrupts transborder commerce and divides binational communities. Stressing the fragility of the desert ecosystems through which the border passes, environmentalists and scientists have criticized the fence as an act of "environmental vandalism" and have warned that both their construction and their continuing disruption of borderland ecosystems could threaten endangered species, including ocelots and Sonoran pronghorns.[25] Although built to inconvenience immigrants and smugglers, it is likely that the new fences will have a more significant long-term effect on the ocelots and pronghorns whose habitats they divide. While high steel walls may be symbols of power, they also limit the states' ability to conditionally and flexibly control transborder movement of a variety of types.

Perhaps, as Senator Patrick Leahy suggested, "Rather than strength, this fence will symbolize weakness."[26] In looking back over the border's history, the U.S. and Mexican governments most often resorted to building fences after other policing efforts failed. By the twenty-first century fences had become politically powerful symbols that in many ways detracted from the nation-states' goal of creating a border control apparatus that would prevent unwanted entries without disrupting other transborder flows. As anyone who has waited in the long lines of border traffic can attest, fences are at the very least an inconvenience to even the most innocent crossers.

And yet people continue to cross. Despite the long lines of traffic faced by legal crossers and the increasingly high stakes confronted by those crossing outside of legal channels, millions of people, as well as cars, trucks, buses, and trains, traverse the U.S.-Mexico boundary line each year in the shadow of the new border fences.[27] These crossings remind us that transborder ties have persisted. Throughout its history, despite the U.S. and Mexican states' attempts to claim the boundary line for their own purposes, they have had to share it with other people, and they continue to do so today. While local people cannot tear down the steel walls that now divide most border cities (even if they wanted to), they can challenge and adapt to state policies and structures and in some ways try to make the fences their own. Since the late 1970s, Mexicans and Americans in Naco, Arizona, and Naco, Sonora, have occasionally organized a binational celebration that has included a transborder game of volleyball in which the border fence serves as the net. In the late 1990s and early 2000s, a group of artists erected a mural on the border wall in Nogales, Sonora. Titled *Paseo de Humanidad* (Parade of Humanity), the mural's brightly painted figures and symbols provide a political critique of capitalism and the United States' border enforcement policies. Performance artists and poets have also incorporated the fences into their artistic protests. Meanwhile, immigrants and smugglers continue to find ways to challenge the nation-states' division of space: tunneling under, climbing over, cutting through, and going around the new barriers.[28]

It remains to be seen what will become of these new border fences. The members of the first Joint United States and Mexican Boundary Commission would never have imagined that the dotted line of boundary monuments that they marked through the desert in the 1850s would someday be crowded with bustling border towns. Nor would the first fence builders have guessed that they were laying the groundwork for the high-tech barriers of today. Similarly, we cannot know what the long-term effects will be of the barriers that the U.S. government is erecting now. While the fence's supporters and critics argue over whether it will lead to less drug smuggling, undocumented immigration, and insecurity or to more environmental destruction, divided families, drug-related violence, and migrant deaths, other possibilities also exist. The history of the boundary line has shown that the border can mean many things—a customs and immigration checkpoint and a divide between political and legal regimes, but also a site of transborder exchange and community formation and a place that people call home. The border has not always been a barrier and there is no reason to think that it will not become something else in the future.

NOTES

INTRODUCTION

1. For descriptions of border fencing see the U.S. Department of Homeland Security, "Southwest Border Fence," U.S. Department of Homeland Security Web site; Von Drehle, "A New Line in the Sand."

2. On the Rio Grande they could rely on the river to do much of this work for them. Although the shallow river was not always a significant obstacle to trans-border movement, it was nonetheless a clearly identifiable marker of national space. Yet the reliance on the river to mark the border also posed distinct problems for the United States and Mexico that they did not have to contend with on the stationary desert line. The propensity of the Rio Grande to shift channels prompted territorial disputes between the U.S. and Mexican governments over the islands and portions of the river's banks, known as *bancos*, that jutted out from the river's banks or were located at the center of a curve such that they were likely to be cut off from the mainland and as a result change position in relation to the river. By contrast, the spatial dimensions of the western, desert border changed, but the line itself stayed in place. See Metz, *Border*, 293–318; Martínez, *Troublesome Border*, 24–29; Utley, *Changing Course*, 77–121.

Although the eastern, river border formed by the Rio Grande and the western, desert border, which is the focus of this book, divide the same two countries, historically they are quite different. In addition to the spatial differences between the eastern/river border and western/desert border, there are also significant historical and historiographical divisions between the two halves of the U.S.-Mexico boundary line. The histories of the Anglo-American colonization of Texas, the Texas Rebellion, and the involvement of Texas in the Civil War set the Texas border apart from the western border. Even when shared events, for instance, the construction of railroads and the Mexican Revolution, occurred on both halves of the border, these events did not always affect the eastern and western halves of the border in the same ways. Historians have also written more about the Rio Grande border and have done so within the context of Texas history. In order to provide a history of the evolution of the western border—a geographic entity in its own right—in this book I have chosen not to revisit this more familiar territory. For histories of the Rio Grande border see, Metz, *Border*; Herrera Pérez, *El lindero que definió a la nación*; Martínez, *Border Boom Town*; Martínez, *Troublesome Border*; Hinojosa, *A Borderlands Town in Transition*; Johnson, *Revolution in Texas*; Young, *Catarino Garza's Revolution on the Texas Border*; Johnson and Gusky, *Bordertown*; García, *Desert Immigrants*; Perales, *Smeltertown*; Tirres, "American Law Comes to the Border."

3. Philips and Comus, *A Natural History of the Sonoran Desert*, 12.

4. Bartlett, *Personal Narrative*, vol. 2, 4.

5. White, *The Middle Ground*; Truett, *Fugitive Landscapes*; Adelman and Aron, "From Borderlands to Borders."

6. Among the classic texts of borderlands history are Bolton, *The Spanish*

Borderlands; Bannon, *The Spanish Borderlands Frontier*; Weber, *The Mexican Frontier*; Weber, *The Spanish Frontier in North America*. Other notable borderlands histories include Truett, *Fugitive Landscapes*; Truett and Young, eds., *Continental Crossroads*; Jacoby, *Shadows at Dawn*; DeLay, *War of a Thousand Deserts*; Hämäläinen, *The Comanche Empire*; Blackhawk, *Violence over the Land*; Gutiérrez, *When Jesus Came, the Corn Mothers Went Away*; Brooks, *Captives and Cousins*; White, *The Middle Ground*; Radding, *Wandering Peoples*; Reséndez, *Changing National Identities at the Frontier*; Alonso, *Thread of Blood*; Montoya, *Translating Property*; Montejano, *Anglos and Mexicans in the Making of Texas*; Tinker Salas, *In the Shadow of the Eagles*; Mora-Torres, *The Making of the Mexican Border*; Johnson, *Revolution in Texas*; Deutsch, *No Separate Refuge*; Young, *Catarino Garza's Revolution on the Texas Border*; Graybill, *Policing the Great Plains*; Benton-Cohen, *Borderline Americans*.

7. For the geographic expansion of borderlands history see Adelman and Aron, "From Borderlands to Borders." For borderlands histories that focus on the U.S.-Mexican borderlands during the national period but do not include significant discussion of the boundary line, see Mora-Torres, *The Making of the Mexican Border*; Reséndez, *Changing National Identities at the Frontier*; Alonso, *Thread of Blood*; Montoya, *Translating Property*; Montejano, *Anglos and Mexicans in the Making of Texas*; Deutsch, *No Separate Refuge*.

8. I am, of course, not the first historian to write about the U.S.-Mexico border. For histories of border towns and general histories of the boundary line see Martínez, *Border Boom Town*; Hinojosa, *A Borderlands Town in Transition*; Price, *Tijuana*; Proffitt, *Tijuana*; Arreola and Curtis, *The Mexican Border Cities*; Ganster and Lorey, *The U.S.-Mexican Border into the Twenty-First Century*; Metz, *Border*; Martínez, *Troublesome Border*; Johnson and Gusky, *Bordertown*; Wood, ed., *On the Border*; Herrera Pérez, *El lindero que definió a la nación*.

9. For studies of other international boundaries see Sahlins, *Boundaries*; Prescott, *Political Frontiers and Boundaries*; Gavrilis, *The Dynamics of Interstate Boundaries*; Nugent, *Smugglers, Secessionists, and Loyal Citizens*; McManus, *The Line Which Separates*; Wilson and Donnan, eds., *Border Identities;* Evans, ed., *The Borderlands of the American and Canadian Wests*; Johnson and Graybill, eds., *Bridging National Borders in North America*; Taylor, "Boundary Terminology;" LaDow, *The Medicine Line*.

10. For an analysis of how communication among border officials and the individual autonomy of border authorities have contributed to cooperation and shared management along a variety of international boundaries see Gavrilis, *The Dynamics of Interstate Boundaries*.

11. Following the conventions of the time and for the sake of clarity, I use *Americans* to refer to citizens of the United States and *Mexicans* to refer to citizens of Mexico. While it is true that both groups are residents of the American continent and could rightfully be called *Americans*, because there is no English equivalent of the Spanish *estadounidenses* I have used the most common and historically accurate terminology.

12. For historiographical discussions of borderlands history see Samuel Truett and Elliott Young, "Introduction: Making Transnational History: Nations, Regions, and Borderlands," in Truett and Young, eds., *Continental Crossroads*;

Weber, "Turner, the Boltonians, and the Borderlands"; Hurtado, "Parkmanizing the Spanish Borderlands"; Adelman and Aron, "From Borderlands to Borders"; Gutíerrez and Young, "Transnationalizing Borderlands History." For recent borderlands histories focusing on the national period see Truett and Young, eds., *Continental Crossroads*; Truett, *Fugitive Landscapes*; Jacoby, *Shadows at Dawn*; Montoya, *Translating Property*; Mora-Torres, *The Making of the Mexican Border*; Johnson, *Revolution in Texas*; Young, *Catarino Garza's Revolution on the Texas Border*; Graybill, *Policing the Great Plains*; Benton-Cohen, *Borderline Americans*; Johnson and Graybill, eds., *Bridging National Borders in North America*.

CHAPTER ONE: A NEW MAP FOR NORTH AMERICA

1. Salazar Ylarregui, *Datos de los trabajos astronómicos y topográficos*, 36.
2. Entry in the Official Journal of the U.S. and Mexican Boundary Commission, September 6, 1851, signed by Thomas H. Webb and Francisco Jiménez, secretaries, Bartlett Papers, Mexican Boundary Commission Records, Reel IX, JCBL.
3. Bartlett, *Personal Narrative*, vol. 1, 377–403.
4. Ibid., 434–43, 455; Werne, *The Imaginary Line*, 86, 103–4, 107, 123.
5. Francis M. Carroll has also characterized surveyors' efforts on the U.S.-Canada border as "searching." Carroll, *A Good and Wise Measure*.
6. Meinig, *The Shaping of America*, vol. 2, 58–144.
7. Weber, *The Mexican Frontier*; Meinig, *The Shaping of America*, vol. 2, 128–44; Reséndez, *Changing National Identities at the Frontier*, 93–123.
8. Cremony, *Life among the Apaches*, 39. See also DeLay, *War of a Thousand Deserts*; Hämäläinen, *The Comanche Empire*.
9. Kelly and Hatcher, eds., "Tadeo Ortíz de Ayala and the Colonization of Texas," 313, 334–35; Brack, *Mexico Views Manifest Destiny*, 65–68; Weber, *The Mexican Frontier*, 283.
10. Stephanson, *Manifest Destiny*; Hietala, *Manifest Design*; Merk, *Manifest Destiny and Mission in American History*; Haynes, *James K. Polk and the Expansionist Impulse*, 91–103.
11. Martínez, *Troublesome Border*, 13; Meinig, *The Shaping of America*, vol. 2, 143.
12. Mier y Terán to the Minister of War, November 24, 1829, in Jackson, ed., *Texas by Terán*, 179.
13. DeLay, *War of a Thousand Deserts*, 27–29; Brack, *Mexico Views Manifest Destiny*, 116–18, 143–45.
14. Meinig, *The Shaping of America*, vol. 2, 142–44; Haynes, *James K. Polk and the Expansionist Impulse*, 95–122.
15. For accounts of the Mexican-American War see Pletcher, *The Diplomacy of Annexation*, 352–521; Henderson, *A Glorious Defeat*; Haynes, *James K. Polk and the Expansionist Impulse*, 123–80.
16. DeLay, *War of a Thousand Deserts*; DeLay, "Independent Indians and the U.S.-Mexican War."
17. Griswold del Castillo, *The Treaty of Guadalupe Hidalgo*, 22–35; Mar-

tínez, *Troublesome Border*, 15–16; Pletcher, *Diplomacy of Annexation*, 517–21; Meinig, *The Shaping of America*, vol. 2, 147–50.

18. Martínez, *Troublesome Border*, 15; Meinig, *The Shaping of America*, vol. 2, 148–49.

19. Horsman, *Race and Manifest Destiny*, 208–48; DeLay, *War of a Thousand Deserts*, 258–70; Griswold del Castillo, *The Treaty of Guadalupe Hidalgo*, 33; Meinig, *The Shaping of America*, vol. 2, 150.

20. Martínez, *Troublesome Border*, 16–17; Pletcher, *Diplomacy of Annexation*, 517–50; Griswold del Castillo, *The Treaty of Guadalupe Hidalgo*, 36–39; Horsman, *Race and Manifest Destiny*, 208–48; Merk, *Manifest Destiny and Mission in American History*, 107–201.

21. Buchanan to Trist, October 25, 1847, in Manning, *Diplomatic Correspondence of the United States*, vol. 8, 217–18; Griswold del Castillo, *The Treaty of Guadalupe Hidalgo*, 36–42; Pletcher, *Diplomacy of Annexation*, 540–50; Haynes, *James K. Polk and the Expansionist Impulse*, 173–80.

22. "Treaty of Guadalupe Hidalgo," "Document 129: Mexico: February 2, 1848," in Miller, ed., *Treaties and Other International Acts of the United States of America*, vol. 5, 207–36.

23. Stegner, *Wolf Willow*, 86.

24. For exploration and surveying see Goetzmann, *Exploration and Empire*; Craib, *Cartographic Mexico*; Rebert, *La Gran Línea*. For more on the importance of mapping in state building see Scott, *Seeing Like a State*, 36–52, 87–88; Mitchell, *Rule of Experts*, 85–93; Winichakul, *Siam Mapped*; McManus, *The Line Which Separates*; Burnett, *Masters of All They Surveyed*.

25. Rebert, *La Gran Línea*, 59–137.

26. Salazar Ylarregui, *Datos de los trabajos astronómicos y topográficos*, 11.

27. Buchanan to Weller, January 24, 1849, Senate Executive Document 34, 31st Cong., 1st sess., 1850, vol. 1 (hereafter SED 34), 3.

28. Salazar Ylarregui, *Datos de los trabajos astronómicos y topográficos*, iv, 9, 16; Werne, *The Imaginary Line*, 100–102, 126–27, 225.

29. Salazar Ylarregui, *Datos de los trabajos astronómicos y topográficos*, iv; Rebert, *La Gran Línea*, 17–27; Sweeney, "Drawing Borders; Giese, "Artist Collaborators."

30. Emory, *Report of the United States and Mexican Boundary Survey*, 10. For a detailed and laudatory account of Emory see Norris, Milligan, and Faulk, *William H. Emory*.

31. Werne, *The Imaginary Line*, 20, 33–34,45–47; Hine, *Bartlett's West*, 3–10; Faulk, *Too Far North . . . Too Far South*, 5–19, 143; Hewitt, "The Mexican Boundary Survey Team," 177–82; Rebert, *La Gran Línea*, 17–26.

32. Joint Boundary Commission Journal, July 7, 1849, Senate Executive Document 119, 32nd Cong., 1st sess., 1852, 57.

33. McPherson, ed., *From San Diego to the Colorado in 1849*, 12; Whipple, *The Whipple Report*.

34. Weller to Clayton, February 3, 1850, SED 34, vol. 2, 2.

35. Lesley, "The International Boundary Survey from San Diego to the Gila River"; Weller to Clayton, November 3, 1849, SED 34, vol. 1, 31; Vargas, "The

Pantoja Map of 1782"; Hughes, "'La Mojonera' and the Marking of California's U.S.-Mexico Boundary Line," 133–36.

36. Buchanan to Weller, February 13, 1849, SED 34, vol. 1, 4.

37. Gray to Weller, November 9, 1849; Gray to Weller, November 14, 1849; SED 34, vol. 1, 47–48. For a detailed discussion of the surveying and mapping techniques used by the commission see Rebert, *La Gran Línea*, 75–85.

38. Gray to Ewing, February 20, 1850, SED 34, vol. 2, 5; Salazar Ylarregui, *Datos de los trabajos astronómicos y topográficos*, 35–36; Hewitt, "The Mexican Boundary Survey Team," 189–91. For an account of some of the U.S. commission's expenses see Buchanan to Weller, February 13, 1849, SED 34, vol. 1, 51.

39. García Conde to Máximo Yáñez, March 11, 1851, Archivo de la Secretaría de Relaciones Exteriores, Exp. 22, p. 226, as quoted in Werne, *The Imaginary Line*, 54.

40. Bartlett, *Personal Narrative*, vol. 1, 201.

41. García Conde to Minsitro de Relaciones, December 24, 1850, Archivo de la Secretaría de Relaciones Exteriores, Exp. 24, p. 37, as quoted in Werne, *The Imaginary Line*, 56.

42. Werne, *The Imaginary Line*, 57. Bartlett also noted that the Mexican settlers in La Mesilla preferred to remain within the Mexican Republic. Bartlett, *Personal Narrative*, vol. 1, 212–15.

43. Registro de Juan B. Espejo, November 21, 1852, in "Diario del General Pedro García Conde sobre los limites de las dos Californias y otros registros de la comisión de los limites," AHGE.

44. Bartlett, *Personal Narrative*, vol. 1, 247.

45. Bartlett, *Personal Narrative*, vol. 2, 4.

46. Cremony, *Life among the Apaches*, 118.

47. Whipple, *The Whipple Report*; Bartlett, *Personal Narrative*, vol. 2, 210–59.

48. For the history of Apache raiding see DeLay, *War of a Thousand Deserts*; Brooks, *Captives and Cousins*; Jacoby, *Shadows at Dawn*, 149–70; Alonso, *Thread of Blood*; Goodwin and Goodwin, *The Apache Diaries*.

49. Bartlett, *Personal Narrative*, vol. 1, 275, 375.

50. "Treaty of Guadalupe Hidalgo," "Document 129: Mexico: February 2, 1848," in Miller, ed., *Treaties and Other International Acts of the United States of America*, vol. 5, 219–22.

51. Bartlett, *Personal Narrative*, vol. 1, 304.

52. Ibid., 402–3. See also ibid., 303–10, 398–405; Cremony, *Life among the Apaches*, 56.

53. Cremony, *Life among the Apaches*, 56–58; Werne, *The Imaginary Line*, 107, 110. For more on Bartlett's views of domesticity see Greenberg, "Domesticating the Border."

54. Bartlett, *Personal Narrative*, vol. 1, 310–11; Cremony, *Life among the Apaches*, 59–66.

55. Bartlett, *Personal Narrative*, vol. 1, 321–22.

56. Ibid., 312.

57. Ibid., 312–17.

58. Cremony, *Life among the Apaches*, 83. Bartlett's and Cremony's accounts

differ on the number of animals stolen. Cremony stated that over 300 had been stolen, while Bartlett placed the number at only 150. Cremony, *Life among the Apaches*, 81–85; Bartlett, *Personal Narrative*, vol. 1, 353.

59. Cremony, *Life among the Apaches*, 119–27.

60. Werne, *The Imaginary Line*, 157–71.

61. Martínez, *Troublesome Border*, 17–21; Utley, *Changing Course*, 25–31.

62. Meyer and Sherman, *The Course of Mexican History*, 353.

63. Werne, *The Imaginary Line*, 193–215.

64. Emory, *Report of the United States and Mexican Boundary Survey*, 120. See also ibid., 34–35.

65. Ibid., 25.

66. "Gadsden Treaty," "Document 163: Mexico: December 30, 1853," in Miller, ed., *Treaties and Other International Acts of the United States of America*, vol. 6, 293–302.

67. Translation of Salazar to Minister of Foreign Relations, October 15, 1855, in Emory, *Report of the United States and Mexican Boundary Survey*, 35.

68. For a discussion of the later disputes over the changing course of the Rio Grande see Martínez, *Troublesome Border*, 24–29; Utley, *Changing Course*, 77–121.

CHAPTER TWO: HOLDING THE LINE

1. Rebert, *La Gran Línea*, 49–50; Officer, *Hispanic Arizona*, 282–83.

2. Werne, *The Imaginary Line*, 179–86; Vázquez and Meyer, *The United States and Mexico*, 57–61.

3. Mowry, *Arizona and Sonora*, 16. See also Officer, *Hispanic Arizona*, 275–83.

4. May, *The Southern Dream of a Caribbean Empire*, 158; Martínez, *Troublesome Border*, 15–23.

5. Faulk, trans. and ed., "Projected Mexican Military Colonies for the Borderlands, 1848," 40.

6. Acuña, *Sonoran Strongman*, 107; Faulk, trans. and ed., "Projected Mexican Colonies in the Borderlands, 1852"; Herring, "A Plan for the Colonization of Sonora's Northern Frontier"; Voss, *On the Periphery of Nineteenth-Century Mexico*, 115–19.

7. Wasserman, *Capitalists, Caciques, and Revolution*; Acuña, *Sonoran Strongman*.

8. Acuña, *Sonoran Strongman*, 14–16; Ruibal Corella, *Perfiles de un patriota*, 1–17. For cultures of honor and violence on the Mexican frontier see Alonso, *Thread of Blood*.

9. Mowry, *Arizona and Sonora*, ix.

10. Acuña, *Sonoran Strongman*, 26–70; Hu-DeHart, *Yaqui Resistance and Survival*, 76–81; Voss, *On the Periphery of Nineteenth-Century Mexico*, 115–19, 148–60.

11. Stout, *Schemers and Dreamers*, x, 15, 55.

12. Report of Reid and the anonymous corporal, reprinted in Woodward, *The Republic of Lower California*, 47.

13. A California court tried Walker for violating neutrality agreements, but despite the abundant evidence of his guilt, a sympathetic jury acquitted him. Woodward, *The Republic of Lower California*; Walker, *The War in Nicaragua*, 18–24; Stout, *Schemers and Dreamers*, 33–37; Wyllys, "The Republic of Lower California"; Wyllys, "William Walker's Invasion of Sonora"; Smith, *Expedición filibustera de William Walker*.

14. "Republic of Sonora, Decree No. 2," reprinted in Woodward, *The Republic of Lower California*, 45.

15. Walker, *The War in Nicaragua*, 18.

16. Acuña, *Sonoran Strongman*, 3–5, 16–25.

17. McPherson, ed., *From San Diego to the Colorado in 1849*, 27.

18. Voss, *On the Periphery of Nineteenth-Century Mexico*, 115–20.

19. Acuña, *Sonoran Strongman*, 19–20; Voss, *On the Periphery of Nineteenth-Century Mexico*, 115–20, 132–42.

20. Wyllys, "Henry A. Crabb," 183–85; Thrapp, *Encyclopedia of Frontier Biography*, vol. 1, 333–34.

21. Islas to the governor and inhabitants of Sonora, August 2, 1856; letter to the governor of Sinaloa, July 12, 1856; both in Fondo Ejecutivo, año 1856, tomo 103, expediente 9, AGES.

22. Letter to the governor of Sinaloa, July 12, 1856, Fondo Ejecutivo, año 1856, tomo 103, expediente 9, AGES. See also Elías to governor of Sonora, July 9, 1856; Prefect of Sahuaripa to governor of Sonora, July 18, 1856; both in Fondo Ejecutivo, año 1856, tomo 103, expediente 9, AGES; Forsyth to Cass, April 24, 1857, "Execution of Colonel Crabb and his associates," February 16, 1858, House Executive Document 64, 35th Cong., 1st sess. (hereafter HED 64), 2–4; Acuña, *Sonoran Strongman*, 33.

23. Translation of Yáñez to the Minister of War and Marine, April 10, 1857, HED 64, 24. See also Translation of Yáñez to Chief Clerk with the War Department, April 10, 1857; Translation of Noriega to General in Chief of the forces of the Western States, March 31, 1857; Translation of Pesqueira to Commanding General of the State, March 28, 1857; Translation of Perez to Prefect of the District of the Town of El Altar, March 24, 1857; all in HED 64, 4–6, 16–17; Acuña, *Sonoran Strongman*, 27.

24. Translation of Valenzuela Orozco to the Prefect of the District of the Town of El Altar, March 23, 1857, HED 64, 15–16.

25. Translation of Gabilondo to Pesqueira, 1857, taken from a pamphlet issued at the time of the dedication of the plaque on the church in Caborca in 1926 and compiled by Jose Clemente Venegas, translated by Harry J. Karns, as reprinted in Forbes, *Crabb's Filibustering Expedition into Sonora*, 32.

26. Crabb to Redondo, March 26, 1857, HED 64, 31. See also Translation of Velasco to the Prefect of the Town of Altar, March 28, 1857, HED 64, 29–30; Translation of Yáñez to the Minister of War and Marine, April 10, 1857, HED 64, 23–25; List of the Personnel of the Crabb Party in Forbes, *Crabb's Filibustering Expedition into Sonora*, 45–46.

27. Translation of Pesqueira to the citizens of Sonora, March 30, 1857, HED 64, 32–33.

28. Forbes, *Crabb's Filibustering Expedition into Sonora*, 21–31; Translation of Gabilondo to Pesqueira, 1857, taken from a pamphlet issued at the time of the

dedication of the plaque on the church in Caborca in 1926 and compiled by Jose Clemente Venegas, translated by Harry J. Karns, as reprinted in Forbes, *Crabb's Filibustering Expedition into Sonora*, 34–35; Forsyth to Cass, April 30, 1857; Translation from Trait d'Union, April 30, 1857; Forsyth to Cass, May 7, 1857; Smith to Forsyth, June 22, 1857; Deposition of Charles Edward Evans, September 14, 1857; all in HED 64, 36–37, 47–48, 64–68.

29. Forbes, *Crabb's Filibustering Expedition into Sonora*, 23, 29–30.

30. Poston, "Building a State in Apache Land, Part III," 291. See also Truett, *Fugitive Landscapes*, 45; Tinker Salas, *In the Shadow of the Eagles*, 94.

31. Forsyth to de la Fuente, May 30, 1857, HED 64, 39–43; Stout, *Schemers and Dreamers*, 48.

32. For later filibustering attempts see Stout, *Schemers and Dreamers*, 60–97; McPherson, "The Plan of William McKendree Gwin"; Hager, *The Filibusters of 1890*; Piñera Ramírez, *American and English Influence on the Early Development of Ensenada*, 75–76, 125–26; Folio Letter Book of Sir Buchanan Scott, MSCL-UCSD.

33. Browne, *Adventures in the Apache Country*.

34. Zúñiga, *Rápida ojeada al estado de Sonora*, 12. For overviews of the history of the Apaches in the borderlands before the end of the Mexican-American War see Jacoby, *Shadows at Dawn*, 142–65; DeLay, *War of a Thousand Deserts*; Spicer, *Cycles of Conquest*, 229–45; Truett, *Fugitive Landscapes*, 13–15, 28–30, 35–37.

35. Goodwin and Basso, *Western Apache Raiding and Warfare*, 43.

36. Griffin, *Beliefs and Holy Places*, 29; Basso, *Wisdom Sits in Places*; Pilsk and Cassa, "The Western Apache Home," USDA Web site; Welch and Riley, "Reclaiming Land and Spirit in the Western Apache Homeland."

37. Goodwin and Basso, *Western Apache Raiding and Warfare*, 63.

38. García, *Apuntes sobre la campaña contra los salvajes en el estado de Sonora*, 6.

39. Geronimo, *Geronimo's Story of His Life*, ed. Barrett, 110. See also ibid., 43–55.

40. Tinker Salas, *In the Shadow of the Eagles*, 63; Hatfield, *Chasing Shadows*, 12; Spicer, *Cycles of Conquest*, 334–40.

41. Bailey to Mix, November 4, 1858, *Annual Report of the Commissioner of Indian Affairs . . . 1858*, 206.

42. Mowry, *Arizona and Sonora*, 68.

43. Greiner to Lea, July 31, 1852, "Letters Received by the Office of Indian Affairs, 1824–1881: New Mexico Superintendency, 1849–1880" (hereafter "Letters of the New Mexico Superintendency"), (M234, roll 546), RG 75, NACP.

44. Greiner to Lea, July 31, 1852, "Letters of the New Mexico Superintendency" (M234, roll 546), RG 75, NACP.

45. Truett, *Fugitive Landscapes*, 40–41; Jacoby, *Shadows at Dawn*, 102–4.

46. Pierce to Seymour, August 29, 1862, Thomas H. Seymour Papers, Connecticut Historical Society, as cited in North, *Samuel Peter Heintzelman and the Sonora Exploring and Mining Company*, 174–75. For the effects of the Civil War on New Mexico and Arizona see Josephy, *The Civil War in the American West*, 8, 31–92.

47. Acuña, *Sonoran Strongman*, 100–101. For the French Intervention see Meyer and Sherman, *The Course of Mexican History*, 385–401.

48. Calhoun to Brown, March 29, 1850, *Annual Report of the Commissioner of Indian Affairs . . . 1850*, 99. See also Spicer, *Cycles of Conquest*, 345–47.

49. "Report of Brigadier-General O. O. Howard," November 7, 1872, *Annual Report of the Commissioner of Indian Affairs . . . 1872*, 176. See also "Report of the Commissioner of Indian Affairs," November 1, 1872; Proclamation by O. O. Howard, October 11, 1872; both in *Annual Report of the Commissioner of Indian Affairs . . . 1872*, 58, 178; Sweeney, *Cochise*, 367–90; Spicer, *Cycles of Conquest*, 250.

50. "Report of Brigadier-General O. O. Howard," November 7, 1872, *Annual Report of the Commissioner of Indian Affairs . . . 1872*, 176.

51. Jeffords to Smith, August 31, 1873, *Annual Report of the Commissioner of Indian Affairs . . . 1873*, 292.

52. M de Zamacona to Swarts, March 16, 1880, "Letters of the New Mexico Superintendency" (M234, roll 582), RG 75, NACP.

53. Gomez Perez to the Acting Secretary of Foreign Relations, February 25, 1876, "Letters Received by the Office of Indian Affairs, 1824–1881: Arizona Superintendency, 1863–1880" (hereafter "Letters of the Arizona Superintendency") (M234, roll 15 or 17 containing the year 1876 files M24-Z1 [note that there is a discrepancy of the numbering of these rolls]), RG 75, NACP.

54. "Report of the Commissioner of Indian Affairs," November 1, 1874, *Annual Report of the Commissioner of Indian Affairs . . . 1874*, 59.

55. Jeffords to Smith, August 31, 1873, *Annual Report of the Commissioner of Indian Affairs . . . 1873*, 292.

56. Bailey to Mix, November 4, 1858, *Annual Report of the Commissioner of Indian Affairs . . . 1857*, 206–7.

57. Calhoun to Brown, March 29, 1850, *Annual Report of the Commissioner of Indian Affairs . . . 1850*, 99.

58. Pope to A. A. General, December 6, 1880, "Letters of the New Mexico Superintendency" (M234, roll 582), RG 75, NACP.

59. "Report of the Commissioner of Indian Affairs," November 1, 1874, *Annual Report of the Commissioner of Indian Affairs . . . 1874*, 59; "Report of the Commissioner of Indian Affairs," October 30, 1876, *Annual Report of the Commissioner of Indian Affairs . . . 1876*, xvii; Clum to Commissioner of Indian Affairs, June 10, 1876; Clum to Kautz, June 8, 1876; both in "Letters of the Arizona Superintendency" (M234, roll 14 or 16 containing the year 1876 files A11-L420 [note that there is a discrepancy of the numbering of these rolls]), RG 75, NACP.

60. McCrary to Sherman, June 1, 1877, "Mexican Border Troubles," House Executive Document 13, 45th Cong., 1st sess. See also Gregg, *The Influence of Border Troubles on Relations between the United States and Mexico*, 48–141; Hatfield, *Chasing Shadows*, 23–37.

61. Forsythe, *Thrilling Days in Army Life*, 120.

62. Gregg, *The Influence of Border Troubles on Relations between the United States and Mexico*, 126, 148.

63. Morrow to Acting Assistant Adjutant General, District of New Mexico,

November 5, 1879, "Letters of the New Mexico Superintendency" (M234, roll 582), RG 75, NACP; "Report of the Commissioner of Indian Affairs," November 1, 1879, *Annual Report of the Commissioner of Indian Affairs ... 1879*, xxxix–xl.

64. Wallace to Schurz, December 20, 1879, "Letters of the New Mexico Superintendency" (M234, roll 580), RG 75, NACP.

65. Pope to Assistant Adjutant General, September 10, 1880, "Letters of the New Mexico Superintendency" (M234, roll 582), RG 75, NACP.

66. Buell and Hatch to Assistant Adjutant General, October 1880, "Letters of the New Mexico Superintendency" (M234, roll 582), RG 75, NACP.

67. Buell to Assistant Adjutant General, October 22, 1880, "Letters of the New Mexico Superintendency" (M234, roll 582), RG 75, NACP. See also Hatfield, *Chasing Shadows*, 36–39.

68. Frederick T. Frelinghuysen, "Mexico: Reciprocal Right to Pursue Savage Indians across the Boundary Line," July 29, 1882, reprinted in Cozzens, *Eyewitnesses to the Indian Wars*, vol. 1, 343–45; Hatfield, *Chasing Shadows*, 53–54, 61, 88, 114, 118.

69. The following account of the pursuit of Geronimo is based on Crook to Sheridan, January 27, 1886, 571–73; Maus to Roberts, February 23, 1886, 576–80; Mariscal to Morgan, May 19, 1886, 589–96; all in *Papers Relating to the Foreign Relations of the United States ... 1886*; Atkins to the Secretary of the Interior, September 28, 1886, *Annual Report of the Commissioner of Indian Affairs ... 1886*, xl; Cozzens, *Eyewitnesses to the Indian Wars*, vol. 1, 346–589; Geronimo, *Geronimo's Story of His Life*, 105–10, 133–82; Sheridan, *Arizona*, 92–97; Hatfield, *Chasing Shadows*, 55–111; Thrapp, *The Conquest of Apacheria*, 267–367; Roberts, *Once They Moved Like the Wind*, 239–98; Utley, *The Indian Frontier in the American West*, 198, 201.

70. Hatfield, *Chasing Shadows*, 113.

71. Ibid., 114.

72. Robinson, *Apache Voices*, 79–85; Goodwin and Goodwin, *The Apache Diaries*.

73. Moreno to Secretary of State, November 23, 1887; Lozarragaz to Secretary of State, November 22, 1887; Mariscal to governor of Sonora, August 3, 1888; unsigned letter from Hermosillo to Secretaría de Relaciones, August 14, 1888; Guerra to Espino, May 20, 1888; all in Fondo Ejecutivo, Ramo Indígenas—Pápagos/Pimas, año 1887–1888, tomo 15, expediente 6, documentos 10945–11035, AGES; "'El Plomo War' Accounts Related by Papago Informants," interviewed by Darrow Dolan, File A-81a, ASMA; Hatfield, *Chasing Shadows*, 120–21.

CHAPTER THREE: LANDSCAPE OF PROFITS

1. Eppinga, *Nogales*, 59–73; Ready, "History of Nogales," 6; Ready, *Open Range and Hidden Silver*, 26–27.

2. Mowry, *Arizona and Sonora*; Poston, "Building a State in Apache Land,

Part II," 203–13; North, *Samuel Peter Heintzelman and the Sonora Exploring and Mining Company*; Truett, *Fugitive Landscapes*, 38–45.

3. Mowry, *Arizona and Sonora*, 62; Truett, *Fugitive Landscapes*, 41–43.

4. Voss, *On the Periphery of Nineteenth-Century Mexico*, 151–52, 212–16; Mowry, *Arizona and Sonora*, frontispiece.

5. Tinker Salas, *In the Shadow of the Eagles*, 41–43; Voss, *On the Periphery of Nineteenth-Century Mexico*, 152; Aguirre, "The Last of the Dons," 243–48.

6. Lingenfelter, *Steamboats on the Colorado River*; Jones to Marcy, July 21, 1869, *Annual Report of the Commissioner of Indian Affairs . . . 1869*, 216; Williams, *The Cocopah People*, 33–37; Poston to Dole, September 30, 1864, *Annual Report of the Commissioner of Indian Affairs . . . 1864*, 152.

7. Browne, *Adventures in the Apache Country*, 258. See also Truett, *Fugitive Landscapes*, 49–50; Sayre, *Ranching, Endangered Species, and Urbanization in the Southwest*, 30.

8. Orsi, *Sunset Limited*, 21–22; Truett, *Fugitive Landscapes*, 58.

9. Ready, "History of Nogales," 6; Ready, *Open Range and Hidden Silver*, 26–27.

10. Orsi, *Sunset Limited*, 21; White, *"It's Your Misfortune and None of My Own,"* 146; Mercer, "Taxpayers or Investors."

11. Lewis, *Iron Horse Imperialism*, 43–44; Boyd, "Twenty Years to Nogales."

12. Law of February 1st, 1856, translated in Hamilton, *Hamilton's Mexican Law*, 11; Book XII, Title I, Chapter I, Article 824, translated in Wheless, *Compendium of the Laws of Mexico*, 526.

13. Hart, *Empire and Revolution*, 106–30; Coatsworth, "Indispensable Railroads in a Backward Economy"; Coatsworth, "Obstacles to Economic Growth in Nineteenth-Century Mexico"; Pletcher, *Rails, Mines, and Progress*.

14. Gray, *When All Roads Led to Tombstone*, 16; Truett, *Fugitive Landscapes*, 60–62.

15. Graeme, "The Queen and Her Court," 43–52; Truett, *Fugitive Landscapes*, 78–80.

16. Truett, *Fugitive Landscapes*, 67–69.

17. Ibid., 69–70, 81; Schwantes, *Vision and Enterprise*, 55–77, 92–95.

18. Sonnichsen, *Colonel Greene and the Copper Skyrocket*, 12, 45–66; Truett, *Fugitive Landscapes*, 88–97; Mathias, "At the Edges of Empire," 18.

19. *Thirteenth Census of the United States Taken in the Year 1910, Volume II*, 82–84; *Thirteenth Census of the United States Taken in the Year 1910, Volume III*, 176; Jeffrey, "The History of Douglas, Arizona," 25.

20. I use the term *ethnic Mexican* to include all people of Mexican descent regardless of their citizenship or residency.

21. J. C. Ryan Testimony in E. W. Powers, ed., "President's Mediation Commission Hearings at Bisbee, Arizona, November 5–11, 1917," U.S. Department of Labor, in *Papers of the President's Mediation Commission, 1917–1919*, ed. Melvyn Dubofsky, rev. ed., microfilm (Frederick, MD, 1986), as cited in Benton-Cohen, *Borderline Americans*, 84.

22. Testimony of Esteban B. Calderon, in González Ramírez, *La huelga de Cananea*, 107. See also Schwantes, "Toil and Trouble," 116–17; González

Ramírez, *La huelga de Cananea*, 34; Byrkit, *Forging the Copper Collar*, 21; Sonnichsen, *Colonel Greene and the Copper Skyrocket*, 178–81. Note that Italians also received the lower pay rate in Bisbee.

23. North, *Samuel Peter Heintzelman and the Sonora Exploring and Mining Company*, 174; *Douglas Daily Dispatch*, February 11, 1904, 1.

24. Report from Filiberto Barroso to the Second Judge of the First Instance at Cananea, June 1, 1906, reprinted in González Ramírez, *La huelga de Cananea*, 33.

25. González Ramírez, *La huelga de Cananea*; Truett, *Fugitive Landscapes*, 144–45.

26. Emmons, *The Butte Irish*; Peck, *Reinventing Free Labor*; Andrews, *Killing for Coal*.

27. Elías Chomina, *Compendio de datos historicos de la Familia Elías*, 26–34; Deed from Elías and P. de Elías to Bryant and Acuña, May 11, 1881; Deed from Elías, Elías, Ainsa, Ochoa, and Tully, to Hall, April 2, 1883; both in box 2, Papers of Francis Henry Hereford, UASC; "Brief Summary of Title History of the Rancho Santa Maria Santisima del Carmen," "Santa Cruz County Ranches," Ephemera Files, PAHS.

28. Copy of "Testimonio of four sitios of land for cattle in the Hacienda of San Bernardino," folder 2, box 1, Slaughter Financial Papers, AHS/T; Erwin, *The Southwest of John Horton Slaughter*, 135–43.

29. Ford to Fulford, May 12, 1892, folder 3, box 2; Cameron to Fulford, November 16, 1899, folder 4, box 2; Statement for the Months of April and May, 1903, May 31, 1903, folder 1, box 3; all in San Rafael Cattle Company Papers (hereafter SRCC Papers), UASC; Hadley and Sheridan, "Land Use History of the San Rafael Valley," 100; Camou Healy, *De rancheros, poquiteros, orejanos y criollos*, 74–76; Haskett, "Early History of the Cattle Industry in Arizona"; Sayre, *Ranching, Endangered Species, and Urbanization in the Southwest*, 30–32, 53–54.

30. Elías Chomina, *Compendio de datos históricos de la Familia Elías*, 26–34; Erwin, *The Southwest of John Horton Slaughter*, 138–39; Hendricks, "Guillermo Andrade and Land Development on the Mexican Colorado River Delta."

31. White, *It's Your Misfortune and None of My Own*, 137–54; Holden, *Mexico and the Survey of Public Lands*.

32. Hu-DeHart, *Yaqui Resistance and Survival*, 78–84, 124; Holden, *Mexico and the Survey of Public Lands*, 79–97.

33. Lumholtz, *New Trails in Mexico*, 26–27.

34. Head to Collier, November 3, 1941, Agency File 062, Henry F. Dobyns Papago-Pima Historical Notes, ASMA; Spicer, *Cycles of Conquest*, 134–39; Honey, "Policy and Politics in the Papaguería," 15–20; Sheridan, *Landscapes of Fraud*, 107–71; Lewis, *Neither Wolf nor Dog*, 136–48; Wilbur-Cruce, *A Beautiful, Cruel Country*.

35. "Testimonio of four sitios of land for cattle in the Hacienda of San Bernardino," 1821, folder 2, box 1, Slaughter Financial Papers, AHS/T.

36. Holden, *Mexico and the Survey of Public Lands*, 105, 154, 187–88; Truett, *Fugitive Landscapes*, 95.

37. Hadley and Sheridan, "Land Use History of the San Rafael Valley," 100–103.

38. Cora Viola Slaughter, "Reminiscences," circa 1937, folders 93–98, box 5, Bernice Cosulich Papers, AHS/T; Bradfute, *The Court of Private Land Claims*, 14–16. See also Montoya, *Translating Property*.

39. Cora Viola Slaughter, "Reminiscences," folders 93–98, box 5, Bernice Cosulich Papers, AHS/T; "In the Court of Private Land Claims, District of Arizona, Involving the property claimed under the San Bernardino Land Grant, Transcript of oral evidence and proceedings," March 18–19, 1895; Judgment of Joseph R. Reed, Chief Justice, in *John H. Slaughter v. The United States*, March 27, 1896; Statement of Allen R. English, Attorney for the Petitioner in *John H. Slaughter* v. *The United States*, March 25, 1896; "Testimony of H. G. Howe in the Court of Private Land Claims," March 18–19, 1895; all in folder 4, box 1, Slaughter Financial Papers, AHS/T; Bradfute, *The Court of Private Land Claims*, 151–52; Walker and Bufkin, *Historical Atlas of Arizona*, 15.

40. Walker and Bufkin, *Historical Atlas of Arizona*, 15; "Brief Summary of Title History of the Rancho Santa Maria Santisima del Carmen," "Santa Cruz County Ranches," Ephemera Files, PAHS; *Ainsa v. U.S.*, 161 U.S. 208 (1896); *Ainsa v. US.*, 184 U.S. 639 (1902); Bradfute, *The Court of Private Land Claims*, 154–55, 163–66, 168–70; folder 3: "Land Grant Papers," box 3, SRCC Papers, UASC; *U.S. v. Green*, 185 U.S. 256 (1902); Hadley and Sheridan, "Land Use History of the San Rafael Valley,"106; *Mexican Grant: San Rafael de la Zanja Rancho*.

41. Elías Chomina, *Compendio de datos históricos de la Familia Elías*, 31; Hadley, "Ranch Life, The Border Country"; Sheridan, *Arizona*, 141–43; Sonnichsen, *Colonel Greene and the Copper Skyrocket*, 24, 102, 237; Hadley and Sheridan, "Land Use History of the San Rafael Valley," 106; Cameron to Ely, May 26, 1903; Fulford to Stockholders, July 7, 1903; both in folder 5, box 2, SRCC Papers, UASC; Deed between Geo. Aston & wife and W. C. Greene, April 8, 1901, box 2, Papers of Francis Henry Hereford, UASC; Miscellaneous files related to the Claims of the Cananea Cattle Company, S.A., in entry 125, box 188, agency file 1149, RG 76, NACP; Deposition of Charles W. Newman, June 9, 1936; Statement of Claimant in the Claim of The United States of America on behalf of *Palomas Land and Cattle Company vs. United Mexican States*; both in Claim File for Palomas Land and Cattle Company, entry 125, box 349a, agency file 1850, RG 76, NACP.

42. Tout, *The First Thirty Years*, 25–98; Rockwood, *Born of the Desert*, 13–14; Cory, *The Imperial Valley and the Salton Sink*, 1252–53, 1262–63; DeBuys and Myers, *Salt Dreams*, 71–95.

43. Otis to Creel, September 3, 1907; Otis to Creel, September 4, 1907; both in folder 37, Anderson Portfolios, Colorado River Land Company Paper (hereafter CRLC Papers), SL; Kerig, "Yankee Enclave"; Herrera Carrillo, *Reconquista y colonización del valle de Mexicali*.

44. Sanginés to Secretaría de Gobernación, February 20, 1901, Fondo IIH: 1901.7 [34:28], Archivo Gobernación, IIH-UABC. See also Jones to Marcy, July 21, 1869, *Annual Report of the Commissioner of Indian Affairs . . . 1869*, 216.

45. Williams, *The Cocopah People*, 42; Tout, *The First Thirty Years*, 273; Inter-Tribal Council of Arizona, Incorporated, "Cocopah Tribe: Introductory Information," Inter-Tribal Council of Arizona Web site.

46. Law of February 1st, 1856, translated in Hamilton, *Hamilton's Mexican Law*, 11; Book XII, Title I, Chapter I, Article 824, translated in Wheless, *Compendium of the Laws of Mexico*, 526; Wasserman, *Capitalists, Caciques, and Revolution*, 84–94; Hart, *Empire and Revolution*, 59–267.

47. Hendricks, "Guillermo Andrade and Land Development on the Mexican Colorado River Delta"; Piñera Ramírez, *American and English Influence on the Early Development of Ensenada*, 49–50. Other historians have put the percentage of lands controlled by colonization companies even higher. See Kearney, "American Colonization Ventures in Lower California," 61.

48. Piñera Ramírez, *American and English Influence on the Early Development of Ensenada*, 47–50, 73; Hendricks, "Guillermo Andrade and Land Development on the Mexican Colorado River Delta," 161–62; Petition from Roach to Coffey, June 6, 1885, folder 24, Anderson Portfolios, CRLC Papers, SL.

49. Department of Fomento to Hacienda, January 19, 1878, folders 14, 15, 16; Letter from Valarta, March 6, 1884, folder 24; both in Anderson Portfolios, CRLC Papers, SL; Piñera Ramírez, *American and English Influence on the Early Development of Ensenada*, 47–63, 75–77; Martínez, *Troublesome Border*, 41–42.

50. Cameron to Fulford, January 24, 1887, folder 5, box 1, SRCC Papers, UASC. See also "In the Court of Private Land Claims, District of Arizona, Involving the property claimed under the San Bernardino Land Grant, Transcript of oral evidence and proceedings," March 18–19, 1895, folder 4, box 1, Slaughter Financial Papers, AHS/T. Some historians have written that Slaughter purchased the San Bernardino Ranch. This may be because they considered the ninety-nine-year lease de facto ownership or because they only considered his ownership of the American portion of the ranch. See Erwin, *The Southwest of John Horton Slaughter*, 139.

51. Cameron to Fulford, May 19, 1890, folder 1, box 2, SRCC Papers, UASC.

52. Hendricks, "Guillermo Andrade and Land Development on the Mexican Colorado River Delta," 41, 66; Hendricks, "Developing San Diego's Desert Empire"; "Historical Background of William Denton"; William Denton's Mexican Naturalization Certificate, August 15, 1894, folder 3, Oversized Box FB-082; Copy of deed of sale of Jacume, stamped March 7, 1877 and March 21, 1872, folder 1, box 1; Certificación, May 5, 1887, folder 5, Oversized Box FB-082; Denton to Co. Juez de Distrito, August 3, 1886, folder 21 box 1; all in Denton Ranch Collection, MSCL-UCSD.

53. Kerig, "Yankee Enclave," 76; "Petition to Mexican Government for a permit in favor of the California-Mexico Land and Cattle Company to acquire property in the prohibited zone of twenty leagues, dated November 18th, 1902, and the Government decision refusing the same, with legal reasons therefore, dated December 16th, 1902," folders 14, 15, 16, Anderson Portfolios, CRLC Papers, SL; Sonnichsen, *Colonel Greene and the Copper Skyrocket*, 102; Rockwood, *Born of the Desert*, 13–14; Lewis, *Iron Horse Imperialism*; Trennert, "The Southern Pacific Railroad of Mexico"; Kirchner, *Baja California Railroads*; "Articles of Incorporation" and "Outline of a Proposed Hunting Reserve in Mexico

near San Diego," folder 2, box 21; Keller to Chandler, February 14, 1916, folder 26, box 21; both in Henry W. Keller Papers (hereafter Keller Papers), HL.

54. Hofsommer, "Making Connections," 89–93; Jeffrey, "The History of Douglas, Arizona," 18–20; Sandomingo, *Historia de Agua Prieta: Tomo I*, 102–3; Lewis, *Iron Horse Imperialism*, 45–49; Kirchner, *Baja California Railways*, 63–69, 74; Trennert, "The Southern Pacific Railroad of Mexico"; Schwantes, *Vision and Enterprise*, 97–100; Greene, Circular, July 16, 1902, folder 52, box 3, Cananea Consolidated Copper Company Papers, AHS/T.

55. Pizarro Suarez to Díaz, June 8, 1910, Folder IIH: [12.11], Archivo Porfirio Díaz, IIH-UABC; Truett, *Fugitive Landscapes*, 80; Wasserman, *Capitalists, Caciques, and Revolution*, 84–94; Hart, *Empire and Revolution*, 59–267.

56. *Douglas Daily Dispatch*, March 30, 1904, 3. See also Anderson Portfolios, CRLC Papers, SL; Sonnichsen, *Colonel Greene and the Copper Skyrocket*, 220–22.

57. Barcenas to Keller, July 5, 1917, folder 2, box 23, Keller Papers, HL. See also Hart to Bruschi, October 28, 1916, folder 20, box 21, Keller Papers, HL; *Oasis*, March 2, 1895, 7; O'Keefe to Young, November 21, 1913, folder 5, box 1, United States Customs Service, District of Nogales, Papers, AHS/T.

58. Martínez, *Border Boom Town*; Hinojosa, *A Borderlands Town in Transition*; Tirres, "American Law Comes to the Border."

59. I use the term *company town* because of the dominance of the mining industry in the economic life of these border towns. None of them, however, was completely owned, planned, or controlled by a single company.

60. Dumke, "Douglas, Border Town," 283; Schwantes, *Vision and Enterprise*, 96; Jeffrey, "The History of Douglas, Arizona," 54; Sonnichsen, *Colonel Greene and the Copper Skyrocket*, 114; Faubien to Morrow, January 21, 1903, folder 58, box 4, Cananea Consolidated Company Papers, AHS/T; Jones to Douglas, June 21, 1907, Jones Letterbook, 1906–1907, Morris Hunter Jones Papers, AHS/T; El Paso and Southwestern Railroad Company Records, AHS/T; *Nogales, Arizona, 1880–1980*, 19.

61. Deposition of Charles W. Newman, June 9, 1936; Statement of Claimant in the Claim of The United States of America on behalf of *Palomas Land and Cattle Company* vs. *United Mexican States*; both in Claim File for Palomas Land and Cattle Company, entry 125, box 349a, agency file 1850, RG 76, NACP.

62. Camacho, McKay, and Pizarro Suárez to Díaz, May 8, 1908, folder 37, Anderson Portfolios, CRLC Papers, SL.

63. *Calexico Chronicle*, July 20, 1905; *Douglas Daily Dispatch*, March 30, 1904, 4; Ada Ekey Jones, Oral history, November 1957, AHS/T; *Oasis*, August 21, 1897, 6; *Oasis*, May 8, 1897, 3.

64. "Registro de las personas en la actualidad . . . ," November 15, 1899, año 1900, tomo 1633, expediente 1, AGES; *Thirteenth Census of the United States taken in the year 1910 Volume II*, 87.

65. Luis Escalada, oral history, March 18, 1972, AHS/T; Tinker Salas, *In the Shadow of the Eagles*, 156; *Douglas Daily Dispatch*, August 26, 1904, 2; *Calexico Chronicle*, July 20, 1905; *Oasis*, December 6, 1894.

66. "Nina," oral history, Ephemera File: Battle of Nogales-1918, PAHS.

67. *Douglas Daily Dispatch*, July 22, 1904, 1.

68. Jones, oral history, November 1957, AHS/T.

69. Ibid. See also Tinker Salas, *In the Shadow of the Eagles*, 158–59.

70. *Oasis*, December 20, 1894, 5; *Douglas Daily Dispatch*, April 3, 1904, 1.

71. Cora Viola Slaughter, "Reminiscences," folder 93–98, box 5, Bernice Cosulich Papers, AHS/T.

72. Tinker Salas, *In the Shadow of the Eagles*, 159; *Nogales, Arizona, 1880–1980*, 37.

73. Slaughter Family History Manuscript, AHS/T.

74. For examples of positive or neutral usage of "Mexican" see *Douglas Daily Dispatch*, May 28, 1903; September 1, 1903; February 7, 1904; May 6, 1904; July 22, 1904; August 28, 1904; October 28, 1904. For examples of negative usage of "Mexican" see *Douglas Daily Dispatch*, February 7, 1904; February 11, 1904; February 12, 1904; June 3, 1904; June 26, 1904; June 30, 1904; January 17, 1904; May 21, 1905; May 23, 1905.

75. *Douglas Daily Dispatch*, May 6, 1905, 1.

76. For another example of how these categories operated in Arizona see Benton-Cohen, *Borderline Americans*, 27–31.

77. *Oasis*, February 29, 1896, 1.

78. *Calexico Chronicle*, July 6, 1905, 1; May 11, 1905, 1; September 22, 1910, 3; Lira y Lira to Díaz, October 6, 1910, Folder IIH: [12.19], Fondo Archivo Porfirio Díaz, IIH-UABC; *Douglas Daily Dispatch*, September 15, 1903, 1; Clausen to the Secretary of State, April 16, 1908, año 1908, tomo 2331, expediente 3: "Festividades y Manifestaciones populares," AGES; *Oasis*, July 4, 1896, 1; July 11, 1904, 1.

79. *Oasis*, September 21, 1895, 4.

CHAPTER FOUR: THE SPACE BETWEEN

1. "Survey and Remarking of the Boundary between the United States and Mexico West of the Rio Grande, 1891–1896," Senate Document 247, 55th Cong., 2nd sess. (hereafter Senate Document 247), Part II, 20.

2. Fernandez to the Minister of Fomento, October 22, 1883, Ref. IIH: 1.9, Fondo Límites México–Estados Unidos, Archivo AGN, IIH-UABC.

3. Senate Document 247, Part I, 13.

4. Senate Document 247, Part II, 178.

5. Browne, *Adventures in the Apache Country*, 159. See also Senate Document 247, Part II, 174.

6. Senate Document 247, Part II, 178.

7. Velasco to Gabilondo, February 17, 1887; Ortiz to the Administrator of Customs at Sasabe, April 8, 1887; both in legajo 1047, gaveta 35-5, AGES.

8. Supplementary Agreement signed by Barlow and Blanco, March 9, 1892, Senate Document 247, Part I, 19. See also Senate Document, 247, Part I, 13, 18.

9. Ibid., 18.

10. Senate Document 247, Part II, 24.

11. Senate Document 247, Part I, 34.

12. Ibid., 49.

13. Senate Document 247, Part II, 20.

14. Ibid., 178.

15. Hamlyn to Raney, June 21, 1971, Ephemera Files: U.S. Boundaries-Mexico, PAHS; Senate Document 247, Part II, 189–90; Morrison to U.S. Attorney General, March 28, 1898, Morrison Letterbook, AHS/T.

16. Vega to Corral, November 16, 1904, Fondo IIH: 1904.27 [36.41], Archivo Gobernación, IIH-UABC.

17. Barlow to Foster, November 29, 1892, Senate Document 247, Part II, 178.

18. *Douglas Daily Dispatch*, May 25, 1904, 1.

19. Hamlyn to Raney, June 21, 1971; Proclamation of Theodore Roosevelt, May 27, 1907; both in Ephemera Files: U.S. Boundaries-Mexico, PAHS.

20. Herrera Pérez, *La Zona Libre*; Bell and Smallwood, *The Zona Libre*, 44–45, 49, 58.

21. "Tariff of 1890 (McKinley Tariff)," in Northrup and Prange Turney, eds., *Encyclopedia of Tariffs and Trade in U.S. History*, vol. 3, 214; Ruíz, *The People of Sonora and Yankee Capitalists*, 140–41. See also Northrup and Prange Turney, eds., *Encyclopedia of Tariffs and Trade in U.S. History*, vol. 1, 248–49; Terrill, *The Tariff, Politics, and American Foreign Policy*; Taussig, *The Tariff History of the United States*, 251–83.

22. Senate Document 247, Part II, 20. See also Tinker Salas, *In the Shadow of the Eagles*, 118. For an overview of customs enforcement see Schmeckebier, *The Customs Service*, 32–78.

23. Tout, *The First Thirty Years*, 273; *Calexico Chronicle*, May 4, 1905; *Calexico Chronicle*, April 18, 1910, 2; Lawler to the President, December 31, 1910; Creel to Otis, January 3, 1911; both in folder 18, Anderson Portfolios, CRLC Papers, SL.

24. Truett, *Fugitive Landscapes*, 85.

25. *Oasis*, October 26, 1895, 4.

26. Cameron to Chalmers, labeled exhibit "B," circa 1887, folder 6, box 1, SRCC Papers, UASC.

27. Milard to Torres, March 2, 1887; Ortiz to the Administrator of Customs, April 8, 1887; Sturges to Corral, January 31, 1889; all in legajo 1047, gaveta 35-5, AGES.

28. Town, Altschul, and Breen to Blaine, December 9, 1890, Despatches from United States Consul in Nogales (M283, roll 1), RG 59, NACP.

29. Chalmers to Cameron Bros, labels exhibit "E," November 20, 1887, folder 6, box 1, SRCC Papers, UASC.

30. Town, Altschul, and Breen to Blaine, December 9, 1890, Despatches from United States Consul in Nogales (M283, roll 1), RG 59, NACP; Clipping: "Problem in Sheep for the Appraiser," *Express*, January 21, 1908, folder 21, Anderson Portfolios, CRLC Papers, SL.

31. Clipping from the *Daily Star*, January 22, 1888, in folder 2, box 1, SRCC Papers, UASC. See also Truett, *Fugitive Landscapes*, 86.

32. Cameron to Chalmers, labeled exhibit "B," circa 1887, folder 6, box 1, SRCC Papers, UASC.

33. Smith to Wharton, July 17, 1890, Despatches from the United States Consuls in Nogales (M283, roll 1), RG 59, NACP.

34. Smith to Aspe, September 23, 1890; Aspe to Smith, September 25, 1890;

Smith to Ryan, October 1, 1890; Fenochio to U.S. Consul, December 31, 1890; all in Despatches from the United States Consuls in Nogales (M283, roll 1), RG 59, NACP; Handwritten Notes re: "Act July 24, 1897—"Dingley" law "Free List," folder 21, Anderson Portfolios, CRLC Papers, SL.

35. Case Entry for Luis Calderon, United States Bureau of Immigration, Record of proceedings in criminal cases, 1905–1907 (hereafter U.S. Immigration, Records of Criminal Cases, 1905–1907), AHS/T; "Complaint: U.S.A. v. Pedro Garcia and Ramona Garcia," August 20, 1909, folder 116; "Complaint: U.S.A. v. Albert Capp," December 27, 1910, folder 118; "Complaints: U.S.A. v. Fred Ferguson and U.S.A. v. William Cluting," January 3, 1911, folder 128; all in box 8, Jared D. Taylor Papers (hereafter Taylor Papers), AHS/T; Cameron to Fulford, January 26, 1885, folder 2, box 1, SRCC Papers, UASC; Smith to Wharton, April 25, 1890, Despatches from the United States Consuls in Nogales (M283, roll 1), RG 59, NACP. For more on transborder smuggling see Andreas, *Border Games*, 15–26; Sahlins, *Boundaries*, 89–93, 240–43; Nugent, *Smugglers, Secessionists, and Loyal Citizens on the Ghana-Togo Frontier*.

36. "Mittimus charging C. E. Biddinger," November 18, 1909, folder 115; "Certificate of Proceedings: U.S.A. v. William Hancock," April 13, 1910, folder 122; "Mittimus: U.S.A. v. George Mullen," June 22, 1910, folder 124; all in box 8, Taylor Papers, AHS/T; Toro, *Mexico's "War" on Drugs*, 5–6; Andreas, *Border Games*, 40; Benton-Cohen, *Borderline Americans*, 48–63; Secretaría de Estado y Despacho to Gobernador de Sonora, March 1, 1900, tomo 1567, expediente 5, año 1900, AGES; Hadley, "Ranch Life," 10–11.

37. Haley, *Jeff Milton*, 148–77; Miller, *The Arizona Rangers*.

38. Erwin, *The Southwest of John Horton Slaughter*, 319. See also Smith Jr., *Emilio Kosterlitzky*, 96–111; Truett, *Fugitive Landscapes*, 139–42.

39. Gobernador de Sonora to Secretaría de Relaciones Exteriores, September 28, 1887, tomo 592, año 1888, Ramo Exportación de Ganado, expediente 7, AGES.

40. McKellar and Hart, "Eradicating Cattle Ticks in California," 283–300; Pulling, "California's Range Cattle Industry," 28. See also Manchado, *The North Mexican Cattle Industry*, 25–26.

41. Masanz, *History of the Immigration and Naturalization Service*, 6–7; Tichenor, *Dividing Lines*, 3. The Mexican government also enacted immigration restrictions, but, as will be discussed in greater detail in chapter seven, these were of less significance on the border. See Translation of Mexican Immigration Law of December 22, 1908, 96th Cong., 2nd sess., Records of the Immigration and Naturalization Service (hereafter Records of the INS), RG 85, Series A, Part 2, reel 17, frames 612–20.

42. Ralph, "The Chinese Leak"; Lee, *At America's Gates*, 165–201; Ettinger, *Imaginary Lines*, 37–122.

43. Smith, "Immigration and Naturalization Service," 305–6; Biographic Note; clippings in Scrapbook of Connell Family, 1901–1906, folder 2, box 1; both in Charles L. Connell Papers (hereafter Connell Papers), AHS/T.

44. "U.S. Immigration Officials Are Busy," "Connell After Wily Chinese," and other clippings, Scrapbook of Connell Family, folder 2, box 1, Connell Papers, AHS/T; Lee, *At America's Gates*, 41, 77–109; Delgado, "In the Age of Exclusion," 199–201; Luibhéid, *Entry Denied*.

45. "Report of Conditions Existing in Europe and Mexico affecting Emigration and Immigration," Records of the INS, RG 85, Series A, Part 2, roll 1, frame 9. See also "Compilation from the records of the Bureau of Immigration of facts concerning the enforcement of the Chinese-exclusion laws," May 25, 1906, House Document 847, 59th Cong., 1st sess., 13.

46. Haley, *Jeff Milton*, 340–55; Rak, *Border Patrol*, 6; Myers, *The Border Wardens*, 15–19; Hernández, *Migra!*, 38–39. For more on the build-up of immigration enforcement on the United States' land borders during this period see Ettinger, *Imaginary Lines*, 90–92.

47. Secretary [of Commerce and Labor] to Root, February 12, 1908, Records of the INS, RG 85, Series A, Part 2, roll 1, frames 301–3.

48. Perkins, *Border Patrol*, 17. See also Paulsen, "The Yellow Peril at Nogales"; "Wrecking the Chinese Underground Route," *San Francisco Bulletin*, Sunday Magazine, August 21, 1904, clipping in Scrapbook of Connell Family, folder 2, box 1, Connell Papers, AHS/T; "Report of Conditions Existing in Europe and Mexico affecting Emigration and Immigration," Records of the INS, RG 85, Series A, Part 2, roll 1, frames 22–23; Ralph, "The Chinese Leak," 524; U.S. Immigration, Records of Criminal Cases, 1905–1907, AHS/T; Delgado, "At Exclusion's Southern Gate," 198–202.

49. Lee, *At America's Gates*, 77–109; Translation of Mexican Immigration Law of December 22, 1908, Records of the INS, RG 85, Series A, Part 2, reel 17, frames 612–20; Hu-DeHart, "Immigrants to a Developing Society," 276–83; Jacques, "Have Quick More Money Than Mandarins," 201–4; Lim, "*Chinos* and *Paisanos*"; Delgado, "At Exclusion's Southern Gate,"187–89, 199; Truett, *Fugitive Landscapes*, 120–24.

50. Secretary [of Commerce and Labor] to Root, February 12, 1908, Records of the INS, RG 85, Series A, Part 2, roll 1.

51. Case records of Ah Sam and Ah Lee, U.S. Immigration, Records of Criminal Cases, 1905–1907, AHS/T. See also Delgado, "At Exclusion's Southern Gate," 185.

52. "How Chinks Were Smuggled," clipping in Scrapbook of Connell Family, folder 2, box 1, Connell Papers, AHS/T; Haley, *Jeff Milton*, 344.

53. U.S. Immigration, Records of Criminal Cases, 1905–1907, AHS/T.

54. "Connell Meets a Wily Chink," undated, clipping in Scrapbook of Connell Family, folder 2, box 1, Connell Papers, AHS/T.

55. "Chinese Inspectors Break Up Gang of Smugglers That Has Operated on Mexican Border," *San Francisco Bulletin*, June 13, 1904. See also "Connell Makes Sensational Raid Captures Counterfeit 'Chok Chees' and Opens Up Many Large Frauds," no date; "Certificates Counterfeited," June 10, 1904; "Certificates Were Bogus," *Los Angeles Times*, June 15, 1904; clippings in Scrapbook of Connell Family, folder 2, box 1, Connell Papers, AHS/T.

56. Secretary [of Commerce and Labor] to Root, February 12, 1908, Records of the INS, RG 85, Series A, Part 2, roll 1, frames 304–15. See also Root to Secretary of Commerce and Labor, February 20, 1908, frames 301–3; "Memorandum in re: Proposed Mexican Agreement," frames 336–49; both in Records of the INS, RG 85, Series A, Part 2, roll 1; Lee, *At America's Gates*, 151–57, 173–79; Ettinger, *Imaginary Lines*, 91–92.

57. Haley, *Jeff Milton*, 147–75.

58. Otis to Díaz, July 28, 1908, folder 37, Anderson Portfolios, CRLC Papers, SL.

59. Rynning, *Gun Notches*, 205–6.

60. Carl M. Rathbun, "Keeping the Peace along the Mexican Border," *Harper's Weekly* (1906), reprinted in Miller, *The Arizona Rangers*, 2; *Douglas Daily Dispatch*, May 11, 1904, 1; *Douglas Daily Dispatch*, July 24, 1904, 1; Salida to Secretaría de Estado, January 15, 1901; Jefe Politico y Militar to Governor of Sonora, October 5, 1901; both in tomo 1695, expediente 1, AGES; Kosterlitzky to Torres, January 18, 1909; Kosterlitzky to Torres, April 13, 1909; Prefect of Magdalena to Secretaría de Estado, October 13, 1909; Hermosillo to District Prefect, Magdalena, October 15, 1909; all in tomo 2525, año 1909, expediente 7, AGES.

61. Truett, *Fugitive Landscapes*, 141.

62. *Douglas Daily Dispatch*, February 11, 1904, 1. See also Erwin, *The Southwest of John Horton Slaughter*, 231–36, 242–48.

63. *Douglas Daily Dispatch*, February 11, 1904, 1.

64. Rynning, *Gun Notches*, 223–25. See also ibid., 223–29.

65. Ibid., 229.

66. *Douglas Daily Dispatch*, March 26, 1904, 1. See also *Douglas Daily Dispatch*, February 20, 1904, 1; February 23, 1904, 1; March 18, 1904, 1; Erwin, *The Southwest of John Horton Slaughter*, 248.

67. *Douglas Daily Dispatch*, April 21, 1904, 1.

68. *Douglas Daily Dispatch*, May 11, 1904, 1; June 10, 1904, 1; July 24, 1904, 1; February 18, 1905, 1; Erwin, *The Southwest of John Horton Slaughter*, 248.

69. *Douglas Daily Dispatch*, February 11, 1904, 1; Rynning, *Gun Notches*, 202, 215; "Arizona Rangers," Douglas *Dispatch*, 1905, reprinted in Miller, *The Arizona Rangers*, 83.

70. For the following description of the Cananea strike and its aftermath see González Ramírez, *La huelga de Cananea*; Truett, *Fugitive Landscapes*, 144–49.

71. Rynning, *Gun Notches*, 292–93. See also Torres to Corral, June 5, 1906, in González Ramírez, *La huelga de Cananea*, 76–77; Truett, *Fugitive Landscapes*, 145–46.

72. Corral to Izábal, June 8, 1906, in González Ramírez, *La huelga de Cananea*, 85; Torres to Corral, June 5, 1906, in ibid., 76–77.

73. Truett, *Fugitive Landscapes*, 146–49.

74. Elías to Secretaría de Relaciones Exteriores, April 22, 1908, tomo 2337, expediente 21, AGES. See also Marsical to the Governor of Sonora, March 23, 1908; Comisario de Policia de Colonia Lerdo to Secretaría de Estado, May 20, 1907; Testimony of Ruiz, Carbajal, and Chiotto before the Mexican Consul at Yuma, February 19, 1907; Judge of First Instance, Altar, to Secretaría de Gobierno, February 13, 1907; all in tomo 2337, expediente 21, AGES.

75. George to Gray, December 4, 1893, Despatches from the United States Consuls in Nogales (M283, roll 2), RG 59, NACP; Dobson, "Desperadoes and Diplomacy."

76. Miller, *The Arizona Rangers*, 188–201; Letters and clippings in folders 3 and 6, Kidder Papers, AHS/T; Arnold to Torres, April 9, 1908; Cubillas to Secretaría de Estado, April 9, 1908; both in tomo 2413, expediente 1, AGES.

77. Olds to Mrs. Kidder, April 9, 1908, folder 3; "Kidder Was Victim of Plot Says Rankin," May 1; "Commissions Are Lifted from Mexicans," April 24, 1909; clippings both in folder 6; "Biographical Note"; all in Kidder Papers, AHS/T; Arnold to Torres, April 9, 1908; Cubillas to Secretaría de Estado, April 9, 1908; both in tomo 2413, expediente 1, AGES; Miller, *The Arizona Rangers*, 196–201.

78. Citizens of Naco to Mrs. Kidder, April 17, 1908; Old to Mrs. Kidder, April 9, 1908; Aley to Mrs. Kidder, June 10, 1909; all in folder 3, Kidder Papers, AHS/T; "Captain Wheeler Pays Tribute to Jeff Kidder, the Dead Ranger," *Arizona Gazette* clipping, folder 6, Kidder Papers, AHS/T; Miller, *The Arizona Rangers*, 74–77, 117, 127–31.

Chapter Five: Breaking Ties, Building Fences

1. Casualty reports varied widely, particularly in regard to the number of Mexican deaths. Creighton, Lewis, and Tidwell to Secretary of Treasury, September 10, 1918, 812.00/22290; "Proceedings of the Board of Officers which met at Nogales to inquire and report on the events of August 27th," August 29, 1918, 812.00/22290; both in (M274, roll 64), RG 59, NACP; *Los Angeles Times*, August 28, 1918, 1; *San Diego Union*, August 28, 1918, 1.

2. For histories of the origins of the Mexican Revolution see Meyer and Sherman, *The Course of Mexican History*, 483–500; Hart, *Revolutionary Mexico*; Knight, *The Mexican Revolution*, vol. 1.

3. Hall and Coerver, *Revolution on the Border*; Ada Jones, "Battle of Nogales, Sonora, March 13, 1913," Ephemera Files, PAHS; Blaisdell, *The Desert Revolution*; Hall, "The Mexican Revolution and the Crisis in Naco"; Martínez, *Fragments of the Mexican Revolution*.

4. O'Keefe to Deputy Collector, Douglas, November 3, 1913, folder 4, box 1; O'Keefe to Deputy Collector, Douglas, November 11, 1913, folder 4, box 1; Mason to Deputy Collector, Douglas, January 24, 1914, folder 6, box 1; Mason to Deputy Collectors at Douglas, Naco, Lochiel, Nogales, Yuma, November 17, 1915, folder 23, box 3; Mason to Deputy Collectors, Douglas and Naco, June 23, 1916, folder 30, box 4; Peters to Collectors of Customs ports on the Atlantic and Gulf Coasts and the Mexican Border, October 19, 1916, folder 34, box 4; Hardy to the Deputy Collectors and others concerned, August 6, 1914, folder 11, box 2; all in United States Customs Service, District of Nogales, Papers (hereafter U.S. Customs Service, Nogales, Papers), AHS/T.

5. "Report of Robert L. Barnes," June 13, 1912; "Report of C. D. Hebert," June 11, 1912, 812.00/4277; both in (M274, roll 19), RG 59, NACP.

6. Press release of the National Association for the Protection of American Rights in Mexico, September 6, in Testimony of Charles Boynton, September 16, 1919, "Investigation of Mexican Affairs," Senate Document 285, 66th Cong., 2nd sess., vol. 1, 467. See also Bowman to Secretary of State, July 30, 1912, 812.00/4568 (M274, roll 19), RG 59, NACP; Hu-DeHart, *Yaqui Resistance and Survival*.

7. Lewis to Deputy Collector, Douglas, November 6, 1913, folder 4, box 1; Customs Service, El Paso, to Collector, Douglas, August 30, 1915, folder 20, box 3; Locke to Collector, Nogales, May 31, 1915, folder 17, box 2; Wheatley to

Locke, February 25, 1915, folder 15, box 2; all in U.S. Customs Service, Nogales, Papers, AHS/T; Knox to Calero, July 9, 1912, 812.00/4348 (M274, roll 19), RG 59, NACP; "Copies of Indictments in the Arizona District Court," folder 120, box 17, Ellinwood Family Papers, AHS/T; Katz, *The Life and Times of Pancho Villa*, 212, 655–59.

8. Petition to President Taft from Nogales citizens, July 23, 1912, 812.00/4560 (M274, roll 19), RG 59, NACP. See also "Consular Report from Douglas, Arizona," July 19, 1920, 812.00/4542 (M274, roll 19), RG 59, NACP.

9. "Note of the Secretary of State of the United States to the Secretary of Foreign Relations of the De Facto Government of Mexico," June 20, 1916, House Document 1237, 64th Cong., 1st sess. (hereafter HD 1237), 14; "Copy of Indictments in the Arizona District Court in the Case of Pedro Torres, Julio Carranza Jr., Lopez Mendoza," November 12, 1914; "Copy of Indictments in the Arizona District Court in the Case of Alfonso Coronado and Joaquin Esquer," May 10, 1915; both in folder 120, box 17, Ellinwood Family Papers, AHS/T; Dye to Secretary of State, August 8, 1912, 812.00/4591 (M274, roll 19), RG 59, NACP; Work, "Enforcing Neutrality."

10. Hart, *Revolutionary Mexico*; Blaisdell, *The Desert Revolution*; Knight, *The Mexican Revolution*, vol. 1, 45–47. Because of the large number of Americans who fought with the Magonistas, some contemporaries accused them of being a front for an illicit filibuster attempt on Baja California. While most historians have concluded that this was not true, it has inspired a great deal of debate. See Sociedad Mexicana Defensores de la Integridad Nacional of San Diego to the Minister of Gobernación, July 1911, folder IIH: [4], Fondo Revolución, IIH-UABC; Blaisdell, *The Desert Revolution*; Griswold del Castillo, "The Discredited Revolution"; Turner, *Revolution in Baja California*; Blaisdell, "Harry Chandler and the Mexican Border Intrigue"; Joseph Richard Werne, "El Periodo del Gobernador Esteban Cantú; 1915–1920," in *Mexicali*, vol. 1, 257–59.

11. Margaret L. Holbrook Smith, "The Capture of Tía Juana," *Overland Monthly* 58, no. 1 (July 1911): 1–7, reprinted in Martínez, *Fragments of the Mexican Revolution*, 99. See also *San Diego Union*, May 11, 1911, 5; Proffitt, *Tijuana*, 188.

12. Angel to Secretaría del Estado y Gobernación, July 11, 1911, IIH: [8]; Vega to Gobernación, July 25, 1911, file IIH: [13]; Vega to Gobernación, July 25, 1911, file IIH: [14]; all in Fondo Revolución, IIH-UABC; Ockerson to Otis, January 30, 1911, folder 18; Otis to Pizarro Suarez, February 13, 1911, folder 18; Ockerson to Otis, February 15, 1911, folder 18; Mexican Department of Foreign Relations to Otis, March 15, 1911, folder 18; Easton to Brant, November 6, 1911, folder 35; all in Anderson Portfolios, CRLC Papers, SL; Waters to Taft, Knox, and Dickinson, April 21, 1911, 711.1214/12 (M314, roll 9), RG 59, NACP.

13. Lamadrid to Keller, August 5, 1913, folder 26, box 27, Keller Papers, HL.

14. Meyer and Sherman, *The Course of Mexican History*, 511–27.

15. Jones, "Battle of Nogales," Ephemera Files, PAHS; Truett, "Transnational Warrior," 241–42, 259–61; Kosterlitzky to Secretary of War, March 19, 1913, reprinted in Smith, *Emilio Kosterlitzky*, 201; Hall and Coerver, *Revolution on the Border*, 31–32. Similar transborder surrenders occurred in Naco and Agua Prieta.

See "Carranza-Wilson Government in Mexico speech of Hon. Albert B. Fall," June 2, 1916," 3, box 33, Ellen Rose Gibbon Bergman Collection (hereafter Bergman Collection), HL; Captain J. E. Gaujot, "Statement given on May 4, 1911," 812.00/1840, Records of the Department State Relating to the Internal Affairs of Mexico, 1910–1929, reprinted in Martínez, *Fragments of the Mexican Revolution*, 72.

16. Meyer and Sherman, *The Course of Mexican History*, 552–61; "Weekly Report on Border Conditions," November 10, 1915, 812.00/16803 (M274, roll 50), RG 59, NACP; "Statement of Frank T. Greene," March 8, 1929, box 188, docket 1149, entry 125; "Mary Greene Wiswall Memorial," 1926, box 188, docket 1149, entry 125; "Memorial prepared by Marshall Morgan," September 1928, box 276, docket 1450, entry 125; "Statement of Claimant in the Claim of The United States of America on behalf of Palomas Land and Cattle Company vs. United Mexican States," box 349a, docket 1850, entry 125; all in Records of the United States–Mexico Claims Commission, (RG 76), NACP.

17. Mascareñas to Banco de Sonora, February 4, 1911; Mascareñas to Banco de Sonora, February 10, 1911; both in Letter Book: January 14, 1911–April 26, 1913, Manuel Mascareñas Papers, UASC; Angel to Secretary of State and Office of Government, July 11, 1911, IIH: [8], Fondo Revolución, 1911, IIH-UABC; Smith, "The Capture of Tía Juana," 1–7, reprinted in Martínez, *Fragments of the Mexican Revolution*, 99, 101; Dye to Secretary of State, July 11, 1912, 812.00/4402 (M274, roll 19), RG 59, NACP.

18. Hall and Coerver, *Revolution on the Border*, 126–27.

19. Hu-DeHart, "Immigrants to a Developing Society," 283–96, 305; Jacques, "Have Quick More Money Than Mandarins," 205–10; Lim, "*Chinos* and *Paisanos*," 67–70.

20. Nelson C. Bledsoe, oral history, April 3, 1961, AHS/T.

21. Ada Ekey Jones, oral history, November 1957, AHS/T; Tully, "Bullets for Breakfast," 10; Smith, "The Capture of Tía Juana," 1–7, reprinted in Martínez, *Fragments of the Mexican Revolution*, 101; Hall and Coerver, *Revolution on the Border*, 130–31.

22. Murphy to Commanding Officer, November 1, 1915; Hale to the Commanding General Provision Division Camp at Douglas, November 3, 1915; both in Assistant Secretary of War to Secretary of State, November 29, 1915, 812.00/16904 (M274, roll 50), RG 59, NACP.

23. Docket Books for the United States and Mexican Claims Commissions, books 1–4, entry 118, RG 76, NACP; *Calexico Chronicle*, December 16, 1913, 1; Truett, *Fugitive Landscapes*, 171. For the Plan de San Diego see Johnson, *Revolution in Texas*.

24. John Hutchison Darling, oral history, AHS/T. See also Bledsoe, oral history, April 3, 1961, AHS/T; Tully, "Bullets for Breakfast," 6–12.

25. "Camp Harry Jones," First Battalion, Twenty-Second Infantry Web site; Eppinga, *Nogales*, 112.

26. Tully, "Bullets for Breakfast," 8.

27. Tipton and citizens of Columbus to Fall, April 27, 1914, folder 5, box 96, Papers of Albert B. Fall, HL. See also *Calexico Chronicle*, December 16, 1913, 1; Dye to Secretary of State, July 17, 1912, 812.00/4458; Dye to Secretary of State,

July 20, 1912, 812.00/4456; both in (M274, roll 19), RG 59, NACP. See also Knight, *The Mexican Revolution*, vol. 1, 188; Hall and Coerver, *Revolution on the Border*, 44–45, 145.

28. Ada Ekey Jones, "Troublesome Days in Old Mexico," March 13, 1913, Ekey Papers, AHS/T; "Chronology of Events—Border Unrest 1910–1929," "Slaughter Family History," AHS/T; Adee, to U.S. Consul, Nogales, July 22, 1912, 812.00/4456 (M274, roll 19), RG 59, NACP; "Weekly Report of Conditions along the Border # 149," February 1, 1916, 812.00/171.94, RG 59 (M274, roll 51), NACP; Truett, *Fugitive Landscapes*, 167.

29. Malburn to the Collector of Customs, Nogales, October 23, 1915, folder 22, box 3; Newton to the Collector of Customs, Nogales, December 10, 1915, folder 24, box 3; Peters to the Collector of Customs, Nogales, December 15, 1915, folder 24, box 3; Mason to Mix, December 13, 1915, folder 24, box 3; all in U.S. Customs Service, Nogales, Papers, AHS/T; *Mexicali*, vol. 1, 256–59; Katz, *The Secret War in Mexico*, 156–202, 298–314.

30. Katz, *The Secret War in Mexico*, 195–202; Knight, *The Mexican Revolution*, vol. 2, 152–62; Meyer and Sherman, *The Course of Mexican History*, 531–34; Hall and Coerver, *Revolution on the Border*, 149; Katz, *The Life and Times of Pancho Villa*, 328.

31. Polk to Caldwell, July 14, 1916, 711.1214/39 (M314, roll 9), RG 59, NACP. See also "Authorizing the President to appoint a commission to conduct negotiations concerning the purchase of certain portions of northern Mexico," July 10, 1916, Joint Resolution 258, 64th Cong., 1st sess., 711.1214/39 (M314, roll 9), RG 59, NACP.

32. *Los Angeles Times*, April 1, 1917, 1, 7.

33. "U.S. State Department weekly report on border conditions for week of July 8–13, 1915," 812.00/15517, *Records of the Department of State Relating to the Internal Affairs of Mexico, 1910–1929*, reprinted in Martínez, *Fragments of the Mexican Revolution*, 151–52.

34. "Weekly Report No. 338, October 4, 1919," 812.00/22844 (M274, roll 66), RG 59, NACP.

35. Katz, *The Life and Times of Pancho Villa*, 309–26, 487–524.

36. John W. Roberts, *Villa's Own Story of His Life*, McClure Newspaper Syndicate publication no. 35 (August 1916), as cited in Katz, *The Life and Times of Pancho Villa*, 526.

37. Cora Viola Slaughter, "Reminiscences," circa 1937, folders 93–98, box 5, Bernice Cosulich Papers, AHS/T.

38. Darling, oral history, AHS/T; Rachel Stephens, oral history, May 13, 1971, AHS/T; Jeffrey, "The History of Douglas, Arizona," 66.

39. John Henry Eicks, oral history, AHS/T.

40. Statement of Dr. R. H. Thigpen, November 7, 1915, Albert B. Fall Papers, University of Nebraska, as quoted in Katz, *The Life and Times of Pancho Villa*, 527.

41. Funston to Adjutant General, November 30, 1915, 812.00/16893 (M274, roll 50), RG 59, NACP.

42. Simpich to Department of State, November 24, 1915, 812.00/16854; Sim-

pich to Department of State, November 26, 1915, 812.00/16869; Sage to Agwar, November 26, 1915, 812.00/16871; Funston to Scott, November 27, 1915, 812.00/16871; Funston to Adjutant General Army, November 27, 1915, 812.00/16886; all in (M274, roll 50), RG 59, NACP; Hall and Coerver, *Revolution on the Border*, 35–36; Ready, *Open Range and Hidden Silver*, 85–87.

43. Katz, *The Life and Times of Pancho Villa*, 525–28, 550–66; Katz, *The Secret War in Mexico*, 302–3.

44. Mary Means Scott, Written memoir; *Password* 20, no. 4 (1975): 163–67, reprinted in Martínez, *Fragments of the Mexican Revolution*, 178–79. See also Katz, *The Life and Times of Pancho Villa*, 560–66; "Investigation of Mexican Affairs," Senate Document 285, 66th Cong., 2nd sess., 1577–627; Clendenen, *Blood on the Border*, 201–12.

45. *New York Times*, March 10, 1916, 1; *Los Angeles Times*, March 10, 1916, 1; *San Francisco Examiner*, March 10, 1916, 1; Cody to Scott, May 15, 1916, box 23; Smith to Scott, June 27, 1916, box 23; Scott to Dunwoody, June 27, 1916, box 23; Scott to Wiley, July 1, 1916, box 24; all in Hugh Lenox Scott Papers (hereafter Scott Papers), LC; "Transportation of Troops to Mexican Border," July 29, 1916, House Document 1311, 64th Cong., 1st sess.; McCann, *With the National Guard on the Border*; Clendenen, *Blood on the Border*, 213–29.

46. Scott, "Written memoir," reprinted in Martínez, *Fragments of the Mexican Revolution*, 181. For more on Pershing's expedition see Stout, *Border Conflict*.

47. Katz, *The Life and Times of Pancho Villa*, 592–93.

48. HD 1237, 18. See also Katz, *The Secret War in Mexico*, 310; Katz, *The Life and Times of Pancho Villa*, 616, 622.

49. Scott to Rickets, June 21, 1916, box 23, Scott Papers, LC.

50. Note from Brown, May 8, 1916, box 23, Scott Papers, LC.

51. HD 1237, 15–16.

52. "Weekly Report No. 338, October 4, 1919," 812.00/22844 (M274, roll 66), RG 59, NACP. See also Katz, *The Secret War in Mexico*, 311–14.

53. Meyer and Sherman, *The Course of Mexican History*, 542–45; Secretaría de Gobernación, *Constitución Política de los Estados Unidos Mexicanos*. An important debate in the historiography of the Mexican Revolution revolves around the extent to which antiforeign sentiment influenced and motivated revolutionary movements. The dominant positions in this debate are expressed in Hart, *Revolutionary Mexico* and Knight, *The Mexican Revolution*. Hart argues that antiforeign sentiment was an essential factor, while Knight downplays the importance of such sentiment. While the various proponents of these arguments differ on many points, the antiforeign provisions of Article 27 of the 1917 Constitution are undeniable.

54. Keller to Chandler, May 10, 1918, folder 26, box 21; Keller to Cantú, April 13, 1918, folder 22, box 21; Horcasitas to Keller, May 10, 1917, folder 15, box 27; all in Keller Papers, HL; "Statement of Claimant in the Claim of The United States of America on behalf of Palomas Land and Cattle Company vs. United Mexican States," box 349a, agency file 1850, entry 125, RG 76, NACP.

55. Brant, Lindsay, Sherman, and Pfaffinger to Gibbon, September 1, 1916, folder 6, box 35, Bergman Collection, HL; "List of Members: National Associa-

tion for the Protection of American Rights in Mexico," June 19, 1919, folder 4, box 29, Keller Papers, HL; Hart, *Empire and Revolution*, 344–45.

56. While it is difficult to pinpoint the "end" of the Mexican Revolution, most historians point to Obregón's election and the resultant consolidation of state power as a critical turning point. Although violent uprisings and political challenges continued throughout the 1920s and many historians highlight the importance of the Cristero Rebellion (1926–29) in particular as a continuation of revolutionary challenges to the Mexican state, both the federal government and the country as a whole experienced greater stability after 1920. See Meyer and Sherman, *The Course of Mexican History*, 550; Hart, *Revolutionary Mexico*; Knight, *The Mexican Revolution*, vol. 2.

57. *Los Angeles Times*, April 1, 1917, part II, 1.

58. Verfassungsgebende deutsche Nationalversammlung, 15. Ausschuss, *Bericht des zweiten Unterausschusses des Untersuchungsausschusses über die Friedensaktion Wilsons 1916/17* (Berlin, 1920), 355, as quoted in Katz, *The Secret War in Mexico*, 354. See also Katz, *The Secret War in Mexico*, 350–78, 511–12; Barron to Gibbon, December 2, 1917, folder 2, box 34, Bergman Collection, HL.

59. *Los Angeles Times*, April 1, 1917, 1.

60. Walmsley, "America's Unguarded Gateway," 314–15.

61. Capt. Harrington V. Cochran, M.I.D., "Data for a Handbook on the Northern District of Baja California," November 23, 1919, 15, SL; Smith to Secretary of State, July 16, 1919, 812.00/22931 (M274, roll 66); "Weekly Report No. 268, June 1, 1918," 812.00/22027 (M274, roll 63); Dyer to Secretary of State, March 27, 1918, 812.00/21838 (M274, roll 63); "Weekly Report No. 264, May 4, 1918," 812.00/21885 (M274, roll 63); Smith to Secretary of State, June 13, 1918, 812.00/22062 (M274, roll 63); "Weekly Report no. 271, June 22, 1918," 812.00/22078 (M274, roll 64); "Proceedings of the Board of Officers which met at Nogales to inquire and report on the events of August 27th," August 29, 1918, 812.00/22290 (M274, roll 64); all in RG 59, NACP.

62. Keller to Throckmorton, April 10, 1919, folder 5, box 32, Keller Papers, HL. See Public Law No. 154, 65th Cong., approved May 22, 1918," in Udell, *Passport Control Acts*, 3–4; Tichenor, *Dividing Lines*, 153–54. For a general overview of the rise of passports in Europe and the United States during the late nineteenth and early twentieth centuries see Torpey, *The Invention of the Passport*, 93–121.

63. Lawton to Secretary of State, August 9, 1918, 812.00/22160 (M274, roll 64), RG 59, NACP. See also Kang, "The Legal Construction of the Borderlands," 22–26.

64. Newton to Collectors of Customs, April 30, 1917, folder 40, box 5, U.S. Customs Service, Nogales, Papers, AHS/T. See also Mason to Deputy Collectors, Douglas, Nogales, Naco, September 29, 1917, folder 45, box 5, U.S. Customs Service, Nogales, Papers, AHS/T.

65. Edwards to Keller, October 14, 1925, folder 13, box 23, Keller Papers, HL.

66. Mason to Collector of Customs, Nogales, March 16, 1914, folder 8, box 1, U.S. Customs Service, Nogales, Papers, AHS/T.

67. Ready, *Nogales, Arizona*, 68, 93. See also Work, "Enforcing Neutrality."

68. Scott, "Written memoir," reprinted in Martínez, *Fragments of the Mexican Revolution*, 180.

69. Rak, *Border Patrol*, 136.

70. Mathews Photo Albums, Album 3, page 6, picture 397, Mathews Photograph Collection, AHS/T. Many soldiers had their photographs taken along the border and made into picture postcards. In addition to the images includes here see Vanderwood and Samponaro, *Border Fury*.

71. Eicks, oral history, June 5, 1970, AHS/T.

72. Creighton, Lewis, and Tidwell, to Secretary of Treasury, September 10, 1918, 812.00/22290 (M274, roll 64); Boyle to Secretary of State, March 11, 1919, 311.112 V23; both in RG 59, NACP.

73. Creighton, Lewis, and Tidwell to Secretary of Treasury, September 10, 1918, 812.00/22291; "Proceedings of the Board of Officers which met at Nogales to inquire and report on the events of August 27th," August 29, 1918, 812.00/22290; both in (M274, roll 64), RG 59, NACP.

74. Creighton, Lewis, and Tidwell, to Secretary of Treasury, September 10, 1918, 812.00/22291; "Proceedings of the Board of Officers which met at Nogales to inquire and report on the events of August 27th," August 29, 1918, 812.00/22290; both in (M274, roll 64), RG 59, NACP; Luis Escalada, oral history, March 18, 1972, AHS/T; Rochlin and Rochlin, "The Heart of Ambos Nogales," 168.

75. Department of State, Division of Mexican Affairs, to Adee, April 10, 1919, 311.112 V23 RG 59, NACP.

76. Boyle to Secretary of State, March 11, 1919, 311.112 V23 RG 59, NACP.

77. Ibid.

78. Boyle to Secretary of State, March 13, 1920, 711.12158 (M314, roll 20), NACP.

79. Scott, "Written memoir," reprinted in Martínez, *Fragments of the Mexican Revolution*, 181; Smith, "The Capture of Tía Juana," reprinted in Martínez, *Fragments of the Mexican Revolution*, 100; Baker to Secretary of State, January 24, 1921, 711.12158/8, (M314, roll 20), NACP; "Investigation of Mexican Affairs," vol. 1, Senate Document 285, 66th Cong., 2nd sess., 1591.

80. Boyle to Secretary of State, April 3, 1919, 311.112 V23, RG 59, NACP.

81. Smith, "The Capture of Tía Juana," reprinted in Martínez, *Fragments of the Mexican Revolution*, 100.

82. For a discussion of the symbolic significance of border fences see Fox, *The Fence and the River*.

83. John Jund, oral history, Ephemera File "Battle of Nogales-1918," PAHS.

84. Lincoln Canfield, oral history, Ephemera File "Battle of Nogales-1918," PAHS.

85. Charley Fowler, oral history; Frank Arcadia, oral history; Charles Wise, oral history; Noriega, oral history; Alberto R., oral history; Josephina, oral history; Allyn Watkin, oral history; all in Ephemera File "Battle of Nogales-1918," PAHS.

86. Fowler, oral history, Ephemera File "Battle of Nogales-1918," PAHS. See also Rochlin and Rochlin, "The Heart of Ambos Nogales," 168; Creighton, Lewis, and Tidwell, to Secretary of Treasury, September 10, 1918, 812.00/22291;

"Proceedings of the Board of Officers which met at Nogales to inquire and report on the events of August 27th," August 29, 1918, 812.00/22290; both in (M274, roll 64), RG 59, NACP; Escalada, oral history, AHS/T.

87. Rochlin and Rochlin, "The Heart of Ambos Nogales," 168. See also Escalada, oral history, AHS/T; Arcadia, oral history, Ephemera File "Battle of Nogales-1918," PAHS.

CHAPTER SIX: LIKE NIGHT AND DAY

1. Cabeza de Vaca and Cabeza de Vaca, "The 'Shame Suicides' and Tijuana," 145–76.

2. San Diego Evening Tribune, February 16, 1926, 1, 6; San Diego Sun, February 13, 1926, 1; New York Times, February 12, 1926, 3.

3. San Diego Union, February 19, 1926, 3.

4. Schantz, "From the 'Mexicali Rose' to the Tijuana Brass"; C. de Baca, "Moral Renovation of the Californias"; French, A Peaceful and Working People; Bliss, "The Science of Redemption"; Woods, "A Penchant for Probity," 101; Trimble, Arizona, 249.

5. Taylor, "The Wild Frontier Moves South," 212–14; Woods, "A Penchant for Probity"; Joseph Richard Werne, "El Periodo del Gobernador Esteban Cantú, 1915–1920," in Mexicali, vol. 1, 268–69; Vanderwood, Satan's Playground, 86–98.

6. San Diego Union, January 2, 1922, 8; Oral History of Miguel Calette Anaya, 108; Alejandro F. Lugo Jr., 114–17; "Testimonios de Personas que Trabajaron en Agua Caliente," 118–28; all in Piñera Ramírez and Ortiz Figueroa, Historia de Tijuana, vol. 1; Leonard Rottman, Oral History Interview, June 18, 1972, SDHC; San Diego Union, January 1, 1930, 3; Price, Tijuana, 49–56; C. de Baca, "Moral Renovation of the Californias," 77–81; Taylor, "The Wild Frontier Moves South," 212–19; Vanderwood, Satan's Playground.

7. Martínez, Border Boom Town, 57–77; Tout, The First Thirty Years, 273; Herrera, El lindero que definió a la nación, 270–76.

8. Grant to Hughes, October 14, 1924, 711.129/13, (M314, roll 28), RG 59, NACP. See also Schantz, "From the 'Mexicali Rose' to the Tijuana Brass," 50.

9. Schantz, "All Night at the Owl," 115–18.

10. Ready, Open Range and Hidden Silver, 81; Douglas Daily Dispatch, August 26, 1904, 2; Vanderwood, Satan's Playground, 138.

11. Fathers and family heads and residents of Mexicali to the President, August 30, 1909, Fondo: Gobernación, Ref: IIH: 1909.41 [40.41], IIH-UABC.

12. McCartney to Coolidge, September 25, 1923, 812.40622/35 (M274, roll 148), RG 59, NACP.

13. Stanfield to Stimson, June 11, 1929, 711.12157/116 (M314, roll 20), RG 59, NACP.

14. Bohr to Secretary of State, September 26, 1928, 812.4054/81 (M274, roll 148), RG 59, NACP.

15. Fathers and family heads and residents of Mexicali to the President, August 30, 1909, Fondo: Gobernación, Ref: IIH: 1909.41 [40.41], IIH-UABC.

16. Von Struve to Secretary of State, December 28, 1922, 812.40622/24 (M274, roll 148), RG 59, NACP. For an analysis of the racial and ethnic make-up of Mexicali's brothels see Schantz, "All Night at the Owl," 106–9. For further discussion of interracial sex in the United States during this period see Mumford, *Interzones*.

17. Ferris to Baker, August 1, 1919, 812.40622/4 (M274, roll 148), RG 59, NACP.

18. Burdett to Secretary of State, August 8, 1921, 812.40622/16 (M274, roll 148), RG 59, NACP.

19. These concerns also tied in with the broader anxieties of many Americans about Mexican bodies and spaces being sources of disease. See Stern, *Eugenic Nation*, 57–81; McKiernan, "Fevered Measures."

20. Ferris to Baker, August 1, 1919, 812.40622/4 (M274, roll 148), RG 59, NACP.

21. Chase, *California Desert Trails*, 292; *Calexico Chronicle*, September 9, 1909, 1.

22. Hughes to Embassy, Mexico City, February 26, 1924, 812.40622/42 (M274, roll 148), RG 59, NACP.

23. Grant to Hughes, October 14, 1924, 711.129/13 (M314, roll 28), RG 59, NACP. See also Connelly, *The Response to Prostitution in the Progressive Era*, 67–90; Bliss, "The Science of Redemption."

24. Ferris to Baker, August 1, 1919, 812.40622/4 (M274, roll 148), RG 59, NACP. See also Fosdick, "The Commission on Training Camp Activities."

25. Fathers and family heads and residents of Mexicali to the President, August 30, 1909, Fondo: Gobernación, Ref: IIH: 1909.41 [40.41], IIH-UABC.

26. Subsecretary to the Secretary of Gobernación, September 7, 1909, Fondo: Gobernación, Ref: IIH: 1909.41 [40.41], IIH-UABC.

27. Damm to Department of State, November 15, 1923, 812.40622/37 (M274, roll 148), RG 59, NACP.

28. Von Struve to Secretary of State, November 28, 1922, 812.40622/25 (M274 roll 148), RG 59, NACP.

29. Grant to Hughes, October 14, 1924, 711.129/13 (M314, roll 28), RG 59, NACP; Werne, "El Periodo del Gobernador Esteban Cantú," in *Mexicali*, vol. 1, 268–69.

30. Vanderwood, *Satan's Playground*; Schantz, "From the 'Mexicali Rose' to the Tijuana Brass," 365–74.

31. "Report re: Development of Pleasure Resorts in the Ensenada District," September 30, 1929, 812.4061/8 (M274, roll 148), RG 59, NACP.

32. Von Struve to Secretary of State, November 28, 1922, 812.40622/25 (M274, roll 148), RG 59, NACP. See also Price, *Tijuana*, 56–57.

33. Grant to Hughes, October 14, 1924, 711.129/13 (M314, roll 28), RG 59, NACP.

34. Burdett to Secretary of State, August 8, 1921, 812.40622/16 (M274, roll 148), RG 59, NACP. For a more detailed discussion of American consumption in the Baja California borderlands, see St. John, "Selling the Border."

35. Yuma Citizens to Hughes, September 27, 1924, 711.129/13, (M314, roll 28), RG 59, NACP. See also *San Diego Sun*, February 17, 1926, 1.

36. Webster to Hughes, September 3, 1928, 711.129/4 (M314, roll 28), RG 59, NACP.

37. *New York Times*, February 22, 1923, 4. See also Jones, *The Eighteenth Amendment and Our Foreign Relations*, 129–30.

38. Schantz, "From the 'Mexicali Rose' to the Tijuana Brass," 178; Von Struve to Secretary of State, November 28, 1922, 812.40622/25; Damm to Department of State, November 15, 1923, 812.40622/37; Burdett to Secretary of State, August 8, 1921, 812.40622/16; all in (M274, roll 148), RG 59, NACP; "Weekly Report No. 332," August 23, 1919, 812.00/22844 (M274, roll 66), RG 59, NACP; Werne, "El Periodo del Gobernador Esteban Cantú," in *Mexicali*, vol. 1, 268–69; Taylor, "The Wild Frontier Moves South," 218.

39. Von Struve to Secretary of State, November 28, 1922, 812.40622/25 (M274, Roll 148), RG 59, NACP; Werne, "El Periodo del Gobernador Esteban Cantú," in *Mexicali*, vol. 1, 268–69; Taylor, "The Wild Frontier Moves South," 212–13, 218; *Calexico Chronicle*, September 30, 1909, 3; Vanderwood, *Satan's Playground*, 141, 148; C. de Baca, "Moral Renovation of the Californias," 81–93.

40. Fathers and family heads and residents of Mexicali to the President, August 30, 1909, Fondo: Gobernación, Ref: IIH: 1909.41 [40.41], IIH-UABC. See also Schantz, "From the 'Mexicali Rose' to the Tijuana Brass," 198–99.

41. As quoted in Piñera Ramírez and Ortiz Figueroa, *Historia de Tijuana*, vol. 1, 100. See also Schantz, "From the 'Mexicali Rose' to the Tijuana Brass," 93, 97–98.

42. Rodríguez, *Memoria administrativa*, 279–82; Piñera Ramírez and Ortiz Figueroa, *Historia de Tijuana*, vol. 1, 100–108, 114–28; Vanderwood, *Satan's Playground*, 235.

43. *Calexico Chronicle*, January 5, 1915, 1. See also Schantz, "From the 'Mexicali Rose' to the Tijuana Brass," 103, 126–45, 164–78, 182; Bliss, "The Science of Redemption."

44. Schantz, "From the 'Mexicali Rose' to the Tijuana Brass," 92–93, 418–24; *San Diego Sun*, February 13, 1926, 1; *San Diego Sun*, February 15, 1926, 1; *San Diego Union*, February 15, 1926, 1–2; *San Diego Evening Tribune*, February 16, 1926, 1; Cabeza de Vaca and Cabeza de Vaca, "The 'Shame Suicides' and Tijuana," 161.

45. Bohr to Secretary of State, September 26, 1928, 812.4054/81 (M274, roll 148), RG 59, NACP.

46. Grant to Hughes, October 14, 1924, 711.129/13 (M314, roll 28), RG 59, NACP.

47. Secretary of State to Embassy, Mexico City, February 26, 1924, 812.40622/42 (M274, roll 148), RG 59, NACP.

48. McCartney to Coolidge, September 25, 1923, 812.40622/35 (M274, roll 148), RG 59, NACP.

49. Grant to Hughes, October 14, 1924, 711.129/13 (M314, roll 28), RG 59, NACP.

50. Webster to Hughes, September 3, 1928, 711.129/4 (M314, roll 28), RG 59, NACP.

51. Hunt to Harding, May 7, 1923, 711.129/2, (M314, roll 28), RG 59, NACP.

52. Von Struve to Secretary of State, December 28, 1922, 812.40622/24 (M274 roll 148), RG 59, NACP. See also Von Struve to Secretary of State, February 12, 1924, 812.40622/42 (M274, roll 148), RG 59, NACP; Toro, *Mexico's "War" on Drugs*, 5–10.

53. Palmer to Ryman, January 19, 1929, folder 50, box 6, U.S. Customs Service, District of Nogales, Papers, AHS/T. See also Chatham to Deputy Collector, Douglas, December 14, 1931, folder 51, box 6; Kleinaman to Collector, Nogales, March 8, 1930, folder 51, box 6; both in U.S. Customs Service, District of Nogales, Papers, AHS/T.

54. Specht to Customs Officers, June 24, 1925, folder 49, box 6; Letter from Specht, November 18, 1930, folder 50, box 6; Edwards to Customs Officers, Arizona, December 28, 1929, folder 50, box 6; all in U.S. Customs Service, District of Nogales, Papers, AHS/T.

55. Division of Customs Circular Letter from Birgfeld, May 19, 1925, folder 49, box 6, U.S. Customs Service, District of Nogales, Papers, AHS/T. See also Andreas, *Border Games*, 30.

56. Circular Letter #59 from Moyle, December 22, 1933, folder 52, box 6, U.S. Customs Service, District of Nogales, Papers, AHS/T.

57. Fowler to customs inspectors, Nogales, Naco, Douglas, January 1, 1923, folder 47, box 5, U.S. Customs Service, District of Nogales, Papers, AHS/T.

58. Stephen Chambers, "The Drought and Tia Juana," *New York Times*, June 6, 1920.

59. Von Struve to Secretary of State, December 28, 1922, 812.40622/245 (M274, roll 148), RG 59, NACP.

60. Grant to Hughes, October 14, 1924, 711.129/13 (M314, roll 28), RG 59, NACP.

61. Von Struve to Secretary of State, no date, 812.40622/37 (M274, roll 148), RG 59, NACP.

62. McCartney to Coolidge, September 25, 1923, 812.40622/35 (M274, roll 148), RG 59, NACP. See also Ashurst to Hughes, April 1, 1924, 812.40622/89; Mellon to Secretary of State, April 19, 1924, 812.40622/74; Resolution of the Calexico Rotary Club, May 10, 1923, 812.40622/27; Glasgow to Hughes, May 11, 1923, 812.40622/31; all in (M274, roll 148), RG 59, NACP.

63. Grant to Hughes, October 14, 1924, 711.129/13 (M314, roll 28), RG 59, NACP.

64. Resolution of the Calexico Rotary Club, May 10, 1923, 812.40622/27; Henning to Secretary of State, June 2, 1923, 812.40622/33; both in (M274, roll 148), RG 59, NACP.

65. State Department Memo re: vice conditions in border towns, February 7, 1924, 812.40622/53 (M274, roll 148), RG 59, NACP.

66. Damm to Department of State, November 15, 1923, 812.40622/37 (M274, roll 148), RG 59, NACP.

67. Hughes to Embassy, Mexico City, February 26, 1924, 812.40622/42 (M274, roll 148), RG 59, NACP.

68. Saenz to Summerlin, March 8, 1924, 812.40622/50 (M274, roll 148), RG 59, NACP; *San Diego Evening Tribune*, February 18, 1926, 1; *San Diego Sun*, February 18, 1926, 1.

69. RCT, Division of Mexican Affairs, to Clark, February 23, 1929,

711.12157/77 (M314, roll 20), RG 59, NACP; Von Struve to Secretary of State, March 31, 1924, 812.40622/65; "Report re: Development of Pleasure Resorts in the Ensenada District," September 30, 1929, 812.4061/8; both in (M274, roll 148), RG 59, NACP; *San Diego Union*, June 3, 1928, 1.

70. Translation of "An Insult to Mexico, *Excelsior*, June 17, 1929, in Morrow to Secretary of State, June 17, 1929, 711.12157/125 (M314, roll 20), RG 59, NACP.

71. Mexicali Chamber of Commerce to Hoover, June 11, 1929, 711.12157/99 (M314, roll 20), RG 59, NACP.

72. Jaffe and Martinez to Hoover, June 18, 1929, 711.12157/122 (M314, roll 20), RG 59, NACP.

73. Memo from ABL (Lane), May 18, 1929, 711.12157/84 (M314, roll 20), RG 59, NACP. See also Marco Antonio Samaniego López, "Prólogo," in Rodríguez, *Memoria administrativa*, 13–14; Ada Ekey Jones, Oral History Interview, November 1957, AHS/T.

74. Von Struve to Secretary of State, March 8, 1924, 812.40622/47 (M274, roll 148), RG 59, NACP.

75. Von Struve to Secretary of State, March 8, 1924, 812.40622/47; Von Struve to Secretary of State, March 31, 1924, 812.40622/65; both in (M274, roll 148), RG 59, NACP.

76. Rodríguez to General Manager of the Tijuana and Tecate Railway Co., June 8, 1929, 711.12157/102 (M314, roll 20), RG 59, NACP.

77. Mercier to Stimson, June 11, 1929, 711.12157/102 (M314, roll 20), RG 59, NACP. See also Swing to Stimson, June 13, 1929, 711.12157/112; State Dept Memo, June 13, 1929, 711.12157/119; both in (M314, roll 20), RG 59, NACP.

78. Mercier to Stimson, June 11, 1929, 711.12157/102; Shoup to Wilbur, June 20, 1929, 711.12157/127; Doherty to Secretary of State, September 18, 1929, 711.12157/152; all in (M314, roll 20), RG 59, NACP.

79. Drowy to Stimson, June 6, 1929, 711.12157/97 (M314, roll 20), RG 59, NACP.

80. Mills and Gorman to Stimson, June 22, 1929, 711.12157/128 (M314, roll 20), RG 59, NACP.

81. Von Struve to Secretary of State, March 8, 1924, 812.40622/47 (M274, roll 148), RG 59, NACP.

82. Rodríguez, *Memoria administrativa*, 293–307; Tout, *The First Thirty Years*, 363–66; Kerig, "Yankee Enclave," 196–98, 271–79; Dumke, "Douglas, Border Town," 296; "The Story in Figures about Nogales," in Nogales Ephemera File, PAHS; Letters in folder 273, box 6, Mose Drachman Papers, AHS/T; Letters in box 6, United States Customs Service, District of Nogales, Papers, AHS/T; Letters in boxes 1,6, 7, 13, 14, and 22, SP de México Collection, HL.

83. Butler to Stimson, no date, 711.12157/87 (M314, roll 20), RG 59, NACP. See also Mexicali Chamber of Commerce to Hoover, June 11, 1929, 711.12157/99; Jaffe and Martinez to Hoover, June 18, 1929, 711.12157/122; Union of Merchants and Manufacturers of Tijuana to Morrow, November 2, 1929, 711.12157/164; all in (M314, roll 20), RG 59, NACP.

84. Henderson to Stimson, June 8, 1929, 711.12157/95 (M314, roll 20), RG 59, NACP.

85. Bohr to Secretary of State, October 26, 1929, 711.12157/155 (M314, roll 20), RG 59, NACP.

86. Memo from ABL (Lane), November 10, 1928, 711.12157/54 (M314, roll 20), RG 59, NACP. See also Tellez to Kellogg, November 10, 1928, 711.12157/54 (M314, roll 20), RG 59, NACP. Unfortunately for the thirsty legionnaires, the telegram authorizing the late closing hours was sent to San Francisco instead of Los Angeles, and the order did not get through in time to keep the border open. Lowman to Lane, November 13, 1928, 711.12157/54 (M314, roll 20), RG 59, NACP. For letters in support of early closing hours see Schuyler to Stimson, June 6, 1929, 711.12157/92; Polhamus and Ingalls to Secretary of State, June 10, 1929, 711.12157/98; Filipino Christian Fellowship of El Centro to Stimson, June 10, 1929, 711.12157/115; and other letters in (M314, roll 20), RG 59, NACP.

87. Lowman to Secretary of State, December 20, 1928, 711.12157/63; Lowman to Lane, November 27, 1928, 711.12157/60; Castro Leal to Kellogg, November 27, 1928, 711.12157/62; Padilla-Nervo to Secretary of State, December 22, 1928, 711.12157/64; Lowman to Secretary of State, January 7, 1929, 711.12157/66; all in (M314, roll 20), RG 59, NACP.

88. Memo from ABL (Lane), June 6, 1929, 711.12157/117 (M314, roll 20), RG 59, NACP. See also Tellez to Kellogg, February 2, 1929, 711.12157/67; RCT to Clark, February 6, 1929, 711.12157/69; Translation of Tellez to Secretary of State, April 25, 1929, 711.12157/80; Tellez to Stimson, August 26, 1929; White to Tellez, September 14, 1929, 711.12157/146; all in (M314, roll 20), RG 59, NACP; Callete and Martínez to the President, December 21, 1930, Fondo: AGN, Ref. IIH: [2.12], IIH-UABC.

89. Memo from ABL (Lane), June 6, 1929, 711.12157/117 (M314, Roll 20), RG 59, NACP. See also RCT, Division of Mexican Affairs, to Clark, February 23, 1929, 711.12157/77; Memo from ABL (Lane), November 10, 1928, 711.12157/54; Memo from ABL (Lane), May 18, 1929, 711.12157/84; all in (M314, roll 20), RG 59, NACP.

90. Memo from ABL (Lane), November 10, 1928, 711.12157/54 (M314, roll 20), RG 59, NACP. See also Memo from ABL (Lane), May 18, 1929, 711.12157/84 (M314, roll 20), RG 59, NACP.

91. Memo from ABL (Lane), June 6, 1929, 711.12157/117 (M314, roll 20), RG 59, NACP.

92. Memo from ABL (Lane), June 10, 1929, 711.12157/120, in (M314, roll 20), RG 59, NACP; President of the Republic to the Camara Nacional Comercio, C. Juárez, December 9, 1933, Fondo: Abelardo L. Rodríguez, Ref. IIH: [2.1], IIH-UABC.

93. Taylor, "The Wild Frontier Moves South," 220–22; Arreola and Curtis, *The Mexican Border Cities*, 77–117; Vanderwood, *Satan's Playground*, 304–21.

CHAPTER SEVEN: INSIDERS/OUTSIDERS

1. Complaint of Charles Geck vs. Nick D. Collear, July 17, 1925, file 55301/217, Entry 9, RG 85, NADC.

2. Ibid.

3. List of Manifest of Alien Passengers, December 1906, 157–58; Florencio Silva Border-Crossing Card, December 1, 1906; Ilia Popovich Border-Crossing Card, December 20, 1906; all in *Border Crossings: From Mexico to U.S., 1903–1957*, Ancestry.com. For a sampling of the places of origin of early twentieth-century border crossers see Lists of Aliens Arriving at Aros Ranch, Douglas, Lochiel, Naco and Nogales, Arizona, July 1906–December 1910 (National Archives Microfilm Publication A3365, 5 rolls); Manifests of Alien Arrivals at Columbus, New Mexico, 1917–1954 (National Archives Microfilm Publication A3370, 7 rolls); Manifests of Alien Arrivals at Naco, Arizona, 1908–1952; (National Archives Microfilm Publication A3372, 18 rolls); Manifests of Alien Arrivals at Ajo, Lukeville, and Sonoyta (Sonoita), Arizona, January 1919–December 1952 (National Archives Microfilm Publication A3377, 2 rolls); Manifests of Alien Arrivals at San Luis, Arizona, July 24, 1929–December 1952 (National Archives Micropublication M1504, 2 rolls); Nonstatistical Manifests and Statistical Index Cards of Aliens Arriving at Douglas, Arizona, July 1908–December 1952 (National Archives Microfilm Publication M1759, 4 rolls); Manifests of Permanent and Temporary Alien Arrivals at Douglas, Arizona, September 10, 1906–October 10, 1955 (National Archives Microfilm Publication M1760, 14 rolls); Manifests of Alien Arrivals at San Ysidro (Tia Juana), April 21, 1908–December 1952 (National Archives Microfilm Publication M1767, 20 rolls); Index and manifests of alien arrivals at Nogales, Arizona, 1950–52; Microfilm Publication M1769, 74 rolls); Index and Manifests of Alien Arrivals at Sasabe/San Fernando, Arizona, 1919–1952 (National Archives Microfilm Publication M1850, 3 rolls); Statistical and Nonstatistical Manifests and Related Indexes of Aliens Arriving at Andrade and Campo (Tecate), California, 1910–1952 (National Archives Microfilm Publication M2030, 5 rolls); all in RG 85, NADC, accessed through *Border Crossings: From Mexico to U.S.*, Ancestry.com.

4. McKeown, *Melancholy Order*, 121–84; Masanz, *History of the Immigration and Naturalization Service*, 96th Cong., 2nd sess., 6–7; Tichenor, *Dividing Lines*, 3; Fairchild, *Science at the Borders*; Translation of Mexican Immigration Law of December 22, 1908, Records of the INS, RG 85, Series A, Part 2, reel 17, frames 612–20.

5. List of Manifest of Alien Passengers, December 1906, 158, *Border Crossings: From Mexico to U.S., 1903–1957*, Ancestry.com.

6. Hall and Coerver, *Revolution on the Border*, 126–41. See also "Weekly Report No. 362, March 20, 1920," 812.00/22844 (M274, roll 66), RG 59, NACP; Cardoso, *Mexican Emigration to the United States*; Reisler, *By the Sweat of Their Brow*, 3–48; Sánchez, *Becoming Mexican American*, 17–62.

7. Cardoso, *Mexican Emigration to the United States*, 46; Hall and Coerver, *Revolution on the Border*, 132; Hutchinson, *Legislative History of American Immigration Policy*, 167; Divine, *American Immigration Policy*, 5.

8. Reisler, *By the Sweat of Their Brow*, 13; Cardoso, *Mexican Emigration to the United States*; Sánchez, *Becoming Mexican American*, 18–19.

9. Berlanga to the Governor, April 23, 1917; Public Notice of this telegram authorized by Urrea, Presidente de Cananea, May 11, 1917; both in año 1917, tomo 3131, expediente 13, AGES. For discussion of the implementation of health

inspections see Sánchez, *Becoming Mexican American*, 55–57; Stern, "Buildings, Boundaries, and Blood; Stern, *Eugenic Nation*, 57–72.

10. Lawler to Secretary of State, November 23, 1917, file 54152/1-E, Entry 9, RG 85 NADC. See also Kang, "The Legal Construction of the Borderlands," 11–12; "Public Law No. 154, 65th Cong., approved May 22, 1918," in Udell, *Passport Control Acts*, 3–4; Beck to Supervising Inspector, El Paso, April 5, 1918, file 54152/1-J, Entry 9, RG 85, NADC; Passport Application Form, file 54152/1-K, Entry 9, RG 85, NADC. For a general overview of the rise of passports in Europe and the United States during the late nineteenth and early twentieth centuries see Torpey, *The Invention of the Passport*, 93–121.

11. Kang, "The Legal Construction of the Borderlands," 22–26.

12. Commissioner General to Flournoy, January 18, 1918, file 54152/1-F, Entry 9, RG 85, NADC.

13. Musgrave to Supervising Inspector, El Paso, April 12, 1918, file 54152/1-J, RG 85, Entry 9, NADC.

14. "Admission of Mexican Agricultural Laborers," 66th Cong., 2nd sess.; Calles to Presidentes Municipales de Nogales, Agua Prieta, Cananea, Nacozari, and the Comisario de Policia de Naco, July 7, 1917; Gomez to Calles, July 29, 1917; Soriano to Presidentes Municipales of Agua Prieta and Nogales and the Comisario de Policia of Naco, August 9, 1917; Soriano to Urrea, August 23, 1917; all in año 1917, tomo 3131, expediente 12, AGES. For a discussion of labor contractors in the North American west see Peck, *Reinventing Free Labor*.

15. *Annual Report of the Commissioner General of Immigration ... 1922*, 3–9; *Annual Report of the Commissioner General of Immigration ... 1924*, 24–30; Ngai, *Impossible Subjects*, 17–55; Reisler, *By the Sweat of Their Brow*, 24–25, 49–71; Tichenor, *Dividing Lines*, 138–49; Hutchinson, *Legislative History of American Immigration Policy*, 168–94; Divine, *American Immigration Policy*, 5–51.

16. Sánchez, *Becoming Mexican American*, 63–67; Gutiérrez, *Walls and Mirrors*, 13–116; Reisler, *By the Sweat of Their Brow*, 77–150; Montejano, *Anglos and Mexicans in the Making of Texas*, 157–254; Foley, *The White Scourge*, 40–63, 118–40; Guerin-Gonzales, *Mexican Workers and American Dreams*, 51–76.

17. Johnson, *Revolution in Texas*.

18. Griswold del Castillo and Larralde, "San Diego's Ku Klux Klan," 71–72. See also Lay, *War, Revolution, and the Ku Klux Klan*.

19. *Congressional Record*, February 9, 1928, 70th Cong., 1st sess., 1928, vol. 69, part 3, 2817–18. See also Statement of Honorable John C. Box, May 13, 1920, in Committee on Immigration and Naturalization, "Admission of Mexican and Other Alien Laborers into Texas and Other States," 66th Cong., 2nd sess. For a general summary of arguments for and against Mexican immigration see Reisler, *By the Sweat of Their Brow*, 151–97. See Peck, *Reinventing Free Labor*, for the larger implications of the argument over free and contract labor.

20. "Temporary Admission of Illiterate Mexican Laborers," 66th Cong., 2nd sess.; "Admission of Mexican Agricultural Laborers," 66th Cong., 2nd sess.; Reisler, *By the Sweat of Their Brow*, 128–32, 176–82; Guerin-Gonzales, *Mexican Workers and American Dreams*, 25–49. Mexican officials also supported the no-

tion that Mexican immigration to the United States would only be a temporary phenomenon. See Cardoso, *Mexican Emigration to the United States*, 60.

21. Reisler, *By the Sweat of Their Brow*, 59. For record of entries see, *Annual Report of the Commissioner General of Immigration . . . 1923*, 27; *Annual Report of the Commissioner General of Immigration . . . 1924*, 36–37; *Annual Report of the Commissioner General of Immigration . . . 1925*, 38; *Annual Report of the Commissioner General of Immigration . . . 1926*, 34; *Annual Report of the Commissioner General of Immigration . . . 1927*, 36; *Annual Report of the Commissioner General of Immigration . . . 1928*, 39; *Annual Report of the Commissioner General of Immigration . . . 1929*, 40.

22. Coleman to Commissioner, Immigration and Naturalization Service, September 16, 1933, file 55877/443, box 708, acc 58A734; Complaint of Charles Geck vs. Nick D. Collear, July 17, 1925, file 55301/217; both in Entry 9, RG 85, NADC. Stern, *Eugenic Nation*, 57–81; Stern, "Buildings, Boundaries, and Blood; Sánchez, *Becoming Mexican American*, 56–58. See also McKiernan, "Fevered Measures."

23. *Annual Report of the Commissioner General of Immigration . . . 1923*, 18.

24. Ibid., 16.

25. "Weekly Report No. 362, March 20, 1920," 812.00/22844 (M274, roll 66), RG 59, NACP. See also Ettinger, *Imaginary Lines*, 150–52.

26. *Annual Report of the Commissioner General of Immigration . . . 1922*, 13.

27. *Annual Report of the Commissioner General of Immigration . . . 1925*, 19. See also *Annual Report of the Commissioner General of Immigration . . . 1923*, 19.

28. *Annual Report of the Commissioner General of Immigration . . . 1923*, 18.

29. *Annual Report of the Commissioner General of Immigration . . . 1924*, 18.

30. Ibid., 19.

31. *Annual Report of the Commissioner General of Immigration . . . 1925*, 16. See also *Annual Report of the Commissioner General of Immigration . . . 1924*, 17, 23–24; *Annual Report of the Commissioner General of Immigration . . . 1925*, 14–21; U.S. Department of Justice, Immigration and Naturalization Service, *The Immigration Border Patrol*, 4; Perkins, *Border Patrol*; Hernández, *Migra!*.

32. Wixon to Hull, February 3, 1926, file 55301/81, Entry 9, RG 85, NADC. For additional discussion see other letters in file 55301/81, Entry 9, RG 85, NADC.

33. *Annual Report of the Commissioner General of Immigration . . . 1924*, 18; *Annual Report of the Commissioner General of Immigration . . . 1928*, 10.

34. *Annual Report of the Commissioner General of Immigration . . . 1929*, 40.

35. Hoffman, *Unwanted Mexican Americans*; Balderrama and Rodríguez, *Decade of Betrayal*; Guerin-Gonzales, *Mexican Workers and American Dreams*; Carreras de Velasco, *Los mexicanos que devolvió la crisis*; Sánchez, *Becoming Mexican American*; Reisler, *By The Sweat of Their Brow*.

36. Elmer Graham, Douglas, Arizona, to Secretary of Labor Frances Perkins, 27 June, 1933; RG 69, Federal Emergency Relief Administration Central Files 1933–36 "State" Series, March 1933–36, 460 Arizona Complaints, G-L, Box 13, NACP, as quoted in Benton, "What about Women in the White Man's Camp?," 579.

37. Hunt to Smith, August 10, 1932, Records of the INS, RG 85, Series A, Part 2, roll 17, frame 785. See also Hunt to Hull, August 10, 1932, frame 783; Smith to Hunt, August 3, 1932, frame 784; Shaugnessy to Secretary of State, April 17, 1934, frame 710; all in Records of the INS, RG 85, Series A, Part 2, roll 17.

38. *Annual Report of the Commissioner General of Immigration . . . 1931*, 11.

39. *Annual Report of the Commissioner General of Immigration . . . 1928*, 39; *Annual Report of the Commissioner General of Immigration . . . 1932*, 18.

40. "Simple Move Would Make City Prosper," clipping from the *Nogales Herald*, May 17, 1932, 1, in Records of the INS, RG 85, Series A, Part 2, roll 17, frame 803.

41. Hayden to Hull, September 2, 1931, Records of the INS, RG 85, Series A, Part 2, roll 17, frames 822–23.

42. Mathews to Commissioner General of Immigration, September 22, 1931, Records of the INS, RG 85, Series A, Part 2, roll 17, frames 817–18.

43. *Annual Report of the Commissioner General of Immigration . . . 1929*, 12. For examples of cases brought against individuals under this law see folders 1–14, United States, District Court (Arizona), Final Mittimus Records, 1931–1932, AHS/T. For discussions of the criminalization of undocumented immigrants see Ngai, *Impossible Subjects*; Nevins, *Operation Gatekeeper*.

44. Coleman to Commissioner of Immigration, September 16, 1933, file 55877/443, box 708, Acc 58A734, Entry 9, RG 85, NADC.

45. Hernández, *Migra!*, 76–77; Ngai, *Impossible Subjects*, 60; Balderrama and Rodríguez, *Decade of Betrayal*, 50–87; Reisler, *By the Sweat of Their Brow*, 230–31; *Annual Report of the Commissioner General of Immigration . . . 1925*, 161; *Annual Report of the Commissioner General of Immigration . . . 1931*, 186.

46. Heyman, *Life and Labor on the Border*, 116–22.

47. Balderrama and Rodríguez, *Decade of Betrayal*, 69–82; Sánchez, *Becoming Mexican American*, 214–15.

48. Coleman to Commissioner General of Immigration, September 16, 1933, file 55877/443, box 708, Acc 58A734, Entry 9, RG 85, NADC.

49. For the Mexican government's response see Coleman to Commissioner of Immigration, September 16, 1933, file 55877/443, box 708, Acc 58A734, Entry 9, RG 85, NADC; John S. Littell, "Mexican National Labor Chamber Requests Legislation for Replacement of American Workers in Mexico by Repatriates," March 26, 1934, Records of the INS, RG 85, Series A, Part 2, roll 17, frames 715–17; Balderrama and Rodríguez, *Decade of Betrayal*, 81; Cardoso, *Mexican Emigration to the United States*, 149.

50. *Annual Report of the Commissioner General of Immigration . . . 1931*, 14.

51. Due to conflicting and incomplete statistical records it is impossible to know the exact number of ethnic Mexicans who returned to Mexico during this

period. Estimates range from as low as 263,000, based on the decline in the number of people born in Mexico living in the United States between 1930 and 1940 according to U.S. census records, to as high as two million based on Mexican news reports from the time. In their studies of Mexican repatriation, both Abraham Hoffman and Camille Guerin-Gonzales estimated that approximately half a million people of Mexican descent left the United States between 1929 and 1939. Meier and Gutiérrez, *The Mexican American Experience*, 343; Balderrama and Rodríguez, *Decade of Betrayal*, 149–51; Hoffman, *Unwanted Mexican Americans*, 2; Guerin-Gonzales, *Mexican Workers and American Dreams*, 8, 74. For histories of repatriation see Hoffman, *Unwanted Mexican Americans*; Balderrama and Rodríguez, *Decade of Betrayal*; Guerin-Gonzales, *Mexican Workers and American Dreams*; Sánchez, *Becoming Mexican American*, 209–26; Carreras de Velasco, *Los mexicanos que devolvió la crisis*.

52. Carr to Commissioner General of Immigration, July 15, 1929, Records of the INS, RG 85, Series A, Part 2, roll 17, frame 279.

53. Hull Memo, September 11, 1930, Records of the INS, RG 85, Series A, Part 2, roll 17, frame 277.

54. Frazer to the Secretary of State, August 5, 1932, Records of the INS, RG 85, Series A, Part 2, roll 17, frames 449–50; Hoffman, *Unwanted Mexican Americans*, 133–51; Balderrama and Rodríguez, *Decade of Betrayal*, 192–211; Herrera, *El lindero que definió a la nación*, 276–78; Sánchez, *Becoming Mexican American*, 212–20; Carreras de Velasco, *Los mexicanos que devolvió la crisis*.

55. Frazer to the Secretary of State, August 5, 1932, Records of the INS, RG 85, Series A, Part 2, roll 17, frame 448. See also Frazer to Secretary of State, July 21, 1931, Records of the INS, RG 85, Series A, Part 2, roll 17, frames 455–57.

56. "Decree Amending Several Articles of the Regulations of the Migration Law," translated from *Diario Oficial*, January 30, 1934, Records of the INS, RG 85, Series A, Part 2, roll 17, frames 423–36; "Translation of the Immigration Law of the United States of Mexico," by decree of Plutarco Elías Calles, January 15, 1926, from *Diario Oficial* 1926 (dated September 28, 1927), Records of the INS, RG 85, Series A, Part 2, roll 17, frames 468–97; Harris to all Commissioners and District Directors of Immigration, May 8, 1931, Records of the INS, RG 85, Series A, Part 2, roll 17, frames 460–61.

57. Immigration Service to Mexican Embassy, July 26, 1927, Records of the INS, RG 85, Series A, Part 2, roll 17, frame 466.

58. González de la Tijera to President, December 18, 1924, folder IIH: [2.2], fondo: Obregón-Calles, IIH-UABC.

59. Sun Yat Sen to Obregón, March 1, 1924, folder IIH: [2.1], fondo: Obregón-Calles, IIH-UABC.

60. Hu-DeHart, "Immigrants to a Developing Society," 286–301; Jacques, "Have Quick More Money Than Mandarins," 210–11; Hernández, *Migra!*, 77–80.

61. Hu-DeHart, "Immigrants to a Developing Society, 301–7; Jacques, "Have Quick More Money Than Mandarins," 212–15; Lim, "*Chinos* and *Paisanos*," 77–79; Spurlock to District Director of Immigration and Naturalization Service, Los Angeles, October 24, 1934; and other letters in file 55855/380, box 506, acc 58A734, Entry 9, RG 85, NADC.

62. Folders 10–14, United States, District Court (Arizona), Final Mittimus

records, 1931–1932, AHS/T; Hu-DeHart, "Immigrants to a Developing Society," 305; Jeffrey, "The History of Douglas, Arizona," 104–7.

63. *Annual Report of the Commissioner General of Immigration . . . 1931,* 53.

64. *Annual Report of the Commissioner General of Immigration . . . 1932,* 5.

Conclusion

1. Secure Fence Act of 2006, Public Law 109-367 (2006).

2. Intelligence Reform and Terrorism Prevention Act of 2004, Public Law 108-458 (2004).

3. Von Drehle, "A New Line in the Sand"; Cryptome Border Photo Essay, November 18, 2007, Cryptome Web site; *Congressional Record,* September 14, 2006, H6586.

4. Malkin, "Send a Brick to Congress," Michelle Malkin Web site; "Minuteman Border Fence," Minuteman Civil Defense Corps Web site; Boudreau and Shiffman, "Minuteman's High-Tech Border Barrier Called 'a Cow-Fence,'" cnn.com Web site.

5. Archibold, "Border Fence Must Skirt Objections from Arizona Tribe," *New York Times* Web site; Bustillo, "In Texas, Little Support for Putting Up Fences," *Los Angeles Times* Web site.

6. "Mexico Anger over U.S. Border Fence," BBC Web site.

7. *Congressional Record,* September 14, 2006, H6585.

8. Ibid., H6583.

9. Ibid., H6586.

10. Ibid., H6589.

11. *Congressional Record,* September 29, 2006, S10610.

12. U.S. Department of Homeland Security, "Southwest Border Fence," U.S. Department of Homeland Security Web site; U.S. Department of Homeland Security, "More on the Southwest Border Fence," Department of Homeland Security Web site; Gaouette, "Border Barrier Approved," *Los Angeles Times* Web site; Gamboa, "House Approves U.S.-Mexican Border Fence," *Washington Post* Web site; Wood, "Where U.S.-Mexico Border Fence Is Tall, Border Crossings Fall," *Christian Science Monitor* Web site; Wood, "Along the U.S.-Mexican Border, an Erratic Patchwork Fence," *Christian Science Monitor* Web site.

13. U.S. Customs and Border Protection, "Locate a Port of Entry—Land, Air, or Sea," U.S. Customs and Border Protection Web site.

14. Anzaldúa, *Borderlands/La Frontera,* 25.

15. For histories of the twentieth-century border see Ruíz, *On the Rim of Mexico;* Ganster and Lorey, *The U.S.-Mexican Border into the Twenty-First Century;* Andreas, *Border Games;* Andreas and Biersteker, eds., *The Rebordering of North America;* Herzog, *Where North Meets South.*

16. Andreas, *Border Games,* 40–84.

17. Ibid., 33–38, 85–112; Ngai, *Impossible Subjects,* 127–66; Hernández, *Migra!,* 109–234.

18. Fox, *The Fence and the River,* 49–51; Hernández, *Migra!,* 130–31; Goin, *Tracing the Line.*

19. Dunn, *The Militarization of the U.S.-Mexico Border*, 174. See also Nevins, *Operation Gatekeeper*, 3–4; Andreas, *Border Games*, vii–x, 94.

20. Wood, "Where U.S.-Mexico Border Fence Is Tall," April 1, 2008, *Christian Science Monitor* Web site. See also United States Department of Homeland Security, "Annual Report: Immigration Enforcement Actions: 2007," December 2008, Department of Homeland Security Web site; Archibold and Preston, "Homeland Security Stands by Its Fence," *New York Times* Web site; Von Drehle, "A New Line in the Sand."

21. *Congressional Record*, September 14, 2006, H6589.

22. *Congressional Record*, September 29, 2006, S10612. For detailed analysis of the effects of the 1990s border build-up on unauthorized immigration see Reyes, Johnson, and Van Swearingen, *Holding the Line?*

23. Andreas, "A Tale of Two Borders," 4.

24. *Congressional Record*, September 29, 2006, S10612; Andreas, *Border Games,* 100.

25. Doyle, "Bush's Border Fence Destroys Wilderness," *The Independent* Web site. See also Roig-Franzia, "Mexico Calls U.S. Border Fence Severe Threat to Environment," *Washington Post* Web site; Eilperin, "Researchers Fear Southern Fence Will Endanger Species Further," *Washington Post* Web site; "The Border Fence: Opposition in Douglas," National Public Radio Web site; "Texas Mayors Threaten Court to Stop Border Fence," *Reuters* Web site; Von Drehle, "A New Line in the Sand."

26. *Congressional Record*, September 29, 2006, S10610.

27. U.S. Bureau of Transportation Statistics, "Border Crossing: Border Crossing/Entry Data," Research and Innovative Technology Administration Web site.

28. "Both Teams at Home in U.S.-Mexico Border Volleyball," *Reuters* Web site; Regan, "Artistic Warning," *Tucson Weekly* Web site; Fox, *The Fence and the River*; Von Drehle, "A New Line in the Sand."

BIBLIOGRAPHY

ARCHIVES

Archivo General del Estado de Sonora, Hermosillo, Sonora (AGES)
Archivo Histórico Genaro Estrada, Mexico City (AHGE)
Arizona Historical Society/Tucson (AHS/T)
  Cananea Consolidated Copper Company Papers
  Connell, Charles L., Papers
  Cosulich, Bernice, Papers
  Drachman, Mose, Papers
  Ekey Papers
  El Paso and Southwestern Railroad Company Records
  Ellinwood Family Papers
  Jones, Morris Hunter, Papers
  Kidder Papers
  Mathews Photograph Collection
  Morrison Letterbook
  Oral History Interviews
    Nelson C. Bledsoe, MD
    John Hutchison Darling
    John Henry Eicks
    Luis Escalada
    Ada Ekey Jones
    Rachel Stephens
  Slaughter Family History Manuscript
  Slaughter Financial Papers
  Taylor, Jared D., Papers
  United States Bureau of Immigration, Record of Proceedings in Criminal Cases
  United States Customs Service, District of Nogales, Papers
  United States, District Court (Arizona), Final Mittimus Records
Arizona State Museum Archives, University of Arizona, Tucson (ASMA)
  "El Plomo War" Accounts
  Henry F. Dobyns Papago-Pima Historical Notes
The Huntington Library, San Marino, California (HL)
  Bergman, Ellen Rose Gibbon, Collection
  Papers of Albert B. Fall
  Keller, Henry W., Papers
  SP de México Collection
Instituto de Investigaciones Históricas, Universidad Autónoma de Baja California, Tijuana (IIH-UABC)
John Carter Brown Library, Providence, Rhode Island (JCBL)
  Bartlett, John Russell, Papers, 1850–1853
Library of Congress, Washington, DC (LC)
  Scott, Hugh Lenox, Papers

Mandeville Special Collections Library, University of California, San Diego (MSCL-UCSD)
  Denton Ranch Collection
  Folio letter book of Sir Buchanan Scott
Pimería Alta Historical Society, Nogales, Arizona (PAHS)
San Diego History Center, San Diego, California (SDHC)
Sherman Library, Corona del Mar, California (SL)
  Colorado River Land Company Papers (CRLC Papers)
U.S. National Archives, College Park, Maryland (NACP)
  Record Group 59 (RG 59): Records of the Department of State
    Despatches from United States Consul in Nogales, 1889–1906, National Archives Microfilm Publication M283
    Records of the Department of State Relating to Internal Affairs of Mexico, 1910–1929, National Archives Microfilm Publication M274
    Records of the Department of State Relating to Political Relations Between the United States and Mexico, 1910–1929, National Archives Microfilm Publication M314
  Record Group 75 (RG 75): Records of the Bureau of Indian Affairs
  Record Group 76 (RG 76): Records of Boundary and Claims Commissions and Arbitrations
  Record Group 77 (RG 77): Records of the Office of the Chief of Engineers
U.S. National Archives, Washington, DC (NADC)
  Record Group 85 (RG 85): Records of the Immigration and Naturalization Service Entry 9
    Records of the Immigration and Naturalization Service, Series A: Subject Correspondence Files, Part 2: Mexican Immigration, 1906–1930. Bethesda, MD: University Publications of America, 1993.
University of Arizona Library, Special Collections, Tucson (UASC)
  Mascareñas, Manuel, Papers
  Papers of Francis Henry Hereford
  San Rafael Cattle Company Papers (SRCC Papers)

NEWSPAPERS AND PERIODICALS

Calexico Chronicle
Christian Science Monitor
Douglas Daily Dispatch
Harper's New Monthly Magazine
The Independent
Los Angeles Times
New York Times
Oasis (Nogales, Arizona)
San Diego Evening Tribune
San Diego Sun
San Diego Union
San Francisco Bulletin

San Francisco Examiner
Time
Tucson Weekly
Washington Post

Published Government Documents

Congressional Record.

Emory, William H. *Report of the United States and Mexican Boundary Survey, Made under the Direction of the Secretary of the Interior.* Senate Executive Document 108, 34th Cong., 1st sess. Washington, DC: A.O.P. Nicholson, Printer, 1857.

Hadley, Diana, and Thomas E. Sheridan. "Land Use History of the San Rafael Valley, Arizona (1540–1960)." General Technical Report RM-GTR-269. Fort Collins, CO: Rocky Mountain Forest and Range Experiment Station, U.S. Department of Agriculture, September 1995.

Intelligence Reform and Terrorism Prevention Act of 2004, Public Law 108-458 (2004).

Manning, William R. *Diplomatic Correspondence of the United States: Inter-American Affairs, 1831–1860.* Vol. 8, *Mexico, 1831–1848 (Mid-Year).* Washington, DC: Carnegie Endowment for International Peace, 1937.

Masanz, Sharon D. *History of the Immigration and Naturalization Service: A Report Prepared at the Request of Senator Edward M. Kennedy, Chairman, Committee on the Judiciary, United States Senate, for the Use of the select Committee on Immigration and Refugee Policy.* 96th Cong., 2nd sess. Washington, DC: U.S. Government Printing Office, 1980.

McKellar, William H., and George H. Hart. "Eradicating Cattle Ticks in California." 26th Annual Report of the Bureau of Animal Industry for the Year 1909. Washington, DC: Government Printing Office, 1910.

Miller, Hunter, ed. *Treaties and Other International Acts of the United States of America*, vols. 5–6. Washington, DC: Government Printing Office, 1937.

Papers Relating to the Foreign Relations of the United States, transmitted to Congress with the Annual Message of the President, December 6, 1886. Washington, DC: Government Printing Office, 1887.

Secretaria de Gobernación. *Constitución Política de los Estados Unidos Mexicanos: Edición Oficial.* Mexico City: Imprenta de la Secretaria de Gobernación, 1917.

Secure Fence Act of 2006, Public Law 109-367 (2006).

U.S. Bureau of the Census. *Thirteenth Census of the United States Taken in the Year 1910. Volume II: Population 1910: Reports by states, with statistics for counties, cities, and other civil divisions: Alabama-Montana.* Washington, DC: Government Printing Office, 1913.

U.S. Bureau of the Census. *Thirteenth Census of the United States Taken in the Year 1910. Volume III: Population 1910: Reports by states, with statistics for counties, cities, and other civil divisions: Nebraska-Wyoming. Alaska, Hawaii, and Porto Rico.* Washington, DC: Government Printing Office, 1913.

U.S. Congress. House of Representatives. "Admission of Mexican and Other Alien Laborers into Texas and Other States." 66th Cong., 2nd sess. Washington, DC: Government Printing Office, 1920.

———. "Mexican Border Troubles." November 13, 1877. House Executive Document 13. 35th Cong., 1st sess. Washington, DC: Government Printing Office, 1877.

———. "Compilation from the Records of the Bureau of Immigration of Facts concerning the Enforcement of the Chinese-Exclusion Laws." May 25, 1906. House Document 847. 59th Cong., 1st sess. Washington, DC: Government Printing Office, 1906.

———. "Execution of Colonel Crabb and associates. Message from the President of the United States, communicating official information and correspondence in relation to the execution of Colonel Crabb and his associates." February 16, 1858. House Executive Document 64, 35th Cong., 1st sess.

———. "Note of the Secretary of State of the United States to the Secretary of Foreign Relations of the De Facto Government of Mexico." June 20, 1916. House Document 1237, 64th Cong., 1st sess. Washington, DC: Government Printing Office, 1916.

———. "Temporary Admission of Illiterate Mexican Laborers." 66th Cong., 2nd sess. Washington, DC: Government Printing Office, 1920.

———. "Transportation of Troops to Mexican Border," July 29, 1916. House Document 1311, 64th Cong., 1st sess.

U.S. Congress. Senate. "Admission of Mexican Agricultural Laborers." 66th Cong., 2nd sess. Washington, DC: Government Printing Office, 1920.

———. "Investigation of Mexican Affairs." Senate Document 285, 66th Cong., 2nd sess. Washington, DC: Government Printing Office, 1920.

———. "Report of the Secretary of the Interior in answer to a resolution of the Senate calling for information in relation to the operation of the commission appointed to run and mark the boundary between the United States and Mexico." Senate Executive Document 34, 31st Cong., 1st sess., 1850.

———. "Report of the Secretary of the Interior made in compliance with a resolution of the Senate calling for information in relation to the commission appointed to run and mark the boundary between the United States and Mexico." Senate Executive Document 119, 32nd Cong., 1st sess., 1852.

———. "Report of the Boundary Commission upon the Survey and Re-Marking of the Boundary between the United States and Mexico West of the Rio Grande, 1891–1896." Senate Document 247, 55th Cong., 2nd sess. Washington, DC: Government Printing Office, 1898.

U.S. Department of Commerce and Labor. *Annual Report of the Commissioner General of Immigration*. Washington, DC: Government Printing Office, 1905–1912.

U.S. Department of the Interior. *Annual Report of the Commissioner of Indian Affairs*. 1850–1887.

U.S. Department of Justice. Immigration and Naturalization Service. *The Immigration Border Patrol: Its Origins, Activities, Accomplishments, Organization, and Personnel*. Washington, DC: Government Printing Office, 1952.

U.S. Department of Labor. *Annual Report of the Commissioner General of Immigration*. 1913–1932.

U.S. Department of the Treasury. *Annual Report of the Commissioner-General of Immigration*. 1892–1903.

PUBLISHED SOURCES, DISSERTATIONS, AND THESES

Acuña, Rodolfo F. *Sonoran Strongman: Ignacio Pesqueira and His Times*. Tucson: University of Arizona Press, 1974.

Adelman, Jeremy, and Stephen Aron. "From Borderlands to Borders: Empires, Nation-States, and the Peoples in between in North American History." *American Historical Review* 104 (June 1999): 814–41.

Aguirre, Yjinio F. "The Last of the Dons." *Journal of Arizona History* 10, no.4 (1969): 239–55.

Alonso, Ana María. *Thread of Blood: Colonialism, Revolution, and Gender on Mexico's Northern Frontier*. Tucson: University of Arizona Press, 1995.

Alvarez, Robert R., Jr. *Familia: Migration and Adaptation in Baja and Alta California, 1800–1975*. Berkeley: University of California Press, 1987.

Andreas, Peter. *Border Games: Policing the U.S.-Mexico Divide*. Ithaca, NY: Cornell University Press, 2000.

———. "A Tale of Two Borders: The U.S.-Canada and U.S.-Mexico Lines after 9-11." In *The Rebordering of North America: Integration and Exclusion in a New Security Context*, edited by Peter Andreas and Thomas J. Biersteker, 1–23. New York: Routledge, 2003.

Andreas, Peter, and Thomas J. Biersteker, eds. *The Rebordering of North America: Integration and Exclusion in a New Security Context*. New York: Routledge, 2003.

Andrés, Benny Joseph, Jr. "Power and Control in Imperial Valley, California: Nature, Agribusiness, Labor and Race Relations, 1900–1940." PhD diss., University of New Mexico, 2003.

Andrews, Thomas G. *Killing for Coal: America's Deadliest Labor War*. Cambridge, MA: Harvard University Press, 2008.

Anzaldúa, Gloria. *Borderlands/La Frontera: The New Mestiza*, 2nd ed. San Francisco: Aunt Lute Books, 1999.

Arreola, Daniel D., and James R. Curtis. *The Mexican Border Cities: Landscape Anatomy and Place Personality*. Tucson: University of Arizona Press, 1993.

Balderrama, Francisco E., and Raymond Rodríguez. *Decade of Betrayal: Mexican Repatriation in the 1930s*. Albuquerque: University of New Mexico Press, 1995.

Bannon, John Francis. *The Spanish Borderlands Frontier, 1513–1821*. Albuquerque: University of New Mexico Press, 1974. First published in 1963.

Bartlett, John Russell. *Personal Narrative of Explorations and Incidents in Texas, New Mexico, California, Sonora, and Chihuahua, connected with the United States and Mexican Boundary Commission, during the years 1850, '51, '52, and '53*. 2 vols. Chicago: Rio Grande Press, 1965. First published in 1854 by D. Appleton.

Basso, Keith H. *Wisdom Sits in Places: Landscape and Language among the Western Apache*. Albuquerque: New Mexico University Press, 1996.

Bell, Samuel, and James B. Smallwood. *The Zona Libre, 1858–1905: A Problem in American Diplomacy*. El Paso: Texas Western Press, 1982.

Benton, Katherine A. "What about Women in the White Man's Camp?: Gender, Nation, and the Redefinition of Race in Cochise County, Arizona, 1853–1941." PhD diss., University of Wisconsin, Madison, 2002.

Benton-Cohen, Katherine. *Borderline Americans: Racial Division and Labor War in the Arizona Borderlands*. Cambridge, MA: Harvard University Press, 2009.

Blackhawk, Ned. *Violence over the Land: Indians and Empires in the Early American West*. Cambridge, MA: Harvard University Press, 2006.

Blaisdell, Lowell L. *The Desert Revolution: Baja California, 1911*. Madison: University of Wisconsin Press, 1962.

———. "Harry Chandler and the Mexican Border Intrigue, 1914–1917." *Pacific Historical Review* 35 (November 1966): 385–93.

Bliss, Katherine. "The Science of Redemption: Syphilis, Sexual Promiscuity, and Reformism in Revolutionary Mexico City." *Hispanic American Historical Review* 79 (February 1999): 1–40.

Bolton, Herbert Eugene. *The Spanish Borderlands: A Chronicle of Old Florida and the Southwest*. New Haven, CT: Yale University Press, 1921.

Bourke, John G. *On the Border with Crook*. New York: Charles Scribner's Sons, 1892.

Boyd, Consuelo. "Twenty Years to Nogales: The Building of the Guaymas-Nogales Railroad." *Journal of Arizona History* 22 (Autumn 1981): 295–324.

Brack, Gene M. *Mexico Views Manifest Destiny, 1821–1846*. Albuquerque: University of New Mexico Press, 1975.

Bradfute, Richard Wells. *The Court of Private Land Claims: The Adjudication of Spanish and Mexican Land Grant Titles, 1891–1904*. Albuquerque: University of New Mexico Press, 1975.

Brooks, James F. *Captives and Cousins: Slavery, Kinship, and Community in the Southwest Borderlands*. Chapel Hill: University of North Carolina Press, 2002.

Browne, J. Ross. *Adventures in the Apache Country: A Tour through Arizona and Sonora, 1864*. Tucson: University of Arizona Press, 1974. First printed in 1869 by Harper and Brothers.

Buffington, Robert. "Prohibition in the Borderlands: National Government–Border Community Relations." *Pacific Historical Review* 63 (February 1994): 19–38.

Burnett, D. Graham. *Masters of All They Surveyed: Exploration, Geography, and a British El Dorado*. Chicago: University of Chicago Press, 2000.

Byrkit, James W. *Forging the Copper Collar: Arizona's Labor-Management War of 1901–1921*. Tucson: University of Arizona Press, 1982.

C. de Baca, Vincent Zachary. "Moral Renovation of the Californias: Tijuana's Political and Economic Role in American-Mexican Relations, 1920–1935." PhD diss., University of California, San Diego, 1991.

Cabeza de Vaca, Vincent, and Juan Cabeza de Vaca. "The 'Shame Suicides' and Tijuana." In *On the Border: Society and Culture between the United States and Mexico*, edited by Andrew Grant Wood, 145–76. New York: S. R. Books, 2004.

Camou Healy, Ernesto. *De rancheros, poquiteros, orejanos y criollos: Los productores ganaderos de Sonora y el mercado internacional.* Hermosillo, Sonora: Centro de Investigación en Alimentación y Desarrollo, 1998.

Cardoso, Lawrence A. *Mexican Emigration to the United States, 1897–1931: Socio-Economic Patterns.* Tucson: University of Arizona Press, 1980.

Carreras de Velasco, Mercedes. *Los mexicanos que devolvió la crisis, 1929–1932.* Mexico City: Secretaría de Relaciones Exteriores, 1974.

Carroll, Francis M. *A Good and Wise Measure: The Search for the Canadian American Boundary, 1783–1842.* Toronto: University of Toronto Press, 2001.

Chamberlin, Eugene Keith. "United States Interests in Lower California." PhD diss., University of California, 1949.

Chase, J. Smeaton. *California Desert Trails.* Boston: Houghton Mifflin, 1919.

Clendenen, Clarence C. *Blood on the Border: The United States Army and the Mexican Irregulars.* Toronto: Macmillan, 1969.

Clum, John. *Apache Days and Tombstone Nights: John Clum's Autobiography, 1877–1887.* Edited by Neil B. Carmony. Silvery City, NM: High-Lonesome Books, 1997.

Coatsworth, John H. "Indispensable Railroads in a Backward Economy: The Case of Mexico." *Journal of Economic History* 39 (December 1979): 939–60.

———. "Obstacles to Economic Growth in Nineteenth-Century Mexico." *American Historical Review* 83 (February 1978): 80–100.

Connelly, Mark Thomas. *The Response to Prostitution in the Progressive Era.* Chapel Hill: University of North Carolina Press, 1980.

Coppey, Hypolite. *El Conde Raousset-Boulbon en Sonora.* Translated by Alberto Cubillas. Mexico City: Librería de Manuel Porrúa, S.A., 1962. First published in 1855.

Cory, H. T. *The Imperial Valley and the Salton Sink.* San Francisco: John J. Newbegin, 1915.

Cozzens, Peter, ed. *Eyewitnesses to the Indian Wars, 1865–1890.* Vol. 1, *The Struggle for Apacheria.* Mechanicsburg, PA: Stackpole Books, 2001–2005.

Craib, Raymond B. *Cartographic Mexico: A History of State Fixations and Fugitive Landscapes.* Durham, NC: Duke University Press, 2004.

Cremony, John C. *Life among the Apaches.* New York: Indian Head Books, 1991. First published in 1868 by A. Roman.

DeBuys, William, and Joan Myers. *Salt Dreams: Land and Water in Low-Down California.* Albuquerque: University of New Mexico Press, 1999.

DeLay, Brian. "Independent Indians and the U.S.-Mexican War." *American Historical Review* 112 (February 2007): 35–68.

———. *War of a Thousand Deserts: Indian Raids and the U.S. Mexican War.* New Haven, CT: Yale University Press, 2009.

Delgado, Grace Peña. "At Exclusion's Southern Gate: Changing Categories of Race and Class among Chinese *Fronterizos*, 1882–1904." In *Continental Crossroads: Remapping U.S.-Mexico Borderlands History*, edited by Samuel Truett and Elliott Young, 183–207. Durham, NC: Duke University Press, 2004.

———. "In the Age of Exclusion: Race, Region and Chinese Identity in the Making of the Arizona-Sonora Borderlands, 1863–1943." PhD diss., University of California, Los Angeles, 2000.

Deutsch, Sarah. *No Separate Refuge: Culture, Class, and Gender on an Anglo-Hispanic Frontier in the American Southwest, 1880–1940*. New York: Oxford University Press, 1987.

Deverell, William, and Tom Sitton, eds. *California Progressivism Revisited*. Berkeley: University of California Press, 1994.

Divine, Robert A. *American Immigration Policy, 1924–1952*. New Haven, CT: Yale University Press, 1957.

Dobson, John M. "Desperadoes and Diplomacy: The Territory of Arizona v. Jesús García, 1893." *Journal of Arizona History* 17 (Summer 1976): 137–60.

Drawing the Borderline: Artist-Explorers of the U.S.-Mexico Boundary Survey. Albuquerque: The Albuquerque Museum, 1996.

Dumke, Glenn S. "Douglas, Border Town." *Pacific Historical Review* 17 (August 1948): 283–98.

Dunn, Timothy J. *The Militarization of the U.S.-Mexico Border, 1978–1992: Low-Intensity Conflict Doctrine Comes Home*. Austin: Center for Mexican American Studies, University of Texas at Austin, 1996.

Elías Chomina, Armando. *Compendio de datos históricos de la Familia Elías*. Hermosillo, Sonora, 1986.

Emmons, David M. *The Butte Irish: Class and Ethnicity in an American Mining Town, 1875–1925*. Champaign: University of Illinois Press, 1989.

Eppinga, Jane. *Nogales: Life and Times on the Frontier*. Chicago: Arcadia Publishing, 2002.

Erwin, Allen A. *The Southwest of John Horton Slaughter, 1841–1922: Pioneer Cattleman and Trail-Driver of Texas, the Pecos, and Arizona, and Sheriff of Tombstone*. Spokane, WA: Arthur H. Clark, 1997.

Ettinger, Patrick. *Imaginary Lines: Border Enforcement and the Origins of Undocumented Immigration, 1882–1930*. Austin: University of Texas Press, 2009.

———. "'We Sometimes Wonder What They Will Spring on Us Next': Immigrants and Border Enforcement in the American West, 1882–1930." *Western Historical Quarterly* 37, no. 2 (2006): 159–81.

Evans, Sterling, ed. *The Borderlands of the American and Canadian Wests: Essays on Regional History of the Forty-Ninth Parallel*. Lincoln: University of Nebraska Press, 2008.

Fairchild, Amy L. *Science at the Borders: Immigrant Medical Inspection and the Shaping of the Modern Industrial Labor Force*. Baltimore: Johns Hopkins University Press, 2003.

Faulk, Odie B. *Too Far North . . . Too Far South*. Los Angeles: Westernlore Press, 1967.

Faulk, Odie B., trans. and ed. "Projected Mexican Military Colonies for the Borderlands, 1848." *Journal of Arizona History* 9 (Spring 1968): 39–47.

———, trans. and ed. "Projected Mexican Colonies in the Borderlands, 1852." *Journal of Arizona History* 10 (Summer 1969): 115–28.

Foley, Neil. *The White Scourge: Mexicans, Blacks, and Poor Whites in Texas Cotton Culture*. Berkeley: University of California Press, 1997.

Forbes, Robert H. *Crabb's Filibustering Expedition into Sonora, 1857, an Historical Account with Map, Illustrations, and Bibliography*. Tucson: Arizona Silhouettes, 1952.

Forsythe, George A. *Thrilling Days in Army Life*. New York: Harper and Brothers, 1900.

Fosdick, Raymond B. "The Commission on Training Camp Activities." *Proceedings of the Academy of Political Science* 7 (February 1918): 163–70.

Fox, Claire F. *The Fence and the River: Culture and Politics at the U.S.-Mexico Border*. Minneapolis: University of Minnesota Press, 1999.

French, William E. *A Peaceful and Working People: Manners, Morals, and Class Formation in Northern Mexico*. Albuquerque: University of New Mexico Press, 1996.

Gamio, Manuel. *Mexican Immigration to the United States*. Chicago: University of Chicago Press, 1930.

Ganster, Paul, and David E. Lorey. *The U.S.-Mexican Border into the Twenty-First Century*. 2nd ed. Lanham, MD: Rowan and Littlefield, 2008.

García, Lorenzo. *Apuntes sobre la campaña contra los salvajes en el estado de Sonora*. Hermosillo, Sonora: Imprenta de Roberto Bernal, 1883.

García, Mario T. *Desert Immigrants: The Mexicans of El Paso, 1880–1920*. New Haven, CT: Yale University Press, 1981.

Gavrilis, George. *The Dynamics of Interstate Boundaries*. Cambridge: Cambridge University Press, 2008.

Gehlbach, Frederick R. *Mountain Islands and Desert Seas: A Natural History of the U.S.-Mexican Borderlands*. College Station: Texas A&M University Press, 1983.

Geronimo. *Geronimo's Story of His Life*. Edited by S. M. Barrett. Bowie, MD: Heritage Books, 1990. First published in 1906 by Duffield.

Giese, Lucretia Hoover. "Artist Collaborators: A Surrogate Hand—Seth Eastman's for Bartlett's." In *Drawing the Borderline: Artist-Explorers of the U.S.-Mexico Boundary Survey*, 79–96. Albuquerque: The Albuquerque Museum, 1996.

Goetzmann, William H. *Exploration and Empire: The Explorer and the Scientist in the Winning of the West*. New York: Alfred A. Knopf, 1966.

Goin, Peter. *Tracing the Line: A Photographic Survey of the Mexican-American Border*. Reno: Library, University of Nevada, Artist's Limited Edition, 1987.

González Ramírez, Manuel. *La huelga de Cananea*. Mexico City: Fondo de Cultura Económica, 1956.

Goodwin, Grenville, and Keith H. Basso. *Western Apache Raiding and Warfare*. Tucson: University of Arizona Press, 1971.

Goodwin, Grenville, and Neil Goodwin. *The Apache Diaries: A Father-Son Journey*. Lincoln: University of Nebraska Press, 2000.

Graeme, Richard W. "The Queen and Her Court: An Industrial History of the Warren Mining District." In *Bisbee: Urban Outpost on the Frontier*, edited by Carlos A. Schwantes, 43–55. Tucson: University of Arizona Press, 1992.

Gray, John Plesent. *When All Roads Led to Tombstone, a Memoir*. Boise, ID: Tamarack Books, 1998.

Graybill, Andrew. *Policing the Great Plains: Rangers, Mounties, and the North American Frontier, 1875–1910*. Lincoln: University of Nebraska Press, 2007.

Greenberg, Amy. "Domesticating the Border: Manifest Destiny and the 'Comforts of Life' in the U.S.-Mexico Boundary Commission and Gadsden Purchase, 1848–1854." In *Land of Necessity: Consumer Culture in the United States-Mexico Borderlands*, edited by Alexis McCrossen, 83–112. Durham, NC: Duke University Press, 2009.

Gregg, Robert D. *The Influence of Border Troubles on Relations between the United States and Mexico, 1876–1910*. The Johns Hopkins University Studies in Historical and Political Science, 55, no. 3. Baltimore: Johns Hopkins Press, 1937.

Griffin, James S. *Beliefs and Holy Places: A Spiritual Geography of the Pimería Alta*. Tucson: University of Arizona Press, 1992.

Griswold del Castillo, Richard. "The Discredited Revolution: The Magonista Capture of Tijuana in 1911." *Journal of San Diego History* 26 (Fall 1980): 256–73.

——. *The Treaty of Guadalupe Hidalgo: A Legacy of Conflict*. Norman: University of Oklahoma Press, 1990.

Griswold del Castillo, Richard, and Carlos M. Larralde. "San Diego's Ku Klux Klan, 1920–1980." *Journal of San Diego History* 46 (Spring/Summer 2000): 68–88.

Guerin-Gonzales, Camille. *Mexican Workers and American Dreams: Immigration, Repatriation, and California Farm Labor, 1900–1939*. New Brunswick, NJ: Rutgers University Press, 1994.

Gutiérrez, David G. *Walls and Mirrors: Mexican Americans, Mexican Immigrants, and the Politics of Ethnicity*. Berkeley: University of California Press, 1995.

Gutiérrez, Ramón A. *When Jesus Came, the Corn Mothers Went Away: Marriage, Sexuality, and Power in New Mexico, 1500–1846*. Stanford, CA: Stanford University Press, 1991.

Gutiérrez, Ramón A., and Elliott Young. "Transnationalizing Borderlands History." *Western Historical Quarterly* 41 (Spring 2010): 27–53.

Hadley, Diana. "Ranch Life, The Border Country, 1880–1940: The Way It Really Was." *Cochise Quarterly* 12 (Spring 1982).

Hager, Anna Marie, ed. *The Filibusters of 1890: The Captain John F. Janes and Lower California Newspaper Reports and the Walter G. Smith Manuscript*. Los Angeles: Dawson's Book Shop, 1968.

Haley, J. Evetts. *Jeff Milton: A Good Man with a Gun*. Norman: University of Oklahoma Press, 1948.

Hall, Linda B. "The Mexican Revolution and the Crisis in Naco, 1914–1915." *Journal of the West* 16, no. 4 (1977): 27–35.

Hall, Linda B., and Don M. Coerver. *Revolution on the Border: The United States and Mexico, 1910–1920*. Albuquerque: University of New Mexico Press, 1988.

Hämäläinen, Pekka. *The Comanche Empire*. New Haven, CT: Yale University Press, 2008.

Hamilton, Leonidas. *Hamilton's Mexican Law: A Compilation of Mexican Legislation Affecting Foreigners, Rights of Foreigners, Commercial Law, Property Real and Personal, Rights Pertaining to the Inhabitants of the Republic, Sales, Prescription, Mortgages, Insolvency, Liens, Rights of Husbands and Wives, Donations, Dower, Quit-Rent, Leases, Inheritance, Commercial Companies,*

Partnership, Agency, Corporations, ETC., ETC., Procedure, Attachment, Levy under Execution, Property Exempt, Registry, ETC., Land Laws and Water Rights—Mexican Constitution—Jurisdiction of Courts—Writ of Amparo—Extracts from Treaties—Mexican Decisions of Federal and State Courts, and Mexican Mining Law, Annotated. San Francisco: Leonidas Hamilton, 1882.

Hart, John M. *Empire and Revolution: The Americans in Mexico since the Civil War.* Berkeley: University of California Press, 2002.

———. *Revolutionary Mexico: The Coming and Process of the Mexican Revolution.* Berkeley: University of California Press, 1987.

Haskett, Bert. "Early History of the Cattle Industry in Arizona." *Arizona Historical Review* 6, no. 4 (1935): 3–42.

Hatfield, Shelley Bowen. *Chasing Shadows: Apaches and Yaquis along the United States–Mexico Border, 1876–1911.* Albuquerque: University of New Mexico Press, 1998.

Haynes, Sam W. *James K. Polk and the Expansionist Impulse.* New York: Addison-Wesley Educational, 1997.

Henderson, Timothy J. *A Glorious Defeat: Mexico and Its War with the United States.* New York: Hill and Wang, 2007.

Hendricks, William Oral. "Developing San Diego's Desert Empire." *Journal of San Diego History* 17, no. 3 (1971): 1–11.

———. "Guillermo Andrade and Land Development on the Mexican Colorado River Delta, 1874–1905." PhD diss., University of Southern California, 1967.

Hernández, Kelly Lytle. *Migra!: A History of the U.S. Border Patrol.* Berkeley: University of California Press, 2010.

Herrera Carrillo, Pablo. *Reconquista y colonización del valle de Mexicali y otros escritos paralelos.* Mexicali: Universidad Autónoma de Baja California, 2002.

Herrera Pérez, Octavio. *La Zona Libre: Excepción fiscal y conformación histórica de la frontera norte de México.* Mexico City: Secretaría de Relaciones Exteriores, Acervo Histórico Diplomático, 2004.

———. *El lindero que definió a la nación.* Mexico City: Secretaría de Relaciones Exteriores, 2007.

Herring, Patricia R. "A Plan for the Colonization of Sonora's Northern Frontier: The Paredes *Proyectos* of 1850." *Journal of Arizona History* 10 (Summer 1969): 103–14.

Herzog, Lawrence A. *Where North Meets South: Cities, Space, and Politics on the U.S.-Mexico Border.* Austin: University of Texas Press, 1990.

Hewitt, Harry P. "The Mexican Boundary Survey Team: Pedro García Conde in California." *Western Historical Quarterly* 21 (May 1990): 171–96.

Heyman, Josiah McC. *Life and Labor on the Border: Working People of Northeastern Sonora, Mexico, 1886–1986.* Tucson: University of Arizona Press, 1991.

Hietala, Thomas R. *Manifest Design: Anxious Aggrandizement in Late Jacksonian America.* Ithaca, NY: Cornell University Press, 1985.

Hine, Robert V. *Bartlett's West: Drawing the Mexican Boundary.* New Haven, CT: Yale University Press, 1968.

Hinojosa, Gilberto Miguel. *A Borderlands Town in Transition: Laredo, 1755–1870.* College Station: Texas A&M University Press, 1983.

Hoffman, Abraham. *Unwanted Mexican Americans in the Great Depression, Repatriation Pressures, 1929–1939*. Tucson: University of Arizona Press, 1979. First published in 1974.

Hofsommer, Don L. "Making Connections: Bisbee and the Railroads of the Southwest." In *Bisbee: Urban Outpost on the Frontier*, edited by Carlos A. Schwantes, 85–99. Tucson: University of Arizona Press, 1992.

Holden, Robert H. *Mexico and the Survey of Public Lands: The Management of Modernization, 1876–1911*. DeKalb: Northern Illinois University Press, 1994.

Honey, James. "Policy and Politics in the Papaguería: A Twentieth Century, Cross-Border History of the Tohono O'odham." Undergraduate history honors thesis, Stanford University, 1997.

Horsman, Reginald. *Race and Manifest Destiny: Origins of American Racial Anglo-Saxonism*. Cambridge, MA: Harvard University Press, 1981.

Hu-DeHart, Evelyn. "Immigrants to a Developing Society: The Chinese in Northern Mexico, 1875–1932." *Journal of Arizona History* 21 (Autumn 1980): 275–312.

———. *Yaqui Resistance and Survival: The Struggle for Land and Autonomy, 1821–1910*. Madison: University of Wisconsin Press, 1984.

Hughes, Charles W. "'La Mojonera' and the Marking of California's U.S.-Mexico Boundary Line." *Journal of San Diego History* 53 (Summer 2007): 126–47.

Hurtado, Albert. "Parkmanizing the Spanish Borderlands: Bolton, Turner, and the Historians' World." *Western Historical Quarterly* 26 (Summer 1995): 149–67.

Hutchinson, E. P. *Legislative History of American Immigration Policy, 1798–1965*. Philadelphia: University of Pennsylvania Press, 1981.

Jackson, Jack, ed. *Texas by Terán: The Diary Kept by General Manuel de Mier y Terán on His 1828 Inspection of Texas*. Translated by John Wheat. Austin: University of Texas Press, 2000.

Jacoby, Karl. *Shadows at Dawn: A Borderlands Massacre and the Violence of History*. New York: Penguin Press, 2008.

Jacques, Leo M. "Have Quick More Money Than Mandarins: The Chinese in Sonora." *Journal of Arizona History* 17 (Summer 1976): 201–18.

Jeffrey, Robert S. "The History of Douglas, Arizona." Master's thesis, University of Arizona, 1951.

Johnson, Benjamin Heber. *Revolution in Texas: How a Forgotten Rebellion and Its Bloody Suppression Turned Mexicans into Americans*. New Haven, CT: Yale University Press, 2003.

Johnson, Benjamin Heber, and Andrew Graybill, eds. *Bridging National Borders in North America: Transnational and Comparative Histories*. Durham, NC: Duke University Press, 2010.

Johnson, Benjamin Heber, and Jeffrey Gusky. *Bordertown: The Odyssey of an American Place*. New Haven, CT: Yale University Press, 2008.

Jones, Robert L. *The Eighteenth Amendment and Our Foreign Relations*. New York: Thomas Y. Crowell, 1933.

Josephy, Alvin M., Jr. *The Civil War in the American West*. New York: Alfred A. Knopf, 1991.

Kang, Shulamith Deborah. "The Legal Construction of the Borderlands: The INS, Immigration Law, and Immigrant Rights on the U.S.-Mexico Border, 1917–1954." PhD diss., University of California, Berkeley, 2005.

Katz, Friedrich. *The Life and Times of Pancho Villa*. Stanford, CA: Stanford University Press, 1998.

———. *The Secret War in Mexico: Europe, the United States, and the Mexican Revolution*. Chicago: University of Chicago Press, 1981.

Kearney, Ruth Elizabeth. "American Colonization Ventures in Lower California, 1862–1917." Masters thesis, University of California, 1944.

Kelly, Edith Louise, and Mattie Austin Hatcher, eds. "Tadeo Ortíz de Ayala and the Colonization of Texas, 1822–1833." *Southwestern Historical Quarterly* 32 (April 1929): 311–43.

Kerig, Dorothy Pierson. "Yankee Enclave: The Colorado River Land Company and Mexican Agrarian Reform in Baja California, 1902–1944." PhD diss., University of California, Irvine, 1988.

Kirchner, John A. *Baja California Railways*. Los Angeles: Dawson's Book Shop, 1988.

Knight, Alan. *The Mexican Revolution*. Vol. 1, *Porfirians, Liberals, and Peasants*. Vol. 2, *Counter-Revolution and Reconstruction*. Lincoln: University of Nebraska Press, 1986.

Kurian, George Thomas, ed. *A Historical Guide to the U.S. Government*. New York: Oxford University Press, 1998.

LaDow, Beth. *The Medicine Line: Life and Death on a North American Borderland*. New York: Routledge, 2001.

Lay, Shawn. *War, Revolution, and the Ku Klux Klan: A Study of Intolerance in a Border City*. El Paso: Texas Western Press, 1985.

Lee, Erika. *At America's Gates: Chinese Immigration during the Exclusion Era, 1882–1943*. Chapel Hill: University of North Carolina Press, 2003.

———. "Enforcing the Borders: Chinese Exclusion along the U.S. Borders with Canada and Mexico, 1882–1924," *Journal of American History* 89 (June 2002): 54–86.

Lesley, Lewis B. "The International Boundary Survey from San Diego to the Gila River, 1849–1850." *Quarterly of the California Historical Society* 9 (March 1930): 3–15.

Lewis, Daniel. *Iron Horse Imperialism: The Southern Pacific of Mexico, 1880–1951*. Tucson: University of Arizona Press, 2007.

Lewis, David Rich. *Neither Wolf nor Dog: American Indians, Environment, and Agrarian Change*. New York: Oxford University Press, 1994.

Lim, Julian. "*Chinos* and *Paisanos*: Chinese Mexican Relations in the Borderlands." *Pacific Historical Review* 79 (February 2010): 50–85.

Lingenfelter, Richard E. *Steamboats on the Colorado River, 1852–1916*. Tucson: University of Arizona Press, 1978.

Luibhéid, Eithne. *Entry Denied: Controlling Sexuality at the Border*. Minneapolis: University of Minnesota Press, 2002.

Lumholtz, Karl S. *New Trails in Mexico: An Account of One Year's Exploration in North-Western Sonora, Mexico, and South-Western Arizona, 1901–1910*. New York: Scribner's and Sons, 1912.

Manchado, Manuel A., Jr. *The North Mexican Cattle Industry, 1910–1975: Ideology, Conflict, and Change*. College Station: Texas A&M University Press, 1981.

Martínez, Oscar J. *Border Boom Town: Ciudad Juárez since 1848*. Austin: University of Texas Press, 1975.

———. *Fragments of the Mexican Revolution: Personal Accounts from the Border*. Albuquerque: University of New Mexico Press, 1983.

———. *Troublesome Border*, 4th ed. Tucson: University of Arizona Press, 1995.

Massey, Douglas S., Jorge Durand, and Nolan J. Malone. *Beyond Smoke and Mirrors: Mexican Immigration in an Era of Economic Integration*. New York: Russell Sage Foundation, 2002.

Mathias, Christine Joy. "At the Edges of Empire: Race and Revolution in the Mexican Border Town of Cananea, 1899–1917." Undergraduate thesis, Yale University, 2007.

May, Robert E. *The Southern Dream of a Caribbean Empire, 1854–1861*. Baton Rouge: Louisiana State University Press, 1973.

McCann, Captain Irving Goff. *With the National Guard on the Border: Our National Military Problem*. St. Louis: C. V. Mosby Company, 1917.

McCrossen, Alexis, ed. *Land of Necessity: Consumer Culture in the United States-Mexico Borderlands*. Durham, NC: Duke University Press, 2009.

McKeown, Adam. *Melancholy Order: Asian Immigration and the Globalization of Borders*. New York: Columbia University Press, 2008.

McKiernan, John Raymond. "Fevered Measures: Race, Communicable Disease, and Community Formation on the Texas-Mexico Border, 1880–1923." PhD diss., University of Michigan, Ann Arbor, 2002.

McManus, Sheila. *The Line Which Separates: Race, Gender, and the Making of the Alberta-Montana Borderlands*. Edmonton: University of Alberta Press; Lincoln: University of Nebraska Press, 2005.

McPherson, Hallie M. "The Plan of William McKendree Gwin for a Colony in North Mexico, 1863–1865." *Pacific Historical Review* 2 (December 1933): 357–86.

McPherson, William, ed. *From San Diego to the Colorado in 1849: The Journal and Maps of Cave J. Couts*. Los Angeles: Arthur M. Ellis, 1932.

Meier, Matthew S., and Margo Gutiérrez, eds. *The Mexican American Experience: An Encyclopedia*. Westport, CT: Greenwood Press, 2003.

Meinig, D. W. *The Shaping of America: A Geographical Perspective on 500 Years of History*. Vol. 2, *Continental America, 1800–1867*. New Haven, CT: Yale University Press, 1993.

Mercer, Lloyd J. "Taxpayers or Investors: Who Paid for the Land-Grant Railroads?" *Business History Review* 46 (Autumn 1972): 279–94.

Merk, Frederick. *Manifest Destiny and Mission in American History: A Reinterpretation*. New York: Vintage Books, 1963.

Metz, Leon C. *Border: The U.S.-Mexico Line*. El Paso: Mangan Books, 1989.

Mexicali: Una historia, vol. 1. Mexicali: Universidad Autónoma de Baja California, Instituto de Investigaciones Históricas, 1991.

Mexican Grant: San Rafael de la Zanja Rancho: Showing Two Surveys That Radically Differ. Florence, AZ: Enterprise Job Rooms, 1891.

Meyer, Michael C., and William L. Sherman. *The Course of Mexican History*, 5th ed. New York: Oxford University Press, 1995.

Miller, Joseph, ed. *The Arizona Rangers*. New York: Hastings House Publishers, 1972.

Mitchell, Timothy. *Rule of Experts: Egypt, Techno-Politics, Modernity*. Berkeley: University of California Press, 2002.

Montejano, David. *Anglos and Mexicans in the Making of Texas, 1836–1986*. Austin: University of Texas Press, 1987.

Montoya, María E. *Translating Property: The Maxwell Land Grant and the Conflict over Land in the American West, 1840–1900*. Berkeley: University of California Press, 2002.

Mora-Torres, Juan. *The Making of the Mexican Border: The State, Capitalism, and Society in Nuevo León, 1848–1910*. Austin: University of Texas Press, 2001.

Mowry, Sylvester. *Arizona and Sonora: The Geography, History, and Resources of the Silver Region of North America*. New York: Harper and Brothers, 1864.

Moyano Pahissa, Angela. *Frontera: Así se hizo la frontera norte*. Mexico City: Ariel México, 1996.

Mumford, Kevin J. *Interzones: Black/White Sex Districts in Chicago and New York in the Early Twentieth Century*. New York: Columbia University Press, 1997.

Myers, John Myers. *The Border Wardens*. Englewood Cliffs, NJ: Prentice-Hall, 1971.

Nevins, Joseph. *Operation Gatekeeper: The Rise of the "Illegal Alien" and the Remaking of the U.S.-Mexico Boundary*. New York: Routledge, 2002.

Ngai, Mae M. *Impossible Subjects: Illegal Aliens and the Making of Modern America*. Princeton, NJ: Princeton University Press, 2004.

Nogales, Arizona, 1880–1980: Centennial Anniversary. Nogales: Nogales Centennial Committee, 1980.

Norris, L. David, James C. Milligan, and Odie B. Faulk. *William H. Emory: Soldier-Scientist*. Tucson: University of Arizona Press, 1998.

North, Diane M. T. *Samuel Peter Heintzelman and the Sonora Exploring and Mining Company*. Tucson: University of Arizona Press, 1980.

Northrup, Cynthia Clark, and Elaine C. Prange Turney, eds. *Encyclopedia of Tariffs and Trade in U.S. History*. Vol. 1, *The Encyclopedia*. Vol. 2, *Debating the Issues: Selected Primary Documents*. Vol. 3, *The Texts of the Tariffs*. Westport, CT: Greenwood Press, 2003.

Nugent, Paul. *Smugglers, Secessionists, and Loyal Citizens on the Ghana-Togo Frontier*. Athens: Ohio University Press, 2002.

Officer, James E. *Hispanic Arizona, 1536–1856*. Tucson: University of Arizona Press, 1987.

Orsi, Robert. *Sunset Limited: The Southern Pacific Railroad and the Development of the American West, 1850–1930*. Berkeley: University of California Press, 2005.

Paulsen, George E. "The Yellow Peril at Nogales: The Ordeal of Collector William M. Hoey." *Arizona and the West: A Quarterly Journal of History* 13 (Summer 1971): 113–28.

Peck, Gunther. *Reinventing Free Labor: Padrones and Immigrant Workers in the North American West, 1880–1930*. Cambridge: Cambridge University Press, 2000.

Perales, Monica. *Smeltertown: Making and Remembering a Southwest Border Community*. Chapel Hill: University of North Carolina Press, 2010.

Perkins, Clifford Alan. *Border Patrol: With the U.S. Immigration Service on the Mexican Boundary, 1910–54*. El Paso: Texas Western Press, 1978.

Philips, Stephen J., and Patricia Wentworth Comus, eds. *A Natural History of the Sonoran Desert*. Berkeley: University of California Press, 2000.

Piñera Ramírez, David. *American and English Influence on the Early Development of Ensenada, Baja California, Mexico*. San Diego: Institute for Regional Studies of the Californias, San Diego State University, 1995.

Piñera Ramírez, David, and Jesús Ortiz Figueroa, coordinators. *Historia de Tijuana, 1889–1989: Edición conmemorativa del centenario de su fundación*, vol. 1. Tijuana: Universidad Autónoma de Baja California, Centro de Investigaciones Históricas, 1989.

Pletcher, David M. *The Diplomacy of Annexation: Texas, Oregon, and the Mexican War*. Columbia: University of Missouri Press, 1973.

———. *The Diplomacy of Trade and Investment: American Economic Expansion in the Hemisphere, 1865–1900*. Columbia: University of Missouri Press, 1998.

———. *Rails, Mines, and Progress: Seven American Promoters in Mexico, 1867–1911*. Ithaca, NY: Cornell University Press, 1958.

Poston, Charles D. "Building a State in Apache Land, Parts I–IV." *Overland Monthly* 24 (July–December 1894): 87–93, 203–13, 291–97, 403–8.

Prescott, J.R.V. *Political Frontiers and Boundaries*. London: Allen and Unwin, 1987.

Price, John A. *Tijuana: Urbanization in a Border Culture*. Notre Dame, IN: University of Notre Dame Press, 1973.

Proffitt, T. D., III. *Tijuana: The History of a Mexican Metropolis*. San Diego: San Diego State University Press, 1994.

Pulling, Hazel Adele. "California's Range Cattle Industry: Decimation of the Herds, 1870–1912." *Journal of San Diego History* 11 (January 1965): 20–32.

Radding, Cynthia. *Wandering Peoples: Colonialism, Ethnic Spaces, and Ecological Frontiers in Northwestern Mexico, 1700–1850*. Durham, NC: Duke University Press, 1998.

Rak, Mary Kidder. *Border Patrol*. Cambridge, MA: Riverside Press, 1938.

Ralph, Julian. "The Chinese Leak." *Harper's New Monthly Magazine* 82 (March 1891): 515–25.

Ready, Alma. "History of Nogales." In *Nogales, Arizona, 1880–1980: Centennial Anniversary*. Nogales: Nogales Centennial Committee, 1980.

———. *Open Range and Hidden Silver: Arizona's Santa Cruz County*. Nogales: Pimería Alta Historical Society, 1986.

Rebert, Paula. *La Gran Línea: Mapping the United States–Mexico Boundary, 1849–1857*. Austin: University of Texas Press, 2001.

Reisler, Mark. *By the Sweat of Their Brow: Mexican Immigrant Labor in the United States, 1900–1940.* Westport, CT: Greenwood Press, 1976.

Reséndez, Andrés. *Changing National Identities at the Frontier: Texas and New Mexico, 1800–1850.* Cambridge: Cambridge University Press, 2005.

Reyes, Belinda I., Hans P. Johnson, and Richard Van Swearingen. *Holding the Line?: The Effect of the Recent Border Build-Up on Unauthorized Immigration.* San Francisco: Public Policy Institute of California, 2002.

Roberts, David. *Once They Moved Like the Wind: Cochise, Geronimo, and the Apache Wars.* New York, Touchstone, 1993.

Robinson, Sherry. *Apache Voices: Their Stories of Survival as Told to Eve Ball.* Albuquerque: University of New Mexico Press, 2000.

Rochlin, Fred, and Harriet Rochlin. "The Heart of Ambos Nogales: Boundary Monument 122." *Journal of Arizona History* 17 (Summer 1976): 161–80.

Rockwood, Charles Robinson. *Born of the Desert.* Calexico, CA: Calexico Chronicle, 1930.

Rodríguez, Abelardo L. *Memoria administrativa del gobierno del distrito norte de la Baja California, 1924–1927.* Tijuana: Universidad Autónoma de Baja California, 1993.

Romero, Fernando. *Hyperborder: The Contemporary U.S.-Mexico Border and Its Future.* New York: Princeton Architectural Press, 2008.

Ruibal Corella, Juan Antonio. *Perfiles de un patriota: La huella del general Ignacio Pesqueira García en el noroeste de México.* Mexico City: Editorial Porrúa, 1979.

Ruíz, Ramón Eduardo. *On the Rim of Mexico: Encounters of the Rich and Poor.* Boulder, CO: Westview Press, 1998.

———. *The People of Sonora and Yankee Capitalists.* Tucson: University of Arizona Press, 1988.

Rynning, Captain Thomas H. [as told to Al Cohn and Joe Chisholm]. *Gun Notches: The Life Story of a Cowboy-Soldier.* New York: Frederick A. Stokes, 1932. First published in 1931 by A. L. Burt.

Sahlins, Peter. *Boundaries: The Making of France and Spain in the Pyrenees.* Berkeley: University of California Press, 1989.

Salazar Ylarregui, José. *Datos de los trabajos astronómicos y topográficos, dispuestos en forma de diario.* Mexico City: Imprenta de Juan R. Navarro, 1850.

Salyer, Lucy. *Laws Harsh as Tigers: Chinese Immigrants and the Shaping of Modern Immigration Law.* Chapel Hill: University of North Carolina Press, 1995.

Sánchez, George J. *Becoming Mexican American: Ethnicity, Culture, and Identity in Chicano Los Angeles, 1900–1945.* New York: Oxford University Press, 1993.

Sandomingo, Manuel. *Historia de Agua Prieta.* Vol. 1, *Primer cincuentenario, 1899–1949.* Hermosillo, Sonora: Editorial Imágenes de Sonora, 1999.

Sayre, Nathan F. *Ranching, Endangered Species, and Urbanization in the Southwest: Species of Capital.* Tucson: University of Arizona Press, 2002.

Schantz, Eric Michael. "All Night at the Owl: The Social and Political Relations of Mexicali's Red-Light District, 1909–1925." In *On the Border: Society and*

Culture between the United States and Mexico, edited by Andrew Grant Wood. New York: SR Books, 2001.

———. "From the 'Mexicali Rose' to the Tijuana Brass: Vice Tours of the United States–Mexico Border, 1910–1965." PhD diss., University of California, Los Angeles, 2001.

Schmeckebier, Laurence F. *The Customs Service: Its History, Activities, and Organization*. Baltimore: Johns Hopkins Press, 1924.

Schmidt, Henry C. *The Roots of Lo Mexicano*. Texas A&M University Press, 1978.

Schwantes, Carlos A., ed. *Bisbee: Urban Outpost on the Frontier*. Tucson: University of Arizona Press, 1992.

———. "Toil and Trouble: Rhythms of Work Life." In *Bisbee: Urban Outpost on the Frontier*, edited by Carlos A. Schwantes, 114–32. Tucson: University of Arizona Press, 1992.

———. *Vision and Enterprise: Exploring the History of Phelps Dodge Corporation*. Tucson: University of Arizona Press, 2000.

Scott, James C. *Seeing Like a State: How Certain Schemes to Improve the Human Condition Have Failed*. New Haven, CT: Yale University Press, 1998.

Sheridan, Thomas E. *Arizona: A History*. Tucson: University of Arizona Press, 1995.

———. *Landscapes of Fraud: Mission Tumacácori, the Baca Float, and the Betrayal of the O'odham*. Tucson: University of Arizona Press, 2008.

Smith, Cornelius C., Jr. *Emilio Kosterlitzky: Eagle of Sonora and the Southwest Border*. Glendale, CA: Arthur H. Clark, 1970.

Smith, Joseph, ed., with an introduction by Jorge Flores. *Expedición filibustera de William Walker en la Baja California*. Mexico City: Vargas Rea, 1944.

Smith, Marian L. "Immigration and Naturalization Service." In *A Historical Guide to the U.S. Government*, edited by George Thomas Kurian, 305–6. New York: Oxford University Press, 1998.

Sonnichsen, C. L. *Colonel Greene and the Copper Skyrocket: The Spectacular Rise and Fall of William Cornell Greene: Copper King, Cattle Baron, and Promoter Extraordinary in Mexico, the American Southwest, and the New York Financial District*. Tucson: University of Arizona Press, 1974.

Spicer, Edward H. *Cycles of Conquest: The Impact of Spain, Mexico, and the United States on the Indians of the Southwest, 1533–1960*. Tucson: University of Arizona Press, 1962.

St. John, Rachel. "Divided Ranges: Transborder Ranches and the Creation of National Space along the Western Mexican-U.S. Border." In *Bridging National Borders in North America: Transnational and Comparative Histories*, edited by Andrew Graybill and Benjamin Heber Johnson, 116–40. Durham, NC: Duke University Press, 2010.

———. "Line in the Sand: The Desert Border between the United States and Mexico, 1848–1934." PhD diss., Stanford University, 2005.

———. "Selling the Border: Trading Land, Attracting Tourists, and Marketing American Consumption on the Baja California Border, 1900–1934." In *Land of Necessity: Consumer Culture in the United States–Mexico Borderlands*, edited by Alexis McCrossen, 83–112. Durham, NC: Duke University Press, 2009.

Stegner, Wallace. *Wolf Willow: A History, a Story, and a Memory of the Last Plains Frontier*. New York: Penguin Books, 2000. First published in 1962 by Viking.

Stephanson, Anders. *Manifest Destiny: American Expansion and the Empire of Right*. New York: Hill and Wang, 1996.

Stern, Alexandra Minna. "Buildings, Boundaries, and Blood: Medicalization and Nation-Building on the U.S.-Mexico Border, 1910–1930." *Hispanic American Historical Review* 79, no. 1 (1999): 41–81.

———. *Eugenic Nation: Faults and Frontiers of Better Breeding in Modern America*. Berkeley: University of California Press, 2005.

Stout, Joseph A., Jr. *Border Conflict: Villistas, Carrancistas and the Punitive Expedition, 1915–1920*. Fort Worth: Texas Christian University Press, 1999.

———. *Schemers and Dreamers: Filibustering in Mexico, 1848–1921*. Fort Worth: Texas Christian University Press, 2002.

Sweeney, Edwin R. *Cochise, Chiricahua Apache Chief*. Norman: University if Oklahoma Press, 1991.

———. *Mangas Coloradas, Chief of the Chiricahua Apaches*. Norman: University of Oklahoma Press, 1998.

Sweeney, Gray. "Drawing Borders: Art and the Cultural Politics of the U.S.-Mexico Boundary Survey, 1850–1853." In *Drawing the Borderline: Artist-Explorers of the U.S.-Mexico Boundary Survey*, 23–77. Albuquerque: The Albuquerque Museum, 1996.

Taussig, F. W. *The Tariff History of the United States*. New York: G. P. Putnam's Sons, 1931.

Taylor, Joseph E., III. "Boundary Terminology." *Environmental History* 13 (July 2008): 454–81.

Taylor, Lawrence D. "The Wild Frontier Moves South: U.S. Entrepreneurs and the Growth of Tijuana's Vice Industry, 1908–1935." *Journal of San Diego History* 48 (Summer 2002): 204–29.

Terrill, Tom E. *The Tariff, Politics, and American Foreign Policy, 1874–1901*. Westport, CT: Greenwood Press, 1973.

Thrapp, Dan L. *The Conquest of Apacheria*. Norman: University of Oklahoma Press, 1967.

———. *Encyclopedia of Frontier Biography: In Three Volumes*. Vol. 1. Lincoln: University of Nebraska Press, 1991.

Tichenor, Daniel J. *Dividing Lines: The Politics of Immigration Control in America*. Princeton, NJ: Princeton University Press, 2002.

Tinker Salas, Miguel. *In the Shadow of the Eagles: Sonora and the Transformation of the Border during the Porfiriato*. Berkeley: University of California Press, 1997.

Tirres, Allison Brownell. "American Law Comes to the Border: Law and Colonization on the U.S./Mexico Divide, 1848–1890." PhD diss., Harvard University, 2008.

Toro, María Celia. *Mexico's "War" on Drugs: Causes and Consequences*. Boulder, CO: Lynne Rienner Publishers, 1995.

Torpey, John. *The Invention of the Passport: Surveillance, Citizenship, and the State*. Cambridge: Cambridge University Press, 2000.

Tout, Otis B. *The First Thirty Years, 1901–1931: Being an Account of the Principal Events in the History of Imperial Valley, Southern California, U.S.A.* San Diego: Otis B. Tout, 1931.

Trennert, Robert A., Jr. "The Southern Pacific Railroad of Mexico." *Pacific Historical Review* 35, no. 3 (1966): 265–84.

Trimble, Marshall. *Arizona: A Cavalcade of History.* Tucson: Treasure Chest Publications, 1989.

Truett, Samuel. *Fugitive Landscapes: The Forgotten History of the U.S.-Mexico Borderlands.* New Haven, CT: Yale University Press, 2006.

———. "Transnational Warrior: Emilio Kosterlitzky and the Transformation of the U.S.-Mexico Borderlands, 1873–1928." In *Continental Crossroads: Remapping U.S.-Mexico Borderlands History,* edited by Samuel Truett and Elliott Young, 241–70. Durham, NC: Duke University Press, 2004.

Truett, Samuel, and Elliott Young, eds. *Continental Crossroads: Remapping U.S.-Mexico Borderlands History.* Durham, NC: Duke University Press, 2004.

Tully, Barbara. "Bullets for Breakfast." *True West* (June 1975): 6–12.

Turner, Ethel Duffy. *Revolution in Baja California: Ricardo Flores Magón's High Noon.* Detroit: Blaine Ethridge Books, 1981.

Udell, Gilman G., ed. *Passport Control Acts.* Washington, DC: Government Printing Office, 1973.

Utley, Robert M. *Changing Course: The International Boundary, United States and Mexico, 1848–1963.* Tucson: Southwest Parks and Monuments Association, 1996.

———. *The Indian Frontier in the American West, 1846–1890.* Albuquerque: University of New Mexico Press, 1984.

Vanderwood, Paul J. *Juan Soldado: Rapist, Murderer, Martyr, Saint.* Durham, NC: Duke University Press, 2004.

———. *Satan's Playground: Mobsters and Movie Stars at America's Greatest Gaming Resort.* Durham, NC: Duke University Press, 2010.

Vanderwood, Paul J., and Frank N. Samponaro. *Border Fury: A Picture Postcard Record of Mexico's Revolution and U.S. War Preparedness, 1910–1917.* Albuquerque: University of New Mexico Press, 1988.

Vargas, Jorge A. "The Pantoja Map of 1782 and the Port of San Diego: Some Answers Regarding the International Boundary in the San Diego–Tijuana Region." *Journal of San Diego History* 46 (Spring/Summer 2000): 119–27.

Vázquez, Josefina Zoraida, and Lorenzo Meyer. *The United States and Mexico.* Chicago: University of Chicago Press, 1985.

Von Drehle, David. "A New Line in the Sand." *Time,* June 30, 2008, 26–35.

Voss, Stuart F. *On the Periphery of Nineteenth-Century Mexico: Sonora and Sinaloa, 1810–1877.* Tucson: University of Arizona Press, 1982.

Walker, Henry Pickering, and Don Bufkin. *Historical Atlas of Arizona.* Norman: University of Oklahoma Press, 1979.

Walker, William. *The War in Nicaragua.* Tucson: University of Arizona Press, 1985. First published in 1860 by S. H. Goetzel.

Walmsley, H. R. [Henry Wray]. "America's Unguarded Gateway." *North American Review* 208 (August 1918): 312–15.

Wasserman, Mark. *Capitalists, Caciques, and Revolution: The Native Elite and*

Foreign Enterprise in Chihuahua, Mexico, 1854–1911. Chapel Hill: University of North Carolina Press, 1984.

Weber, David J. *The Mexican Frontier, 1821–1846: The American Southwest under Mexico.* Albuquerque: University of New Mexico Press, 1982.

———. *The Spanish Frontier in North America.* New Haven, CT: Yale University Press, 1992.

———. "Turner, the Boltonians, and the Borderlands." *American Historical Review* 91 (February 1986): 66–81.

Welch, John R., and Ramon Riley. "Reclaiming Land and Spirit in the Western Apache Homeland." *American Indian Quarterly* 25 (Winter 2001): 5–12.

Wells, Reba B. "The 'Mormon House.'" *Cochise Quarterly* 15 (Winter 1985): 36–41.

———. "The San Bernardino Ranch." *Cochise Quarterly* 15 (Winter 1985): 3–29.

———. "Slaughter Ranch Outpost." *Cochise Quarterly* 15 (Winter 1985): 30–35.

Werne, Joseph Richard. *The Imaginary Line: A History of the United States and Mexico Boundary Survey, 1848–1857.* Fort Worth: Texas Christian University Press, 2007.

Wheless, Joseph. *Compendium of the Laws of Mexico,* vol. 2. St. Louis: The F. H. Thomas Law Book, 1910.

Whipple, A. W. *The Whipple Report: Journal of an Expedition from San Diego, California, to the Rio Colorado, from Sept. 11 to Dec. 11, 1849.* Los Angeles: Westernlore Press, 1961.

White, Richard. *"It's Your Misfortune and None of My Own": A New History of the American West.* Norman: University of Oklahoma Press, 1991.

———. *The Middle Ground: Indians, Empires, and Republics in the Great Lakes Region, 1650–1815.* New York: Cambridge University Press, 1991.

Wilbur-Cruce, Eva Antonia. *A Beautiful, Cruel Country.* Tucson: University of Arizona Press, 1987.

Williams, Anita Alvarez de. *The Cocopah People.* Phoenix: Indian Tribal Series, 1974.

———. *Travelers among the Cucupá.* Los Angeles: Dawson's Book Shop, 1975.

Wilson, Thomas M., and Hastings Donnan, eds. *Border Identities: Nation and State at International Frontiers.* Cambridge: Cambridge University Press, 1998.

Winichakul, Thongchakul. *Siam Mapped: A History of the Geo-Body of a Nation.* Honolulu: University of Hawai'i Press, 1997.

Wood, Andrew Grant, ed. *On the Border: Society and Culture between the United States and Mexico.* New York: SR Books, 2001.

Woods, Gerald. "A Penchant for Probity: California Progressives and the Disreputable Pleasures." In *California Progressivism Revisited,* edited by William Deverell and Tom Sitton, 99–113. Berkeley: University of California Press, 1994.

Woodward, Arthur, ed. *The Republic of Lower California, 1853–1854: In the Words of Its State Papers, Eyewitnesses, and Contemporary Reporters.* Los Angeles: Dawson's Book Shop, 1966.

Work, David K. "Enforcing Neutrality: The Tenth U.S. Cavalry on the Mexican

Border, 1913–1919." *Western Historical Quarterly* 40 (Summer 2009): 179–200.

Wyllys, Rufus Kay. "Henry A. Crabb—A Tragedy of the Sonora Frontier." *Pacific Historical Review* 9 (June 1940): 183–94.

———. "The Republic of Lower California, 1853–1854." *Pacific Historical Review* 2 (June 1933): 194–213.

———. "William Walker's Invasion of Sonora, 1854." *Arizona Historical Review* 6 (October 1935): 61–67.

Young, Elliott. *Catarino Garza's Revolution on the Texas Border*. Durham, NC: Duke University Press, 2004.

Zorrilla, Luis G. *Historia de las relaciónes entre México y los Estados Unidos de América, 1800–1958*. Mexico City: Editorial Porrúa, 1977.

———. *Monumentación de la frontera norte en el Siglo XIX*. Mexico City: Secretaría de Relaciones Exteriores, 1981.

Zúñiga, Ignacio. *Rápida ojeada al estado de Sonora dirigida y dedicada al supremo gobierno de la nación*. Mexico City: Impreso por J. Ojeda, 1835.

ONLINE SOURCES

Archibold, Randal C. "Border Fence Must Skirt Objections from Arizona Tribe." September 20, 2006. *New York Times* Web site. Available at http://www.nytimes.com/2006/09/20/washington/20fence.html, accessed June 20, 2009.

Archibold, Randal C., and Julia Preston. "Homeland Security Stands by Its Fence," May 21, 2008. *New York Times* Web site. Available at http://www.nytimes.com/2008/05/21/washington/21fence.html, accessed May 28, 2008.

Ainsa v. U.S., 161 U.S. 208 (1896). Available at http://laws.findlaw.com/us/161/208.html, accessed April 11, 2005.

Ainsa v. U.S., 184 U.S. 639 (1902). Available at http://laws.findlaw.com/us/184/639.html, accessed April 11, 2005.

Ancestry.com. Available at http://www.ancestry.com, accessed May 1, 2010.

"The Border Fence: Opposition in Douglas." October 26, 2006. National Public Radio broadcast, National Public Radio Web site. Available at http://www.npr.org/templates/story/story.php?storyId=6387502, accessed June 20, 2009.

"Both Teams at Home in U.S.-Mexico Border Volleyball." April 14, 2007. *Reuters* Web site. Available at http://www.reuters.com/article/idUSN14215597 20070414, accessed May 31, 2010.

Boudreau, Abbie, and Ken Shiffman. "Minuteman's High-Tech Border Barrier Called 'a Cow-Fence.'" November 7, 2007, cnn.com Web site. Available at http://www.cnn.com/2007/US/11/07/border.fence/, accessed June 29, 2009.

Bustillo, Miguel. "In Texas, Little Support for Putting Up Fences." October 1, 2006. *Los Angeles Times* Web site. Available at http://articles.latimes.com/2006/oct/01/nation/na-border1, accessed June 20, 2009.

"Camp Harry Jones." First Battalion, Twenty-Second Infantry Web site. Available at http://1-22infantry.org/history/harryjones.htm, accessed June 10, 2009.

Cryptome Border Photo Essay. November 18, 2007. Cryptome Web site. Available at http://eyeball-series.org/border-wall/border-wall.htm, accessed June 23, 2009.

Doyle, Leonard. "Bush's Border Fence Destroys Wilderness." April 3, 2008. *The Independent* Web site. Available at http://www.independent.co.uk/news/world/americas/bushs-border-fence-destroys-wilderness-804005.html, accessed June 20, 2009.

Eilperin, Juliet. "Researchers Fear Southern Fence Will Endanger Species Further." April 20, 2008. *Washington Post* Web site. Available at http://www.washingtonpost.com/wp-dyn/content/article/2008/04/19/AR2008041900942.html, accessed June 20, 2009.

Gamboa, Suzanne. "House Approves U.S.-Mexican Border Fence." September 14, 2006. *Washington Post* Web site. Available at http://www.washingtonpost.com/wp-dyn/content/article/2006/09/14/AR2006091401153.html, accessed June 28, 2009.

Gaouette, Nicole. "Border Barrier Approved." September 30, 2006. *Los Angeles Time* Web site. Available at http://articles.latimes.com/2006/sep/30/nation/na-immig30, accessed June 28, 2009.

Inter-Tribal Council of Arizona, Incorporated. "Cocopah Tribe: Introductory Information." Inter-Tribal Council of Arizona Web site. Available at http://www.itcaonline.com/tribes_cocopah.html, accessed April 8, 2005.

Malkin, Michelle. "Send a Brick to Congress." April 17, 2006. MichelleMalkin Web site. Available at http://michellemalkin.com/2006/04/17/send-a-brick-to-congress/, accessed June 22, 2009.

"Mexico Anger over U.S. Border Fence." October 27, 2006. BBC Web site. Available at http://news.bbc.co.uk/2/hi/americas/6090060.stm, accessed June 29, 2009.

"Minuteman Border Fence." Minuteman Civil Defense Corps Web site. Available at http://www.minutemanhq.com/bf/, accessed June 27, 2009.

Pilsk, Seth, and Jeanette C. Cassa. "The Western Apache Home: Landscape Management and Failing Ecosystems." USDA Forest Service Proceedings RMRS-P-36. 2005. Available at http://www.fs.fed.us/rm/pubs/rmrs_p036.pdf, accessed September 28, 2010.

Regan, Margaret. "Artistic Warning." May 13, 2004. *Tucson Weekly* Web site. Available at http://www.tucsonweekly.com/tucson/artistic-warning/Content?oid=1076154, accessed June 29, 2009.

Roig-Franzia, Manuel. "Mexico Calls U.S. Border Fence Severe Threat to Environment." November 16, 2007. *Washington Post* Web site. Available at http://www.washingtonpost.com/wp-dyn/content/article/2007/11/15/AR2007111502272.html, accessed June 20, 2009.

"Texas Mayors Threaten Court to Stop Border Fence." October 12, 2007. *Reuters* Web site. Available at http://www.reuters.com/article/topNews/idUSN1141879320071012?feedType=RSS&feedName=topNews&rpc=22&sp=true, accessed June 20, 2009.

U.S. Bureau of Transportation Statistics. "Border Crossing: Border Crossing/Entry Data." Research and Innovative Technology Administration Web site. Available at http://www.transtats.bts.gov/Fields.asp?Table_ID=1358, accessed June 30, 2009.

U.S. Customs and Border Protection. "Locate a Port of Entry—Land, Air, or Sea," U.S. Customs and Border Protection Web site. Available at http://www.cbp.gov/xp/cgov/toolbox/contacts/ports/, accessed May 31, 2010.

U.S. Department of Homeland Security. "More on the Southwest Border Fence."
    Department of Homeland Security Web site. Available at http://www.dhs.gov/
    xprevprot/programs/gc_1207842692831.shtm, accessed April 28, 2009.
————. "Southwest Border Fence." U.S. Department of Homeland Security
    Web site. Available at http://www.dhs.gov/xprevprot/programs/border-fence
    -southwest.shtm, accessed June 28, 2009.
————. "Annual Report: Immigration Enforcement Actions: 2007." Decem-
    ber 2008. Department of Homeland Security Web site. Available at http://
    www.dhs.gov/xlibrary/assets/statistics/publications/enforcement_ar_07.pdf,
    accessed June 28, 2009.
U.S. v. Green, 185 U.S. 256 (1902). Available at http://laws.findlaw.com/
    us/185/256.html, accessed April 12, 2005.
Wood, Daniel B. "Along the U.S.-Mexican Border, an Erratic Patchwork Fence,"
    April 3, 2008. *Christian Science Monitor* Web site. Available at http://www
    .csmonitor.com/2008/0403/p01s02-usgn.html, accessed June 20, 2009.
————. "Where U.S.-Mexico Border Fence Is Tall, Border Crossings Fall." April
    3, 2008. *Christian Science Monitor* Web site. Available at http://www.csmon
    itor.com/2008/0401/p01s05-usgn.html, accessed June 20, 2009.

ONLINE PERIODICALS

BBC Web site, http://news.bbc.co.uk. Accessed June 29, 2009.
Christian Science Monitor Web site, http://www.csmonitor.com. Accessed June
    29, 2009.
CNN Web site, http://www.cnn.com. Accessed June 29, 2009.
The Independent Web site, http://www.independent.co.uk. Accessed June 29,
    2009.
Los Angeles Times Web site, http://www.latimes.com. Accessed June 20–28,
    2009.
National Public Radio Web site, http://www.npr.org. Accessed June 20, 2009.
New York Times Web site, http://www.nytimes.com. Accessed May 28, 2008 and
    June 20, 2009.
Reuters Web site, http://www.reuters.com. Accessed June 20, 2009 and May 31,
    2009.
Tucson Weekly Web site, http://www.tucsonweekly.com. Accessed June 29, 2009.
Washington Post Web site, http://www.washingtonpost.com. Accessed June 20–
    28, 2009.

INDEX

Note: Illustrations are indicated by page numbers in italic type.